Lecture Notes in Computer

Edited by G. Goos, J. Hartmanis, and

Springer
Berlin
Heidelberg
New York
Barcelona
Hong Kong
London
Milan
Paris
Tokyo

Jyrki Kontio   Reidar Conradi (Eds.)

Software Quality –
ECSQ 2002

Quality Connection – 7th European Conference on Software Quality
Helsinki, Finland, June 9-13, 2002
Proceedings

 Springer

Series Editors

Gerhard Goos, Karlsruhe University, Germany
Juris Hartmanis, Cornell University, NY, USA
Jan van Leeuwen, Utrecht University, The Netherlands

Volume Editors

Jyrki Kontio
Nokia Research Center, Nokia Group
P. O. Box 407, 00045 Nokia Group, Finland
E-mail: jyrki.kontio@nokia.com

Reidar Conradi
Norwegian University of Science and Technology (NTNU)
Department of Computer and Information Science (IDI)
Gloeshaugen, 7491 Trondheim, Norway
E-mail: conradi@idi.ntnu.no

Cataloging-in-Publication Data applied for

Die Deutsche Bibliothek - CIP-Einheitsaufnahme

Software quality : quality connection - 7th European conference on software quality;
proceedings / ECSQ 2002, Helsinki, Finland, June 9 - 13, 2002. Jyrki Kontio ;
Reidar Conradi (ed.). - Berlin ; Heidelberg ; New York ; Barcelona ; Hong Kong ;
London ; Milan ; Paris ; Tokyo : Springer, 2002
    (Lecture notes in computer science ; Vol. 2349)
    ISBN 3-540-43749-5

CR Subject Classification (1998): D.2, K.6.3, K.4.3, K.6, J.1, H.5.3

ISSN 0302-9743
ISBN 3-540-43749-5 Springer-Verlag Berlin Heidelberg New York

Springer-Verlag Berlin Heidelberg New York
a member of BertelsmannSpringer Science+Business Media GmbH

http://www.springer.de

© Springer-Verlag Berlin Heidelberg 2002
Printed in Germany

Typesetting: Camera-ready by author, data conversion by Steingräber Satztechnik GmbH, Heidelberg
Printed on acid-free paper   SPIN 10870017   06/3142   5 4 3 2 1 0

Preface

Software professionals and companies live in a new world today. Increasingly complex systems need to be built faster and cheaper. While many of the established approaches in software quality are still valid, the software quality community is going through a paradigm shift that requires a re-assessment of our current method and tool portfolio, as well as creating new and more effective solutions.

We have selected two themes for this conference to highlight this paradigm shift. Our first theme, *"production of attractive and reliable software at Internet speed"* sums up the dilemma many software organisations face. In order to be competitive, software should contain advanced features and run reliably – yet it should be developed quickly and cost effectively for the right market window. Finding the right balance between these objectives is a critical question that will determine business success in the years to come.

Our second theme, *"production of software with a dynamic partnership network"* highlights the current trend of using partnerships and subcontractors as integral players in the software development process. Partnerships sometimes need to be created quickly to respond to a market opportunity, yet the costs and speed of cooperation must be competitive. Different companies have different processes, quality tools and cultures, yet they should cooperate seamlessly for the best result.

The 7th European Conference on Software Quality – Quality Connection – addresses these challenges as the papers in these proceedings show. We received a total of 78 technical and experience-based papers and two to three referees reviewed each paper. The papers were selected based on how well they satisfied six evaluation criteria: relevance to the conference themes; novelty of contribution; industrial significance; empirical validation; positioning with other work; and writing style and correctness. After a rigorous review process, 31 papers were accepted and are printed in these conference proceedings. These papers provide a solid technical foundation for the conference and offer novel contributions to the community. In addition, the proceedings include keynote and invited papers that provide timely perspectives in this transition.

In addition to the material included in the proceedings, the programme committee selected noteworthy contributions to be presented at the Quality Forum during the conference. These contributions are published by the conference organiser as *Quality Connection - 7th European Conference on Software Quality 2002 - Conference Notes* (ISBN 952-5136-24-8). These contributions present interesting new issues and ideas, as well as practical experiences, on key approaches in achieving software quality.

One of our targets was to establish this conference as the main European forum for providing and sharing the latest and most reliable information on software quality. Thus, we aimed at improving the scientific quality of the accepted papers, while maintaining the practical orientation of the conference. Having completed the review process, we feel that this objective has been reached.

The greatest thanks belong to the authors who have conducted the research and are willing to share their results and insights. In addition, the programme committee did a very thorough and objective job in reviewing and discussing each paper and by providing detailed feedback to the authors.

This conference series is supervised by the European Organization for Quality and its Software Group, currently chaired by Mr. Finn Svendsen. We are grateful to them for providing this forum for these contributions. The General Chair of the conference, professor H. Dieter Rombach, has also been an excellent source of advice and guidance in making this conference happen. We would also express our gratitude to Center for Excellence Finland, and especially to the General Secretary of the conference, Ms. Maija Uusisuo, who has done an excellent job in hosting and organising the conference.

These proceedings are published as the conference takes place. At the same time, the software quality community is entering an era of new challenges. The selected presentations give indications of what the new software quality paradigm will look like. We would like to welcome you and your partners to peruse and apply the knowledge and insight contained in these papers to develop attractive and reliable software even faster.

Helsinki and Trondheim, March 15, 2002

Dr. Jyrki Kontio & Prof. Reidar Conradi
ECSQ2002 Programme Committee Co-Chairs

Organisation

The 7th European Conference on Software Quality (ECSQ2002) is organised by the Center for Excellence Finland in co-operation with the European Organization for Quality – Software Group (EOQ-SG).

General Chair

Professor H. Dieter Rombach, Fraunhofer IESE, Germany

Programme Committee Co-Chairs

Dr. Jyrki Kontio, Nokia Reseach Center, Finland
Professor Reidar Conradi, Norwegian University of Science and Technology, Trondheim, Norway

General Secretary of the Conference

Maija Uusisuo, Center for Excellence Finland, Finland

EOQ-SG Executive Committee

President:	Finn N. Svendsen, Grundfos A/S, Denmark
Member:	Walter Wintersteiger, Management and Informatik, Austria
Member:	Francois de Nazelle, QUAL-AS, France
Member:	Karol Frühauf, Infogem AG, Switzerland
Member:	Mika Heikinheimo, Flander Oy, Finland

Organising Committee

Chair:	Jyrki Kontio, Nokia Research Center, Finland
Coordinator:	Maija Uusisuo, Center for Excellence Finland, Finland
Member:	Casper Lassenius, Software Business and Engineering Institute (SoberIT), Helsinki Univ. of Tech., Finland
Member:	Petri Lehtipuu, Center for Excellence Finland, Finland
Member:	Markku Oivo, University of Oulu, Finland

Programme Committee

Main Sponsor

Nokia Oyj, Finland

Other Sponsors

American Society for Quality
Finnair Oyj
Helsinki University of Technology
QPR Software Oyj Plc.
SecGo Group Oy
Siemens Oy
Solid Information Technology Oy
Sonera Oyj
Stonesoft Oyj
TietoEnator Oyj

Table of Contents

Keynotes and Invited Presentations

Software Quality versus Time-to-Market:
How to Resolve These Conflicts? 1
    H. Dieter Rombach (IESE Fraunhofer)

Mobile Web Services and Software Quality 2
    Mikko Terho (Nokia Oyj)

Solid Software: Is It Rocket Science? 7
    Shari Lawrence Pfleeger (Systems/Software Inc.)

Is Process Improvement Irrelevant to Produce New Era Software? 13
    Stan Rifkin (Master Systems Inc.)

Model-Driven Business Operations 17
    Einar Dehli (Computas AS)

Product Quality in Software Business Connection 25
    Juhani Anttila (Sonera Corporation)

Breakthrough in Delivering Software Quality:
Capability Maturity Model and Six Sigma 36
    Gregory H. Watson (Business Systems Solutions, Inc.)

Accepted Papers
quality@web

Using Mobile Agents for Security Testing in Web Environments 42
    Wen-Kui Chang, Min-Hsiang Chuang, Chao-Tung Yang
    (Tunghai University)

Quality Control Techniques for Constructing Attractive Corporate Websites:
Usability in Relation to the Popularity Ranking of Websites 53
    Toyohiro Kanayama (Advantest Corporation),
    Hideto Ogasawara (Toshiba Corporation),
    Hiroshi Kimijima (Fujitsu Learning Media Ltd.)

Evaluating the Performance of a Web Site via Queuing Theory 63
    Wen-Kui Chang, Shing-Kai Hon (Tunghai University)

Requirements Engineering and QA

Lessons Learned from Applying the Requirements Engineering
Good Practice Guide for Process Improvement 73
    Marjo Kauppinen, Tapani Aaltio, Sari Kujala
    (SoberIT, Helsinki University of Technology)

Quality Assurance Activities for ASP Based on SLM in Hitachi 82
  Masahiro Nakata, Katsuyuki Yasuda (Hitachi Corporation)

Improving Software Quality in Product Families
through Systematic Reengineering 90
  Gopalakrishna Raghavan (Nokia Research Center)

Process Improvement Experiences

SPI Models: What Characteristics Are Required
for Small Software Development Companies? 100
  Ita Richardson (University of Limerick)

Experience Based Process Improvement 114
  Kurt Schneider (Research Center, DaimlerChrysler AG)

How to Effectively Promote the Software Process Improvement Activities
in a Large-Scale Organization 124
  *Hideto Ogasawara, Atsushi Yamada, Takumi Kusanagi, Mikako Arami
  (Corporate Research & Development Center, Toshiba Corporation)*

Risk and Cost Management

Consideration of EVMS Technique Application to Software Development .. 135
  *Yoshihiro Kitajima (NTT Comware Corp.),
  Hitoshi Fuji (NTT Information Sharing Platform Laboratories),
  Seiichiro Satou (FUJITSU Ltd.),
  Hitoshi Ohsugi (Tokiomarine Systems Development Co. Ltd.),
  Isao Gotou (INTEC Inc.), Hitoshi Oono (Japan Novel Corp.)*

Performing Initial Risk Assessments in Software Acquisition Projects 146
  *Esa Rosendahl (R&D-Ware Oy),
  Ton Vullinghs (Research and Technology, DaimlerChrysler AG)*

UML Developments: Cost Estimation from Requirements 156
  Philippe Larvet (Alcatel CIT), Frédérique Vallée (Mathix)

Personal Software Process

The Personal Software Process in Practice:
Experience in Two Cases over Five Years 165
  *Georg Grütter (Line Information GmbH),
  Stefan Ferber (Robert Bosch GmbH)*

Personal Software Process: Classroom Experiences from Finland 175
  *Pekka Abrahamsson (VTT Electronics),
  Karlheinz Kautz (Copenhagen Business School)*

Partnering for Quality

GARP – The Evolution of a Software Acquisition Process Model 186
  *Thomas Gantner (Research and Technology, DaimlerChrysler),
  Tobias Häberlein (University of Ulm)*

Cooperation and Competition with Partner Companies:
Practices for Quality Control through Competition among Teams 197
    Yasuko Okazaki (Software Development Laboratory, IBM Japan, Ltd.)

Cooperate or Conquer?
A Danish Survey of the Customer-Supplier Relationship 207
    Robert Olesen, Jørn Johansen (DELTA)

Defect Management

Introduction of the Software Configuration Management Team
and Defect Tracking System for Global Distributed Development 217
    Shinji Fukui (OMRON Corp.)

Software Development Bug Tracking:
"Tool Isn't User Friendly" or "User Isn't Process Friendly" 226
    Leah Goldin (Jerusalem College of Engineering),
    Lilach Rochell (NICE Systems Ltd.)

I-P-O/Multilateral Design Quality Evaluation Methods:
Process Improvements and Effects 236
    Nobuyuki Hashino, Satoshi Kurokawa, Mamoru Wakaki, Junji Nakasone
    (NTT Comware Corp.)

The COTS Market

Classifying COTS Products 246
    Letizia Jaccheri, Marco Torchiano
    (Norwegian Univ. of Science and Technology)

Understanding Software Component Markets:
The Value Creation Perspective 256
    Nina Helander, Pauliina Ulkuniemi, Veikko Seppänen
    (University of Oulu)

Collaboration between a COTS Integrator and Vendors 267
    Tuija Helokunnas (Nokia),
    Marko Nyby (Tampere University of Technology)

XP and/or Maturity

Creation of a Guideline for Tailoring Development Processes
Using Project Metrics Data 274
    Kazutoshi Shimanaka, Masato Matsumoto, Junji Koga, Hiroyuki Domae
    (NTT Comware Corp.)

Comparison of CMM Level 2 and eXtreme Programming 288
    Jerzy R. Nawrocki, Bartosz Walter, Adam Wojciechowski
    (Poznan University of Technology)

An Empirical Study with Metrics for Object-Relational Databases 298
    Coral Calero (University of Castilla-La Mancha),
    Houari Sahraoui (Université de Montréal),
    Mario Piattini (University of Castilla-La Mancha)

New Approaches to Testing

Extended Model-Based Testing toward High Code Coverage Rate 310
    Juichi Takahashi (SAP Labs),
    Yoshiaki Kakuda (Hiroshima City University)

Restricted Random Testing 321
    Kwok Ping Chan (University of Hong Kong),
    Tsong Yueh Chen (Swinburne University of Technology),
    Dave Towey (University of Hong Kong)

Quality-Adaptive Testing: A Strategy for Testing
with Focusing on Where Bugs Have Been Detected 331
    Yasuharu Nishi (SQC Inc.)

Effective Inspection

Peer Reviews as a Quality Management Technique
in Open-Source Software Development Projects 340
    Jacqueline Stark (Griffith University)

An Evaluation of Inspection Automation Tools 351
    Vesa Tenhunen, Jorma Sajaniemi (University of Joensuu)

Author Index 363

Software Quality versus Time-to-Market: How to Resolve These Conflicts?

H. Dieter Rombach

Fachbereich Informatik, Universität Kaiserslautern, Germany
and IESE Fraunhofer, Germany,
rombach@iese.fhg.de

Abstract. As software becomes more and more part of revenue generation processes in all industrial domains, and as development cycles shorten significantly, the challenges of producing high reliability and quality as well as adhering to shorter time-to-market requirements have hit the software community. As unsuccessful cases demonstrate, the solution is neither to throw unreliable software on the market prematurely, nor to be late with high quality software. The key seems to be choosing the appropriate development model, selecting partnership models based on strengths and weaknesses, and using development processes in a goal-driven way. There is a big difference between product and process oriented development models. Which one is appropriate under what circumstances?
The new Internet age offers so far unknown opportunities for collaboration – which collaborations add value and which ones are counterproductive? All software methods and processes can be used in different ways. If used rigorously (as defined in theory) they take a long time. How can we use 'light' versions of methods to save time, but do not sacrifice essential quality requirements? All these questions will be discussed and illustrated with examples. The goal of this presentation is to understand some of the options for achieving reliability and quality under tight time constraints.

J. Kontio and R. Conradi (Eds.): ECSQ 2002, LNCS 2349, p. 1, 2002.
© Springer-Verlag Berlin Heidelberg 2002

Mobile Web Services and Software Quality

Mikko Terho

Senior Vice President, Strategic Architecture, Mobile Software, Nokia

Abstract. Convergence and changes in the business environment are bringing together the traditional telecom, datacom and consumer electronics industries. Rapid evolution period is taking place in this "infocom" industry where mobile technologies are offering consumers the choice of many new services. In the mobile world the traditional voice communication is being augmented with mobile data services that is making possible the access to any data, on any device, any time. Solving this inherent complexity in a way that enables consumers to have personal view for their own mobile world is a key ingredient in creating future proof solutions. This imposes new requirements to quality to address the whole end-to-end chain for enabling e.g. mobile web services. Realisation of the mobile world requires innovation and co-operation among industry to achieve jointly agreed open specifications and technical solutions that interoperate with each other. Managing the increasing complexity of the software systems combined with stringent time-to-market requirements on product level poses a challenge to software processes. It's evident that the fundamentals of software engineering (i.e. processes, tools, management) need to be in good shape, but that's not enough. Software development challenges of tomorrow call for collaboration in the industry, strong focus in mobile Internet technical architecture, and an advanced software platform approach. This keynote focuses on these topics.

1 Introduction

In the mobile world the traditional voice communication is being augmented with mobile data services, which is making possible the access to any data, on any device, any time. We have witnessed the market growth when voice has gone wireless; now it is time for content to go mobile.

2 IP Convergence – Making a Connection between Telecom, Datacom and Consumer Electronics

Converging IP networks and changes in the business environment are bringing together the traditional telecom, datacom and consumer electronics industries. Rapid evolution period is taking place in this "infocom" industry where a wide spectrum of mobile services will be offered to the users of mobile devices. Mobile services created for the converging IP networks need to be highly user-friendly,

J. Kontio and R. Conradi (Eds.): ECSQ 2002, LNCS 2349, pp. 2–6, 2002.
© Springer-Verlag Berlin Heidelberg 2002

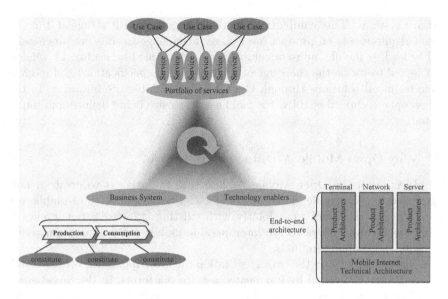

Fig. 1. Enabling Mobile Services

enabling flexibility in the business models, while hiding complexities related to underlying technologies.

There are three main factors that affect commercial success of mobile services. These factors are shown in Fig. 1:

- Gaining user acceptance for the *portfolio of services*, achieved through matching user needs with services.
- Ensuring that *business systems* are ready for both creation of the services, and for service provisioning. The readiness depends on creating business models with clear value.
- Understanding *technology enablers* and their lifecycles, and matching technology enablers accordingly to the evolution of user needs and business systems.

Solving this in a way that enables consumers to have personal view for their own mobile world is a key ingredient in creating future proof solutions. This imposes new requirements for quality to address the whole end-to-end chain for enabling mobile services.

3   Industry Collaboration

Creating the end-to-end chain for enabling mobile services requires industry collaboration between telecom, datacom and consumer electronics industries. Co-operation is needed to jointly agree on open specifications and interoperable technical solutions. The extended scope leads to increasing complexity of the software systems. This complexity combined together with stringent time-to-market requirements on product level poses a challenge to software processes.

The leading mobile industry companies, accompanied by leading IT vendors have agreed to tackle the challenge of achieving open specifications and interoperable technical solutions through Open Mobile Architecture initiative. In this process open technical enablers for mobile services are being defined and implemented.

3.1   Why Open Mobile Architecture Initiative?

The objective of the Open Mobile Architecture initiative is to create a non-fragmented, interoperable global market for the next generation of mobile services. The initiative will work jointly with existing standardisation bodies to enable mobile subscribers to use interoperable mobile services across markets, operators and mobile terminals.

As shown in Fig. 2, in the current situation the growth potential of the mobile services market is limited by fragmented service platforms. In the target situation, numerous suppliers will be able to develop products and solutions based on architecture with open interfaces and technologies. Uniform service platforms and interoperable terminals will allow branded and personalised mobile services to be available from many operators and service providers, and over a wide range of terminals.

The principles of the Open Mobile Architecture initiative are:

- Products and services are based on open and global standards.
- Service platform is agnostic of the communications layer (GSM/GPRS, CDMA, WCDMA).

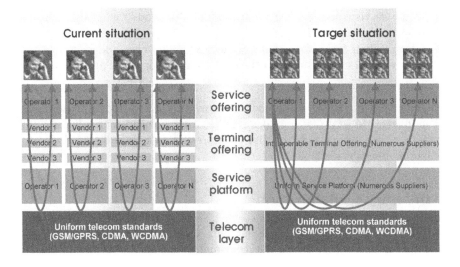

Fig. 2. Current situation and target situation of the mobile services market

- Architecture and its interfaces are open.
- Application programming interfaces for creating services are open.
- Geographical and generational roaming is seamless.
- *Ease of use* is ensured for the users.
- *Interoperability* of independent implementations is possible in multi-vendor environment.
- No lock in is created to technologies available only from single source.

4   SW Quality Becomes Increasingly Important

In converged IP networks there are multiple business roles and interlinked technologies with inherent complexity. It is important to emphasise the software quality to ensure the success in this new business and technical environment.

The traditional view that software quality equals to SW *reliability* does not sufficiently reflect the scope of software quality for mobile services and applications. In the environment depicted above, all the attributes for external and internal quality specified by e.g. ISO/IEC 9126–1 need to be addressed.

As the OMA principles emphasise – good *usability* is also of vital importance when it comes to wide acceptance of new mobile services. Regardless of the technical complexity of any service implementation, users must find the services to be easy to learn and pleasant to use.

Achieving high quality user experience requires that the whole chain of devices and network elements – the terminals, accessories, servers and other network infrastructure components – work together in a reliable way. This implies that all interfaces to other devices must be properly managed, and there needs to be effective means to ensure *interoperability* between components – many of which are not made by a single vendor. This is one of the OMA principles.

Software *reliability* becomes increasingly important in products that enable mobile services. The complexity of terminal software alone has increased rapidly

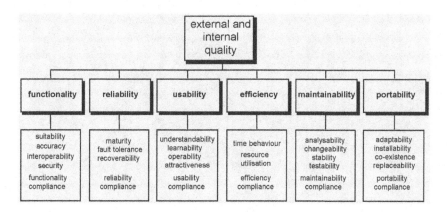

Fig. 3. ISO/IEC 9126–1: Quality Model for External and Internal Quality

during the past years and continues to do so as technically complex service enablers (e.g. Multimedia Messaging) and fascinating applications (e.g. imaging) are being introduced to mobile devices. It is essential to continuously improve the reliability of software to keep the high standard of perceived quality. This requires persistent efforts to improve software development practices, quality assurance, quality culture and all means to prevent defects.

5   Conclusions

It's evident that the fundamentals of software engineering (i.e. processes, tools, and management) need to be in good shape, but that's not enough. Software development challenges of tomorrow call for collaboration in the industry, strong focus in mobile Internet technical architecture, and producing high-quality services for end-users.

Solid Software: Is It Rocket Science?

Shari Lawrence Pfleeger

Systems/Software Inc., 4519 Davenport St. NW, Washington DC 20016-4415,
s.pfleeger@ieee.org

Abstract. Over the years, software engineers have created and applied many technologies to monitor and improve the quality of the software we produce. At the same time, the demands on that software have been increasing: our clients want better and predictable software for less cost in shorter time frames. This presentation will present several techniques for producing "solid software": software that is reliable, predictable and easy to maintain. We will explore whether these techniques are enough to guarantee high quality every time.

1   Introduction

We often discuss software quality and assume everyone wants it and knows how to build it. But in fact high-quality software is easier said than done. In this paper, we look at the notion of "solid software," software whose high quality is critical to a person or organization's business or mission. This idea is discussed more fully in Pfleeger, Hatton and Howell [6]. Here, we look at:

- What is solid software?
- Why is it so hard to build?
- Can we build solid software for the United States' proposed Strategic Missile Defense system?

2   What Is Solid Software?

As defined by Pfleeger, Hatton and Howell [6], solid software is software that is reliable, secure, has predictable performance, and is easy to upgrade. But we don't always do a good job of building such software. Indeed, Dijkstra [2] recently pointed out that we do an abysmal job:

> "The average customer of the computing industry has been served so poorly that he expects his system to crash all the time, and we witness a massive worldwide distribution of bug-ridden software for which we should be deeply ashamed."

For example, Blair [1] describes a situation shortly after the end of the Cold War when the United States discovered that Russia was tracking its nuclear weapons materials using a paper-based system. That is, the materials tracking

J. Kontio and R. Conradi (Eds.): ECSQ 2002, LNCS 2349, pp. 7–12, 2002.

system consisted of boxes of paper filled with paper receipts. In a gesture of friendship, the Los Alamos National Lab donated to Russia the Microsoft software it uses to track its own nuclear weapons materials. However, experts at the renowned Kurchatov Institute soon discovered that over time some files become invisible and inaccessible! In early 2000, they warned the US. To solve the problem, the US told Russia to upgrade to the next version of the Microsoft software. But the upgrade had the same problem, plus a security flaw that would allow easy access to the database by hackers or unauthorized parties.

Dijkstra, commenting on situations such as this one, says that computing's central challenge is "how not to make a mess of it," and we have certainly not met that challenge. He sees complexity as one of the root causes of our inability to build good software: "... most of our systems are much more complicated than can be considered healthy, and are too messy and chaotic to be used in comfort and confidence" [2]. Dijkstra's remarks seem to be based on clear evidence, not merely on perception. Neumann and Parnas [5] note that:

> "Evidence over the past decade of Inside Risks and other sources suggests that we are not responding adequately to that challenge. Humans have repeatedly demonstrated our predilection for short-term optimization without regard for long-term costs."

3   Why Is It So Hard to Build?

Pfleeger, Hatton and Howell [6] have pondered this question, and they suggest four reasons:

- Programmer optimism vs. gutless estimation
- The difference between discrete and continuous systems
- The combination of immaturity and rapid change
- Repeating our mistakes

Programmer optimism follows a predictable pattern. We are enthusiastic about our new project, and we are asked to estimate how long it will take us to complete it. We employ gutless estimation: basing our estimate not on historical data and sensible models but on optimistic projections of how we might finish the project if we anticipate no hiccups or setbacks. Our estimates then become targets, with no flexibility if something comes up that we didn't expect–such as a new requirement, a change in resources, or a difficulty in design that we didn't foresee. Our unrealistic budgets and schedules lead to unsustainable time pressures, and eventually we find ourselves cutting corners and compromising quality.

At the same time, the nature of the system itself, as a discrete system rather than a continuous one, suggests significant differences in sensitivity to small errors, limited interpolation, and the absence of safety margins. Software engineering is not like other engineering. Whereas we might have some "slack" when we build a one-inch nail to be 1.001 inches or 0.999 inches, an off-by-one error is devastating to software. That is, software is much more sensitive to small errors than other kinds of engineered items. Similarly, when engineering other things, we can test at one level (say, a weight on a bridge at 1000 pounds) and another level (a weight on a bridge at 10,000 pounds) and, if the bridge doesn't collapse, we can assume that the bridge can hold any weight between 1000 and 10,000. But we can't test software with values of 1000 and 10,000 and assume that it works for all values in-between. Finally, we can't build in safety margins the way other engineers can. When John Roebling calculated the size and strength of the cables he needed for building the Brooklyn Bridge, he doubled his result to account for any manufacturing errors or miscalculations. But we cannot easily "double" or over-engineer the quality of our software in the same way.

We like to think that we build our products based on sound technical principles. But in fact market pressures may force us to adopt new technologies well before they are ready for prime time. We use a new tool, platform or technique because our developers want to learn new things, even if the technology is inappropriate for the application. At the same time, we are building complex systems as solutions to problems we have never before solved. The combination is a risky recipe.

Complexity is a particularly difficult ingredient in the mix.

> "While we all know that unmastered complexity is at the root of the misery, we do not know what degree of simplicity can be obtained, nor to what extent the intrinsic complexity of the whole design has to show up in the interfaces. We simply do not know yet the limits of disentanglement. We do not know yet whether intrinsic intricacy can be distinguished from accidental intricacy. We do not know yet whether trade-offs will be possible" [2].

Lehman's [4] notions of S-, P- and E-systems can help us to understand the nature of the complexity, and perhaps to deal with it. An S-system is one where we completely understand the problem and have a closed-form solution that is not likely to change. For example, matrix inversion is well-defined, well-understood, and we can build an S-system to solve it. A P-system is more difficult to deal with. We cannot always characterize the problem and its solution completely, so we build an abstraction and implement that as a solution. For instance, a chess-playing program must be based on an abstraction, since it cannot calculate all possibilities for every move. So a chess-playing program is a P-system, inherently more complex than an S-system. An E-system is the most complex, because the system is itself embedded in the real world and must reflect the changes invoked when the system runs. To see how, consider a stock trading program. As it runs and initiates stock trades, it actually changes the real-world in which it is embedded. So this E-system must learn from changes in the environment it influences. Many of the solid software systems we want to build are E-systems.

Moreover, we don't often try to localize and isolate the complexity. In addition, "most of us are so busy advancing and applying technology that we don't look either back or forward" [5], so we keep repeating our mistakes, or worse, enhance our misunderstandings. Neumann and Parnas suggest that:

"We should look back to recognize what we have learned about computer-related risks. We must look forward to anticipate the future effects of our efforts, including unanticipated combinations of apparently harmless phenomena."

Instead, we often suffer from two common software engineering diseases: *analysis paralysis* and *buzzword du jour*. That is, we get stuck analyzing a system to death, or we jump on the latest technological bandwagon in the hope that it will solve all our problems–the silver bullet that Fred Brooks warns does not exist.

In the book, *Solid Software*, Pfleeger, Hatton and Howell [6] suggest eleven steps that a project manager can take to reduce the risks when building an application requiring solid software:

- Understanding what you mean by quality
- Risk analysis
- Hazard analysis
- Careful testing
- Good design
- Effective prediction
- Peer review
- Static analysis
- Configuration management
- Using appropriate tools
- Trust but verify

These actions do not guarantee that the software will be solid, but they certainly address many of the issues that make the software so hard to build.

4   Example: Strategic Missile Defense

Clearly, George W. Bush's proposed Strategic Missile Defense (SMD) system requires solid software; the failure of a missile can threaten human life and health. Let us look at the kinds of questions we must ask about SMD to determine whether the state of software engineering is ready to build such a system.

The SMD is to be located in Alaska. Designed to destroy attack missiles targeted at the United States (sometimes described as a bullet hitting a bullet because destruction is done by direct impact), the system has 25 minutes to destroy the attack missile from the time it is launched. The SMD must distinguish the real warhead on the attack missile from any decoys that have been released at the same time.

Nobel Prize-winning physicist Burton Richter [7] poses three important questions about the SMD:

- How reliable does the system have to be?

- How do we know how reliable it is?
- How does it handle decoys?

He examines each question in turn. To determine system reliability, suppose an attack has five missiles. Assume further that the chance of one SMD interceptor finding and destroying real warhead is 4 out of 5. Then the chance of destroying all five warheads is (0.8)*5, or about 1 in 3. That is, there is a 2 out of 3 chance that a warhead get through the SMD missile shield.

But what if we increase the reliability of the SMD interceptors? If a single interceptor is 90% reliable (that is, we can be assured of its hitting its target 9 out of 10 times), then the risk of an attack missile's getting through is reduced to 1 chance in 3. That risk may still be considered unacceptable by some people. To bring the risk of a warhead's getting through down to 1 in 10, the single interceptor reliability has to be at least 98%.

No space launch system has ever achieved a reliability of 98%. So how can we improve the reliability in some other way? One approach is to fire more than one defensive missile for each attacking missile. For example, to reach a 1-in-10 risk, a single interceptor needs only 85% reliability if two interceptors are fired for each attacking missile, and only 73% if three interceptors are fired, and so on. But these numbers work only if each failure has a different cause. If all failures arise from the same problem, there is no increase in reliability when more interceptors are fired. Knight and Leveson [3] have shown that software designers tend to make the same kinds of mistakes, because they are taught design in the same or similar ways. So it is unlikely that several software-related failures in an SMD interceptor will have different causes.

Richter goes on to ask how we can tell how reliable the SMD actually is. The answer has two parts: testing and measurement. In the plans for testing SMD, the developers are using a sequential set of tests. That is, each test represents one hurdle; the system passes one hurdle and go on to the next test. Richter notes that passing one hurdle implies two things:

- The good news: We have 100% confidence that the system is more than 0% effective.
- The bad news: We have 0% confidence that the system is 100% effective.

The natural question to ask in this circumstance is: How many tests do we need? By passing only one test, we have 50% confidence that the system is 50% reliable. Richter does the math: To reach 1 in 10 odds that a warhead will get through the missile shield with two defenders for each attacking missile, we would need 18 tests (with a 95% confidence that each interceptor is at least 85% reliable) with no failures of the full system.

Finally, Richter examines the nature of the decoys, since the SMD must also be able to distinguish a decoy from a real attack missile. He explains that there are three types of decoys: dumb, intelligent and genius. A dumb decoy looks the same as a warhead to the radar system trying to identify it. For instance, the enemy might send up balloons with the warheads, so that the radar sees lots of blips and cannot tell one from the other. However, the warhead would be hot and the balloons cold, so a temperature-sensing system might solve this decoy problem.

A decoy of average intelligence, though, might have the same shape and the same temperature as a warhead. For example, a decoy might consist of a balloon with a light bulb and battery, fooling the temperature-sensors and the radar. A genius decoy may be more similar to a warhead. For example, the warhead may be surrounded by a cooled balloon, so that now the decoys and the warheads are indistinguishable.

What are the requirements for SMD? The proposed system considers only dumb decoys.

From Richter's point of view, he concludes that "The proposed system is not ready to graduate from development to deployment, and probably never will be." From a software engineering point of view, we must ask ourselves if we can build software this solid. The requirements for this kind of system are well beyond any software that has ever been built. One step in the analysis is to decide how good our software is now. Another is to see what lessons we can learn from our failures. Normally, we insist that a safety-critical system run for 10^9 hours of failure-free operation. But such a constraint would mean we would have to test the system for over 114,000 years! We might consider simulation as an option, assuming that we know enough about the situation in this E-system to be able to incorporate all the right variables and relationships.

The best we can do is be aware and be responsible. Neumann and Parnas [5] tell us:

> "We must strive to make sure we maximize the benefits and minimize the harm. Among other things, we must build stronger and more robust computer systems while remaining acutely aware of the risks associated with their use."

References

1. Bruce G. Blair, "Nukes: A lesson from Russia", *Washington Post*, Wednesday, July 11, 2001, page A19.
2. Edsger W. Dijkstra, "The end of computing science?" *Communications of the ACM*, 44(3), March 2001, page 92.
3. John Knight and Nancy Leveson (1986). "An empirical study of failure probabilities in multi-version software". In *Digest of the Sixteenth International Symposium on Fault-tolerant Computing*, pp. 165-70. Los Alamitos, CA: IEEE Computer Society Press.
4. M. M. Lehman, "Programs, life cycles and the laws of software evolution", *Proceedings of the IEEE*, 68(9), 1980, pages 1060-1076.
5. Peter G. Neumann and David L. Parnas, "Computers: Boon or bane?" *Communications of the ACM*, 44(3), March 2001, page 168.
6. Shari Lawrence Pfleeger, Les Hatton and Charles C. Howell, *Solid Software*, Prentice Hall, Upper Saddle River NJ, 2001.
7. Burton Richter, "It doesn't take rocket science; to test missile defense, start with basic math", *Washington Post*, Sunday, July 23, 2000, page B2.

Is Process Improvement Irrelevant to Produce New Era Software?

Stan Rifkin

Master Systems Inc., 2604B El Camino Real #244, Carlsbad, California 92008 USA,
sr@Master-Systems.com

Abstract. Narrow focus is the key to success for organizations of all kinds and sizes. Focus can be diluted by emphasizing the "wrong kind" of software process improvement. That's right: traditional software process improvement may impede the successful development and deliver software, particularly innovative and total solutions. In fact, adherence to traditional software process improvement can cause an organization to become blind to competitive forces. This presentation gives a preview of a new set of improvements that are tailored to the new styles of software development and to the new market realities about time to market, our tolerance of quality concerns, and relentless focus on convenience.

1 Introduction

Many other commentators, including distinguished ones at this Conference, have observed the tension between high software quality and demands of the Internet Age. To some degree, we have all been vindicated because the pressure to produce software at Internet speed has diminished as the dot-coms have receded into the economic landscape. On the other hand, we will always have the tension between high quality and the other non-functional attributes of software projects, such as effort, duration, and features.

Therefore, we have to find a permanent solution to the question of how to instill quality into software that must be developed quickly. I have found the answer in an odd place: the management literature on strategy.

2 Focus on What?

How many strategies are there? Three, according to *The Discipline of Market Leaders*. The best organizations focus on only one of these three, while maintaining threshold levels of the other two. The three strategies are:

1. **Operational excellence**: These organizations have a "formula" for their service or product. Their menu of choices is small, limited, and with that menu they deliver excellently. They are usually the lowest cost providers because they are the highest quality producer for their market segment. Standard examples are McDonalds and Federal Express.

J. Kontio and R. Conradi (Eds.): ECSQ 2002, LNCS 2349, pp. 13–16, 2002.

2. **Product innovativeness**: These organizations pride themselves on maximizing the number of turns they get in the market. They introduce many new products, selling innovation and features as opposed to, say, price. Examples are Intel, 3M, Sony, and Bell Labs. They measure their success by the number of new product introductions, the number of patents, and/or the number of Nobel prizes.

3. **Customer intimacy**: These organizations seek to be a total solution. Whatever the customer wants gets added to the menu. The menu is (infinitely) long and custom-made for each engagement. "Schmoozing" is an important part of customer intimacy.

Each of these three strategies offers something completely different to the clients of the organizations, and therefore each performs its operations in support of its strategy in completely different ways. This is critical to quality professionals because high quality is not what all of the clients expect. Therefore, it does not make strategic sense to every kind of organization to have high quality.

Specifically, operationally excellent organizations offer high quality as an integral part of their strategy. It is not optional, not just desirable. These organizations love and use the Software Engineering Institute's Capability Maturity Model (SEI CMM), and ISO 9000, and all other quality standards. Quality is, in fact, how operationally excellent differentiate themselves, so quality is critical. And it is worth mentioning that while operationally excellent organizations do not innovate products (they have a small, stable menu), they are very process innovative.

Product innovative organizations distinguish themselves by imaginatively assembling features, so that their products and services are unique. From product innovative organizations we buy creativity, features, sexiness. Quality is important, but it is not what we clients are buying. In fact, we are quite tolerant of quality problems in new products and services. Just think about how we love to hate Microsoft!

And customer intimate organizations are not the cost, quality or innovation leaders. Rather they take care of all functions in a certain area. For example, large global accounting firms not only audit books, but also give tax advice and prepare tax forms, suggest and implement accounting systems, recruit accounting people, and even implement all computer systems. They will do everything related to the finances of organizations, even stretch the truth!

From a process perspective, customer intimate organizations need to have an architecture. The architecture facilitates the quick addition of features and offerings to the "base," the backplane.

At the risk of repetition, there are only three strategies, and each one offers a different thing of value to clients. Operationally excellent organizations offer quality, product innovative organizations offer a unique combination of features, and customer intimate organizations offer an infinite menu of features. And therefore, each type of organization values quality generally and process improvement specifically very differently.

3   Quality Is Directly Related to Strategy

The Discipline of Market Leaders notes that (1) firms that try to offer more than one strategy are not as successful as those that focus on one and only one, and (2) all organizations must present at least a threshold level of the two disciplines that they do not focus on. Therefore, quality is important to all strategies, but only really important to one (operational excellence). The other two strategies should have "good enough" or "just enough" quality and that is appropriate, as much as it makes our skins crawl!

How much is "good enough" or "just enough" quality? The marketplace specifies these values, so benchmarking and customer satisfaction surveys tell us. To have quality in excess of what the marketplace values is a waste of resources and dilutes focus from the strategic advantage of the organization.

This can be illustrated by looking at planning. Planning is the key to the SEI CMM and all operationally excellent organizations. Predictability is highly valued. But how would you plan innovation in a product innovative organization? And how valuable is planning in a customer intimate organization when the requirements are intentionally vague? After all, for innovative and customer intimate organizations, the plan is not a deliverable!

4   The New Quality: Convenience

So, what is the quality function in an organization to do? The short answer is to represent the end-customer, to be the voice of the customer. The quality organization is a filter that lets only "good" products and services into the marketplace. One of the "ilities" (that is, quality attribute) this new era of systems and software is *convenience*, and clearly there is too little of it.

Why, for example, would a person watch a movie on a little computer screen rather than a larger one, as on a television or in a movie theatre? Why would a person read a book on a grayish, reflective little screen rather than a white, flat paper? Why would a person type out a message when he or she could just as easily pick up the (mobile?) phone and talk? Why would a person wear an always-on e-mail device on his/her belt? One that has teeny, tiny keys? Why would a person get on an airplane and travel across an ocean to attend a conference instead of sitting at his or her computer screen and interact that way?

The answer, of course, is convenience. Convenience is a feature, one sought in all strategies. And it is a differentiator in all strategies, too. We might think of convenience as an innovation, but many of us eat at an operationally excellent firm, McDonald's, precisely because of convenience. Or we might use a Nokia product, clearly innovative, precisely because it so convenient.

Convenience is a new "ility" that we quality professionals will have to learn about and then encourage our organizations to adopt, define, and operationalize. We will become the gate through which only convenient systems pass, and that will become the new reality of the new economy.

Acknowledgements

I learned most of this by working with John Title of Computer Sciences Corporation. The quality leader who made me ask myself why quality implementation is difficult is David Card. Many SEI SEPG conference keynote speakers/cheerleaders who claim that those who resist have bad character have irritated me into writing this. Their failure to ask (and answer) "Why?" stimulated me. And I am grateful to the program committee, particularly Reidar Conradi, for the honor to present. The content of this paper has profited from being presented in other forums, such as *IEEE Software* and an SEI SEPG conference.

References

1. Fred Crawford and Ryan Mathews. (2001). *The Myth of Excellence: Why Great Companies Never Try to Be the Best at Everything*, Crown Pub. ["To research purchasing behavior, the authors surveyed 5,000 consumers, but the responses they got surprised them and prompted their title's contrary proposition. Crawford and Mathews found that values (respect, honesty, trust, dignity) were more important to consumers than value. This discovery led the pair to develop a new model of 'consumer relevancy.' They explain in detail the importance of price, service, quality, access, and experience for the consumer. They then suggest that for companies to be successful they need to dominate on only one of these five factors. On a second of the five they should stand out or differentiate themselves from their competitors; and on the remaining three they need only to be at par with others in their industry."]
2. Stan Rifkin. (July/August 2001). "Why software process innovations are not adopted." *IEEE Software*, vol. 10, no. 4, pp. 110-112.
3. Stan Rifkin. (May/June 2001). "What makes measuring software so hard?" *IEEE Software*, vol. 10, no. 3, pp. 41- 45.
4. Michael Treacy and Fred Wiersma. (1995). *The Discipline of Market Leaders: Choose Your Customers, Narrow Your Focus, Dominate Your Market.* Addison-Wesley.
5. Fred Wiersema. (1996). *Customer Intimacy: Pick Your Partners, Shape Your Culture, Win Together.* Knowledge Exchange.
6. Chris Zook and James Allen. (2001). *Profit From the Core: Growth Strategy in an Era of Turbulence*, Harvard Business School Press. ["Spawned by a 10-year study of 2,000 firms conducted at Bain & Company, a global consultancy specializing in business strategy, Profit from the Core is based on the fundamental but oft-ignored maxim that prolonged corporate growth is most profitably achieved by concentrating on a single core business."]

Model-Driven Business Operations

Einar Dehli

Computas AS, Vollsveien 9, P.O. Box 482, 1327 Lysaker, Norway
ed@computas.com

Abstract. Most software-focused improvement efforts, including OMG's recent *Model Driven Architecture* initiative, stop short of addressing the challenging knowledge-level integration and interoperability issues organizations will be faced with in the emerging knowledge society. In this keynote, an extended view of *model-driven* is presented. Knowledge models and modeling activities are envisioned to drive future organizational development and business operations in real time, encompassing and integrating activities at all levels, from top management to the floor. A new breed of powerful and flexible enablers will be required to capture, represent, and bring knowledge to life in visual models and operational work solutions. Several real-world cases already demonstrate the benefits of this holistic model-driven approach to business planning and operations, with resulting dramatic productivity gains and unsurpassed alignment of IT and business.

1 The Business-Aligned IT Challenge

Leading professionals in the knowledge management field have for years been arguing that the basic economic resource is and will be knowledge [1]. Tomorrow's agile organizations need to continuously grasp new business opportunities, respond to changes in their competitive environment, and take advantage of new technological enablers. Business managers will demand business-aligned enterprise IT architectures, infrastructures and solutions that are supportive of constantly changing work processes and knowledge sharing needs. IT Managers, IT Architects and software application developers will have to respond.

Business Managers and IT people will often find they have different views and opinions on what business-aligned IT means and implies. Establishing a common understanding of goals and requirements is the first part of the challenge. Coming to grips with what it takes to achieve business-aligned IT is the second part. It is easy to become occupied looking for answers to the wrong problem. We will briefly touch on some potential fallacies.

As people are becoming the dominant cost factor in enterprises, employees at all levels in the organizational hierarchies are under pressure to take on more work and perform tasks more effectively.

A common assumption in many circles seems to be that once perfect access to information resources is enabled, it will bring about a situation where all relevant information is taken into account in work execution and decision-making. Such

J. Kontio and R. Conradi (Eds.): ECSQ 2002, LNCS 2349, pp. 17–24, 2002.
© Springer-Verlag Berlin Heidelberg 2002

expectations are dangerous. Human capacity to perform intellectual work and digest information has stayed virtually unchanged in modern-time history. People have for a long time had access to more information than they can make use of. Being presented with too much information tends to paralyze, rather than improve performance. Clever search engines are helpful, but information retrieved must still be read and understood by humans. The simplicity of being able to mass-distribute emails at the click of a button is a double-edged sword. It is an excellent example of recent performance-detrimental innovations.

Many workaround solutions are being attempted to solve the growing information overload problems. Unfortunately, most are based on the fallacy that better information management is the answer. Observing any organization closely will soon reveal that it takes a lot more than just making information accessible before people start acting according to the organization's best documented knowledge.

Organizational behavior results from the complex interactions of planned and uncoordinated individual behavior. To solve organizational challenges, it is helpful to analyze what changes are required at the individual level, and initiate actions that maximize the likelihood of theses changes to come about. As people are generally resistive to change, motivating for change is always challenging. Much has been written on organizational development, and most conceivable configurations and solutions have been tried [2], with varying success. Sustainable and repeatable advances generally requires introduction of new technologies. In the last century, communication technologies and computing have had dramatic impacts on organizational design and behavior. To achieve similar advances in knowledge sharing behavior, it is reasonable to assume that new knowledge technologies are required.

2   Model-Driven Business Operations

If investments in conventional information management solutions and organizational development programs are no longer cost-effective ways of improving performance and knowledgeable behavior in most organizations, what alternatives are there? How can organizations get away from just managing more and more dust-gathering information, and get to a situation where individuals rapidly get up to speed and act with competence in new settings?

We claim that adopting a model-driven business operations approach to IT has substantial advantages, and that this approach will soon be the prevalent way of supporting business IT needs. In the coming decade, model-driven knowledge technologies are likely to open up whole new avenues for organizational design, allowing novel configurations and new ways of distributing tasks and responsibilities. We will increasingly find that model-driven knowledge systems are offloading and assisting human workers with a growing number of knowledge-intensive tasks and decisions.

The key enabler of this approach is the concept of an active and executable knowledge *model*.

Modeling is an age-old endeavor. The concepts of *models* and *modeling* mean different things to people in different fields. Building architects use models to visualize, study and communicate alternative designs before launching construction projects. Scientists and engineers rely heavily on mathematical models to explain complex relationships in all aspects of their work. The advent of computing has further expanded the scope and utility of models. Software architects and designers use information and data models to describe software systems. Business consultants have devised a plethora of modeling approaches for documenting and analyzing organizations and business processes. And in the eighties, expert systems researchers pioneered the use of knowledge models to mimic and support human reasoning.

Recently, the term *model-driven* has received widespread attention. OMG's move to concentrate its standardization efforts on Model Driven Architectures (MDA) is noteworthy [3]. MDA is a new approach to managing the integration of objects, components, and middleware, with the aim of achieving platform-independent software interoperability. Though this is a worthwhile goal, it stops short of addressing the challenging knowledge-level integration and interoperability issues facing business managers in the emerging knowledge society.

In this keynote, an extended interpretation of *model-driven* is used. Knowledge models and modeling activities are envisioned to drive future organizational development and business operations in real time, encompassing and integrating activities at all levels, from top management to the floor. The visual knowledge models at the heart of this approach are live reflections of all important aspects of the enterprise, intended both for visual communication with humans, and for formal interpretation and execution by computers. The result is Visual Enterprise Integration™, an all-embracing and far-reaching new approach for achieving business-aligned IT.

3.1 Visual Enterprise Integration

The term *Visual Enterprise Integration* highlights the benefits of advanced visualization as a key to leverage human knowledge comprehension, as well as the much-improved integrated enterprise behavior that becomes visible to everyone in organizations that adopt the new technological enablers for operational work management and execution.

This unique model-driven approach to harmonized business and software development has been extensively researched, matured and field-tested for seventeen years by the innovative Scandinavian knowledge engineering company, Computas. Its two complementary product families, Metis® and FrameSolution™, incorporate experience from more than twenty European level research projects and hundreds of commercially deployed solutions with tens of thousands of daily users.

Early adopters are already reaping the benefits of model-driven business operations. The following sections present characteristics of available tools and fielded systems to illustrate what can be achieved with model-driven technologies today. Experience with current research prototypes promises many additional synergies and benefits of this approach to appear over the next 2-3 years [4].

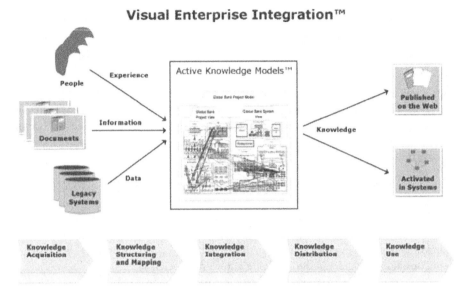

Fig. 1. The diagram shows how visual modeling tools can be used to acquire, structure and map knowledge from all kinds of sources, and distribute the resulting integrated knowledge models on the web and in intelligent systems. Publishing visual knowledge models on the web significantly enhances common understanding of complex issues and relationships. Deploying operational knowledge models in software applications ensures that best practices are adhered to everywhere and everytime. The result is true *Visual Enterprise Integration*™

4   Active Knowledge Modeling with Metis®

Metis® is a tool for building and using advanced visual models. Visual models in Metis may be used to represent any aspects of an enterprise, including but not limited to strategies, goals, programs, initiatives, projects, organizations, processes, products, resources, requirements, architectures, applications, information, data, etc. Visual models are built from typed objects and relationships. The semantics and visual appearance of these objects and relationships are defined in metamodels. Metis can be configured to support any desired standard and methodology just by defining a corresponding metamodel.

Models in Metis differ from models built with conventional modeling tools in several important ways:

1. Models may have any number of model views. Views are extensively used to present relevant model extracts tailored to the needs of different audiences, with desired changes to language, symbols and layout. End users browsing the models can generate new model views dynamically. All views immediately reflect changes in the underlying logical object models.
2. Models and model views can be arbitrarily large, containing tens of thousands of objects, constrained only by memory size.

3. Models can include any number of other models. Relationships and views can be created across submodel boundaries. Submodels can be opened in lazy-load mode, allowing arbitrarily large model structures to be managed and browsed in a drill-down manner.
4. All types of visual models can coexist and be interrelated in the same modeling and browsing environment. The tool automatically configures itself to work with different model types, based on specifications in the model's metamodel. Metamodels define types, symbols, methods, constraint, scripts, menu entries, and more.
5. Models are persisted as XML structures and can be dynamically browsed and interrogated from standard web browsers with a Metis downloadable component.
6. Models can be maintained in secure web services based model repositories, with extensive permission, version and configuration management support.
7. Mappings can be defined from Metis models to any external database, application, or information store, allowing Metis models to be generated or augmented on the fly from data and information residing in other systems.
8. Model objects can link to any accessible application service or information object on the web, allowing the tool to be used as a corporate knowledge portal.

These characteristics illustrate the extreme flexibility of modeling in Metis. Models can be created, integrated, and maintained in a way that gives anyone with the required permissions access to unprecedented overviews of enterprise information and data. Employees can navigate and drill down from high-level strategic enterprise views to detailed visual models of almost any aspect or activity of relevance to the enterprise. Models can be used for structured interrogation and analysis, as a portal to all enterprise knowledge and information, and for many other purposes.

Metis models contribute structure to unstructured information. Its visual style and dynamic navigation capabilities effectively communicate at a level of understanding that the written word is incapable of.

As discussed in Chapter 1, building and deploying visual models does not automatically imply that the models will be used to the extent desired. Only the diligent can be expected to make frequent use of the models. Creating enterprise models and keeping the models up-to-date is in itself a process that requires contribution from a large number of people. Motivating for and coordinating work at this scale across the enterprise is never an easy undertaking. It requires operational process support.

5 Just-in-Time Knowledge Support with FrameSolution™

Many organizations have started to deploy workflow applications for coordinating and streamlining their work processes. Conventional workflow systems coordinate work at a course level of granularity, with only rudimentary capabilities for knowledge sharing and task support. They have little to contribute when it comes to getting organizations to act more knowledgeably.

Experience with a new breed of operational knowledge support applications has proven that it is both feasible and cost-efficient to model tasks and activities at a very fine-grained level of detail, thereby allowing workflow capabilities to be extended with Just-in-Time Knowledge Support™ [5]. Since the mid-nineties, more than twenty such model-driven workplace solutions have successfully been developed and fielded by Computas. The systems range in size from supporting the needs of small workgroup teams to being the primary work environment for organizations with thousands of users. These systems are all based on the FrameSolution™ family of integrated, component-based knowledge execution frameworks.

FrameSolution architectures are characterized by a clear separation of concern between declarative knowledge and functional behavior implemented in program code. Behavior is defined and implemented as fine-grained object-oriented services. Knowledge models define how these services are dynamically configured and composed at runtime into sequences of activities to support work execution.

Implementation of the object-oriented services is a programming task, while defining all the rules and constraints for the composition of services into activities and processes is a knowledge engineering task. All actions and decisions to be supported by the system need to be modeled, in terms of preconditions, post-conditions, required information and tools, and relevant knowledge support. The knowledge definitions are interpreted at runtime by generic knowledge execution engines in the framework. Models allow for introspection into execution states and reasoning traces, an essential advantage over compiled code for providing contextualized knowledge support.

Declarative knowledge is structured in four interacting, executable models:

1. The *organization* model represents users, roles and organizational structures, along with relevant relationships and attributes, including permissions, competencies and authority.
2. The *domain* model is a generic object-oriented model of all the *things* and *concepts* that the system is capable of handling. Domain objects, relationships and attributes are modeled in UML. Applications may use both object-oriented databases and relational databases. FrameSolution efficiently maps domain objects to persistent storage, while ensuring transactional data integrity and execution performance in large distributed systems.
3. The *process* model represents the business processes supported by the system. Processes are modeled from a use perspective, as sets of declarative representations of pertinent actions and decisions, arranged in dynamic, context-sensitive, checklists.
4. The *rule base* represents conditions and constraints between representations in the other models. Rules can be used for both backward and forward chaining, and are expressed using first-order predicate calculus statements, i.e. statements built up using the familiar connectives *and*, *or*, and *not* as well as bounded versions of the quantifiers *forall* and *exists*.

Development of FrameSolution applications follows a proven incremental and iterative development process, with frequent interactive sessions that bring together user representatives, software engineers, domain experts and business managers.

Early FrameSolution projects primarily targeted public sector case management applications and other well-structured domains with a large number of repetitive cases, a complex set of established rules and regulations, and well-defined sets of basic activities and possible actions. Some examples from Norway include:

- a system assisting more than 6000 police officers in handling all administrative work processes related to criminal proceedings
- a system for the management of court cases in the Supreme Court of Justice, with a much larger solution for all lower courts in Norway currently under development.
- support to immigration officers for handling applications from immigrants and refugees
- a system for the foreign services managing Visa applications according to the Schengen convention
- a comprehensive application for the Labor Market Administration, assisting 3000 officers in servicing job seekers and employers

FrameSolution frameworks are not constrained to be used with the structured processes and predefined activity sequences characterizing these public sector solutions. FrameSolutions are applicable wherever knowledge supported work execution is desired, including intelligent e-business and intranet solutions, business-to-business process automation, ERP functionality, engineering design, project management, quality management, etc. Unstructured work processes also consist predominantly of well-defined basic activities and operations that are repeatedly performed. When FrameSolutions are used in settings where work planning and execution go hand in hand, users can define, select, arrange, schedule, delegate and execute activities and services on the fly, with extensive support from the intelligent reasoning engines.

5.1 Metis Modeling and FrameSolution Knowledge Support

Both Metis and FrameSolution are model-driven environments. Synergies between the environments exist at several levels:

1. The Metis Team Server repository is itself a FrameSolution application. The Team Server provides knowledge support to teams of modelers and data owners.
2. All knowledge contents and definitions of services in FrameSolution applications can be built and maintained as regular Metis models. Installing the FrameSolution metamodel configures Metis as a knowledge engineering environment for FrameSolution.
3. Model management processes used by the Metis Team Server are supplied as Metis models. The processes can be augmented and extended by customers to address local needs and for integration with other customer defined business processes.

6 Conclusion

The feasibility and value of the model-driven approach to knowledge-level integration of business operations and IT have been thoroughly demonstrated in real world settings. Metis and FrameSolution already go a long way towards achieving Visual Enterprise Integration.

The stable infrastructure, rich functionality and methodology-neutral approach have also made the tools attractive to many research groups, including several large R&D collaboration projects funded by the European Commission. The many extensions and new concepts now being researched promise an exciting future for Model-Driven Business Operations.

References

1. Drucker, P.F.: Post-Capitalist Society. Harper Collins, New York (1993)
2. Groth, L.: Future Organizational Design, The scope for the IT-based Enterprise. John Wiley & Sons Ltd., England (1999)
3. Object Management Group: Model Driven Architecture. http://www.omg.org/mda
4. Dehli, E., Coll, G.J.: Just-in-Time Knowledge Support. In: Roy, R. (ed.): Industrial Knowledge Management: A Micro-level Approach. Springer Verlag London Berlin Heidelberg (2001) 299–315
5. Lillehagen, F., Karlsen, D.,Tangen, K.A.: The four layers of EE and VO Infrastructures. In: Proceedings, e-Business and e-Work Conference , Venice (2001)

Trademark Notices

Computas and Metis are registered trademarks belonging to Computas AS. Frame-Solution, Visual Enterprise Integration (VEI), Active Knowledge Modeling (AKM), and Just-in-Time Knowledge Support (JIT KS) are trademarks used by Computas AS. Model Driven Architecture (MDA) is a registered trademark belonging to OMG.

Product Quality
in Software Business Connection

Juhani Anttila

Sonera Corporation, P.O. Box 740, FIN-00051 Sonera, Helsinki, Finland,
juhani.anttila@sonera.com,
http://www.QualityIntegration.net, http://www.sonera.com

Abstract. Product and its quality are clarified in this paper at first conceptually. After a clear general understanding of product-concept and a product's inherent characteristics, satisfaction of users (customers) and the other interested parties is considered. This general insight is applied to the software industry's business needs where the products are strongly service and information or knowledge content. Within software industry there are many quite different business areas. Practical experiences presented in this paper where the general described principles have been applied are from an e-business software engineering application for a B2B case.

1 Product Concept for the Software Industry

As a whole the software industry does not fundamentally differ from any other business branch. Any company as well as a software company has its own business mission, vision, and correspondingly own approach for management and leadership. Business is run as projects or processes in order to produce outputs to the needs and expectations of markets or individual customers. Software industry is strongly based on projects. However, when plenty of projects are being simultaneously and continuously carried out, the business can be effectively and efficiently done only through processes, project-processes.

Within software industry there are many quite different types of businesses, where typical buyer-supplier relationships are characteristically different. Examples include software products, such as commercial-off-the-shelf software applications, system products or components for them, and software realization services, such as software engineering services, platform tailoring and other modification services, and embedded software businesses, and pure application services, such as ASP. These businesses may be either B2C or B2B cases. Emphasis of the practical example of this paper is on the software system engineering for B2B cases.

Very often software industry is not very familiar with generally recognized quality methodology but they have developed and lived with their own dedicated procedures and methods. Neither in the development of general quality methodologies the needs of the software industry have been strongly under consideration. This may cause problems when integrating software elements into

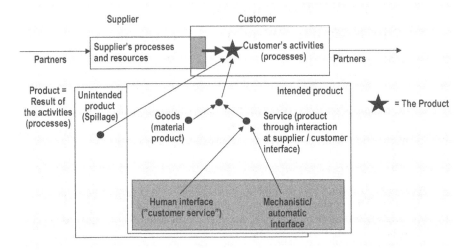

Fig. 1. Product is the linking item between parties of a business connection

larger system products. In fact, in practice software is always a part of some bigger entity, and nowadays almost all products may include software modules.

The product issues of software companies have been considered typically in practice and in research studies in an inadequate way. Therefore it is better to go back to the basics. According to the standard vocabulary and definition of the recognized ISO 9000:2000 standard a product as a concept is in general "a result of a process" to be delivered from the supplier to the customer (see Fig. 1). This definition of a product is valid for all kinds of businesses. Services are nowadays the most important products or parts of the products of any company including software industry. In addition to services, those companies may produce also goods. A service may consist of human and mechanic (automatic) service elements. Thus, also a software company is factually and primarily a service company.

Understanding the concept of service has proved to be difficult in practice. According to the standard definition of ISO 9000 for service-concept, 'service' refers to the result of a company's actions (processes) to the customer, who also participates in this result through his or her own actions. The action itself does not constitute a service, but a service is rather a more permanent result (e.g. the memorable experience produced by a travel agency) which the customer retains even after the activity ends.

Software industry is very strongly a knowledge-based business. Knowledge is the major element in all products (both in goods and services) and in the business processes of a software company. Therefore this context requires a clear understanding of knowledge in general and in particular related to the product concept.

In general the concept of knowledge may be understood in many different ways. It has been considered deeply e.g. by many recognized philosophers during centuries. The pragmatic knowledge-concept is suitable for business purposes. It implies that knowledge means a belief on the nature of some item relevant to a business context. As a consequence of genuine knowledge one can act in a new meaningful way. Knowledge is a real thing only if it is tested by an action and thus changed into a useful activity. In that way also the importance of knowledge is emphasized as a major feature of a product. Thus, knowledge can never be objective.

Knowledge can never exist as such but it has always some kind of "carrier". Examples of the different types of knowledge and its knowledge-carrier include:

- fact – phenomenon, activity, process
- data – measurement or data acquisition network
- information, explicit knowledge – information file or data base, report, procedure document, book
- tacit knowledge – person, expert system
- wisdom – community, mankind

It is not meaningful to talk about a particular knowledge or information product. Knowledge and information exist always embedded with their carriers, and in fact, all products (goods and services) always consist of some kind of information. As examples one may mention a disc with information or software program, IT system with business information, quality records on intranet pages, conference paper, consulting service of an expert, skills of a professional at work, etc. Products of the software industry benefit software and electronic digital technologies for knowledge and information business. Thus, as the carrier always has a crucial role and effect in the provision of knowledge and information, the knowledge-product can always be restored to the consideration of traditional goods and services or their combinations. Knowledge and information are inherent characteristics of any product.

2 Quality of a Software Related Product

When considering the quality of a product, also knowledge and information should be considered together with the major parts of the product (goods and services) taking into account the purpose, users and usage environments of the product. Neither here there are any fundamental differences between the products of software industry and the other business branches. The differences are due to the different technologies. Common general principles and practices are needed because nowadays many different technologies intermingle in the products. Therefore the standard definition of quality-concept of the ISO 9000:2000 is very relevant and useful also for software related products. Thus, product-quality means the degree to which the set of inherent characteristics of the product fulfils the requirements of all interested parties (especially the users) of the product. Requirements consist of needs or expectations that are stated, generally implied or obligatory. Satisfaction follows from the benefits or added-value to the user of the product. Customer value is based on the three major product elements

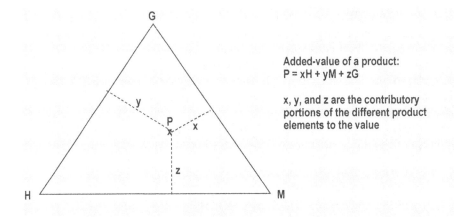

G: Goods from supplier to customer
H: Human service: Results from human activities at the customer/supplier interface
M: Mechanistic service: Results from automatic or mechanical activities at the customer/supplier interface

Fig. 2. Added-value of a product to a customer. All kinds of products can be presented as points within the tringle

(goods, human service, and mechanistic or automatic service – see Fig. 1) and their overall characteristics and performance. Depending on the composition of a product, the different elements have different contribution to the customer value (see Fig. 2).

For handling product-quality the characteristics of the product should be considered comprehensively taking into account the product as a whole and all its characteristics. Systematically the characteristics of any product may be categorized according to international standard principles as follows:

- "technical" performance
- operability (easy to use)
- serviceability (including product dependability)
- safety
- esthetic performance
- ethical characteristics
- price

This is a general grouping of the high-level product-properties, and from this one can approach to more detailed definitions according to the needs of particular cases. All these characteristics may contain information and knowledge and can be realized by goods or services based on software technology. However, there is no general standardized systematical and detailed concept-hierarchy for the characteristics applicable for all products. Also for different expertise areas there have been developed different specialized systems to describe particular product performance. One example is the terminology of information security that

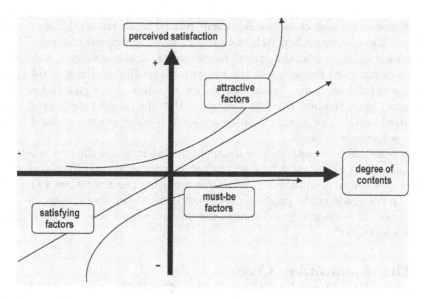

Fig. 3. Creating customer's satisfactions through different kinds of product characteristics (Kano's model)

is very essential in many software-related ICT products. Information security performance can be understood as a sub-group in the above mentioned product performance structure and typically it consists of integrity, dependability and confidentiality. Especially important characteristics that relate to the networked digital ICT services include authenticity and authority performance.

Prof. Kano's model is very recognized for taking into account customers' needs and expectations when designing product characteristics aiming at customers' satisfaction. According to that model products have the following three different kinds of characteristics or factors regarding to their effects to the customers' satisfaction (see Fig. 3):

1. Dissatisfier or must-be characteristics
2. Satisfier characteristics
3. Delighter or attractive characteristics

These view-points are very relevant for all software-related products, too. However, all product-features also influence to each other. E.g. easiness to use the product is always linked to the information security features of the product.

Product-quality is created when product features are designed during the product development. In the specification phase there should be in use a methodology that takes into account Kano's satisfaction phenomena based on the information from customers' needs and expectations. When considering quality of the product it is essential in relationship to the performance characteristics to know (to agree) what is good (acceptable) and what is not good (not acceptable). In this context nonconformity (cf. ISO 9000:2000) is defined as non-fulfilment of a requirement and defect as non-fulfilment related to an intended use or specified use. There is very often lack of clarity in these important concepts. Thus, nonconformity relates to the stated requirements of the customer and defect to perceptions from the usage of the product. According to the general terminology non-fulfilments may be critical, major, or minor. Managing fulfilment of the requirements requires consistent action within the product supplier. Normal recognized practices of quality management and quality assurance may be used also in software businesses.

There should be a clear understanding of the fundamental difference between two concepts, "quality" and "grade". Before starting any product development project and before establishing product requirements one must have a clear decision on the grade of the product performance. Grade implies the chosen category or rank of performance relevant to the needs of the focused market segment (cf. ISO 9000:2000).

3   The Application Case: e-Quality Portal of the "Killer Grade"

For getting practical experiences, the general principles presented above in this paper have been applied in an e-business application for a B2B case. The e-Quality Portal is a cutting-edge gateway to quality-related business reality for enhancing quality awareness, improved use of expertise, performance management and interested party confidence. It was initiated as joint venture of Sonera Corporation seeing the importance to provide a generic solution for the units of its business community and Finnevo Ltd. being interested to satisfy the similar needs in the market. To the portal owner organization, the e-Quality Postal is a software engineering product and to the end users (members of the portal organization and its interested parties) the Portal provides automatic quality management and quality assurance services.

Targeted grade of performance of the e-Quality Portal was to create a killer application to enable to bring about a disruptive and regenerating improvement compared with the following sustaining quality management and quality assurance practices:

1. Conventional poserish activities of a kind of service provided by quality managers
2. "Quality System" as a distinct system with inadequate integration with business management to aim at quality of management
3. Quality Manual as a distinct collection of disciplinary written procedure etc. documents, which are typically more harmful than useful or then forgotten to bookshelves for auditors of certifying bodies
4. Third Party Certificate as a piece of paper with the purpose to end interaction instead of promoting to confidence by creating discussions with customer.

The biggest challenge for the e-Quality Postal is the poor use of business related knowledge and information that may appear in many forms (see Fig. 4).

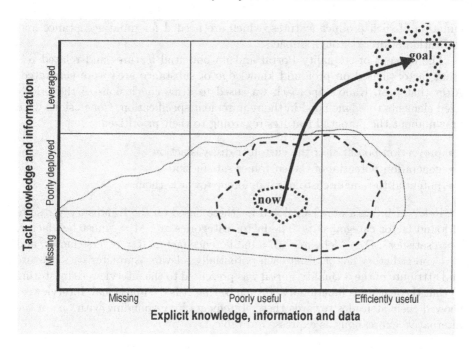

Fig. 4. Challenge of the e-Quality Portal to enhance the effectiveness and efficiency of the use of knowledge and information

Knowledge may be missing in general, or just internally. It may be unused because the needed tacit or relevant explicit knowledge is not available or accessible at the moment of truth or is not in a useful form. It may be used but not appropriately or at opportune time and place, or it may be misused. As we see, a greater challenge than to stretch the usefulness of explicit knowledge, information and data to its extreme is to bring about a radical improvement of utilization of tacit knowledge and information. This is a strong strive for eliminating "tacit ignorance" (Ref. H. Haapio).

4   Surveying and Analyzing the Requirements of the Customer for an Innovative Application

Product quality refers to how well product features correspond to the requirements. This must create value to customer and generate customer satisfaction. The innovation called for a successful killer solution satisfies even latent needs and poorly articulated requirements. Quality of innovation is determined before product development by the creative use of profound knowledge of the poorly preventable problems brought on by conventional practices. During product development this calls for eliminating risks of eventually inappropriate assumptions by effective investigations of potential customer requirements and simulative validation of preliminary solutions. These activities can be concurrent with determination of such product features, which are needed for rapid acceptance and realization of breakthrough impacts.

The concept of e-Quality Portal and its potential features and related relevant factors based on profound knowledge of substance area were generated. After that prof. Kano's approach was used to draw conclusions of the prioritized elements to be included in the requirement specification. Conclusions were drawn about the potential features regarding to their prioritized

- prevention potential of the customer dissatisfaction
- generation potential of the customer satisfaction
- potential to remain customer indifferent towards them

Relevant indexes were calculated for these based on the Kano-survey results of found factor category hits. The factor categories are: M = "must be" factor, S = "satisfier", D = "delighter", I = indifference factor, R = reverse factor, and C = contradictory factor. First each potentially relevant characteristics, feature and attribute of the e-Quality Portal was presented to the interviewees by stating a) that the feature is functional and then b) that it is dysfunctional. Interviewees showed their attitudes towards these statements by responding with one of the alternative expressions as expressed in table 1.

Table 1. Surveying and categorizing customer requirements according to the Kano Model

Feature		Dysfunctional				
		I like it	It is expected to be that way	I don't feel anything	There is no other choice	I don't like it
Functional	I like it	C	D	D	D	S
	It is expected to be that way	R	I	I	I	M
	I don't feel anything	R	I	I	I	M
	There is no other choice	R	I	I	I	M
	I don't like it	R	R	R	R	C

For instance one of the potential features was that "e-Quality Portal enables use of location-based information". Based on the survey 40% of hits was in favor of this factor being classified as S (satisfier), 20% portions were in favor of D (delighter), I (indifferent) and that the dysfunctional feature is a must-be factor. The calculated index was based 75% for generation potential of the customer satisfaction, 50% potential for customer dissatisfaction and 25% for remaining customer indifferent. This resulted to leave this feature with rather low priority (the 4th of 6 priority classes). However, the need to provide location-based services, enabling applications to take a device's location into account was stated as one of the technical requirements. (This decision reflected the interest to leave this feature to be a part of marketing mix regarding to the willingness-to-pay of targeted segments.) So called Control Module was specified as a part of the Content-Related Static Portal Logic. That is for the automatic reasoning for operations and is needed to ensure that a user is supported and alerted appropriately in operations according to the use cases (eventually depending on authorization and personalization for as well as location of the user). A software interface requirement was as an example that the e-Quality Portal can be in interaction with Corporation's Positioning Service to define the location of a mobile user.

5   Product Characteristics and the Brand Characterization

The general systematic hierarchy of the product characteristics described above was used in the requirement specification of the e-Quality Portal. The most essential specified characteristics of the e-Quality Portal product include the following items:

1. Technical performance (cashing succeeds): Context and business events of e-Quality Portal in intranet, extranet and Internet, software interfaces, and documentation
2. Operability (easy and nice operation): Ease of use, ease of learning, operational performance characteristics
3. Serviceability (accessibility: access is available, and retainability: as long as needed): Quantitative sufficiency (capacity available), dependability: reliability performance (no defects), maintainability performance (defects can be eliminated): maintainability characteristics, maintainability of contents, maintainability of personalizations, maintainability of tailorings, maintainability of customizations, and maintenance support performance (organizational support available)
4. Environmental compatibility (environment does not disturb cashing)
5. Safety (no hazards)
6. Aesthetic (beautiful): Brand, style and outlook, balance
7. Ethical (good): Cultural and political requirements, legal requirements
8. Price (win/win is realized): Investment and operating costs, monetary expenditures and non-monetary sacrifices

In addition to these characteristics also several important multidimensional performance characteristics were specified including security (accuracy, availability, confidentiality, authenticity, and authority), and portability.

Brand outcome of the e-Quality Portal was based on the requirement survey. In generating customer satisfaction one must excel customer expectations appropriately. The base of expectations is the brand of the product. As a result of the survey was the conclusion of the brand value statement of e-Quality Portal: "factual quality anywhere anytime" based on the brand authority: "a cutting-edge gateway connecting us to everything and everybody we need to excel in quality-related business reality". As the rational part of its brand personality it was emphasized: "assuring, knowledgeable, helpful, 'killer application'" and as the emotional part "clear, trustable, smart, disruptive way to improvement". The benefits are: "more gain with less pain" as gain increase: new type of value-added experience and breakthrough options and as pain decrease: ease, cost reductions. The brand service is: "support, facilitation, sharing, learning, collaboration, improvement".

6   Conclusions

Experiences behind this paper prove that generally recognized quality management and quality assurance principles and methodology may be very useful also in software-related businesses and for considering quality of their products in a professional way. This is also beneficial when integrating software modules in large system products. Naturally in the context of software technology also specialized quality methodology is needed. Key issue is the consistency with the different methods used.

Product issues are very essential topics when considering quality of software business connections. Products should be understood and handled in a broad sense including both goods, and human and automatic services. Software businesses are primarily service organizations.

e-Quality Portal is a challenging product to demonstrate the practical use of recognized quality methodology in the business areas of software system design and engineering, and specialized automatic service for e-business.

Acknowledgements

The sustained cooperation with Mr. Jorma Vakkuri, Finnevo Ltd., has significantly influenced many views and details of this paper. Many fruitful discussions and debates with him are very much acknowledged and appreciated.

References

1. Anttila J., Vakkuri J.: Business integrated e-quality, e-Business Research Forum, Tampere 2001
2. Anttila J., Vakkuri. J: Good Better Best, Sonera Corporation, Helsinki (2000)
3. Anttila J., Vakkuri. J: ISO 9000 for the Creative Leader, Sonera Corporation, Helsinki (2001)
4. Anttila J.: www.QualityIntegration.net: "Internet pages for the business integrated quality approach", Sonera Corporation, 2001
5. International Standardization Organization: ISO 9000. Quality Management Systems. Fundamentals and Vocabulary, ISO, Geneve (2000)
6. Shiba S, Graham A., Walden D.: A new American TQM, Center for Quality Management, Cambridge MA (1993)
7. Downes L., Mui C.: Unleashing the Killer App, Harvard Business School Press, Boston (2000)

Author Information

Mr. Juhani Anttila has been over 30 years in different quality related tasks in the leading Finnish telecommunication company, Sonera Corporation, and its predecessors. Now he is Vice President Quality Integration of the Corporation. 1984-87 he was also President of the Finnish Society for Quality (now The Center for Excellence), since 1998 Honorary Member of the Society, 1994-96 Vice President of EOQ (European Organization for Quality), and since 1995 International Academician for Quality (i.e. member of the International Academy for Quality). He has been broadly involved with national and international standardization of telecommunications systems, and quality and dependability management and assurance, e.g. since 1980 a member of the international standardization committee ISO TC 176 (ISO 9000) and of the corresponding Finnish national committee. He was four years the chairman of the criteria committee of the Finnish National Quality Award and also acted as an assessor. He has been also as an assessor for the European Quality Award. He was chairman of the technical program committee of the EOQ'93 Helsinki World Quality Congress sponsored by EOQ, ASQC, JUSE and IAQ.

Breakthrough in Delivering Software Quality: Capability Maturity Model and Six Sigma [1]

Gregory H. Watson

Business Systems Solutions, Inc.
10460 Roosevelt Blvd. North PMB#316
St. Petersburg, FL 33716 USA
gregbss@aol.com

Abstract. Since the 1980s software engineering and the quality profession
have been on an intellectual collision course. Software quality has been assured
through the same approach that was first used in hardware manufacturing –
inspection of quality at the source of production. The emphasis on software
quality was originally focused on the programmer and the process of software
development. This effort culminated in a set of documented quality maturity
levels to define the progress of an organization in developing a structured
approach to programming. The Capability Maturity Model (CMM) was
developed by the Software Engineering Institute at Carnegie Mellon University
based on the best practices of a number of leading companies such as IBM and
Hewlett-Packard. Also during the 1980s quality improvement became more
focused with the advent of the Malcolm Baldrige National Quality Award (in
the USA and a parallel effort in Europe with the European Quality Award) as
well as global acceptance of ISO9000 as the basic quality management system
standard. As the practices of quality became more focused, so did the methods
used in application of statistics and industrial engineering, culminating in a
breakthrough refinement of the Total Quality Management (TQM) operating
philosophy that is called Six Sigma. The Six Sigma approach was initiated by
Motorola and subsequently defined by the members of the Six Sigma Research
Institute, followed by application developments at ABB, AlliedSignal, General
Electric and many other leading organizations that have applied the Six Sigma
methods since late 1995. In this speech, the presenter proposes an approach to
drive software breakthroughs by integrating CMM and Six Sigma to improve
software quality performance.

1 Introduction to Software Quality

Software quality is an elusive term. It may be defined internally from the viewpoint
of software developers, or it may be define externally from the viewpoint of end users
of the software. Both perspectives have a unique contribution to defining 'goodness'

---

[1] The copyright for this keynote address is held by Business Systems Solutions, Inc. Permission
has been granted to Springer-Verlag to publish this speech in the proceedings of the Seventh
European Conference on Software Quality. Further publication requires permission of the
author or an officer of Business Systems Solutions, Inc.

J. Kontio and R. Conradi (Eds.): ECSQ 2002, LNCS 2349, pp. 36–41, 2002.
© Springer-Verlag Berlin Heidelberg 2002

in software and both of these perspectives are necessary in order to have 'world class' levels of quality performance. It is equally important to note that neither viewpoint is sufficient, by itself, to achieve the highest levels of software quality. This thesis starts the redefinition of software quality as a holistic objective in product development that combines both a programmer's desire for defect-free (bug-less) lines of programming code and the end user's desire for ease of use and functionality that makes their jobs easier and faster. It is not to the benefit of software developers to ignore either of these two objectives because, combined, they create one of three business errors:

- Produce a product that provides a buggy product with full functionality,
- Produce a bug-less product that doesn't provide desired functionality, or
- Produce a buggy product that has less than desired functionality.

Of course, this third option is totally non-competitive. A company that performs in this way does not belong in business. In the first two options, the company may be able to limp along, provided its competitors do not have a superior offering in terms of software quality that are important in the market. One advantage of software products over hardware products is that there is more consumer tolerance to problems because of the high technology of living at the leading edge. However in today's highly competitive world the leading edge becomes the "bleeding edge" and it is the customers who are bleeding! The software product that meets their need best is the one that the market will favor. Software quality has moved from 'good-to-do' to one of the most significant software development imperatives. Only when the product is able to deliver on both of these objectives, will it be truly competitive. The question for software developers becomes: how to assure competitive software quality?

2   Software Quality and the Capability Maturity Model

Software engineers have traditionally taken an approach to software quality that is inspection-based using code-inspection and testing to assure that products are free of any defects in logical structure. However, users of software applications have taken a much broader view of software quality and included such additional product aspects as functionality, usability, portability, reliability and utility. These additional quality dimensions are initially assured in design and maintained through an upgrade process. Thus, the assurance of software quality requires a commitment that encompasses the entire life cycle of the product. In order to achieve this broad quality requirement for a software product, design engineers have experimented with different approaches to deliver a quality product from both the engineering and the applications viewpoints.

One approach that has been taken is the Capability Maturity Model (CMM) that was developed by the Software Engineering Institute (SEI) of Carnegie-Mellon University in Pittsburgh, PA. The CMM focuses on assuring software product quality through the development of a comprehensive product development infrastructure that is based on best practices in software engineering from many leading companies. CMM gives assurance of performance through a certification program that provides management with confidence that their program is performing at a specified level of proficiency.

The CMM features a model that has five levels of indexed maturity growth. The five levels will take an organization from an entry level in quality performance to the place where quality becomes a competitive advantage:

- Level 1: The initial or entry level is the state where quality is unpredictable and poorly controlled. Improvement beyond this level focuses on the application of project management methods to add discipline to software development.
- Level 2: The second level of maturity characterizes repeatable performance. It occurs when previously mastered tasks are executed in a reliable manner that is consistent with prior performance. Moving beyond this performance level requires integrated engineering processes to produce a standard, consistent process for software development.
- Level 3: The third level of maturity results in a defined approach where the design process characteristics are very well understood. Maturity beyond this level emphasizes product and process quality to create predictable outcomes from design processes.
- Level 4: The fourth level of quality maturity in software development is the state where quality is managed using performance measurement and software design process control in order to achieve consistent outcomes that are characteristic of predictable processes. To move beyond this maturity level requires continuous improvement with an emphasis on managing strategic change in product development processes.
- Level 5: The fifth level of quality maturity optimizes performance in design and software product development through process improvement. At this level of maturity, continuous improvement is ingrained in an organization and has become a way of life.

The CMM philosophy applies process management and quality improvement ideas to the development of software. It identifies three concepts that are woven among these five levels of performance:

- Process capability – the range of expected results that can be achieved by following a process. Achieving process capability will allow the prediction of future project performance.
- Process performance – measures the actual results from following an agreed upon software development process.
- Process maturity – recognizes the extent to which a software development process is explicitly defined, managed and measured to achieve effective performance that meets business objectives.

CMM relies on this general model to achieve process development maturity, but as the prominent statistician Dr. George E. P. Box once quipped: "All models are wrong, but some models are useful." By embedding the concept of process capability into its approach to achieving maturity in performance for measured quality characteristics, the CMM approach provides a good linkage point for Six Sigma thinking.

3   Quality System Management and Six Sigma

During the 1980s the traditional approaches to quality took two developmental pathways. One approach represented a classical approach to quality control and assurance by design of a quality management system that provided customers with the assurance that the provider had a minimal level of quality performance as validated by a third-party assessment. This is the fundamental rationale for ISO9000 as a quality management system. ISO9000 has a unique global application for assuring customers that their suppliers will maintain a quality system. However, the standard for performance is low. Only the basics are required, so the adherence to ISO9000 does not assure that quality can provide a competitive advantage to a supplier over other sources being considered for a specific product application. A second approach taken in the 1980s is represented by the self-assessment undertaken to evaluate an organization's performance against a criteria for business excellence, such as the European Quality Award criteria or the USA's Malcolm Baldrige National Quality Award criteria. In this self-assessment approach management evaluates its performance using the criteria for business excellence that have been established based on successful strategic and operational practices of leading organizations that are codified in a formal self-assessment criteria. This approach to quality provides a "stretch" for the organization as it aspires to perform among the 'best-of-the-best' organizations. Both of these methods of assessment produce gaps in an organization's performance –gaps from ISO9000 tend to be tactical concerns focused on the daily work process and the gaps identified by the self-assessment are more strategic in nature. Both of these systems identify gaps, but neither one provides a method for closure of the gaps.

Six Sigma is a business improvement approach that seeks to find and eliminate causes of mistakes or defects in products and business processes by focusing on outputs that are significant to customers. The concepts underlying Six Sigma deal with the fact that process and product variation are known to be strong factors affecting product production lead times, product and process costs, process yields, and, ultimately customer satisfaction. One of the most important aspects of the work of a Six Sigma "Black Belt" is to define, identify and measure sources of variation with the intent of discovering causes and developing efficient operational means to control and reduce this variation. The heart of the Six Sigma approach lies within its rigorous problem-solving approach, the dedicated application of trained business analysts to well-structured process or product improvement projects, and the attention of management for delivering bottom-line results and sustaining those results over time.

To achieve the performance excellence that is inherent in a Six Sigma process, Black Belts will apply two methods to deliver predictable results. One of these Six Sigma methods is called DMAIC – for the five-step define, measure, analyze, improve and control problem- solving process. The outcome of this method is to revolve a problem and put its process into a state of control where the process capability is consistently delivered. The second of the Six Sigma methods is called DFSS – or Design for Six Sigma. DFSS is used to develop new products or reengineer business processes. DFSS creates enhanced process capability that keeps ahead of market and technology changes by innovating to design and deliver new product features that anticipate changing market needs and customer requirements. It is DFSS that assures the future competitiveness of an organization by maintaining both its inherent process capability and its performance results on the leading edge of its industry. Sustainable performance of Six Sigma processes delivers long-term organizational maturity of a business.

While this explanation of Six Sigma is brief and inadequate in many respects, it does illustrate its ability to act as the gap-closing methodology to support both ISO9000 and the business excellence self-assessment. Six Sigma can also be linked with the CMM concepts for assuring the quality of software. How can conceptual integration of these methods be approached efficiently?

4   Integrating CMM and Six Sigma

Perhaps the best way to illustrate how to integrate CMM and Six Sigma is to begin by discussing the distinctions between these two approaches. There are a few interesting comparisons may be made:

- While Six Sigma relies on analytical tools and statistical methods to drive its performance improvement, these methods are only implied as an intention that is associated with the CMM approach to measurement, and is most often not well implemented.
- While Six Sigma begins by building process capability using DMAIC as the method for improving business, CMM emphasis is on technology application that is more consistent with application of the DFSS method of Six Sigma.
- While Six Sigma improvement projects should be drawn from a portfolio of problems that are identified during strategic planning by business leaders, the CMM linkage to strategy is weak and often ignored.
- While Six Sigma emphasizes the development and certification of the Black Belts, CMM emphasizes development of CMM assessors and certification of organizations.

Based on this comparative analysis, it is clear that the methods of Six Sigma are most complementary with the CMM Level 4 and Level 5 organizations that emphasize the use of quantitative measurements for defect reduction in order to achieve business outcomes that are predictable. Six Sigma methods fulfill the requirement of CMM for quantitative methods and tools, thereby fulfilling a requirement for certification of an organization to the CMM.

What are some of the benefits that can be obtained by forging a link between CMM and Six Sigma? Just to name a few, consider the following list:

- Establish a common language between hardware and software developers.
- Define a shared objective for product design performance improvement.
- Build a set of processes that applies the systems approach to product design.
- Provide a consistent framework for assessing project performance.
- Assure the integration of product development and business strategy.

5   Conclusion

Among the drivers of business success in the high technology industry are both time-to-market and customer satisfaction. To have high product development productivity, an organization must eliminate wasted actions and redundant activities, streamlining the work that it performs to rapidly design and release a product that out-performs its competitors and meets its window of market opportunity. This is a tall order to do on a single occasion; but sustained success in business is achieved only when this can be accomplished on a predictable basis. The business requirement of sustainable success implies that the software development process needs to be structured efficiently so that it meets product delivery requirements, integrated with business plans so that it meets commercial requirements, and focused on true market needs so that it meets the customer requirements. The quality system must be capable of assuring that all three of the requirements are met. Based on the observations in this paper, how can such a quality system be structured?

The suggested approach to business system wide performance improvement:

- Align the ISO9000 approach to improvement with CMM Levels 1 through 3.
- Align a Six Sigma approach to improvement with CMM Levels 4 and 5.
- Conduct a holistic assessment of business excellence within the framework of the European Quality Award criteria.
- Implement improvements from either tactical or strategic changes into the basic work process documents and combine these improvements with the ISO9000 quality system work instructions and standard operating procedures that define the routine tasks an organization performs to design and develop both the hardware and software components of its products.

Taking this integrated approach to software quality provides the opportunity to make breakthrough business performance happen by planning the innovation of products to meet market expectations and predictably delivering these products on schedule. The quality management system, when properly structured, integrates with a development process to assure that the business objectives and market objectives are met. When an integrated approach to software quality is taken, quality is no longer – rather quality is visible in the organization's dual bottom lines: business financial results and customer satisfaction.

Using Mobile Agents
for Security Testing in Web Environments

Wen-Kui Chang, Min-Hsiang Chuang, and Chao-Tung Yang

Dept. of Computer Science & Information Engineering, Tunghai University, Taiwan,
{wkc,ctyang}@mail.thu.edu.tw, sg892819@cis.thu.edu.tw

Abstract. In this paper, we first introduce the concepts of mobile agent technology, and then look at some related research on mobile agent technology. Mobile agent technology is introduced as a solution for the critical problem of limited bandwidth we face nowadays, and its autonomy characteristic helps solve the problem of inability of the system administrators to stand by 24 hours a day. Next we study the issues related to security testing. In addition, we link these issues to today's websites, and study how we can examine the security functionalities of websites.
Finally, we combine the verdicts from different sections of this paper and produce the framework of a mobile agent for testing website security. We also discuss the expected output.

Keywords: mobile agent technology, limited bandwidth, autonomy, security testing

1 Introduction

Surfing the web has become a daily activity for many people. Furthermore, almost everything can be put onto the web without much cost and effort. This is especially helpful for businesses that want to have a deeper reach and wider range of customers. However, there is an adverse effect of such popularity. If the site is unstable and becomes unavailable at times, the potential visitors will be deterred from going to the website. In other words, there will be less customers to the website to either shop for goods or look for information. Therefore, we see the importance of website quality.

In order to have a quality website, we need to test the site to ensure everything is working properly. By performing security tests on those websites that require logging in, we can ensure that the log in function is working well. There are several ways to test this functionality, and we have chosen to use mobile agent technology as the solution.

By utilizing a mobile agent to perform security testing, we are able to significantly cut down the bandwidth that we need to achieve the same test coverage. The mobile agent requires a minimum amount of bandwidth to send the agent out to the client, and once the agent starts to perform the tests, it will be on its own and require no connection with the server. Furthermore, the agent will be able to perform the tests automatically after the system administrator has adjusted settings. This decreases the workload of the workers and increases their efficiency in the long run.

J. Kontio and R. Conradi (Eds.): ECSQ 2002, LNCS 2349, pp. 42–52, 2002.

First we introduce the concepts of mobile agent technology. This technology is introduced so as to save the already-limited bandwidth we have today. Next we will highlight the security issues of current websites. Finally we will combine the essence from these two sections to construct a framework for using mobile agents to perform security testing in web environments.

2 Description of Mobile Agent Technology

2.1 Basic Structure

In essence, an agent [2,3] is a computerized (that is, hard- and/or software) or human entity that, according to the "weak agency" notion [Woolridge and Jennings, 1995] has the following properties:

- Autonomy - Agents operate without the direct intervention of humans or others, and have some control over their actions.
- Social ability - Agents can interact with other agents and possibly humans.
- Reactivity - Agents respond in a timely fashion to changes they perceive in their environment which may be a representation of the physical world, a user via a graphical user interface, a collection of other agents, the Internet, etc.
- Pro-activeness - Agents do not simply act in response to their environment; they are able to exhibit goal-directed behavior by taking the initiative.

In addition, the agent can also be considered as an intelligent entity that possesses the ability to learn, cooperate, and move.

Considering a mobile agent as a moving software agent, it may generally consist of the following components as illustrated in Fig. 1.

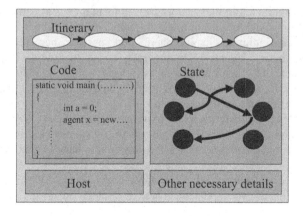

Fig. 1. The basic structure of a mobile agent

Itinerary – This is the place where the route of the agent is recorded. Not only does it record the route, it also records the current position, so that we know exactly where the agent is. This is an essential part of a mobile agent; since the agent is moving, it needs to know where to start and where to go next and ultimately, where to end. We also have to know its current position so that we can trace it and it will not get lost.

Code – This is the part where fragments of the program code are stored. By definition, an agent is a computational entity, which also means it is a program that can be executed. Therefore, this is the part that cannot be neglected. Without this code part, an agent will not be able to perform any tasks, not even traveling. Moreover, this part controls all other parts of the agent, making it more important than it seems.

State – The status of the agent is recorded here. In our case it means the status of the tested hyperlinks will be recorded here. With this part, the agent then will be able to report to both the server and client about the status of the hyperlinks.

Host – This is the place where the server position will be stored. It is quite vital since an agent is only running on the Agent Transfer Protocol (ATP) [9]. The agent will have to remember where it came from so that it will be able to return to the server after the assigned tasks are completed. If not, it will be lost in the network and perhaps be jamming up the network.

Other necessary details – The agent needs to show who created it, and this is the place to put that. Other information related to this agent is stored in the same place so that people will know what this agent does and who the owner is.

2.2 Related Research

Though the mobile agent is quite a new technology, it has been utilized in several areas in computer science. We will look at related studies on mobile agents for network management [3], and the NASA human planetary exploration plan [11].

The authors of the research note on mobile agents for network management [3] realized that the mobile agent framework is an emerging standard as early as 1998, and they tried to utilize it in the network management area. Basically they categorized basic network management into three different management areas, namely fault management, configuration management, and performance management. They wanted to use mobile agents in these areas, so as to automate what we would normally do manually. The ultimate goal is to have a plug-and-play network that will automatically configure itself under different circumstances. This is also what the new technologies are hoping to achieve recently.

Next is the NASA human planetary exploration plan. Future NASA missions will require robust and flexible Web-based information systems that designers can rapidly develop, extend, and customize. Therefore they have adopted agent-oriented software engineering and agent components to allow them to achieve this. A successful agent-based system can enhance human performance during planetary exploration in hostile environments. This is a very specialized area of research on agent systems.

3 Issues Related to Security Testing

3.1 Basic Information

Security requirements [5,6,7,13] define the security services that the system must provide and help to guide the allocation of security functionality to components. Security requirements are analyzed to determine whether they comprise a complete set and whether they adequately reflect the concerns of the customers. Requirements analysis also determines whether functionality has been identified and allocated to a component to satisfy the requirements. Requirements, threat, architecture analysis, and penetration tests will attempt to identify how the system may be exploited (i.e., hacked, attacked, or broken into) and the potential impact of that exploitation.

Weaknesses are generated where no functionality exists to enforce a security requirement or where testing and analysis reveal a deficiency in the effectiveness of security mechanisms. Weaknesses against which a threat is levied are classified as vulnerabilities. Weaknesses and vulnerabilities are differentiated in order to focus and prioritize the decision maker's limited resources on items that will yield the greatest improvement in security when addressed. Finally, security guidance is offered to mitigate or eliminate vulnerabilities through the customer's decision-making processes.

There are security risks that affect web servers, the local area networks that host Web sites, and even innocent users of web browsers. >From the point of view of the network administrator, a Web server represents yet another potential hole in your local network's security. The general goal of network security is to keep strangers out. Yet the point of a web site is to provide the world with controlled access to your network. Drawing the line can be difficult. A poorly configured web server can punch a hole in the most carefully designed firewall system. A poorly configured firewall can make a web site impossible to use. Things get particularly complicated in an intranet environment, where the Web server must typically be configured to recognize and authenticate various groups of users, each with distinct access privileges.

To the end-user, web surfing feels both safe and anonymous. It's not. Active content, such as ActiveX controls and Java applets, introduces the possibility that web browsing will introduce viruses or other malicious software into the user's system. Active content also has implications for the network administrator, insofar as web browsers provide a pathway for malicious software to bypass the firewall system and enter the local area network. Even without active content, the very act of browsing leaves an electronic record of the user's surfing history, from which unscrupulous individuals can reconstruct a very accurate profile of the user's tastes and habits.

Finally, both end-users and web administrators need to worry about the confidentiality of the data transmitted across the Web. The TCP/IP protocol was not designed with security in mind; hence it is vulnerable to network eavesdropping. When confidential documents are transmitted from the Web server to the browser, or when the end-user sends private information back to the server inside a fill-out form, someone may be listening in.

There are basically three overlapping types of risk:

• Bugs or misconfiguration problems in the Web server that allow unauthorized remote users to steal confidential documents not intended for their eyes and execute commands on the server host machine, allowing them to modify the system. The remote users can also gain information about the web server's host machine that will allow them to break into the system and launch denial-of-service attacks, rendering the machine temporarily unusable.

- Browser-side risks, including active content that crashes the browser, damages the user's system, breaches the user's privacy, or merely creates an annoyance, and the misuse of personal information knowingly or unknowingly provided by the end-user.
- Interception of network data sent from browser to server or vice versa via network eavesdropping. Eavesdroppers can operate from any point on the pathway between browser and server including the network on the browser's and server's side of the connections, and Internet Service Providers for end-users and servers.

It is important to realize that "secure" browsers and servers are only designed to protect confidential information against network eavesdropping. Without system security on browser and server sides, confidential documents are vulnerable to interception.

3.2 CGI Scripts

The problem with CGI scripts [12] is that each one presents yet another opportunity for exploitable bugs. CGI scripts should be written with the same care and attention given to Internet servers themselves, because, in fact, they are miniature servers.

CGI scripts can present security holes in two ways. First, they may intentionally or unintentionally leak information about the host system that will help hackers break in. In addition, scripts that process remote user input, such as the contents of a form or a "searchable index" command, may be vulnerable to attacks in which the remote user tricks them into executing commands.

CGI scripts are potential security holes. A subverted CGI script not running as root still has enough privileges to mail out the system password file, examine the network information maps, or launch a log-in session on a high numbered port.

4 Testing Methodology

4.1 Testing Framework

In this section, we describe in detail the desired framework for developing a mobile agent for security testing. The steps are described in the following paragraphs and are illustrated in Fig. 2.

1. Initiate the test

The target website initiates the testing process by accessing the web page of the agent server. The agent can determine at this stage where it will go after being dispatched. Since the main purpose of the agent is to test the security scripts of the

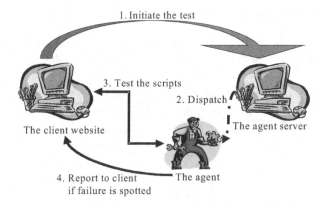

Fig. 2. The desired testing framework

web server, other attributes that the agent requires will only be obtained just before the agent starts the testing process.

2. Dispatch

The agent server will then create an agent and send the agent out. After the agent has been sent out, it is on its own. The agent will be responsible for testing the security scripts of the targeted server and will report on failures automatically. During the process, the agent need not be connected to the server.

3. Test the scripts

The agent will perform some fairly simple tests to collect data. The agent will first obtain the test data from the system administrator of the web server. The test data includes two sets of user names and passwords. One is the valid set of user names and passwords whereas the other set is the invalid one. The agent will be responsible for applying these two sets of data for testing the validity of the security scripts.

4. Report to client if failure is spotted

The agent will continue testing the scripts alternatively with time intervals that can be set by the system administrator. The main purpose of the agent is to make sure that there is no security breakdown. If the valid set of user names and passwords does not allow the agent to log in successfully or the other way round, this is an indication that the security system is down. The agent will then record the time that the breakdown took place and after a period of time, it will send the log file to the system administrator. The system administrator will then know about the problem and fix it before the system is further damaged.

One thing to note is that since mobile agents only travel on ATP as discussed in the earlier section, the clients will have to install the IBM Aglets Software Development Kit (ASDK) [9], and have it properly set up. Only with it can the mobile agent know where it is going, and the testing framework work properly.

4.2 Testing Techniques

We now illustrate the testing techniques necessary to produce the security report for the clients. The steps are described in the following paragraph and are illustrated in Fig. 3.

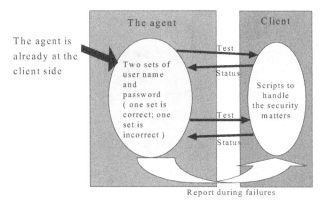

Fig. 3. The testing techniques

To describe the testing techniques, we assume that the mobile agent is already at the client side. Once the agent is at the client side, it will automatically start the testing techniques. It will first obtain the two sets of test data from the system administrator as described earlier.

Next the agent will start to feed the scripts that handle the security with the two different set of data. If the scripts are working as expected, a valid set of user name and password will allow the agent to log in to the system, whereas an invalid set of user name and password will forbid the agent to log in. To achieve the autonomy characteristic of the mobile agent, the agent will be designed to perform the test automatically. Furthermore, in order to report the failures near real time, the system administrator will be able to adjust the frequency with which the mobile agent needs to perform the test.

Once the agent encounters unexpected situations, such as being prohibited from logging in even when the user name and password are correct, or being allowed to log into the system even when the user name and password are invalid, the agent will report the failure to the system administrator. By default, the email address of the system administrator is where the warning will be sent to since in most cases, the system administrator is the one who is in charge of the system.

However, it will be impossible for the system administrator to stay 24 hours a day. Therefore this is what the security testing agent is designed to do. The agent will continuously test the security of the log in system, and report any failures to the system administrator. The agent will keep a log of the failures if the problems are not addressed before the next test, and it will send the daily log file to the system administrator when he starts work.

4.3 Advantages

There are several advantages [8] that our approach supplies. The basic and the most obvious advantage is the bandwidth. Generally, if we want to perform any test from the test server, we will require huge bandwidth that can handle all the tests requested by different clients. Furthermore, in our approach for security testing, we are able to perform the test continuously, which needs even bigger bandwidth. With the mobile agent approach, we are able to cut down the bandwidth tremendously. The agent server will only require a small amount of bandwidth to send the agent out. Once the agent is at the client side, there will be no need for the server to communicate with the agent. In other words, no bandwidth will be required after the agent is sent out. Hence, we see that applying mobile agent technology to the testing area will save lots of bandwidth, especially when we are facing problems with bandwidth so often today.

In addition, the mobile agent will perform the security testing automatically. In other words, the system administrator will not have to stay 24 hours a day to watch for any service failure. The mobile agent will test the security functions all by itself once the settings have been adjusted by the system administrator. Once the mobile agent detects failures, it will straightaway email the system administrator and log the failures. The logged report will be shown to the system administrator every morning when he steps into the office. This effort in achieving autonomy helps to decrease the workload of the people involved. In the long run, the efficiency of work will improve.

5 Demonstration Example

We will first look at one simple example and decide what we want to do about it. Without loss of generality, we take the MSN Hotmail website as an example. Fig. 4 shows a snapshot of the one of the most popular Internet email account providers.

Fig. 4. Snapshot of MSN Hotmail

Fig. 5. The conceptual test path

Since we used the IBM Aglets Software Development Kit (ASDK) as our tool to create our mobile agent, we will need to install the ASDK onto the server for the mobile agent to arrive there and perform the tests. However, at the present moment we are not able to install the agent server onto the Hotmail website, and therefore we decided to take an alternative approach. We installed ASDK on another computer within our control, and let it test the Hotmail website. When the test server makes a request to the agent server to test the security functions, the agent server will send an agent, with the testing abilities, to it.

Once the agent is at the test server, it will start to test the Hotmail website. The test server will provide the agent with two sets of test data as described in the earlier sections of this paper. The valid set of sign-in name and password will allow the agent to log into the server and access the emails, which is not the main function of this testing agent. On the other hand, the invalid set will lead the agent to a page that will display the error. Fig. 5 shows the conceptual test path.

The agent will repeat the testing process as required. In this example, we have set the agent to perform the test every hour and report the results everyday. The sample log file is illustrated in Fig. 6.

Number	Date	Time	ID : password	Status
1	2001/10/22	10:45	thuselab : 12345678	Success
2	2001/10/22	10:45	thuselab : 123	Fail
3	2001/10/22	11:45	thuselab : 12345678	Success
4	2001/10/22	11:45	thuselab : 123	Fail
5	2001/10/22	12:45	thuselab : 12345678	Success
6	2001/10/22	12:45	thuselab : 123	Fail
7	2001/10/22	13:45	thuselab : 12345678	Success
8	2001/10/22	13:45	thuselab : 123	Success
9	2001/10/22	14:45	thuselab : 12345678	Success
10	2001/10/22	14:45	thuselab : 123	Success
11	2001/10/22	15:45	thuselab : 12345678	Success
12	2001/10/22	15:45	thuselab : 123	Success

Fig. 6. The sample log file

From the log file, we can see that the failure cases start at case number 8. By rights, when the supplied sign-in name (ID) is **thuselab**, the only password that will allow the agent to log in is **12345678**. However, in this case, when the password is **123**, the agent is still able to log into the system without prompting the error message. This will indicate that the security functionalities are not working as expected and therefore failure occurs.

Once the system administrator receives this log file, he will be able to address the problem as soon as possible, and further security leaks will be prevented.

6 Conclusion

Testing has long been an issue of discussion. Good testing can save a huge amount of development time and cost. On the contrary, mobile agent technology is pretty fresh to the computing scene. Only recently has mobile agent technology started to show its potential. Mobile agent technology has been utilized in many diverse areas, ranging from network management to NASA space plans. However, only in a small number of papers did we see that mobile agent has actually been utilized in the field of testing. Hence there are limited resources in this area.

With mobile agent technology being applied in security testing, we are trying to achieve a method that is both low in bandwidth and high in performance. The nature of the mobile agent allows us to significantly decrease the bandwidth needed for testing, and the characteristics of the software agent enable us to perform the tests automatically resulting in high performance testing.

In the future, we will want to study the security issues related to mobile agents so as to create mobile agents that are both secure and harmless to the execution environments. There will be more and more research on mobile agent technology, and it will be a rising star in the future.

Acknowledgement

The authors gratefully acknowledge financial support from the National Science Council, Taiwan, Republic of China, under project NSC 90-2213-E-029-005, entitled "A mobile agent for testing distributed applications."

References

1. Asaka Midori, Okazawa Shunji, Taguchi Atsushi, Goto Shigeki, A Method of Tracing Intruders by Use of Mobile Agents, web page: http://www.isoc.org/inet99/4k/4k_2.htm.
2. Agent Characteristics of Java, homepage: http://agent.cs.dartmouth.edu/workshop/1997/slides/lange/tsld002.htm, (last visited: 2001.8).
3. Bieszczad, Andrzej, Pagurek, Bernard and White, Tony, Carleton University, Mobile Agent for Network Management, 1998.

4. Concordia-Java Mobile Agent Technology, homepage: http://www.concordiaagents.com/, (last visited: 2001.5).
5. Farmer Darn, Testing methodology, homepage: http://www.fish.com/survey/testing.html, (last visited: 2001.9).
6. Mosley, Daniel J., Client-Server Testing on the Desktop and the Web, Prentice Hall, 2000.
7. Tripunitara Mahesh V., Dutta Partha, Security Assessment of IP-Based Networks: A Holistic Approach, web page: http://www.isoc.org/inet99/4k/4k_3.htm.
8. Nwana, Hyacinth and Ndumu, Divine, An Introduction to Agent Technology, 1996.
9. IBM Aglets Software Development Kit Home, homepage: http://www.trl.ibm.com/aglets/index.html, (last visited: 2001.3).
10. Lowe, David, Hypermedia and the Web-An Engineering Approach, Wendy Hall, 1999.
11. Griss, Martin L. and Pour, Gilda, Accelerating Development with Agent Components, Computer, May 2001, Volume 34, Number 5, p37-43.
12. The WWW Security FAQ, homepage: http://www.w3.org/Security/Faq/index.html#contents, (last visited: 2001.8).
13. Trusted Computer Solutions, homepage: http://www.tcs-sec.com/welcome.html, (last visited: 2001.9).

Quality Control Techniques
for Constructing Attractive Corporate Websites:
Usability in Relation
to the Popularity Ranking of Websites

Toyohiro Kanayama[1], Hideto Ogasawara[2], and Hiroshi Kimijima[3]

[1]e-Commerce Initiatives, Advantest Corporation,
Shinjuku-NS Bldg., 2-4-1, Nishi-Shinjuku, Shinjuku-ku, Tokyo 163-0880, Japan,
kanayama@ns.advantest.co.jp

[2]Corporate Research & Development Center, Toshiba Corporation,
1, Komukai Toshiba-cho, Saiwai-ku, Kawasaki-shi, Kanagawa 212-8582, Japan
hideto.ogasawara@toshiba.co.jp

[3]Customer Satisfaction Promotion Office, Fujitsu Learning Media Limited,
Kamata Green Building, 37-10, Nishikamata 7-chome, Ota-ku, Tokyo 140-8623, Japan
kimijima.hirosi@jp.fujitsu.com

Abstract. Content and usability are important in the context of efforts to raise the attractiveness of a corporate website. Regarding the content, there must be information indispensable for a corporate website. Regarding the usability, it is necessary to establish a usability test method. This paper describes the results of an investigation of the Japanese-language corporate websites of Japanese companies in order to specify the content necessary for a corporate website. Furthermore, a scenario-based usability test technique was applied and the relationship between the popularity of a website and its usability was examined. Based on the results obtained, we propose a framework for constructing a corporate website by tailoring the WBS (Work Breakdown Structure) and checklist for static quality assurance, and usability and function test for dynamic quality assurance.

1 Introduction

In view of the widespread use of the Internet, it is important to raise the usability of websites. Also, websites have an increasingly important bearing on the ability of corporations to achieve their goals. Moreover, by building and updating a website quickly, opportunities for business can be increased. However, the methods for constructing websites are in their infancy and establishment of construction techniques for attractive websites is needed.

J. Kontio and R. Conradi (Eds.): ECSQ 2002, LNCS 2349, pp. 53–62, 2002.

2   Problems in Constructing Corporate Websites

Websites have become important elements in corporate strategy. However, the following problems impede effective utilization of websites.

Problems of Content. It is unclear what information a corporate website should contain. For example, for an investor, financial information is required. Moreover, for a recruiter, jobs and careers information is indispensable. But, it is unclear what kind of information is required, or how detailed the information should be, for a corporate website to support the various types of users.

Therefore, the content of websites varies within the same industry, making it difficult for users to use corporate website efficiently.

Problems of Usability. The usability of websites is a significant element in the context of efforts to increase the number of users who repeatedly access websites. However, in many cases, usability is not considered from the viewpoint of users. For example, many websites have deficiencies in terms of font size or color scheme. Moreover, some websites are deficient in terms of operability, i.e., it is difficult for users to reach the content they want.

3   Indispensable Content and Usability Test Method

In order to solve the above-mentioned problems concerning content, we performed an analysis of many corporate websites in order to ascertain the content indispensable for a corporate website. It is useful to embody the results of this analysis in a checklist. Designers can use the checklist to build in quality at an early stage. Therefore, we investigated a usability test method and evaluated it. In this chapter, we explain the results of the investigation and the evaluation.

3.1   Actual Condition of Japanese-Language Corporate Websites of Japanese Companies

First, we conducted an investigation to identify key features of the composition of corporate homepages, in order to better understand the actual condition of Japanese-language corporate websites of Japanese companies. In September 2000, we investigated whether it would have the common information and function of 22 items obtained by the preliminary survey about the corporate homepages which were working. We selected ten companies for investigation from eight industries, and 80 companies in all, including notable companies from each industry. The types of information contained in the corporate homepages we investigated are listed in Table 1.

Table 1. The results of investigation (unit : %)

Information / Common Items	Electrical Machinery	Supplier of Industrial Material	Measuring Instrument	Construction	Department Store	Travel	Securities Brokerage	Press
1 Company Information (Map, Tel.)	100	100	100	80	70	100	100	90
2 Jobs and Careers	80	100	100	80	60	90	90	70
3 Products and Ordering Informati	100	100	100	100	100	100	90	70
4 Services	100	20	80	10	70	50	80	20
5 Financial Affairs and Stocks	100	100	60	40	30	30	70	20
6 News (Flash)	80	100	100	90	90	80	100	100
7 Instructions	40	0	50	30	40	30	50	90
8 Contact Information	50	30	100	20	50	70	60	60
9 Business Opportunity (Bid etc.)	50	40	10	0	0	0	80	0
10 Search	90	60	70	0	10	30	50	60
11 Link	30	0	100	40	40	90	60	60
12 Stores, Dealers	0	30	50	10	90	90	60	0
13 Eye Catcher	80	90	70	90	70	40	60	80
14 Catchphrase	60	70	60	70	0	40	40	20
15 Site Map	40	50	80	40	30	60	70	50
16 Ownership, Customer Logon	10	0	30	30	90	30	80	0
17 Calendar	0	0	0	0	30	20	0	0
18 Corporate Logo	100	80	100	90	50	100	100	100
19 Highlight Mark 'New'	30	30	70	10	40	60	30	60
20 Scrolling	50	80	70	50	100	100	100	90
21 Multiframes	0	60	60	50	30	30	50	80
22 Multilingual	100	90	70	60	10	40	50	80

This result showed that there was information indispensable for a corporate website, regardless of the industry. For example, "Company Information", "Jobs and Careers", "Products and Ordering Information", "News", and "Corporate Logo" were contained in almost all homepages. These are important items for building a company homepage. "Scrolling" means the percentage of the homepage, which cannot be seen without scrolling, when maximizing the web browser at the display size of 640x480. From the viewpoint of usability, it is desirable that all content of the homepage be displayable on the screen simultaneously; however, for about 80% of the homepages scrolling is necessary in order to see all the information.

When building a corporate website, it is important to confirm whether indispensable information is offered.

3.2 Usability Test Technique

Usability refers to the ability to display information skillfully, in order to aid the user's decision-making. That is, if the site is such that the information which the user is looking for can be found easily, usability is good. We assumed that attractive sites have high usability.

Conventionally, usability has been evaluated mainly by a functional test. Reliance on a functional test is unsatisfactory from a user's viewpoint. Considering that usability of websites is becoming more important, usability must be maintained by using methods other than a functional test. So, we selected a usability test method and evaluated it. In order to judge the validity of the selected test method, we hypothesized that an attractive site has high usability. That is, there is a correlation between the popularity ranking of a website and the result of the usability test. To verify that, we carried out a usability test on Japanese-language EC sites of Japanese companies that had received high popularity rankings.

3.2.1   Scenario-Based Usability Test

Although there are various techniques advocated for usability tests, the techniques of the usability test in reference [1] are a good example based on a user's real experience. They can be summarized as follows:

Enforcement Method: Showing subject material (scenario) to a tester who completes a questionnaire (7-point evaluation) after exposure to an object site. There are 8 Post-Task Questions, and 16 items of Post-Test Site Comparison. (Fig.1)

Evaluation Method: Calculating the score using the degree of stress (Q3), the time required (Q4), and reliability (Q6). A perfect score is 100 points.

Tester: Users familiar with the operation of a web browser.

A scenario consists of the following four viewpoints:
1. Simple Fact Questions
2. Judgment Questions
3. Comparison of Fact Questions
4. Comparison of Judgment Questions

These four subjects can cover most aspects of decision-making in everyday life.

3.2.2   Popularity Ranking of Websites

How can we judge the popularity of websites? We think that "The ranking of EC sites selected by 1200 users" by Nikkei Network Business shows the popularity of websites. (http://nnb.nikkeibp.co.jp/nnb/ranking/f_index.html)

We decided to select the sites for investigation from among sites whose popularity was already established. The ranking was decided on the basis of four factors: Familiarity, expectations, availability and user evaluation. A full score was 20 points. The overview of "The ranking of EC sites selected by 1200 users" is shown as follows:

Enforcement: October 2000.
Object Site: EC sites (books, personal computers, travel etc.)

Post-Task Questions

Q3 While completing this task, did you

feel completely frustrated **1 2 3 4 5 6 7** always know what
to do next

Q4 Compared to what you expected, did this task go

much slower **1 2 3 4 5 6 7** much faster

Q6 How confident are you that you found all the relevant information?

not at all confident **1 2 3 4 5 6 7** very confident

Post-Test Site Comparison

1 Ease of finding specific information	very unsatisfied **1 2 3 4 5 6 7** very satisfied
2 Ease of reading data	very unsatisfied **1 2 3 4 5 6 7** very satisfied
3 Ease of the concentrating on the data search (distractions)	very unsatisfied **1 2 3 4 5 6 7** very satisfied
4 Logic of navigation	very unsatisfied **1 2 3 4 5 6 7** very satisfied
5 Ease of search	very unsatisfied **1 2 3 4 5 6 7** very satisfied
6 Appearance of site	very unsatisfied **1 2 3 4 5 6 7** very satisfied
7 Quality of graphics	very unsatisfied **1 2 3 4 5 6 7** very satisfied
8 Relevance of graphics to site subject	very unsatisfied **1 2 3 4 5 6 7** very satisfied
9 Speed of data display	very unsatisfied **1 2 3 4 5 6 7** very satisfied
10 Timeliness of data (is it current?)	very unsatisfied **1 2 3 4 5 6 7** very satisfied
11 Quality of language	very unsatisfied **1 2 3 4 5 6 7** very satisfied
12 Fun to use?	very unsatisfied **1 2 3 4 5 6 7** very satisfied
13 Explanations of how to use site	very unsatisfied **1 2 3 4 5 6 7** very satisfied
14 Overall ease of use	very unsatisfied **1 2 3 4 5 6 7** very satisfied
15 Completeness with which the site's subject is treated	very unsatisfied **1 2 3 4 5 6 7** very satisfied
16 Your overall productivity with the site	very unsatisfied **1 2 3 4 5 6 7** very satisfied

Fig. 1. The contents of the questionnaire after a test end (extract)

Participants: Internet users with experience of EC sites. (1212 persons)
Evaluation Items:
- Familiarity: Do you know the site well?
- Expectation: Which site do you want to use next?
- Availability: Which site do you use the most?
- User Evaluation: Abundance of products offered, user-friendliness, evaluation of the payment method, and customer correspondence service.

3.2.3   Implementation of the Scenario-Based Usability Test

From the above-mentioned ranking site, we selected 3 sites selling books, because sites of that type are widely used. In order to prevent a result inclining in the order of test implementation of the three sites, testing was carried out in arbitrary order. At the time of the test, we collected the following information: Age, sex, history of PC use, web use frequency (times per week), the degree of subject achievement, and test log (a memorandum of speech and conduct by the tester, consideration of observer). This information was used in order to probe the aspects of a site requiring improvement after execution of the usability test. Since an observer may not record the perfect log in the test period, it is ideal to carry out video recording and be able to view it later.

The same questionnaire shown in Fig. 1 was used. After the test we compared the results of the scenario-based usability test with the popularity ranking.

Since it was the first time we had performed the usability test, we tried simulations of the test by ourselves before using it with the test subjects (Table 2). We made minor adjustments to the difficulty of the questions and the contents of information gathering at the time of the test.

Table 2. Questions in the usability test

Type of Question	Questions
Simple Facts	How much is "book A"?
Judgment	Would "book B" be a suitable present for a child at elementary school?
Comparison of Facts	Which is the cheapest of the "title C" books?
Comparison of Judgment	Which book would be the best present for your boss?

The four types of questions were selected in order to express actions of the decision-making process when purchasing goods in imitation of the technique in reference [1]. We thought that these four questions could cover most aspects of decision-making in everyday life.

After selecting the target websites for the test and making questions, we asked 14 testers to test the selected websites with an observer.

3.2.4   Results of the Scenario-Based Usability Test

The results of the Post-Test Site Comparison are shown using labels S1, S2, and S3 from a high-ranking site (Fig.2). As can be seen from the following graph, if the ranking of an EC site was high, the score of the usability test was also high.

When the relation between the popularity (the site ranking score of an EC site) and usability (score from the questionnaire of the usability test) was examined, it was found that the score of the usability test was high if the score of popularity was high (correlation coefficient = 0.98). In this case, a correlation exists between popularity and usability (Fig. 3).

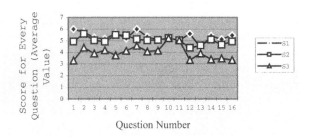

Fig. 2. Results of Post-Test Site Comparison

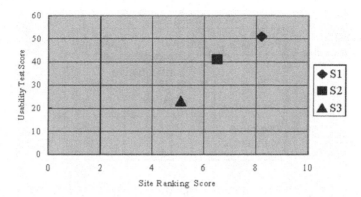

Fig. 3. Relation between Site Ranking & Usability test score

Regarding the test method, we think that the ease and measurability of a test are important. That is, it is desirable to lower costs to the minimum level and obtain useful results.

Regarding the ease of a test, it takes about 15 minutes for one site. For three sites, it is estimated to take about 1 hour, including completion of questionnaire. If the workload is at this level, we estimate that it is easy for the tester to participate in the test.

Since evaluation is expressed as a score in the usability test, it becomes an accurate measure when the same site has been improved. It is an effective guide for continuing improvement.

4   Quality Control for Constructing a Corporate Website

Since website construction involves many work items, a simple means of creating a website is needed. We used the conventional software quality control techniques as the base, and arranged them as the quality control techniques of website construction. In this chapter, we explain the quality control framework for constructing a corporate website.

To develop corporate websites effective and efficiently, we proposed the framework shown in Fig. 4.

This framework has the following some features.

1.   The content of a corporate website can be checked by using the checklist.
2.   There are 2 quality assurance methods: static quality assurance and dynamic quality assurance.
3.   Usability of a website can be confirmed effectively and efficiently by using the scenario-based usability test.

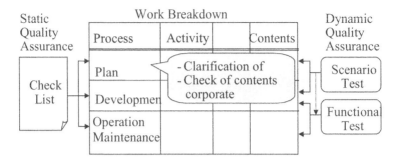

Fig. 4. Quality control framework for constructing a corporate website

4.1   WBS for Constructing a Corporate Website

The classification of WBS defined work of website development and operation by three classes (a process, an activity, a task) based on SLCP (Software Life Cycle Process), a common frame for system development activities. In the processing of an object, three processes of a plan, development, and operation and maintenance are considered from the viewpoints of continuous management and improvement of a corporate website. The devised points are shown below.

1. The work related to the website does not end once the content of the website is made. The item of operation and maintenance is included in a plan phase of the WBS since daily operation and maintenance are important. (Ex. clarification of a content management process)
2. Each process of a plan, development, and operation and maintenance describes the detailed item further. The responsibility of the section in charge of each process was also clarified. (Ex. clarification of a content design policy, announcement to the related sections)
3. The design of a website, issue of a website, and management of a website were also taken into consideration. (Ex. content registration, user correspondence)

4.2   Usability Checklist for Constructing a Corporate Website

The usability checklist for website construction was made so as to correspond to the detailed items, which were defined by WBS and prepared for every process. This approach enables a required check in a required scene to be performed using this checklist. In the check process column of an actual checklist, the development process is subdivided into such items as design, creation, and test. An actual checklist consists of 10 large items and 95 small items.

4.3 Utilization of Usability Test

Since the proposed usability test techniques are easy to prepare and can be performed quickly, they can be used in various processes repeatedly. It is recommended that the test be applied to a prototype before website development and to the website once it is developed. By repeating a usability test and improving the website cyclically, the website will become more attractive. In that case, the accumulated scores of usability tests are quality control data, and we think it is effective to determine a score for use as a standard.

5 Future Work

Although it was found that the usability test based on the scenario is effective, the following subjects remain to be resolved.

1. Experiences of PC use, etc. varies among testers. This is why the usability test varies among testers. So, many examiners are needed in order to test the testers.
2. It is difficult to devise a consistent scenario covering all questions.

Regarding the test method, we want to lower costs to the minimum level and obtain useful results by using a scenario-based usability test. But we cannot establish a test method for this purpose. In order to solve the problems, we introduced the concept of persona within the scenario-based usability test [10]. We are considering clarifying the intention by defining a typical user image. This approach, which will realize a cheaper usability test with no actual user, is currently under trial.

We intend to apply these techniques to a larger number of websites and check their validity in detail. Moreover, once the essential work and check items have been determined, we intend to add them to WBS and the checklist of website construction.

6 Conclusion

The application of a usability test, which incorporated the intentions of the provider and the user of a website, revealed that there is a correlation between the popularity ranking of a website and its usability.

The following quality control techniques for constructing websites were presented: WBS of website construction, usability checklist corresponding to the WBS, and usability test. Application of the usability test to various processes of website construction facilitates the implementation of improvements leading to realization of a more attractive corporate website.

References

1. Jared M. Spool and others : Web Site Usability: A Designer's Guide, Morgan Kaufmann Publishers, Inc., 1998.
2. Masaaki Kurosu and others : A Guide to User Engineering, Kyoritsu Publishing, and 1999.
3. Shinohara Toshikazu : Information and Design: An Actual Guideline for Information Design and Web Design, The Journal of Information Science and Technology Association, Vol.49, 1999.
4. Mary Jo Fahey : A Design Guide for Commercial Web Site, Nikkei BP Soft Press, 1998.
5. Mary Haggard : A Successful Web Site Development Guide, Nikkei BP Soft Press, 1998.
6. The Notes of Web Application Development, Nikkei Internet Technology, April 1999.
7. Ryoichi Fukuda : Actual Situation of a Homepage Manufacturing, AI Publishing, 1996.
8. Kate Dobroth and others : Organizing Web Site Information: Principles and Practical Experience, SIGCHI Bulletin, Volume 32, Number 1, and 2000.
9. Joel Sklar : Web Design, Course Technology, 2000.
10. Alan Cooper : The Inmates are Running the Asylum, SAMS, 1999.

Evaluating the Performance of a Web Site via Queuing Theory

Wen-Kui Chang and Shing-Kai Hon

Dept. of Computer Science & Information Engineering, Tunghai University, Taiwan
wkc@mail.thu.edu.tw, g882826@student.thu.edu.tw

Abstract. In recent years, many people have devoted their efforts to the issue of Web site quality. Web performance testing can be divided into many categories; it is usually performed in different aspects such as user interface, functionality, interface compatibility, load/stress, security, etc.
After carefully reviewing the current literature of website evaluation up to this stage, we find that performance issues of web sites now attract much more attention than before. This research investigates performance evaluation of the website under the World Wide Web environment. In the World Wide Web environment, we measure real data and obtain response time via the evaluation algorithm.
In this paper, we propose an enhanced equation to evaluate the performance of a web site via a queuing network model, and improve the evaluation algorithm. We demonstrate a practical equation for applying the suggested mechanism to the Internet. To get results on the performance of a Web server, we measure some data from the Internet environment, such as propagation time and service time. We use different tools to capture those data. In the final section, we show the relationship between mean response time and number of users.

Keywords: Web site quality, web performance testing, World Wide Web, Internet, Web server

1 Introduction

As Internet applications grow explosively in recent years, the number of websites is increasing tremendously. However, more web sites emerging will imply more problems encountered and pricklier situations to manage. Specifically, a Web manager wants to know how the performance of a Web site affects the number of users.

In this paper, queuing theory is employed to measure the performance of a Web server. In principle, queuing models characterize various operational paths of user service. First, we introduce the attributes of network performance testing, quality and performance of Web site. In the second section, we introduce related work about queuing networks and the modeling process. Then, we apply Little's queuing theory to measure the response time of a Web server. After measuring the required data, we calculate the number of users logging into the database system and evaluate the

J. Kontio and R. Conradi (Eds.): ECSQ 2002, LNCS 2349, pp. 63–72, 2002.

amount of time the Web server needs to process those users. In the final section, we strengthen the equation and discuss other evaluations that we plan to do in the future.

2   Related Research

2.1   Attributes of Network Performance Testing

WWW and Web sites cause unique software testing challenges. For the developers and managers of web sites, all they need is new technology and a tool to test web sites. Test requirement preparation is a process of communication among tester, clients, and users for defining a new system. Failure to communicate and understand each other's domains results in a system that is difficult to use [1].

Within minutes of going live, a WWW application can have many thousands more users than a conventional, non-WWW application. The immediacy of the WWW creates expectations of quality and rapid application delivery, but the technical complexities of a Website and variances in the browser such as JavaScript, ActiveX and Flash, etc., make testing and quality control much more difficult [2].

Performance testing can be divided into many categories, including load testing, stress testing, and smoke testing, etc. Using testing tools has many advantages. For example, time-delay on a linking process may usually cause link failure [3].

Internet-based client-server applications service a much larger group of audiences than the conventional C-S applications. Including graphics, audio, and video files embedded in web pages severely affects performance. Especially in the early development of the Internet, these large files can seriously affect the performance of a web site. Other factors, such as popularity of a web site, will impact performance during times of peak usage.

2.2   Quality and Performance Issues

As a Web site attracts more visitors, the server starts to slow down in delivering pages. It is difficult to figure out where the bottlenecks of a web server are and at what point the browsing experience becomes unacceptable for users. Furthermore, network administrators may not be aware that a web server is under an unstable situation. Because of these factors, many large-size or popular web sites need performance testing.

The Web is an unstable situation and many factors may influence it, such as a heavy load in the network that usually generates long response time and a lot of throughput. Those factors make web site tests more complicated and difficult.

In recent years, the sudden emergence of the World Wide Web is bringing this issue to the forefront. In many respects, performance in web sites today is tied to the future of the Web and the technology base that has been used to develop incremental improvement in performance. With more and more web sites, the emerging generation of critical Internet and Web technologies will require very high levels of performance, and we must explore the implications of this for distributed computing technologies in the Web environment.

3 Queuing Theory

3.1 General Description

Queuing theory emphasizes the analysis of systems that involve waiting for a particular service. The model usually includes one or more servers that provide the service, possibly an infinite number of customers, and some description of the arrival and service processes. If there is more than one queue for the servers, there may also be some policy regarding queue changes for the customers. In queuing systems, it is easiest to analyze the system in the steady state. A network in which a new user enters whenever a user leaves the system can also be considered as a closed queuing network [4].

Performance testing is based on the maxim that overall system performance is limited by the performance of the most restrictive component of the system. Finding such components is one of the key benefits of performance testing regardless of the system under test. Testing an application involves a variety of skills. Developing and maintaining a team that has the expertise to thoroughly handle in depth web performance testing is expensive and effort intensive. Performance testing can be accomplished in parallel with volume and stress testing because tester or network administrators want to assess performance under all load conditions. Network performance is generally assessed in terms of response times and throughput rates under differing processing and configuration conditions [5].

3.2 The Modeling Process

There are two steps in computing the mean response time of queuing systems. First, assign the number of customers present in a state as the reward rate to that state, and compute the measures as required. Second, it can be proven that there exists a linear correspondence between mean response time and mean number of customers present. Little's theorem can be used for the computation of the mean response time from the mean number of customers [6].

To interpret these measures, reward definitions for a simple CTMC (continuous time Markov chain) are considered. Customers are arriving at a system with exponentially distributed interarrival times, with mean $1/\lambda$. In the system they compete for service from a single server station. Since each customer exclusively receives service, if more than one customer is in the system at the same time, the others have to wait in line until their turn comes. Service times are independently exponentially distributed with mean $1/\mu$. In the following example, the system is described by the MRM (Markov reward model) and the number of customers is limited to three in the system.

Each state in $S = \{3, 2, 1, 0\}$ of the MRM represents the number of customers in the system. Arc μ represents the completion of a customer's service by the service station, and arc λ indicates that a new customer arrives.

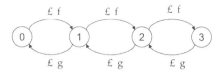

Fig. 1. CTMC with Arrivals and Services

4 Applying Queuing Theory in the Internet

4.1 Redefinition

In a queuing system, response time is defined as data transfer time plus server time, as shown in the following expression.

$$\text{response time} = \text{waiting time} + \text{service time}$$

According to the original definition, we redefined the content of response time. The redefinition of response time can be divided into two phases. The first phase is propagation time, which is the time required for a signal to travel from one point to another. The points can be seen as client and server. The second phase is service time, which is the time it takes the server to process the requests of the clients.

The whole framework of response time is illustrated in Fig. 2.

According to the above illustration, the propagation time is the sum of t1, t2, t4 and t5. The service time is t3; so the response time is the sum of these times. Thus,

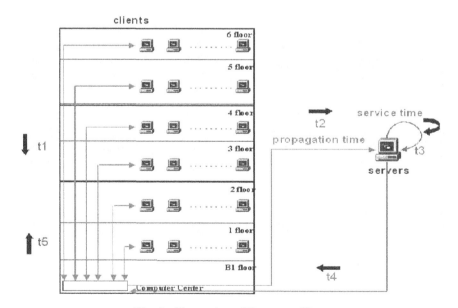

Fig. 2. Illustration of Response Time

waiting time can be seen as propagation time. The original expression for response time can be redefined as the following expression:

$$\text{response time} = \text{propagation time} + \text{service time}$$

When a queuing system is applied on the Internet, the queuing model can be seen as in Fig. 3. In the figure, theoretical models are based on a random distribution of service duration. "Arrival" defines the way customers enter these Web servers. "Output" represents the way customers leave the system. Theoretical models mostly ignore output, but the users will leave the server and enter the queue again in the Internet. In queuing theory, systems with more servers are called multi-channel systems.

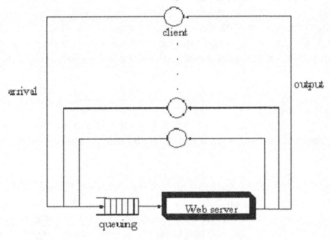

Fig. 3. Queuing model of the Internet

4.2 Enhancement

Little's theorem is valid for all queuing disciplines. According to Little's theorem, the mean number of jobs in the queuing system K and the mean queue length Q can be calculated using one of the most important theorems of queuing theory [7], as shown in equation 1.

$$K = \lambda \, T \, . \tag{1}$$

If we use Little's theorem to apply in the Internet, we define P as users who connect to a Web server. In equation 2, λ is the mean arrival rate.

$$P = \lambda T \, . \tag{2}$$

Mean response time T can be represented as Tt + Ts, which is shown in equation 3.

$$P = \lambda (Tt + Ts) \, . \tag{3}$$

5 Evaluating the Load of Web Sites in the Internet

5.1 Test Process

5.1.1 Building a Web Site for this Testing Work

We used IIS 5.0 (Microsoft Internet Information Services) to build the web site for this testing work. This Web site contains a database, which is basically a collection of software names. We used SQL Server to create the database system, because SQL Server provides agility to the data management and analysis, allowing the organization to adapt quickly and gracefully to derive competitive advantage in a fast-changing environment.

A user can search the contents of the software and download the software. The function of this homepage is to let users log into the database system.

When a user logs into this database system, the system will show another HTML page. In this page, the user can enter the name of the software that he wants to find. The other way is that the user selects the correct category and downloads the software.

5.1.2 Measuring Time

Because the response time has been redefined, to calculate it, we need to measure the propagation time and the service time separately by using a tool.

5.1.2.1 PropagationTtime

We use a tool to measure the response time of the web site. The tool is HostMonitor, which is a network monitor program. It can monitor any TCP service, ping a host, retrieve an URL, check the available disk space, check integrity of files and web site, test SQL servers, NT services, and much more [8]. After measuring it, we found the propagation time in this case is 10ms.

5.1.2.2 Specification of the Web Site

To show the capability of the Web server, we list the hardware specification as the following table.

Table 1. Hardware and Software Specification

CPU	Pentium III
CPU frequency (MHz)	550
RAM (M)	256
HDD rpm	7200
HDD buffer (M)	2
Netcard	10/100Mbps

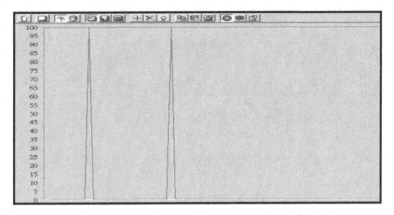

Fig. 4. Microsoft Management Console

5.1.2.3 Service Time

After building the web site, we sent out 500 requests to the Web server and used MMC to view and record the performance of IIS 5.0, which is shown in Fig. 4.

The full name of MMC is Microsoft Management Console. It is one of Microsoft's products. MMC—previously known by the code name "Slate"—is an ISV-extensible, common console framework for management applications. The MMC will be released as part of the next major release of the Windows NT system.

MMC itself does not provide any management behavior, but it provides a common environment for Snap-Ins, which will be written by both Microsoft and ISVs. Snap-Ins provide the actual management behavior. The MMC environment provides for seamless integration between Snap-Ins, even those provided by different vendors.

Administrators will create tools from various Snap-Ins, from various vendors. Administrators can then save the tools they have created for later use, or for sharing with other administrators. This model provides the administrator with efficient tool customization and the ability to create multiple tools of different levels of complexity for task delegation, among other benefits.

To measure the capability of the server, we let MMC monitor the performance of IIS 5.0 in this example. At first, we simulate 500 users connecting to the web sites two times. Then, by observing the IIS 5.0, we can learn how long it needs to handle it. We find IIS 5.0 takes an average of 2 seconds to process the 500 connections.

According to the result of this measurement, we find IIS 5.0 takes 2 seconds to process the 500 connections. In other word, the IIS 5.0 Web server can service 250 users each second.

5.2 Test Results

After measuring the propagation time and service time, we calculate the result from the first second to the eighth second, and show the number of users in each second. This is shown in Fig. 5. The Y-axis represents "number of users" and the X-axis represents "mean response time".

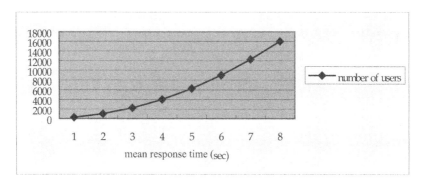

Fig. 5. The result of forecast

5.3   Comparison with Another Tool

In this section, we used the Webserver Stress Tool [9] to analyze the performance of the server, as show in Fig. 6, using those data to compare with the result of our measure data. Functionally the Webserver Stress Tool is a kind of load and performance test tool. It can simulate concurrent uses of different URLs on the server to check for cross page problems and steadily increase the number of simulated users to find out the limits of a web application and web server. The main principle of the Webserver Stress Tool is to keep 100% load on a server for hours and determine system capacity to find the bottleneck of the server.

According the result of the analysis tool, we find that the curve of performance is not perfect. Performance data can also be deduced by theory and calculated by the tool.

The detailed comparison is shown in Table 2. It shows that there is much difference between the proposed approach and other methods, although there exist many factors that can affect the performance data. In the future, we hope to reduce the influence of these factors and deduce more precise performance results.

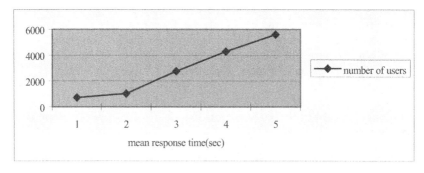

Fig. 6. The result of the testing tool

6 Research and Work in the Future

Web applications are complex. It is necessary to test performance under real environments. The result of testing will reveal more precise information. It is also necessary to test the system in conjunction with a second system utilizing the same server and accessing the same database. Hence, the difficulty in Web testing is that we must have some assumptions.

In this paper, we apply Little's theory to evaluate the performance of a web server. In other words, this is the first time that queuing theory is applied on the Internet. In the original queuing theory, some systems may not be soluble at all, so the only technique that may be applied is simulation. Hence, we redefine some assumptions of Little's theory and measure the response time in reality. This revised Little's theory can be used to predict the capability of Web server without using much hardware resource. Furthermore, since we obtain the forecasting result directly from the derived formula, the proposed framework is ready to be applied in industrial community.

The result of testing which is inferred by equation has a drawback. In our method, the curve is perfect, because the result is inferred by equation. In the real case, each Web server has a maximum capability. Once the number of requests exceeds the maximum capability of the Web server, many clients will not be able to receive responses from the web server. That is the bottleneck of the web server. Each web server must have a bottleneck. In our method, we still cannot forecast the bottleneck of web servers. In the future, we hope that we have a more precise equation to forecast the bottlenecks of web servers.

7 Conclusions

For web site performance testing, there are many factors that can affect the result of testing, such as the usage of the network, status of loading, the bandwidth of the network, etc.

Although there are many factors that can affect the result of testing, we still try to apply queuing network theory on the Internet. To measure the real bottleneck of web sites, we hope to develop more suitable queuing network theory that can forecast the response time and bottlenecks of web sites.

We are the first who have applied queuing theory in the Internet. A Web site performance testing method is investigated in this paper, and a new procedure for using queuing theory to evaluate performance of web site is developed.

Acknowledgement

The authors gratefully acknowledge financial support from the National Science Council, Taiwan, Republic of China, under project NSC 90-2213-E-029-005, entitled "A mobile agent for testing distributed applications."

References

1. Bernd Bruegge and Allen H. dutoit, (1999), Prentice Hall International Editions, Object-Oriented Software Engineering-Conquering Complex and Changing systems,
2. sISBN:0-13-017452-1, 25- 46.
3. Edward Miller (1999): "WebSite Testing", Software Research, Inc.
4. Chang, Wen-Kui, Hon Shing-Kai and Ching-Chun Fu (2000), 13th Annual International Software/Internet Quality Week, "A System Framework for Ensuring Link Validity under Web Browsing Environments" San Francisco.
5. Cunter Bolch, Stefan Greiner, Hermann de Meer, and Kihor S. Trivedi (1998): "Queueing Networks and Markov Chains – Modeling and Performance Evaluation with Computer Science Applications".
6. Daniel J. Mosley, (2000), Client-Server Testing on the Desktop and the Web.
7. American National Standard for Telecommunications, Telecom Glossary 2000.
8. J. Little. A Proof of the Queuing Formula L = λW. Perations Research, 9(3):383-387, May 1961.
9. HostMonitor, host monitor tool Website (October 2001: http://www.ks-soft.net/hostmon.eng/index.htm).
10. Webserver Stress Tool Website
11. (November 2001: http://www.Web-server-tools.com/tools/.)

Lessons Learned from Applying the Requirements Engineering Good Practice Guide for Process Improvement

Marjo Kauppinen, Tapani Aaltio, and Sari Kujala

Helsinki University of Technology, Software Business and Engineering Institute,
P.O. Box 9600, FIN-02015 HUT, Finland
{marjo.kauppinen,tapani.aaltio,sari.kujala}@hut.fi

Abstract. The systematic definition and management of requirements is becoming increasingly important in product development. Many software organizations are interested in improving their requirements engineering processes but they do not know where to begin. Sommerville et al. have developed a framework known as the Requirements Engineering Good Practice Guide (REGPG) for incremental process improvement. We applied the REGPG in four Finnish organizations and evaluated its strengths and weaknesses. The most important strengths of the REGPG are that it raises personnel awareness of requirements engineering and it includes relevant requirements practices allowing organizations to select practical improvement actions. The main weakness of the REGPG is that it offers a very limited set of general process improvement guidelines. Therefore, organizations that want to develop their requirements engineering processes systematically need to support the use of the REGPG with other improvement frameworks.

Introduction

An increasing number of organizations are interested in improving their requirements engineering (RE) processes. In theory, requirements engineering applies proven principles, techniques, languages and tools [1]. In practice, organizations need guidance as to where to start the improvement of their RE processes. Two of the basic questions that practitioners ask are what requirements engineering means and which requirements models, methods, and practices are recommended for organizations undertaking improvement in their RE processes.

The REAIMS (Requirements Engineering Adaptation and IMprovement for Safety and dependability) project has developed a framework for RE process improvement. The framework is known as the Requirements Engineering Good Practice Guide (REGPG) [8]. The REGPG is unique in focusing particularly on requirements engineering. It contains sixty-six good requirements practices covering eight RE areas [7,8]. The REGPG additionally includes a REAIMS maturity model and an assessment process.

As far as we know, no published empirical studies have been conducted on the REGPG. The goal of this study is to evaluate the strengths and the weaknesses of the

J. Kontio and R. Conradi (Eds.): ECSQ 2002, LNCS 2349, pp. 73–81, 2002.
© Springer-Verlag Berlin Heidelberg 2002

REGPG. To obtain empirical data, we applied the REGPG in four organizations that have started to improve their RE processes systematically. The main contribution of this paper is to describe lessons learned from these four cases.

The paper is structured as follows. In the following section, the REGPG is explained briefly. Then, we introduce the four cases. The lessons learned from these cases are described in the fourth section. Finally, we state our conclusions.

Overview of the REGPG

The REGPG is a process improvement framework for the systematic, incremental adoption of good requirements practice [7]. The framework is unique in focusing on requirements engineering, and it builds on existing software process improvement (SPI) models and standards. The REGPG includes the REAIMS maturity model, an assessment process, and a set of improvement guidelines that are based on the good requirements practices (Fig. 1).

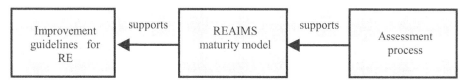

Fig. 1. The main components of the REGPG

The REGPG covers eight RE areas, and it includes sixty-six good requirements practices that have been abstracted from existing standards, reports of requirements practices, and the experience of the practitioners [8]. The framework describes the good requirements practices in the form of improvement guidelines. Each guideline provides the following information: 1) the key benefits of the practice, 2) the cost of introducing the practice, 3) the cost of applying the practice, and 4) some advice on how to implement the guideline [7,8].

For organizations starting RE process improvement, the REGPG offers the top ten guidelines. These ten guidelines are so important that they should be implemented in all organizations, and organizations should start their process improvement program by implementing them [8].

The REGPG contains a three-level REAIMS process maturity model. The maturity levels of the REAIMS model are called initial, repeatable and defined, and they help organizations to characterize their RE processes [7,8]. The REGPG additionally describes an assessment process involving five steps [8].

The Cases

The REGPG was applied in the RE process improvement of four Finnish organizations. All the organizations were product development units of medium-size or large companies and the number of the employees of these units varied from 25 to 160. The companies focus mainly on market-driven products but occasionally, they develop customer-specsific systems. The companies represent four different kinds of application domain (Table 1). Organization A develops products that have both real-time embedded and interactive components. The systems of Organization B, C, and D are interactive.

Table 1. Description of the participating companies

Organization	Company size [employees]	Type of systems	Application domain
A	23 000	Market-driven	Transportation systems for buildings (elevators and escalators)
B	1100	Market-driven	Measurement systems for meteorology, environmental sciences and traffic safety
C	500	Market-driven	Information management systems for building, public infra and energy distribution designers
D	3200	Market-driven	Patient monitoring systems for anesthesia and critical care

We discovered one of the weaknesses related to the REGPG at the beginning of the study. The REGPG offers only very general suggestions for facilitating process change [8]. To guide the systematic RE process improvement of the case organizations, we defined a simple process improvement procedure (Figure 2). The procedure combines tasks from the IDEAL model [3] and the ISO/IEC 15504 standard [2]. In this report, we concentrate on the first two activities of the procedure and the tasks supported by the REGPG (Table 2).

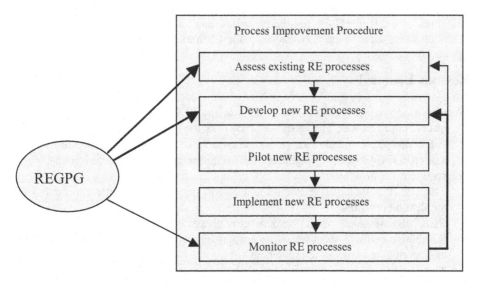

Fig. 2. Process improvement procedure of the study and the activities supported by the REGPG

Table 2. Tasks involved in the first two activities of the process improvement procedure. The tasks supported by the REGPG are in italics.

Activities	Tasks
Assessing existing RE processes.	<ul><li>Planning the assessment.</li><li>*Collecting data.*</li><li>*Analyzing data.*</li><li>Reporting assessment results.</li></ul>
Developing new RE processes.	<ul><li>*Planning improvement actions.*</li><li>Forming project improvement teams.</li><li>*Defining new RE processes.*</li><li>Documenting new RE processes.</li><li>Reviewing new RE process documents</li></ul>

The current state of the requirements practices was evaluated using the REAIMS model in all the case organizations. The main purpose of the assessment was to identify the strengths and weaknesses of the existing RE practice. The REAIMS interviews were the first step of the data collection and were conducted in all the case organizations. The purpose of these interviews was to define quickly the current state of the RE process and discover whether the practitioners found the sixty-six requirements practices of the REGPG relevant for their organizations. In the three organizations that wanted to use assessment results for long-term monitoring, the REAIMS interviews were supplemented with document analyses and more detailed interviews. Based on the collected information, we analyzed the state of the requirements practices using the improvement guidelines of the REGPG.

Organizations A, B and C selected the RE areas to be developed and decided the practical improvement actions by discussing the assessment results. Organization D had identified the RE improvement actions before the assessment, and it used the assessment results to supplement the development activities. The improvement guidelines of the REGPG offered the basic information for the selected requirements practices. More detailed information was gathered from other RE literature.

Lessons Learned

We identified six strengths and weaknesses of the REGPG when it was applied for RE process improvement. The lessons learned from the four cases are:

- A REAIMS assessment raises personnel awareness of requirements engineering.
- The REGPG supports organizations in defining a first process model for requirements definition.
- The REGPG includes relevant requirements practices for different kinds of application domains.
- REAIMS assessment results are dependent on assessors.
- Selecting a realistic set of improvement actions requires expertise in requirements engineering and process improvement.
- The REGPG offers very limited set of general process improvement guidelines.

All the other lessons are described in this section except the last one that is explained in detailed in the previous section.

Strengths of the REGPG

A REAIMS assessment raises personnel awareness of requirements engineering. Conducting a REAIMS assessment gives information about how systematically an organization is defining and managing requirements, and what can be done better if the organization wants to improve its requirements practices. REAIMS interviews and assessment results increase understanding of what requirements practices are recommended, and they motivate practitioners for RE process improvement.

The participants of the REAIMS interviews gained a quick overview of the nature of the good requirements practices by answering the REAIMS questionnaire. It took an average of 46 minutes to answer the questionnaire individually. The REAIMS group interview lasted 32 minutes for the thirty-six basic practices of the REGPG, and 105 minutes for the whole set of the sixty-six practices.

The assessment results showed the personnel how widely the practices of the REGPG were already used in their organization. By going through the RE strengths of the organization, experience of the good requirements practices was shared across the departments and the projects. For example, one project manager commented during the assessment: "We didn't know that the software group had already developed a template for requirements documents." The assessment results showed not only the state of the sixty-six individual practices but also the state of the eight RE areas of the REGPG. This helped practitioners to gain an overall, structured view of requirements engineering.

The REGPG supports organizations in defining a first process model for requirements definition. The REGPG recommends that a good RE process includes the following activities: elicitation, analysis combined with negotiation, and validation. These activities seem to suit organizations that want to define a first process model in order to facilitate their personnel's understanding of the basics of requirements engineering.

Three organizations used the RE activities of the REGPG as a basis for their first RE process model. Organization D decided to tailor the requirements subprocess of the rational unified process (RUP) for its purposes. The process models of the three case organizations are compared with the RE activities of the REGPG in Table 3.

Table 3. The RE process models of the case organizations compared with the RE activities of the REGPG

RE activities of REGPG	Organization A	Organization B	Organization C
Elicitation	Elicitation and analysis	Gathering	Collection
Analysis and negotiation	-	Analysis	Analysis
-	Documentation	-	Specification
Validation	Verification and validation	Review	Validation

Table 4. Improvement actions selected by the organizations. X represents a clear decision and (x) indicates preliminary discussion about the practice to be implemented in the organization.

Improvement action selected from the REGPG	Organization			
	A	B	C	D
Define a standard document template for requirements	x	x	x	x
Define a process for requirements definition	x	x	x	x
Define standard templates for requirements description	x	(x)	(x)	x
Uniquely identify each requirement	x	x	(x)	(x)
Prioritize requirements	x	x	x	(x)
Use a database to manage requirements	(x)	x	x	(x)
Define a process for requirements change management	x	x	-	(x)
Record requirements rationale	x	x		x
Record requirements source	x	x		
Document the links between requirements and system models	x	x		
Define traceability policies		x		x
Include the business objective for the system into requirements documents	x		x	
Define specialized terms	x		x	
Define guidelines for formal requirements inspections	x			
Define checklists for requirements validation	x			

The REGPG also helped the case organizations to define new practices in the requirements definition process. Table 4 summarizes the good requirements practices of the REGPG that the case organizations selected as their improvement actions.

The REGPG includes relevant requirements practices for different kinds of application domains. Almost all the practices of the REGPG appear to suit all the case organizations that represent four different application domains.

Evidence of the relevance of the REGPG requirements practices is based on the REAIMS interviews. In these interviews, the participants evaluated how widely a certain practice had been used in their organization or whether it was irrelevant for their organization. Firstly, Table 5 shows that the interviewees found only a small number of the REGPG requirements practices irrelevant. In Organization A and B, no practice was judged by all the interviewees to be irrelevant. Therefore, the status of all the sixty-six practices was assessed. In Organization C, the group found all nine safety practices irrelevant. Further evidence of the relevance is that the organizations have already used many of the requirements practices to some extent, according to the REAIMS interviews (Table 5).

Table 5. Results of the REAIMS interviews that are based on individual interviews in Organization A and B, and on a group interview in Organization C and D. The assessment covered all the 66 practices of the REGPG in Organization A, B and C, and the basic 36 practices of the REGPG in Organization D.

Classification of requirements practices of the REGPG	Organization			
	A	B	C	D
Number of irrelevant practices	1	5	10	2
Number of practices never used	20	40	20	13
Number of practices sometimes, usually, or systematically used	46	26	36	21

The most important evidence of the relevance of the requirements practices is that the case organizations have used them as a basis for practical improvement actions. Table 4 summarizes the practices of the REGPG that the case organizations have already selected as improvement actions or have discussed in terms of potential development and implementation in their organization.

Weaknesses of the REGPG

REAIMS assessment results are dependent on assessors. The REGPG has three shortcomings that decrease the reliability of assessment results. These reliability problems limit the use of assessment results for long-term monitoring.

The main reason for the reliability problems was that the REGPG does not offer unambiguous assessment guidelines. We had to interpret the improvement guidelines of the REGPG to set the assessment criteria for each requirements practice. If the REGPG included assessment criteria for each RE practice, the assessment results would be more independent of assessors.

Secondly, the assessment process of the REGPG was too informal for our purposes because it offers too little guidance for reliable assessments. The reliability of the assessment results can be improved using a systematic assessment process [3].

The third reason for the reliability problems was that the REGPG does not define clearly the type of requirements that is assessed. The REGPG mentions two sets of requirements: 1) stakeholder requirements and 2) system requirements, but it combines them into one set of requirements and it offers an ambiguous definition for it. This ambiguous definition caused some interviewees to describe the status of user requirements, and others to talk about technical requirements. We have observed that technical requirements are often defined and managed more systematically than user requirements. This caused reliability problems because the assessors had to interpret the inconsistent answers of the interviewees.

Selecting a realistic set of improvement actions requires expertise in requirements engineering and process improvement. The REGPG introduces sixty-six practices and organizations can select too many of them to be implemented at the same time. This can cause an improvement cycle to take too long, in which case people can become frustrated or even lose interest in RE process improvement.

Table 4 shows that the case organizations selected ambitious sets of improvement actions. The REGPG offers useful information for improvement planning such as benefits and costs of implementing individual requirements practices, but practitioners require more guidance for prioritizing RE improvement actions. We have discovered that certain requirements practices of the REGPG are interdependent. It would help practitioners to prioritize the requirements practices if their interdependencies were clearly defined. Based on the four cases, we also emphasize two general process improvement guidelines. Firstly, a process improvement project must align improvement efforts with available resources. Secondly, it is important to include actions that yield short-term benefits, particularly if the organization is new to RE process improvement.

Conclusions

In this paper, we have described the lessons learned in four Finnish organizations that have started to improve their RE processes systematically. To support RE process improvement, the requirements engineering good practice guide (REGPG) [8] was applied. The goal of this study was to evaluate the strengths and the weaknesses of the REGPG.

Conducting an RE assessment with the REGPG is useful for organizations that are just starting to improve their RE processes because it raises personnel awareness of requirements engineering, and offers valuable information about good requirements practices. This result of the study does not support one of the assessment problems described by Fayad et al., according to whom assessments can be a waste of money and time for organizations just starting because, in an immature organization, the results are meaningless [2]. Fayad et al. also report that all assessment models are artificially derived and include idealized list of practices [2]. According to our study, the REGPG includes relevant requirements practices where organizations can select improvement actions.

The REGPG additionally offers information based on which organizations can define a first RE process model. According to Houdek et al., RE activities such as validation and elicitation are heavily intertwined, and the authors questioned whether a differentiation between those activities yields benefit [3]. Three case organizations of this study found beneficial to define a process model that includes elicitation, analysis and validation activities as recommended by the REGPG.

The main weakness of the REGPG is that it offers only a few general guidelines for process improvement. Therefore, organizations that want to develop their RE processes systematically need to support the use of the REGPG with other improvement frameworks. The REGPG can be developed further by removing two other weaknesses. Firstly, assessment criteria for each requirements practice are required to make assessment results more reliable for long-term monitoring. Secondly, a dependency flowchart that defines the interrelationships of the requirements practices would help practitioners to prioritize improvement actions.

The improvement projects of the case organizations are still in progress and are the subjects of a longitudinal study. Currently, we are following the piloting and implementation of the new requirements practices. Our main research goal in the future is to evaluate the impact of the selected improvement actions.

References

1. Davis, A. M., Hsia, P.: Giving Voice To Requirements Engineering. IEEE Software, Vol. 11, Issue 2 (1994) 12-15
2. Fayad, M., Laitinen, M.,: Process Assessment Considered Wasteful, Communications of the ACM, Vol 40, No. 11, (1997) 125-128
3. Houdek, F., Pohl, K.,: Analyzing Requirements Engineering Processes: A Case Study, Proceedings of 11th International Workshop on Database and Expert Systems Applications, (2000) 983 - 987
4. Information technology – Software process assessment – Part 7: Guide for use in process improvement, Technical report, ISO/IEC TR 15504-7:1998(E) (1998)

5. Kauppinen, M., Kujala, S.,: B.: Assessing Requirements Engineering Processes with the REAIMS Model: Lessons Learned, Proceedings of 11th International Symposium of INCOSE, Melbourne (2001)
6. McFeeley, B.: IDEAL: A User's Guide for Software Process Improvement. Handbook CMU/SEI-96-HB-001. Software Engineering Institute, Carnegie Mellon University, Pittsburgh, PE, USA (1996)
7. Sawyer, P., Sommerville, I., Viller, S.: Capturing the Benefits of Requirements Engineering. IEEE Software, Vol. 16, Issue 2 (1999) 78-85
8. Sommerville, I., Sawyer, P.: Requirements Engineering – A Good Practice Guide. John Wiley & Sons, New York (1997)

Quality Assurance Activities for ASP Based on SLM in Hitachi

Masahiro Nakata[1] and Katsuyuki Yasuda[2]

[1] 890 Kashimada, Saiwai, Kawasaki, Kanagawa, 212-8567 Japan
manakata@itg.hitachi.co.jp
[2] 5-12 Minamiaoyama 5-chome,Minato-ku,Tokyo,107-0062 Japan
yasuda@itech.hitachi.co.jp

Abstract. With the spread of the Internet, new business models have arisen. Application Service Provision (ASP) is one of those new services and its market is expected to grow rapidly. Many players have entry into this new market. However, it is risky for both customers and Application Service Providers (ASPs) to introduce ASP on their critical applications if quality of service is not sufficient. Service Level Management (SLM) is a solution to this problem but most IT organizations do not practice SLM as a clearly defined and continuous process, particularly for new applications or services, such as ASP. In this situation, Hitachi developed integrated SLM process (iSLM) standards for ASP and started to apply this process for real services. SLM is a quality management process itself and it is most effective, performed with continuous, organized improvement actions (KAIZEN). In the present paper, introduce SLM methodology and practice with making good use of KAIZEN experience in Hitachi.

1   Introduction

Network Service Provider (NSP) and Internet Data Center (IDC) have been introduced as Service Level Agreements (SLA) to assure their Quality of Service (QoS). Service Level Management (SLM) is a methodology used to ensure that adequate levels of service are delivered to end-users. Now, many service providers recognize the importance of SLM and SLA. However, "in general the current state of service management, particularly for newer applications and services across distributed enterprises, is somewhat immature"[1], such as Application Service Provision (ASP). Most service providers do not practice SLM as a clearly defined, continuous quality management process. One of the major reasons is that there are no industry-accepted standards for SLM, SLA and its metrics. ASPIC[1] and JEITA[2] research on end-users and IT organizations in purpose of standardization of those subjects.

Hitachi studied these research reports, and developed integrated SLM process (iSLM) standards based on existing quality management process for system integration/outsourcing with KAIZEN experiences in Hitachi. After introduction of iSLM, an availability of application service has improved from 99.5% to 99.9%.

---

[1] ASP Industry Consortium; http://www.aspindustry.com/

[2] Japan Electronics and Information Technology Industries Association; http://www.jeita.or.jp/

J. Kontio and R. Conradi (Eds.): ECSQ 2002, LNCS 2349, pp. 82–89, 2002.

2   Quality Assurance Process for ASP Based on SLM

2.1   ASP Layer Model and SLM Schema

As ASPIC definition of ASP is: "An ASP deploys, hosts and manages access to a packaged application to multiple parties from a centrally managed facility. The applications are delivered over networks on a subscription basis."

ASP business consists of various components or functions, such as center facilities, servers, network, applications, etc. The layer model is often used to express the ASP business model. Various providers exist corresponding to each layer, e.g. NSPs, IDCs, ASPs, Call Centers, etc. Although it has been general accepted that these providers set their SLAs separately and perform their SLM in their own way (layer by layer SLM), 84.8% of end-users expect that application service providers manage every layer (end-to-end SLM)[2]. From this research report, we examined end-to-end SLM schema, that is, application service provider integrates management activities of every layer to assure whole application service to end-users. The reason why we take end-to-end SLM schema is that; (a) It is expected that end-to-end SLM schema improves understandability of SLAs for end-users; and (b) it is possible to optimize each layer's management cost effectively. Fig.1 shows an ASP layer model and SLM schemas.

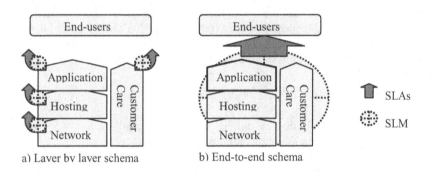

Fig. 1. ASP Layer Model and SLM schemas

2.2   Integrated SLM Process (iSLM)

We identified all quality activities which appear to relate to ASP, from our existing process, for example, system integration service, application package development, help desk, system operation service, etc. In addition, we arranged them layer by layer, cut or unified the if the same activities existed, connected one activity to another and then integrated the SLM process (iSLM) for ASP and set it as a standard quality process for ASP in our company.

Table 1 shows an outline of an application service process with an iSLM process. Every activity in these process should be managed by "ASP service development plan" and "SLM plan" which are tailored according to each application service.

Table 1. Application Service Process with iSLM Process

Phase		Plan	Development	Operation
Application Service Process		-define service scope -basic design -prototyping	-system development -service process design	-system operation -system maintenance -customer support
iSLM Process		-SLA planning	-SLM in development	-SLM in operation
		-SLM audit		
	Plan		-ASP service development plan	-SLM plan

Service Level Management Policy

It is not necessary that all service level management items should be included in the agreement (see Fig.2). An excess of service levels has an impact upon a provider's finance and it might cause an increase in service fees. Service level objectives should be limited to critical ones taking into consideration the characteristics of the service or marketing strategy. The important thing is to clarify which service level item is assured and which is not, in order that the provider and customer can share/understand the risks involved. On the other hand, it is recommended some service level items should be managed even if those items don't be expressed in SLA.

Whether SLA exist or not, proper SLM brings better customer satisfaction, and makes service providers manage their service more cost effective. SLA is just a tool (or enabler) for SLM.

2.2.1   SLA Planning

In this process, service policy is defined and documented as an "ASP service development plan" based on the scope definition of service.

Procedure

Step1: Identify service level items

List up service level items of each layer (network, hosting, application, customer care) based on the service scope definition.

Service Level Objective
⇨ Commit to customer by SLA

Service Level Management
⇨ Defined and managed by SLM plan

Service Level Item

Mapping
Metrics

Fig. 2. Service Level Management Policy

Step2: Map service level items to each metrics
Break down service level items listed above into as many measurable elements (metrics) as possible. Some items may have qualitative metrics and some may have quantitative ones.

Step3: Define service level management items and set target level
Select service level management items from service level items listed in step1, and set target value for each service level management items, taking into consideration the costs and risks of each service level being achieved. This is a trade-off.

Step4: Define requirements to development and operation phase
Document service level management items with its target level and requirements to design for every layer to satisfy defined service level.

Deliverables
1. ASP Service Development Plan

Tools
1. Service Level Template
It is difficult to identify service level items and to map those items to metrics. This process requires a lot of time, and the competence of the work depends on personal skill. We developed a Service Level Template to solve this problem.

2.2.2   SLM Process in the Development Phase
In the development phase, the IT system and service process are designed or developed based on an ASP service development plan.

Procedure
Step1: Develop IT system and design service process based on ASP service development plan
Design or develop an IT system and service process according to ASP service development plan to satisfy requirements.

Step2: Evaluate service level
Examine and evaluate service level management items if each service level meets the required level. Take improvement actions if necessary.

Step3: Negotiate SLA
Negotiate for SLA with the company's marketing staff, QA staff, financial staff or other. Decide service level objectives, i.e., service level management items and the service levels of agreement. Document service level objectives as a SLA, which is a part of a contract.

Deliverables
1. Service Level Agreement

2.2.3   SLM Process in Operation Phase

Harvard Business School has proposed that the value of a service is determined by the following equation, and it is said that the process quality is a very important factor for the quality of service.

$$\text{Value of Service} = [\text{Quality of Service (Result, Process)}]/ [\text{Initial Cost} + \text{Running Cost}] \quad (1)$$

Hence, it is important for the provider to create, maintain and administer the service delivering process.

Procedure

Step1: Set service level management actions

Set service level management actions based on ASP service development plan to keep required service level for each service level management items before placing the service in operation. Document these actions to the "SLM plan".

Step2: Perform service level management actions

Perform service level management actions according to the SLM plan continuously while in service.

Step3: Monitor service level

Regularly monitor/capture metrics for each service level management item. Report service level to the customer in case it is required in SLA.

Step4: Evaluate service level

Evaluate difference between service level expected and service level monitored. Analyze the cause of any differences.

Step5: Improve service level

Take improvement actions. This possibly requires re-negotiation or modification of the SLA or SLM plan.

Deliverables

1. SLM Plan/SLM Plan Updates
2. Service Level Report
3. Requirements to Improvement
4. SLA updates

Tools

1. Service Level Management Action Template

In order to support SLM planning, a template for service level management actions has been prepared. This template defines common actions that every application service should have. Table 2 shows examples of action items from this template. Details of these actions are tailored (ex. cycle or accuracy) by every application service.

Table 2. Examples of Service Level Management Actions

Service Level Management Actions	
-operation logging	-H/W regular maintenance
-monitoring	-S/W updating
-problem solving	-personnel training/education
-configuration management	-regular meeting ... etc.

2.2.4 SLM Audit

In order to ensure that every ASP team carries out their SLM properly, an SLM audit is performed. An audit team consists of an ASP team manager, QA section manager and other stakeholders. A standard checklist for the SLM audit is prepared. The SLM audit is planned annually and detected problems will be followed up at the next audit. In case of the possibility of common problems among every application service, iSLM standard would be revised.

3   SLM Practice in Hitachi

3.1   Reality of iSLM

We examined 19 application services and classified each service level for these services. Table 3 shows how many of these 19 services have a service level objective (committed by SLA) and service level management item (not committed but internally managed). A number of service level management items of each application service, on average, is 2 to 3 while that of service level objectives is 1 to 2. Generally, it is rare to commit SLA except for workload levels at the present time.

Table 3. A Number of Services which Service Level Elements is defined for

	Service Level Objective		Service Level Management Item	
	Defined	Not defined	Defined	Not defined
Availability	2	17	2	17
Recoverability	1	18	18	1
Response	0	19	5	14
Workload	19	0	19	0

Availability/Recoverability
Availability is presented by following equation.

$$\text{Availability} = (\text{expected working time} - (1 - \text{Reliability})*\text{MTTR})/\text{expected working time} \qquad (2)$$

Reliability of H/W components is relatively high and stable today, while MTTR tends to be unstable and long because it depends on various factors, such as system configuration and recovery procedure, human skills, etc. Therefore, recoverability is considered to be critical and is set as a service level management item.

Response/Workload
No application service commits response in SLA. Even in this case it is considered that the application service should satisfy high performance. There are two major reasons to this situation.

At first, for end users, response means end-to-end response. However, most NSPs provide a best-effort type service and the transfer speed on the network cannot be assured. Therefore, ASP cannot commit end-to-end response to their customer.

Second, most of H/W facility, such as servers, is shared to multiple customers in order to cut costs and set lower service fees. If response is required to commit, it should be optional with additional charge as it requires a special facility such as exclusive server or private network for the customer. Response problem is difficult for ASP but is the most important factor next to availability/recoverability for the customer. Some ASPs manage server response time to tune-up and deliver balanced-performance to customer as necessary. Most application services set a workload level in SLA because a workload level is a basic factor to performance/capacity planning.

3.2   Effect of iSLM

Fig.3 shows both availability and number of users of our financial ASP service, which started running in April 1999. This service provides Internet banking services for several local banks and their depositors. Availability of this service has been stable after an initial error period, but went wrong as a result of an increased number of users.

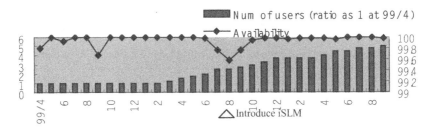

Fig. 3. Effect of iSLM

We analyzed the factor of availability falling and observed that an increase of users caused errors in system configuration changes, errors in system operations, or shortages of server performance. This meant a lack of appropriate management for this service. We assembled a special team to introduce the iSLM process into this service in August 2000. The team analyzed the service process, and listed 117 improvement items, and has been carrying out these improvement items. After the introduction of iSLM, availability was restored and became stable.

4   Problems to be Solved

As an ASP business is a new business model, some problems are presented in practice. First, a standard contract model for ASP is required. While the standard contract model for the system integration service has already proposed by JEITA but the contract for ASP varies from provider to provider now. This makes negotiating SLA difficult for both provider and customer. JEITA is now working at studying and making a common standard contract model for ASP. Second, it is difficult to realize end-to-end service level agreement for ASP in some case, as mentioned in 3.1. To assure an end-to-end service level, it is strongly required that all providers in the ASP value chain should have a SLA for their service. ASP should urge co-working providers to have SLA on their service.

5   Conclusion

SLM is a quality assurance process for providers to give their customers great satisfaction, and as a result, their ASP business will grow. We defined an integrated SLM process (iSLM) standard for ASP and have been practicing the process in real ASP business. Further practice and case studies is required to make SLM more effective. We will continue to improve our SLM process while catching-up with trends of standardization.

References

1. Rick Sturm, Wayne Morris, Mary Jander: Foundation of Service Level Management. Sams, A Division of Macmillan, USA (2000)
2. ASPIC Best Practice Committee: White Paper on Service Level Agreements. ASP Industry Consortium, USA (2000)
3. JEITA Solution Business Committee: Research Report on Solution Business. Japan Electronics and Information Technology Industries Association, Japan (2001)
4. Andrew Hills: The Complete Guide to IT Service Level Agreements 1999-2000Edition. Rothstein Associates Inc, USA (1999)
5. Adrian Payne: Marketing Planning for Service. Butterworth-Heinemann (1996)
6. Kondo, Takao: Service Management. Japan Productivity Center, Japan (1995)

Improving Software Quality in Product Families through Systematic Reengineering

Gopalakrishna Raghavan

Nokia Research Center,
5 Wayside Road, Burlington MA 01803, USA
gopal.raghavan@nokia.com

Abstract. Software quality is a very subjective attribute and is a complex mixture of several factors. There is no universal definition or a unique metric to quantify software quality. It is usually measured by analyzing various factors that are significant to the domain or application. It is evident that the end user of a product realizes substantial benefits due to improved software quality. Therefore many software industries strive hard to improve the quality of their product by investing in quality control and quality assurance activities like inspections, reviews, testing and audits. However, many software companies do not endeavor into reengineering activities to reap quality improvements. Product families that share legacy components, which have a lot of common features, could be reengineered in a systematic manner to consolidate knowledge and produce common components that can accommodate future applications. A significant by-product of this systematic reengineering activity would be an improved software quality. This paper presents a systematic reengineering approach and also identifies different quality factors that could be improved during this process. The proposed reengineering technique was used at Nokia Research Center to reengineer existing mobile systems in an efficient manner so that more applications and operating modes could be supported.

1 Introduction

It is challenging to characterize and measure the quality of a software product. Physical objects displays various quality attributes like, texture, color, material and shape. On the contrary, software quality characteristics like, cyclomatic complexity, cohesion, function points and lines of code, are not visible to the customer for evaluation. The end user only experiences the correctness, efficiency and usability of a software product. But there are several other quality factors that should be considered to evaluate software [1]. McCall et al., have identified eleven different quality factors [2][3]. Similarly, the ISO 9126 identifies six key quality attributes [4]. Also, a research from Hewlett-Packard defines five major factors for software quality [5]. Nevertheless, software developers seldom consider any of these quality factors during product creation. During product development, major emphasis lies on functional implementation. The software for a product family is conventionally developed based on a proprietary framework. The core components are maintained common and

J. Kontio and R. Conradi (Eds.): ECSQ 2002, LNCS 2349, pp. 90–99, 2002.

possibly remain unmodified for a long time. However, network interfaces and applications undergo significant changes over a period of time. In many cases, new projects borrow the entire source code from a similar product and modify it to meet the new requirements. This is done in order to speed-up the development process. As a result different products are maintained exclusively although several components are common across products. Over a period of time, component sources from different products that are designed to meet similar requirements are implausibly disparate, due to which inter-operability of components between products becomes unfeasible. Such dissimilarities are very difficult to avoid unless appropriate componentization and configuration management schemes are followed [6]. When the market expects drastically new products that support an enhanced technology, unifying features from several existing products, it isn't easy for the developers to deal with the situation. The demands are high, resources are limited and the need for inter-operability within a product family brings everything to state of disarray. However, with all this chaos things wouldn't really come to a standstill. There are always ways out of such situations, but only with compromise to quality.

This paper presents a systematic reengineering approach that is quality driven and practical on product families that share some common features. In Section 2, a framework for reengineering is presented. A systematic procedure for reengineering, composed of six discrete steps, is described in Section 3. In Section 4, the effect of reengineering on different quality factors is explained. Conclusions and future work in this direction are provided in Section 5.

2   A Reengineering Framework

The proposed reengineering framework is represented using Unified Modeling Language (UML) notation in Fig 1 [7]. The interface I_1 offered by two different products in the family is represented as P_1I_1 and P_2I_1. The source code implementations that exist for these interfaces are actually the interface realizations.

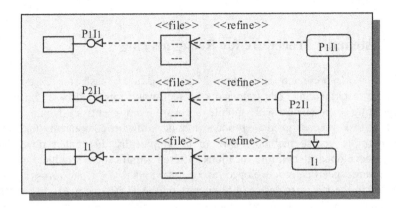

Fig. 1. Reengineering framework

From the implementations, the interface behaviors are elicited and represented as state machine models. P_1I_1 and P_2I_1 are behavior representations that have corresponding implementation sources as refinements. The interface behavior models are conceptual models that can be visually analyzed and unified to produce a common interface behavior I_1. Refinement of the unified interface behavior model would produce the necessary implementation, which realizes the common interface I_1.

This reengineering framework uses knowledge from existing systems to produce another enhanced system. In the process, not only is the existing system re-designed to result in a better version of the system but also allowance is provided for future enhancements and applications. The reengineering activity is systematically carried out in several discrete steps. Initially, different software components and interfaces are studied to understand their behavior. Implementation level analysis for functional similarities is extremely tedious, mainly because of the differences in programming styles. The use of source code analysis tools usually does not alleviate the situation, as they are not always successful in uncovering similarities in functionality. If the source code comparison tool reports similarities between multiple implementation of a component then it positively means that there are similarities, but if it does not produce a lot of similarities then it does not necessarily mean that the two components are dissimilar. The source line of code (LOC) that is similar between two different implementations is therefore not a very reliable measure to observe commonalities. On the other hand, similarities in design models are easier to visualize as they provide necessary abstraction and are conceptually straightforward to understand. The only caveat with this type of cognitive approach is that design decisions are purely based on visual observation since there are no quantitative measures to compare the design models. One possible way, which we are still exploring, of measuring this is by eliciting a number of requirement traces for the component and by analyzing a number of such traces that are satisfied by each design model. Based on the similarities, conceptual models can be unified to produce a common model that satisfies necessary requirements. This model can be validated and verified using requirement traces and when the models are satisfactorily consistent, source code can be automatically generated. The resulting source will offer a reengineered interface that can operate across the product family.

3   A Systematic Procedure for Reengineering

The framework presented in Section 2 is the primary basis for executing this systematic reengineering. The framework as such was formulated based on practical reengineering experiences with mobile software components at Nokia Research Center. A task was assigned to produce mobile software components that operate under multiple access methods. Due to geographically distributed development, products developed at multiple locations differed significantly. Products created in Europe were specifically developed to operate under GSM networks and those developed in the US were designed to operate on the TDMA networks [8]. Although application layer components are not supposed to be different in multiple access environments, several factors like individual development styles, team specific coding standards, configuration synchronizations etc., could result in variance. Legacy components accrue such disparities over a period of time and make it difficult to converge two logically similar components. Systematic reengineering is a prudent approach for producing highly efficient systems that also accommodates the needs of future applications [9]. All the rich experiences form the past are carried along without having to invest heavily in re-developing the system from scratch [10]. Also, quality improvements would be discernible as legacy components are re-designed to operate in an optimal and efficient manner. However, software reengineering can be rewarding only if it is executed in a systematic manner. The proposed reengineering process involves six discrete steps and should be carried out with appropriate support from Domain Experts and the Management [11]. While the domain expert assists in the knowledge elicitation process, the management plays a significant role in allocating and providing access to resources. Without the latter, it would be impossible to realize any profitable results. The next few sub-sections provide more details on the reengineering steps.

3.1 Identifying Common Components

This is the first and foremost activity and is more in lines with problem-oriented domain analysis [12]. It involves collection of resources such as source code, design documentation and suggestions from domain experts. Also, the system boundaries are clearly defined during this process. Multiple products in the family are analyzed at an abstract level to identify all the components that are involved in the product. Common components that are used in multiple products are carefully studied to discern their potential use in future products. Such candidates are identified by their name, signature or even their description. In some cases it might be necessary to explore their operational semantics to understand what they actually perform. When a family of mobile phone products are considered it can be observed that components like phone book, calendar, voice call application etc., are supported under multiple products. On the other hand, there may be certain components, for example: Bluetooth, which are support only on specific products. The goal of this step is to primarily identify such common components that offer possibilities for reusing certain functional similarities across the product family.

3.2 Elicit Common Interface

In this step, multiple implementations of an interface are studied to identify commonalities. Based on the similarities and differences, the behavior of the interface is re-designed to accommodate the needs of multiple product implementations. A component would usually offer several interfaces and these interfaces can be realized as API implementations in the form of functions. The candidate component that is identified for reengineering may have several interfaces that are common across products. In addition, there may be interfaces that are specific to a product. The interfaces that are common are of particular interest from reengineering perspective. These candidate interfaces are selected based on the interface signature or the feature that they support. It is possible that a feature that is provided by an interface in one product may be implemented as several interfaces in another product. Identification of these common interfaces is the main concern of this step and is undeniably a protracted process. Expert advice from the domain specialist could definitely expedite this process.

For example, the voice call application of the mobile phone software offers several interfaces, like call origination, call termination, call holding etc. These interfaces are supported under multiple implementations of the component, on various products in the family. Ideally their source codes should be alike as they perform similar functionality. But as pointed out earlier, large variances can be observed in such legacy interfaces. Reengineering these interfaces would facilitate reuse of call interfaces across various mobile phone products.

3.3   Reverse Engineer the Interfaces

The source code that represents a function is carefully studied to understand the logic and various states that are involved during the flow. Implementation details such as buffer allocation, variable declarations, string manipulation, etc., are ignored. Different states, transitions to states, communication of events and decision logic are captured and translated to state machine diagrams or activity diagrams. State information is usually stored in structures and these values are changed accordingly, during transitions. Events are composed and sent to different objects in the system via system specific API's. Condition loops clearly provide the decision flow and can be mapped as transition guards at a higher level [13][14]. The effort involved in this step can be considerably reduced if the interface behavior is already documented. In which case, the models are merely inspected to make sure they accurately represent the implementation. However, if the models are not up to date, then they have to be updated to accurately reflect the most recent implementation.

3.4   Compare and Unify the Conceptual Models

This is one of the most challenging parts of reengineering and involves cognitive reasoning in order to develop a unified model. Various design models are compared visually, since there are no automatic tools available to aid in this process. Also there are no measures to quantify the commonalities at the design level [15]. Nevertheless, the distance between specifications could be measured using certain formal techniques and used to quantify design similarities [16]. However, most decisions are based on the Architect's expertise in model building and knowledge about the domain. This activity is basically an art that involves visual examination, assimilation of various behaviors and construction of mental models of a common behavior. However, if models are constructed using state machine simulation tools, like Telelogic Tau [17], it is possible to use requirements trace as a good measure to identify commonalities. In order to do this, requirements for the common component interface are modeled using Message Sequence Charts (MSC). The interface behaviors under multiple implementations are modeled as communicating finite state machines using Specification and Description Language (SDL) [18]. The MSCs are traced against these SDL models. The number of MSCs that are satisfied by a model and the percentage of the design covered by them are good indicators of the commonalities that exist between models. Using this, factor design models are unified to form a common representation that meet common requirements, which are represented as MSCs. However if requirements and designs are modeled using UML diagrams, tools like I-Logix Rhapsody can be used to trace the design and simulate the models [19].

3.5 Verify and Validate Models

Formal verification is an activity that ensures that the specification satisfies system properties and formal validation is an activity that ensures that the specification captures user's needs [20]. In the simplest form, verification can be conducted by design walkthrough and code inspections. In a more elaborate form it involves rigorous testing and simulation. At the highest level, formal verification involves application of mathematical deduction for proving system properties. Based on the experience and skills, different techniques may be used for verifying a system to ensure correctness. Many commercial tools, like Telelogic Tau, have a built in validator that can perform extensive state space validation. They also support verification of different requirements MSCs against the design. Validation tools are preferred in industrial set-up as opposed to manual mathematical proof techniques because they provide easier user interfaces and do not demand high mathematical skills. This definitely motivates developers who are not specifically trained to prove systems properties, to use such tools to prototype and simulate the system before actually implementing it. This activity not only eliminates ambiguities but also assists in early discovery of defects.

3.6 Generate the Source

This is a straightforward activity that is achieved with the help of appropriate tool support. After validating and verifying the design models, they need to be refined by providing cleaner structures and including appropriate header definitions. The refined model can then generate source code automatically in the desired implementation language, which of course depends primarily on the code generation support provided by the tool. For example, Telelogic Tau provides capability for generating C++, C or Cmicro from SDL specifications. There are numerous tools that provide auto-code-generation capability, which vary in model and language support. The downside of auto generation is the poor readability of source code and future maintenance. In addition to maintaining the source code, the design level models need to be updated to reflect the most recent implementation. Whether to modifying the source code to accommodate future requirements or to make necessary changes to the design and regenerate the code is always debatable. From the maintenance perspective, re-generation seems to be a prudent solution since all maintenance efforts can be concentrated only on design models. However, minor implementation details and linking with legacy components necessitates code changes. Factors like delivery schedule, knowledge in design modeling, tool capability, development cost and several other management concerns drive the adoption of code generation.

4   Effect on Software Quality

There are several factors that contribute towards software quality. Since quality cannot be easily computed using some mathematical formulae, different factors are used to estimate the quality of a product. McCall et al., have identified eleven factors, namely correctness, reliability, efficiency, integrity, usability, maintainability, flexibility, testability, portability, reusability and interoperability [2]. The ISO 9126 suggests six key quality attributes: functionality, reliability, usability, efficiency, maintainability and portability [4]. The FUPRS quality factors proposed by Hewlett-Packard are functionality, usability, reliability, performance and supportability [5]. Some of the quality attributes considered by Basili et al., includes correctness, readability, testability, ease of modification and performance [10]. Different quality factors discussed in these studies are quite similar and are broadly covered by McCall's factors. The proposed reengineering approach was therefore evaluated on the basis of McCall's quality factors, as presented in Table 1. Accordingly, a grading scheme with 0 representing low and 10 representing high scale was used as a metric. In Table 1, the abbreviation RE refers to the reengineering approach discussed in Section 3.

As illustrated in Table 1, the proposed reengineering approach in Section 3 plays an imperative role in improving the software quality. Although, it can be argued that the grade metrics used here are very subjective. Unfortunately, there aren't any direct measures to quantify the quality of software. Higher-grade values for various quality factors only suggest that the reengineering approach addresses diverse aspect of the software that contributes to quality improvements. The grading provided above is based on experiences gathered while reengineering certain mobile phone components at Nokia Research Center. The metric values were primarily derived from various small and focused discussions. The approach and results were presented internally to various product creation experts and researchers. Although, an extensive survey was not done, personal interaction and verbal feedbacks have contributed to the assessment of this approach. Such feedback definitely provides constructive criticism, which adds value to the improvement process. However, more survey needs to be done to capture the views of diverse audience.

Table 1. Effect on software quality due to reengineering

Quality Factor	Description	Grade	Comments
Correctness	Capability of a software to satisfy its specification and meet customers needs	9	RE step 5 would ensure correctness via formal verification and validation
Reliability	Ability to tolerate various severe conditions and perform intended functions	6	RE step 5 would validate the state space but several other aspects like hardware, platform, external interfaces etc., could affect reliability
Efficiency	Optimal use of system resources	8	RE steps 1-4, contributes towards optimization of resources like memory, time, etc., by combining common functionalities and interfaces
Integrity	Controlled access to software and data	2	RE does not provide any tools to facilitate integrity
Usability	Ease with which system could be studied, understood and operated	8	RE provides appropriate design documentation to understand the system concepts and operation
Maintainability	Ability to keep the system in operating condition after development	9	RE unifies several common components in step 4 and eliminates repeated maintenance activity
Flexibility	Ability to modify operational components	7	RE facilitates replacement or upgrade of components that conform to the interface
Testability	Ability to check that the software performs intended functionality	9	RE step 5 allows design level simulation and validation. The suggested tools help in generating extensive test cases and scenarios.
Portability	Capability to operate in multiple platform environments	8	RE abstracts several product family components that operate in different environment
Reusability	Ability to use the same component in different applications	9	Various steps of RE identifies reusable parts and combines common components
Interoperability	Ease with which different modules could be interconnected	8	RE steps 1-4 focus on reducing interface complexity

5   Conclusion

Reengineering is an activity that involves redesigning of existing systems to improve them and to make them operate efficiently in future systems. This activity is usually overlooked by many organizations since it involves large amount of effort and time in modifying existing systems that are already functional. Most of the effort of product development goes towards introducing new applications and supporting latest technologies, while very little is spared towards revisiting existing implementations and making them more efficient and maintainable. Several legacy components exist in large systems that are unmodified for a long period of time. Unlike a desktop system, resources are very restricted in an embedded system and hence it is very critical to make efficient use of them. Especially if functionalities from multiple products in a family are combined and supported under one platform it is vital to coalesce commonalities and re-organize components to efficiently utilize memory and other resources. Postponing or ignoring this activity could only accrue un-organized software components that could be susceptible to faulty behavior due to drastic adjections driven by some demanding technological revolutions. Reengineering activities should therefore be considered part of development process and scheduled periodically.

A systematic approach for reengineering is proposed in this paper that involves six discrete steps. Several quality improvements that could be achieved as a result of systematic reengineering are identified and evaluated. This approach is based on practical experimentation on mobile phone systems, which was found to be very efficient and result oriented. Accordingly management support and domain expert's feedback were identified as key elements to the success of reengineering. Using lightweight formalism that does not involve heavy mathematical deductions could attract developer's attention to assist in the process and motivate them to follow the guidelines in order to maintain the reengineered components. Comparing design models is still a cognitive and manual process that involves visual examination by experts who are familiar with both the domain as well as model building techniques. A good metric for measuring the similarities at this level could be valuable in developing design comparison and merging tools, which could accelerate the design unification process. Also, quality factor measurements are extremely subjective and any domain specific metrics could help in evaluating the product. At Nokia Research Center, we are exploring in this direction and investigating different metrics that could aid in reengineering software to produce quality products in an efficient and practical manner.

Acknowledgement

I gratefully acknowledge the support from members of Software Architecture Group at Nokia Research Center. I would also like to extend my sincere thanks to several product creation experts who provided excellent domain support.

Reference

1. R. S. Pressman, Software Engineering A Practitioner's approach, 5th ed. McGraw-Hill Series in Computer Science (2001)
2. J. McCall and P. Richards, G. Walters, Factors in Software Quality, three volumes, NTIS AD-A049-014, 015, 055 (1977)
3. J.P. Cavano and J.A. McCall, A Framework for Measurement of Software Quality, Proceedings of ACM Software Quality Assurance Workshop (1978)
4. ISO/IEC 9126, Information Technology – Software Product Quality, Part 1-4, ISO/IEC JTC1/SC7/WG6 (1998)
5. R.B. Grady and D.L. Caswell, Software Metrics: Establishing a Company-Wide Program, Prentice-Hall (1987)
6. G. Raghavan, Reduce Maintenance Cost In Product Families Using Multi-Platform Development Scheme, Proceedings of IASTED Software Engineering and Applications, Anaheim, California (2001)
7. G. Booch, J. Rumbaugh and I. Jacobson, The Unified Modeling Language: User Guide, Addison-Wesley Longman, Inc., Reading, Massachusetts (1999)
8. L. Harte, S. Prokup and R. Levine, Cellular and PCS: The Big Picture, McGraw-Hill, New York (1997)
9. V. R. Basili and H.D. Rombach, Support for Comprehensive Reuse, Software Engineering Journal, September (1991)
10. G. Caldiera and V. R. Basili, Reengineering Existing Software for Reusability, Technical report UMIACS-TR-90-30, Institute of Advance Computer Studies and Department of Computer Science, University of Maryland, MD (1990)
11. W. Tracz, Software Reuse: Motivators and Inhibitors, Proceedings of COMPCONS (1987)
12. G. Arango and R. Prieto-Diaz, Domain Analysis and Software System Modeling, IEEE Press (1991)
13. G. Raghavan and M. Boughdadi, Mapping UML Object Model and Statechart to SDL, Software Engineering Symposium, Motorola Conference, Arizona (2000)
14. K. Verschaeve and A. Ek, Three Scenarios for Combining UML and SDL 96, SDL'99: The Next Millennium, Elsevier Science, Netherlands (1999)
15. W. Frakes and C. Terry, Software Reuse and Reusability Metrics and Models, TR-95-07, Computer Science Department, Virginia Techn (1995)
16. L.L. Jilani, J. Desharnais and A. Mili, Defining and Applying Measures of Distance Between Specifications, IEEE Transactions on Software Engineering, vol. 27, no. 8, (2001)
17. Telelogic AB., Telelogic Tau 4.2: SDT Manual (2000)
18. J. Ellsberger, D. Hogrefe and A. Sarma, SDL: Formal Object-Oriented Language for Communicating Systems, Prentice Hall (1997)
19. Rhapsody I-Logix, http://www.ilogix.com
20. G. Raghavan, Industrial Strength Formalization of Object-Oriented Real-time System, PhD Dissertation, Florida Atlantic University, Boca Raton, Florida (2000)

SPI Models: What Characteristics Are Required for Small Software Development Companies?

Ita Richardson

Dept. of Computer Science and Information Systems, University of Limerick
Limerick, Ireland
ita.richardson@ul.ie

Abstract. Internationally, as an aid to the improvement of software quality, there is a growing interest in the improvement of software process. This initiative, if ignored, may contribute to a reduction in the advantage which Irish companies have had in the international marketplace in recent times. As much of the software in Ireland is developed by small companies, this sector not only should be aware of, but must become involved in available software process improvement initiatives. This paper presents a list of characteristics which must exist for software process models to be useful to such companies. A model, the Software Process Matrix, which demonstrates these characteristics and is based on Quality Function Deployment and has been developed and implemented. The development of the model and its implementation in one small software development company is discussed.

1 Introduction

There is a need for small indigenous software companies to improve their software process. It has been recognised that the Irish Software Sector is valuable to the Irish economy, and that it continues to grow and should contribute further to the economy in future. Sales from the Irish Software Sector increased at approximately 25% faster than international software markets from 1991-1995, and the growth in software sector employment during 1995-1999 would indicate that this trend has continued [1]. However, due to the nature of software products and the growth in the use of the internet, country markets are faced with increasing global competition. While there continues to be growth in traditional software producing countries such as the United States of America and the United Kingdom, other countries such as India, Israel, the Philippines and the Eastern European countries have demonstrated that they have an educated staff available to work in the software sector for lower wages. In Ireland, therefore, software companies need to stay very competitive.

One way to do this is to ensure that the software produced and the process by which it is produced is of higher quality than other countries. Small software companies are even more vulnerable because they are perceived as not being able to produce this level of quality. This is evidenced in a quote from the customer of a company involved in this study, when the company requested a delay in software installation due to the illness of a team member:

J. Kontio and R. Conradi (Eds.): ECSQ 2002, LNCS 2349, pp. 100–113, 2002.

"CS expressed concern over Software Solutions's inability to 'turn up the burner' recognising that this was an inherent risk when dealing with small suppliers".

While one wonders if this perception is justified considering the well-publicised projects which have not been implemented on time nor with the quality required by the customer, this is indeed the reality for many small companies.   Therefore, small Irish indigenous software sector must not only should be aware of software process improvement, but must become involved in it. The views of Combelles and DeMarco [2] should not be taken lightly: "the issues Software Process Improvement raises are important, if not vital, to the future of your organisations".

Much has been written highlighting the deficiencies in the more popular SPI models where the small company is concerned, for example in [3], [4], [5], [6]. However, there has been little discussion about the characteristics that should be included in SPI models to make them useful for the small company.

2   Appropriate Improvement Model

Assessment is an important element of any software process improvement initiative. However, there must be more from an assessment than just a record of how good or how bad the processes are at that point in time. The main requirement is that the company must be able to identify what improvements are needed. But, in the case of the small company is such an improvement plan enough?   Because of financial constraints [7], [8] and the availability of fewer people [9], for maximum effect in a small company an appropriate improvement model should display the following characteristics:

- **Relate to the Company's Business Goals:** Within the small company, funding is very limited and there is usually a large personal commitment by the owner/manager. Therefore, it is important that any projects undertaken, including software process improvement projects, have the company's business goals in focus.
- **Focus on the Most Important Software Processes:** It is important that when new or modified practices are implemented, they are making changes which will have the greatest effect on those software processes most important to the company. These process improvements should give the greatest business benefits.
- **Give Maximum Value for Money:** No company, regardless of whether they are large or small, is willing to undertake any project without being assured that the resources expended will in fact give maximum value for money.   In small companies, there are fewer areas that can absorb losses, therefore this becomes more important than in large companies.
- **Propose Improvements Which Have Maximum Effect in as Short a Time as Possible:** Obviously, finance is a factor here. Another significant factor is that, in a small company, the software process improvement project is most likely to be worked on part-time by the software engineers. They will not have the luxury of a full-time software quality assurance engineer to drive the project. Therefore, if

they do not see improvements to the process in a relatively short space of time, it is likely that the project will lose momentum.

- **Provide Fast Return on Investment:** Due to the relative shortage of finance in a small company, it is unreasonable to expect any owner/manager to spend money unless improvements are seen within a short period of time. The improvement model must be able to cope with this.
- **Be Process-Oriented:** Many of the publicised software process models are based on assessment of the process, but do not focus on modifications to the process. In a small company, while the issue of how well the company is currently doing is important, what improvements can be made to the process which will ultimately improve product quality is more important.
- **Relate to Other Software Models:** While some of the software development companies with which the author has been involved are interested in software process improvement as a means to improving the quality of their product, many companies are interested in certification by outside bodies, particularly ISO. Therefore, an improvement model used by the company must take cognisance of the requirements of these external bodies.
- **Be Flexible and Easy-to-Use:** Because of the nature of small companies, it is unlikely that they will have specialists in software process available within the organisation, unless someone with a background in this discipline has been employed there. It is much more likely that they will be software developers with little experience in software process. Therefore, unless the model is flexible and easy-to-use, it will involve training, which is usually limited in small companies and more likely to be given to engineering training. This could render a model to be not useful within the company.
- **Demonstrate Multi-dimensionality:** When a company makes changes to a process by modifying current practice, this could have a significant effect on other processes within the organisation.   Currently, there is no record of such possibilities. Such a record would be useful to an organisation.

3   What Is the Software Process Matrix (SPM)?

The Software Process Matrix (SPM), which displays the required characteristics as listed above, was developed during this research project. The SPM can be used to establish an improvement strategy based on Quality Function Deployment. Quality Function Deployment (QFD) has been defined as a "way to assure the design quality while the product is still in the design stage" [10] and as a "quality system focused on delivering products and services that satisfy customers" [11]. Used mainly in manufacturing, its use has spread more recently to services and software development. Originating in Japan, QFD is now used in many countries worldwide.

3.1   What Is Quality Function Deployment?

In order to collect and maintain the voice of the customer throughout the production life-cycle, QFD usually uses a series of matrices which convert the customer's voice into a final product. Different models are available for use, and according to Cohen [12], the model adapted by the American Standards Institute (Four-phase model) and containing 4 matrices [13] is "probably the most widely described and used model in the United States". The Software Process Matrix (SPM) is based on the first matrix of this model, the House of Quality.

3.2 The Four-Phase Model

In the four-phase QFD model there are four matrices as shown in Figure 1. These are:

- Product planning matrix (House of Quality);
- Parts Deployment;
- Process Planning;
- Production Planning.

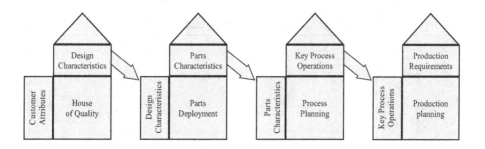

Fig. 1. Four-Phase model for Manufacturing

Initially, the 'voice of the customer' is collected, and the relative importance of each customer requirement is measured. In house of quality matrix, these requirements are used to identify design characteristics which have the greatest impact on customer requirements. Although QFD consists of many matrices, the main focus is often this matrix, as using it alone can have a significant effect on the product development process [14]. The matrix is normally broken down into six 'rooms' as shown in Figure 2:

- Customer requirements (WHATs)
- Design characteristics (HOWs)
- Overall importance of customer requirements
- Relationships between customer requirements and design characteristics
- Importance of design characteristics
- Inter-relationships between design characteristics.
-

Overall Importance of Customer Requirements. The overall importance of customer requirements is used to identify priorities of these requirements. Generally, the accepted numerical data included in this calculation are:

- Current capability of product in providing the requirements
- Measurement of competitive analysis
- Proposed capability of future product in providing the requirements
- Improvement factor required to get from current to future status
- Importance of each customer requirement to the product
- Market leverage – specific market information which should be taken into account.

For both the current capability and proposed capability, the value used in this project ranged from 1-5, where 1 represented doing badly and 5 represented doing very well. Market leverage had values of 1.0, when no market leverage existed, 1.2 for medium market leverage, and 1.5 for strong market leverage.

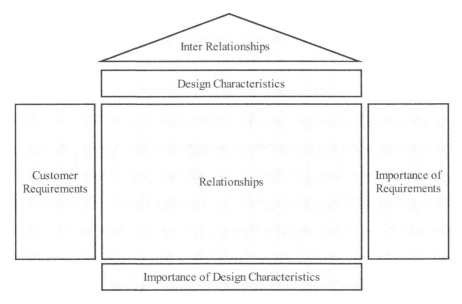

Fig. 2. Outline House of Quality

Relationships between Customer Requirements and Design Characteristics. The underlying theory of using Quality Function Deployment matrices is that design characteristics have an effect on one or more of the customer requirements. Therefore, customer requirement vs design characteristic relationships must be established.

These relationships are often stated at four levels of effect: strong, medium, weak and none. The values given to these are 9, 3, 1 respectively and on QFD charts they are normally represented by the symbols: ● or ◎ (strong), O (medium), and Δ (weak). There is no scientific basis for the values used, except that practitioners felt the need to have a wide gap between the value of 'Strong' and 'None'. It is now common practice to use the values as stated. As these values have emerged from over 30 years of use in Japanese industry, and 16 years of use in the United States, Europe and the rest of the world, they now have a universal currency. Consequently, they were used in the current research. Figure 3 shows an abstract from the Software Process Matrix, showing these relationships.

Importance of Design Characteristics. The importance of design characteristics is calculated, by using the strong, medium and weak relationship values combined with the overall importance of customer requirements.

3.3 Quality Function Deployment for Software Process

Using QFD, the software process model is treated as the customer where software processes are the customer requirements. These processes were identified from software process literature. Examples of processes are:

- Define and document processes
- Systematic assessment of suppliers' software process suitability
- Systematic implementation of software design
- Systematic planning of project work flow and estimates.

The design characteristics are the practices which must be followed for processes to be successful. These practices were also identified from the software process literature. Examples of practices are:

- Test the customer's operation before software implementation
- Prototype or simulate critical elements of the software
- Maintain and trace product item histories.

In developing the Software Process Matrix, a total of 135 practices were identified. A crucial part in the development of the software process matrix was to identify the relationships between processes and practices. Those which are explicitly mentioned in the literature were easily identified. For example:

> **Practice:** To ensure software's traceability to requirements
> has a strong effect on
> **Process:** The systematic development of detailed design.

Using expert opinion and various statistical techniques, other relationships between processes and practices were identified, resulting in the development and verification of the software process matrix which was then validated in industry. A sample of relationships which were identified as a result of this exercise is shown in Figure 3.

These include:

> **Practice:** To map requirements to future releases
> has a medium effect on
> **Process:** The development of software requirements;

> **Practice:** To specify interfaces between software units
> has a weak effect on
> **Process:** System acceptance testing.

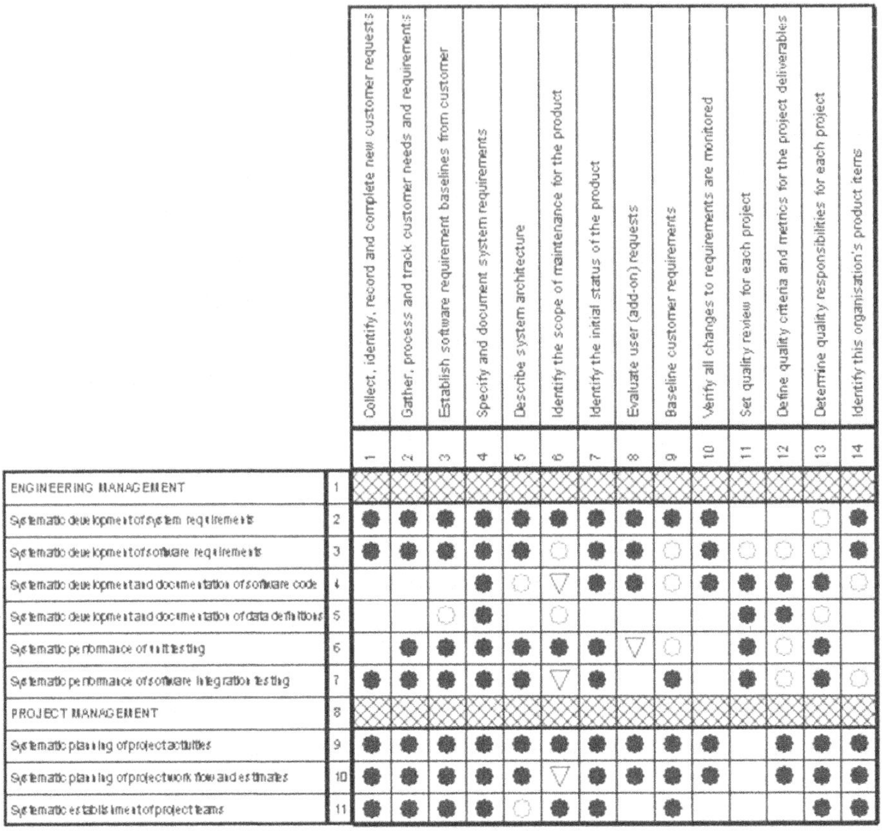

		Collect, identify, record and complete new customer requests	Gather, process and track customer needs and requirements	Establish software requirement baselines from customer	Specify and document system requirements	Describe system architecture	Identify the scope of maintenance for the product	Identify the initial status of the product	Evaluate user (add-on) requests	Baseline customer requirements	Verify all changes to requirements are monitored	Set quality review for each project	Define quality criteria and metrics for the project deliverables	Determine quality responsibilities for each project	Identify this organisation's product items
		1	2	3	4	5	6	7	8	9	10	11	12	13	14
ENGINEERING MANAGEMENT	1	▨	▨	▨	▨	▨	▨	▨	▨	▨	▨	▨	▨	▨	▨
Systematic development of system requirements	2	●	●	●	●	●	●	●	●	●	●			○	●
Systematic development of software requirements	3	●	●	●	●	●	●	●	●	○	●	○	○	○	●
Systematic development and documentation of software code	4				●	○	▽	●	●	○	●	●	●	●	○
Systematic development and documentation of data definitions	5		○		●		○					●	●	○	
Systematic performance of unit testing	6		●	●	●	●	●	●	▽	○		●		●	
Systematic performance of software integration testing	7	●	●	●	●	●	▽	●		●		●	○	●	○
PROJECT MANAGEMENT	8	▨	▨	▨	▨	▨	▨	▨	▨	▨	▨	▨	▨	▨	▨
Systematic planning of project activities	9	●	●	●	●	●	●	●	●	●	●	●		●	●
Systematic planning of project work flow and estimates	10	●	●	●	●	●	▽	●	●	●	●		●	●	●
Systematic establishment of project teams	11	●	●	●	●	○	●	●		●				●	●

Fig. 3. Extract from Software Process Matrix

For a small company to use any software process model to their advantage, it is imperative that the effort expended is minimal. The Software Process Matrix provides them with a generic section that has been completed previously and can be used in their company. From the company's point of view, all they need to provide are the measurements for calculating the overall importance of the software process. These are:

- Current capability as assessed using a self-assessment questionnaire;
- Future capability as input from management;
- Importance of the software process to the business;
- Competitive analysis;
- Market leverage for company specific requirement e.g. ISO-certification.

These measurements combined with the relationship values (9,3,1,0) can then be used to calculate the overall importance of each practice, providing the organisation with a ranked list of actions which can be input to their software process improvement strategy.   This ranked list can be combined with cost figures and time-effective calculations thus taking these factors into account when determining the action plan for the organisation. Further detail on calculations is given in Richardson [15].

3.4 Self-assessment

The basis for the model is that organisations will be able to carry out a self-assessment of their own software development process. Concern about using the self-assessment approach is expressed by Stevenson [16] after he completed a study of self-assessment by managers in organisations. He states that "an individual's cognitive perceptions of the strengths and weaknesses of his organisation were strongly influenced by factors associated with the individual and not only by the organisation's attributes". As the questions are all focused within one organisation and software process, any bias will exist in all answers from that respondent, and therefore, will not compromise the validity of using the questionnaire. Furthermore, in the company studied, the researchers carried out an independent assessment to validate the results obtained from the questionnaire.

However, even this independent assessment is not without criticism. Research conducted by El Eman et al. [17] on the reliability of SPICE assessments by independent assessors demonstrates that in the investigation of 21 process instances covering 15 processes, six of the processes did not meet their initial benchmark for interrator agreement and a further eight processes could improve their reliability. The study concludes that "while some would like to believe that assessments are sufficiently reliable, our results indicate that this is not always the case." They also note that SPICE has been built upon the experience of previous assessment models, therefore expect that this disagreement would extend to other software process models. If this is in fact the case, then bringing in an independent person may not provide more reliable results to an organisation than the self-assessment questionnaire.

4 Research Project

The challenge undertaken by the researcher was to develop an improvement model which could be easily and successfully used by companies when embarking on a software process improvement strategy through the provision of a prioritized list of practices. Once the model was developed and verified, the researcher validated the model in two small Irish software development companies, while, at the same time investigating process improvement in two other companies (action research with control companies). To maintain confidentiality, the company names used are pseudonyms. Two companies, Computer Craft and DataNet, were involved in longitudinal action research over two years. Two companies, Software Solutions and Ríomhaire, were treated as control companies. Initially, personnel within the action research companies completed a self-assessment questionnaire. Results were entered into the SPM, and an action plan devised within each company. Implementation of actions and outcome within DataNet are discussed in detail in this paper, with particular emphasis on organisation, customer management and project management processes, all of which were affected as a direct result of the project.

4.1 DataNet

There were nine people employed in DataNet, four in the software development group. DataNet were interested in acquiring ISO9000 certification. The researcher investigated improvements to their software process subsequent to the use of the SPM within the organisation.   Research methods used included participation during meetings, interviewing, observation, self-assessment questionnaires and examination of documentation for two projects within the company. She became a participant observer in the process, taking on a dual role of "outsider and insider" giving her the opportunity "to participate and to reflect on the data that is gathered during participation" [18].

Starting Scenario. Initially, in DataNet, there were no documented procedures, and employees stated that they were *"attempting to follow a process"* which was based on their own personal experience. At this point no attempt had been made to introduce formal processes into the organisation but they were considering ISO9000 certification with input from an external consultancy company. The Managing Director was enthusiastic about improving the software process, and the software engineers were aware of this.

In DataNet, the main product, CD-Base, was being developed in conjunction with Dealbhna, their main customer: *"more a joint venture than sub-contract"*. From a customer management viewpoint, the situation within DataNet was unusual. Both the Managing Director and the Technical Director were ex-employees of Dealbhna. Because of this connection, the software engineers viewed the Managing Director as the customer. The DataNet software engineers believed that the final customer for the product was Dealbhna's responsibility.   A functional specification, which the customer and Managing Director signed off, was written. The software engineers had no contact with Dealbhna employees during the early stages of the project, nor had they contact with Dealbhna's customers until Beta testing, which caused problems during development.

Changes were requested at all stages of the development lifecycle, which continually affected due-dates. Many updates and modifications in the latter stages did not go through any formal change control procedure, although this procedure did exist.

In DataNet, the development group within the company was very small, and, as all software engineers were going to be involved in the project, there was no requirement for setting up a project team. No project plans were written at project start, and tasks were allocated to individual engineers by the Managing Director, but no due dates were assigned. Project schedules were available at times throughout the project. There was no continuity to these schedules, but when they were available, they listed the developers to whom tasks had been allocated and the due dates of the tasks. There was no update of schedules based on feedback from developers.

Intervention Using Software Process Matrix. Assessment questionnaires were completed by the Managing Director, Technical Director and two software engineers. The SPM matrix was completed for DataNet and the top five processes that should be concentrated on by the company were identified as:

1. Systematic preparation of new product versions
2. Define standard software process for the organisation
3. Establishment of contracts with sub-contractors
4. Systematic development and documentation of data definitions
5. Systematic planning of project work flow and estimates.

To have an effect on these process areas, the top nine practices listed in priority order to be used as the basis for an software process improvement action plan were identified as:

1. Assign a person with SQA responsibilities
2. Establish product baselines for each product supplied
3. Specify and document system requirements
4. Identify this organisation's product items
5. Verify all changes to requirements are monitored
6. Collect, identify, record and complete new customer requests
7. Assign responsibility for software development plan, work products and activities
8. Identify facilities and estimate resource needs for project
9. Define delivery contents (media, software, documentation) for customer from subcontractor / development group

Although the company was given the option for their inclusion, the priorities given above did not take into account such factors as whether ISO9000 or some other requirements should take precedence. The actions were not costed nor was the effort involved quantified. Following a meeting with company management and employees, it was agreed that the actions as given would be the priorities for the Software Process Improvement action plan for the company. One of the software engineers took responsibility for Software Quality Assurance within the company tasked with the implementation of procedures.

Actions Implemented. The SPM actions in DataNet were identified close to the time that the company had an ISO9000 audit completed, so the priority for them was to implement ISO9000 actions. Many of the actions which resulted from the ISO9000 audit paralleled those from the SPM.

The first action to be implemented was the *assignment of a person with software quality assurance responsibilities*. The fact that this position had been filled was one of the positive elements mentioned during the ISO9000 audit. The software engineer responsible was allowed 2-3 hours per week to work on quality issues, and was the person who drove the implementation of procedures within the company. He also *identified the organisation's product items* and attempted to *establish baselines for each product supplied* (actions 2 and 4).

Complying with action 3, one of the procedures written in DataNet was for the *specification and documentation of requirements*, and this was adhered to during their latest project. It included meeting with the customer and gathering their requirements, writing the documentation and updating the history file. Although there were attempts made to follow this procedure, some difficulties arose, such as getting customer feedback. Action 6, the *collection, identification, recording and completion of new customer requests*, was also covered by this procedure.

The fifth action identified was to *verify that all changes to requirements are monitored*. This was done mainly through the use of the version control on the specifications, and changes to requirements still caused problems during development.

The *assigning of responsibility for the software development plan, work product and activities* had improved significantly (action 7). Although it had not been proceduralised, there had been modifications to the project management process, giving engineers involvement in the establishment of tasks and due dates, and continual updating of the plan. These modifications were also influenced by action 8 – *to identify the facilities and estimate the resource needs for the project*. As could be seen by the delay in testing the product, there were further refinements to be made to this, but certainly, there was evidence to show that this had indeed improved. For this improved process to become embedded in the organisation, it would be important that it is documented.

Action 9 was not completed during the course of the research – the *definition of delivery contents for the customer*, mainly because they did not have time to do so, and it was not seen to be of great importance to the company.

While not implemented solely because of the use of the SPM, but also driven by the Managing Director's goal of the company becoming ISO9000-certified, eight of the actions identified by SPM within DataNet were implemented, one of them partially.

Processes at End of Research Period. The software development group in DataNet had developed ISO9000 procedures which were approved and implemented within the organisation. These procedures were developed mainly by the Software Quality Assurance engineer, who had been appointed as a direct result of action 1. Six out of an expected nine procedures were approved, implemented and followed.

In conjunction with a business partner, the main software product in development at the end of the research period in DataNet was Hitech. Although this product was being built for a specific market rather than a specific customer, the software developers were very clear that *"(business partner) is our customer"* and gathered the customer requirements from him during meetings. DataNet knew the technical side; the business partner knew the business side and extensively reviewed the specifications. He was also available for clarification on issues.

Even with regular meetings and contact between the business partner, there was a *"bit of confusion"* around the requirements. Reasons given for this were because a *"lot of the requirements turned out to be very complex"*, *"misunderstanding of terminology"* between the developer and business partner. This subsequently caused problems for the software engineers, in that some features were changed *"quite late in the process"*.

In DataNet, once the Hitech project began, project schedules were implemented following discussion with the software group and were well-managed. They drew up a project plan with a finishing date that they thought would be reasonable, but this had been modified and the schedule re-written. The schedule was "*tight in the time sense but loose in tasks*". For example, one engineer knew that he had four tasks to complete in the following two weeks, but the order in which he did them was not important once they did not impact anyone else involved in the project. Because of the size of the group, they did not use a formal means of reporting the status of their work.

Analysis of Change in DataNet. Within DataNet, a quality ethos was evident, and as it was a young company, the Managing Director was determined that it would develop software based on good quality standards. To do this, he contacted the researcher about participating in her project and was working towards ISO9000 certifications. The improvements discussed above were made as a result of these interventions, but were also a consequence of the input by the employees to the development of processes and procedures.

Practices focused on during the research period were customer contact, the specification of requirements and monitoring changes to the requirements. These had been identified as an area of improvement within the SPM and subsequently as part of the ISO9000 audit. Although they did not introduce specific requirements gathering techniques the software developers were able to establish requirements from their identified customer, provide him with written specifications, and receive feedback on those requirements. There were still some problems, such as delay in getting feedback and changes to requirements in the later stages of the project, but DataNet had a much more controlled process than when the researcher first visited the company.

The other main area of improvement was Project Management. They had introduced planned and controlled project schedules, and updated these regularly. They discussed delays when they occurred, and removed a number of features from the product so that they could meet the required deadlines.

The actions in DataNet were identified as a result of using the Software Process Matrix. The software process improvement effort concentrated round the prioritized actions and the company had success in implementing the actions.

5   Were Required Characteristics Displayed by the Software Process Matrix?

The Software Process Matrix supported the implementation of the software process improvements in the researched organisations. But did the model display the required characteristics for an appropriate improvement model in small software development companies?

- **Relate to the Company's Business Goals:** Using Quality Function Deployment as a basis for the Software Process Matrix allows the organisation to include a measure for the importance of the process to the business when calculating practice priorities.

- **Focus on the Most Important Software Processes:** Using QFD calculations in SPM not only allows for the inclusion of the business importance, but also calculates priorities based on those processes where most improvement is required, based on the current performance and the proposed performance within the organisation.
- **Give Maximum Value for Money:** When practice priorities are calculated using the SPM, a cost for each practice can be given. This allows the organisation the opportunity to re-prioritise the practices based on cost.
- **Propose Improvements Which Have Maximum Effect in as Short a Time as Possible:** As with the previous point, length of time for each practice can be provided for inclusion in calculating practice priorities. This helps the organisation to focus on 'quick-return' improvements.
- **Provide Fast Return on Investment:** Combining the cost and length of time discussed in the previous two points ensures that the organisation can prioritise their practices to be improved based on fast return on investment.
- **Be Process-Oriented:** The practices prioritised through using the Software Process Matrix will gain priority because of the effects they have on the processes which are seen as most important to the business, be these because of business goals or the improvement required by management.
- **Relate to Other Software Models:** The market leverage element of the Software Process Matrix allows the organisation to increase the weight on processes which are more likely to affect their chosen model e.g. ISO9000. This will shift the practice priorities towards the requirements of the model.
- **Be Flexible and Easy-to-Use:** The SPM provides flexibility by allowing the organisation to decide which of the previous points it is interested in. The model can be used effectively whether or not these are used. Ease-of-use is provided through the existence of a generic model which can be used across organisations provided the self-assessment has been carried out.
- **Demonstrate Multi-dimensionality:** The Software Process Matrix has been developed based on the multi-dimensionality that exists. By looking at the model closely, management can identify that improvements in practices will affect particular processes.

6 Conclusion

This research examined the suitability of developing a software process improvement model based on Quality Function Deployment. While it makes use of self-assessment, it does not concentrate on creating another assessment model. Rather, it provides a model, the SPM, which will take the assessment and other factors into account, and then supply the organisation with a list of improvements it should action. This model fulfils the initial requirements of the research, which was to develop a model demonstrating the nine characteristics listed at the beginning of the paper. Moreover, it also demonstrates how the model was used in an industrial setting.

References

1. McIver Consulting: Manpower, Education and Training Study of the Irish Software Sector, A Report submitted to the Software Training Advisory Committee and FAS, Dublin, Ireland (1998).
2. Combelles, Anne and DeMarco, Tom: Viewpoint, Software in Focus, published by the ESSI News Project Team, Issue 1, March (1998).
3. Buchman, Caroline D. and Larry K. Bramble: Three-Tiered Software Process Assessment Hierarchy, Software Process - Improvement and Practice, Vol 1, Issue 2, December (1995).
4. Geyres, Stephane, Gualtiero Bazzana and Gemma Deler: Exchanging SPI Experience across SMEs by Internet Conferencing in Proceedings of SPI 97, How to Improve: Practice and Experience, The European Conference on Software Process Improvement, 1-4 December, Barcelona, Spain (1997).
5. Horvat, Romana Vajde, Rozman, Ivan and Gyorkos, Jozsef: Managing the Complexity of SPI in Small Companies. Software Process – Improvement and Practice, Vol 5, Issue 1, March, (2000) 45-54.
6. Zahran, Sami: Software Process Improvement, Practical Guidelines for Business Success, Addison-Wesley, U.K (1998).
7. Kuvaja, Pasi, Jouni Simila, Kech Krzanik, Adriana Bicego, Gunter Koch and Samuli Saukkonen: Software Processes Assessment and Improvement: The BOOTSTRAP Approach, Blackwell Publishers, U.K. (1994)
8. Kilpi, Tapani, 1997: Product Management Challenge to Software Change Process: Preliminary Results from Three SMEs Experiment, Software Process - Improvement and Practice, Volume 3, Issue 3, September, (1997) 165-175.
9. National Competitiveness Council: Annual Competitiveness Report, Dublin, Ireland (1999).
10. Akao, Yoji: QFD, Integrating Customer Requirements into Product Design, Productivity Press. U.S.A. (1990)
11. Mazur, Glenn: QFD for Small Business – A Shortcut through the 'Maze of Matrices'" in Transactions from the Sixth Symposium on Quality Function Deployment, Novi, Michigan, U.S.A., June 13-14th, (1994) 375-386.
12. Cohen, Lou: Quality Function Deployment, How to Make QFD Work for You, Addison-Wesley, U.S.A. (1995)
13. Hauser, John R. and Don Clausing: The House of Quality, Harvard Business Review, May-June, (1988) 63-73.
14. Fortuna, Ronald M.: Beyond Quality: Taking SPC Upstream, Quality Progress, June (1988) 23- 28
15. Richardson, Ita: Software process matrix: A small company SPI model, Software Process Improvement and Practice, Volume 6, Number 3, September (2001) 157-165.
16. Stevenson, Howard H.: Defining Corporate Strengths and Weaknesses in David Asch and Cliff Bowman (editors), Readings in Strategic Management, Macmillan in association with the Open University, London, U.K., (1989) 162-176.
17. El Eman, Khaled, Lionel Briand and Robert Smith: Assessor Agreement in Rating SPICE Processes, Software Process Improvement and Practice, Volume 2, Issue 4, December, (1996) 291-306.
18. Burgess, R.G.: Some Role Problems in Field Research in Field Research: a Sourcebook and Field Manual, Robert G. Burgess, editor, George Allen & Unwin (Publishers) Ltd., London, (1982) 32-45.

Experience Based Process Improvement

Kurt Schneider

DaimlerChrysler AG, Research Center Ulm, P.O. Box 2360, 89013 Ulm, Germany
Kurt.Schneider@DaimlerChrysler.com

Abstract. Software process improvement is often defined and framed by general maturity models such as CMM or SPICE. Those models are applicable over a wide range of companies and contexts. However, specific experiences can make important contributions of a different kind to process improvement. It may not be obvious, though, how experience-based elements can be effectively integrated into software process improvement activities. At DaimlerChrysler, we have applied experience-based concepts to software process improvement for a number of years. During that time, we learned many lessons about experience-based PI approaches that were more or less successful. In this paper, a number of areas are described in which experiences can be highly advantageous to use. The exploitation of experiences is deeply ingrained into PI activities and goes beyond experience package writing and publishing in a database or a web-tool. Risk management is used as process improvement example from practice.

1 Experience-Based Process Improvement at DaimlerChrysler

Process improvement has seen a phase of wide-scale interest in industry during the last decade. Maturity models like CMM [1], SPICE (ISO 15 504) and more current variants like CMMi or SA-CMM [2] have guided many companies in their efforts towards better processes for software development and acquisition [3]. At DaimlerChrysler, we have applied several concepts from those models, and we have complemented them with an approach that is based on experiences made in our own business units. Unlike CMM et al., our experiences may not apply in general, but they reflect the specific situation in each respective business unit very well. We claim those experiences can contribute a lot to an effective and efficient process improvement initiative. This is even more true when there is no opportunity for a wide-scale top down initiative, but when smaller departments need to run their own software process improvement (SPI) programs.

The experience-based process improvement initiative "SEC" at DaimlerChrysler is coordinated by Research&Technology. It involves several participating business units and departments. As a long-term initiative SEC aims to foster systematic learning from experience in the software domain. SEC stands for *Software Experience Center*. The research project is supposed to find out more about the potential of experiences in software process improvement: how can experiences be acquired [4], how can they be stored and organized [5], and how can they be (re-) used [6]? Preliminary work has started in 1997. Since then, SEC has established working relationships with several

J. Kontio and R. Conradi (Eds.): ECSQ 2002, LNCS 2349, pp. 114–123, 2002.

business units and application projects. Through local SEC groups in the business units, we emphasized the decentralized approach situated in each particular department context. When the initiative started in 1997, its initial concepts were mainly those of the experience factory [7]. Our early adoption and interpretation of this concept first led us to

- a focus on GQM-based (Goal Question Metric [8]) measurement programs as the primary source of input;
- development of mechanisms and prototypes of an Experience Base. According to Basili [7], an Experience Base is the persistent storage location or device that acts as organizational memory for an experience factory.

During our work, we identified substantial differences between the situation at NASA-SEL [9], where the experience factory concept had been first applied, and our situation in DaimlerChrysler business units: see [10] for a comparison. For example, we used many more qualitative experience packages than the original EF. Despite all differences, a general focus on exploiting experiences during process improvement still characterizes our work in SEC [11]. And there is a separate organizational unit, SEC, that supports a number of projects and business units in their SPI efforts.

This paper describes how experiences can be used in process improvement. There are several different uses all of which have been tried out in SEC. In this paper, the elicitation and collection of experiences is only briefly referenced, but not highlighted or discussed in any detail. This paper is rather devoted to actively *using and reusing experiences*. Section 2 raises aspects of selecting appropriate SPI activities, assisted by prior experiences. Once an activity or a process to improve has been selected, the improvement needs to be supported by training and learning (Section 3). In Section 4, one example of SPI is analyzed in more detail, looking at the phases through which one goes when introducing a new or improved process. Risk management is used as a running example of an improvement activity we have implemented in practice.

2   Selecting Appropriate SPI Activities

Process improvement requires management commitment [12]. However, management often needs to be convinced by visible short-term benefits to fund a long-term improvement initiative. The choice of activities during the low-funding period is crucial. Recommendations from literature (like CMM capability maturity key process areas [1]) cannot be fully covered under these constraints. One needs to pick a very focused set of initial improvement activities. This selection is critical, since its short-term success determines long-term funding and improvement opportunities.

2.1   Capability Models and Selection of Concrete Activities

The CMM approach with its five-level maturity concept has a very good reputation among management. Especially when higher management can be convinced to grant and maintain serious commitment for a larger initiative, the five-level rating scheme provides a sense of accomplishment as the organization moves up the levels. CMM recommends an explicit set of improvement activities, listed in the key process areas (KPAs).

In our business units, there is hardly a chance to systematically perform all CMM key process areas in the way they are recommended. In this situation, CMM can serve as a checklist and even as a framework for improvement activities, but the *art is in the picking*! We appreciate CMM as a treasure of condensed experiences in the field and as a collection of good checklists. They indicate process areas and potential activities for improvement. However, unless actively supported by top-level management commitment, the full list of KPAs (even for level 2 or 3) demands too much at a time and does not indicate to middle-level management how to provide short-term benefit. Obviously, we need to select from the KPAs, according to our situation - and usually there are additional *specific areas* a business unit should work on (e.g., usability engineering as part of the whole software development process). The KPAs can roughly be seen as checklists that frame the choice of recommended improvement areas. Experiences help to pick single activities that get implemented (first). Once these initial improvement activities succeed in producing visible benefit, there will be more management commitment to continue.

2.2   The Usual Suspects: 3 R

Over a period of three years, we have identified three activities that are light-weight and short-term effective starters for experience-based process improvement [13]. At the same time, they support a seamless upgrade to systematic long-term improvement *based on experience reuse*. Our experience tells us that it is always rewarding to look at those three fields once a department or business unit wants to embark on a process improvement effort. Even without an in-depth assessment, we have learned that a lot of benefit can be generated if any of those three fields can be improved. The three areas of support that turned out to be particularly rewarding are:

- **R**equirements clarification (a part of requirements engineering, RE) [14].
- **R**isk Management [15, 16].
- **R**eviews and inspections [17].

Since all three terms start with an "R", we came to briefly call this set of techniques "**3R**". Obviously, we invented none of the three. They are fairly well-known for their individual impact on software projects (experts at the 1999 ISERN meeting agreed on the individual merit of each [18]). For some time we saw them as three separate activities that shared little more than a good influence on projects. However, we do now believe that there is more to 3R.

As a first and immediate consequence, we consider it good practice (learned from our experiences) to recommend those three areas when we are called into a business unit that has not been part of a major, systematic improvement effort yet. Since time and visible benefit are crucial during the first weeks and months of an improvement initiative, it is a valuable lesson learned to know three activities that can start without – or in parallel with – an assessment of any kind. In addition, all 3R activities help to surface deeper problems, i.e. they work like "special aspect mini-assessments" themselves. Findings can then be used to select new follow-up activities, as described in Section 2.1.

2.3   More General: Active Probes as Starters for SPI

We analyzed why 3R worked so well and found two principal reasons:

- 3R are a set of mature basic techniques that have proven their usefulness.
- 3R share a set of properties: One of their secrets seems to be a combination of local usefulness and the ability to identify deeper problems.

Properties of 3R: Active Probes
The 3R techniques are *not* an arbitrary set of activities that just happen to be useful. It is due to a set of properties that they are so successful in experience-based process improvement:

- they produce short-term benefit in visible terms (reduced deficits, clearer requirements, mitigated project risks);
- they actively elicit highly valuable experiences from projects;
- they perform this elicitation at almost no extra cost, and they provide project supporters with valuable context information as a by-product of their support.
- This synergy of experiences must be actively exploited or it will be lost.
- If the synergy is used, activities like 3R are long-term effective by contributing to an orderly overall process.

We call an improvement technique with these properties an "active probe" of the process: It is *active* in improving the process, and it *probes* it at the same time.

We coined the term "Active Probes" [13] to refer to activities which share that same profile. Active probes are *actively* generating short-term benefit and at the same time they *probe* the process for deeper insights and experiences. This synergy makes active probes special.

We now consider 3R three concrete initializations of the active probe concept. Of course, 3R may not be the only active probes there are. A different environment may come up with a different list. But no matter what is on the list: When looking for an appropriate door-opener activity for process improvement, techniques with the active probe properties should be given preference over techniques without built-in feedback (such as configuration management or usability engineering).

The desirable properties of active probes (providing low threshold to start with, and a high ceiling to strive for) match the pattern of constraints and challenges we usually face in business units.

3   Experience-Based Training and Learning

Once an improvement activity (or a set of activities) was selected, we observed a common phenomenon: The high need for training or coaching of the workforce during all variants of SPI. Training programs are acknowledged as a key process area at CMM level 3 (defined). However, it is hard to raise by any level without some – tailored – training. Almost each improvement activity in every project required (mostly informal) training to the project participants. We have learned to accept this fact and have now integrated a training step in all our SPI activities. We did not want to repeat the same kind of small-scale instructions over and over again, in each individual project (e.g., about inspections). When a technique needs to be spread beyond one (pilot) project, more formal teaching becomes an issue.

There are many institutions offering training to software professionals. Employees can be sent to those courses. In addition, large companies usually offer in-house training programs that convey the most crucial messages, and sometimes company-specific know how. As discussed above, an experience-based SPI initiative will try to identify those areas that show most deficits, and find out where an improvement could make the biggest impact. As an integral part of improving a process or technology (e.g. 3R, configuration management, testing), corresponding training should be offered. Since external or company-wide training programs cannot consider the situation in a specific business unit, SPI organizers need to select from those general programs and try to add what is missing. In some cases, a whole new training program is set up.

Our SEC project aims at exploiting experiences. Among its products are so-called "Experience Bases" [5]. They store relevant experiences and related information about a "best practice" process, e.g. for reviews or for risk management. We considered training a good opportunity to spread a best practice together with experiences. Experiences lend more credibility to a practice. Beyond spreading and offering experiences as such, we also use them for tailoring training courses. For some topics there are complete training courses offered in the training market (e.g., inspections, risk management). Of course, such a generic course does not contain any specific processes or experiences made in our company. Therefore, courses often need to be tailored and enriched. At least, experiences must be added to the generic material taught everywhere. Experiences often come in so-called "experience packages" [19]. However, the exploitation of experiences in experience-based process improvement goes beyond experience package trading: Experiences *are built into* many steps.

For example, in-depth tailoring was needed in many cases:
- In all cases, there was an in-house process (e.g., for a special risk management method [16]), or a manual or company standard for the respective topic. It was the purpose of the course to convey exactly this material and not just anything similar under the same heading.
- Many of the given processes or standards are not difficult to understand in the abstract. Problems occur during practical implementation. Participants of several courses asked for more hints and tips on those practical aspects – and they were willing to sacrifice some of the abstract explanations. We always used the Experience Bases as reference in a course, and even taught three smaller formal courses by just guiding participants through the Experience Base material on-line instead of presenting slides.
- Experiences and best practices are deeply rooted in the company and business unit culture. In order to understand and appreciate reported experience, people need to be introduced to some particularities of a business unit – unless audience and experiences come from the same environment anyway (identical context).

- External training providers may use a questionnaire to measure general satisfaction. When training is just one element in a system of different learning elements, feedback needs to become a permanent channel for learners. Through feedback, they can reach peers and coaches before, during, and after courses. Therefore, appropriate feedback channels need to be opened in order to encourage and sustain collaborative learning. We integrate them in our courses [6] and our Experience Base [5].

The following list summarizes how we have used experiences with respect to training and learning during an improvement activity:
- Selection of an appropriate improvement activity (see above)
- The decision to offer training whenever an activity is started (lesson learned)
- Training courses use exactly our specific process description, material, and related experiences collected (in the Experience Base).
- Experiences are conveyed as an asset by themselves (ref. to Experience Base),
- and experience used as a catalyst for learning, to emphasize credibility and applicability of taught issues and processes.
- Like in every professional training environment, course feedback is used to improve the educational quality of offered training courses.

We saw this new brand of experience-enriched training courses reaching significantly higher acceptance ratings with the business unit attendants. In particular, the "applicability of process" aspect was rated much higher than in more traditional courses which did not integrate experiences from the respective environment. Respondents appreciated the Experience Base that holds all relevant material. The additional effort to stage a (e.g. risk management) course, was two days by the professional training provider, and about one day for two SEC researchers to transfer and explain core experiences.

In addition, one SEC person attended part of the risk management course to answer in-depth questions. This moderate effort seems very well spent.

4   Phases of Experience-Based SPI

For the introduction of an improvement activity, we have established a (meta-) process. We followed this process in two business units and for different improvement areas. The meta-process of experience-based software process improvement (EBPI) starts before a topic has been selected, and it proceeds until a process (like risk management in Figure 1) has been improved, taught, and supported.

EBPI goes through several phases and integrates experiences. Of course, each phase may be implemented differently, but the general timeline and the sequence of steps stay the same. For example, we hired a professional training provider to give a series of risk management courses to over one hundred project leaders and quality managers, whereas training for a local improvement of a requirements engineering technique was carried out by only two introductory talks given by SEC researchers.

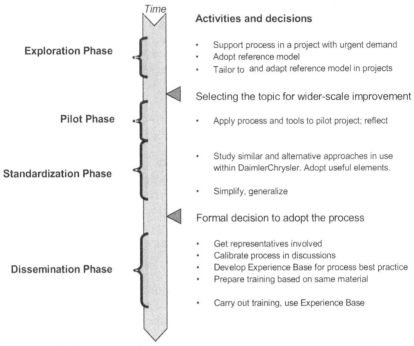

Fig. 1. Phases, decisions, and activities in an experience-based SPI

At first glance, the four phases look straight-forward. It is interesting what happens in terms of concrete actions, and what kinds of experiences are used and produced:

- During the ***exploration phase***, supporting and coaching project by project is the focus. There has yet no decision been made to make this improvement a department-wide effort, but the topic is considered a candidate. There is usually little management attention, and the immediate project benefit is crucial. Important experiences get collected as by-products to coaching projects. Starting with the second or third project, a reference model is chosen (e.g. from a textbook, in the risk management case: [15, 20]) for the process to be improved [16]. Variations and adaptations of the reference model are captured and analyzed. The experience collected during the exploration phase influences the experience-based selection of wider-scale improvement activities. Once a topic is selected for improvement, the pilot phase starts.

- The ***pilot phase*** is devoted to explicit, critical reflection on all process steps and support materials related to the reference model. A "pilot project" is selected in which the revised reference model is applied and – where possible – simplified and made easier to use. This phase requires intense interaction between the PI team and the pilot project. Like in a case study, the outcome and lessons learned are carefully collected and analyzed. The emphasis lies on both supporting the pilot project, and on finding flaws and potentials for improvement. A pilot project should be a "typical" project with high visibility.

- In the ***standardization phase***, the improved reference model is checked for more general applicability and understandability. The purpose of this phase is to make it general enough for the entire business unit to use, *but not more general than necessary!* Specific adaptations that represent lessons learned in that environment should not be sacrificed. This is also the time to consider alternative approaches that are used in other DaimlerChrysler business units (like FMEA [21], failure mode and effect analysis in the case of risk management) and interface to other techniques.

- The standardization phase ends with a ***formal decision by high-level management*** to adopt the derived process and tools for the entire department or business unit.

- Given this decision, the SPI activity enters into the ***dissemination phase***. A last round of *calibration* of process steps and checklists is carried out, including representatives from different parts of the business unit. This step usually introduces few drastic changes but active involvement at this point is extremely important for the acceptance of an improved process. In parallel to the above calibration step, an *Experience Base* is created. We follow a defined process of what to include and how to structure material. Some of the steps are currently being automated, so that Experience Base creation will be even faster in the future. Finally, a series of *teaching courses* and information elements (email, newsletter, talks) are delivered. They are scheduled after the formal management decision and prepared in parallel with Experience Base and calibration steps.

When looking at the steps and phases, please note:
- During exploration, a topic may be dropped and never make it to the pilot phase. All that remains is the benefit to the supported projects.

- One role of SEC researchers (as SPI coaches) was to support and coach projects and to prepare management decisions.

- The entire EBPI process for topics like risk management extended over more than two years, plus an exploration phase of more than a year! Experience is not a material that can be compressed a lot; it takes some patience to let it unfold its full potential. However, we have seen several *impatient* attempts failing that have not taken the specific constraints and concerns of a business unit into account.

- In SEC, there was usually more than one instance of the above meta-process on the way: we introduced all 3R techniques, and additional quality management approaches (like quality gates) along overlapping timelines.

Of course, there is a learning curve involved in EBPI: When we first followed the experience-based PI meta-process we made more mistakes, and it took longer. In the meantime, we are much faster with the Experience Base and training preparation steps. However, discussions still take a long time – and they always will.

5   Conclusions

The role of experiences in software process improvement is often neglected or only mentioned implicitly. In this paper, experiences have been highlighted throughout several tasks that are part of systematic process improvement.

In particular, experiences can be used to

- select appropriate improvement areas (e.g., from a framework like CMM);
- tailor and enrich training courses that need to support SPI in order to be effective in daily work;
- improve and tune process and tools during several steps in a systematic SPI introduction process.

The phases and steps of our EBPI process include several feedback loops and extends over a long period of time. Especially in an environment like ours, where large-scale top-down SPI initiatives are rare, such a process can be carried out for only a limited number of crucial improvement items. Pruning or compressing the process would endanger its acceptance and is, thus, no real option. Therefore, experiences should be exploited to choose the most rewarding set of improvement activities; and experiences should influence the entire improvement effort in order to keep it contextualized, applicable, and on track.

References

1. Paulk, M.C., *et al.*, *The Capability Maturity Model: Guidelines for Improving the Software Process.* 1 ed. SEI Series in Software Engineering, ed. M.C. Paulk, *et al.* Vol. 1. 1994, Reading, Massachusetts: Addison Wesley Longman, Inc. 441.
2. CMU-SEI, *Software Acquisition Capability Maturity Model (SA-CMM),* . 1996, Carnegie Mellon University, Software Engineering Institute.
3. Daskalantonakis, M., *Achieving higher SEI levels*, in *IEEE Software.* 1994. p. 17-24.
4. Schneider, K. *LIDs: A Light-Weight Approach to Experience Elicitation and Reuse.* in *PROFES 2000.* Oulo, Finland: Springer.
5. Schneider, K. and T. Schwinn, *Maturing Experience Base Concepts at DaimlerChrysler.* Software Process Improvement and Practice, 2001. **6**: p. 85-96.
6. Schneider, K. ***Experience-based Training and Learning as a Basis for Continuous SPI.*** in *European SEPG.* 2001. Amsterdam.
7. Basili, V., G. Caldiera, and D.H. Rombach, *The Experience Factory.* Encyclopedia of Software Engineering. 1994: John Wiley and Sons.
8. Basili, V., G. Caldiera, and H. Rombach, *Goal question metric paradigm*, in *Encyclopedia of Software Engineering*, J.J. Marciniak, Editor. 1994, John Wiley & Sons: New York. p. 528-532.
9. Basili, V.R., *et al. The Software Engineering Laboratory - An operational Software Experience Factory.* in *14th Int. Conf.e on Software Engineering (ICSE'92).* 1992.
10. Houdek, F. and K. Schneider, *Software Experience Center. The Evolution of the Experience Factory Concept.*, in *International NASA-SEL Workshop.* 1999.
11. Landes, D., K. Schneider, and F. Houdek, *Organizational Learning and Experience Documentation in Industrial Software Projects.* International Journal on Human-Computer Studies (IJHCS), 1999. **51**(Organizational Memories).
12. Fletcher, I. and G. Urqhart. *Process Engineering for Rapid Growth.* in *SPI99 conference.* 1999. Barcelona, Spain.

13. Schneider, K. *Active Probes: Synergy in Experience-Based Process Improvement.* in *PROFES 2000.* Oulo, Finland: Springer.
14. Macaulay, L.A., *Requirements Engineering.* 1995: Springer.
15. Hall, E.M., *Managing Risk: Methods for Software Systems Development.* 1997, Reading, MA: Addison-Wesley.
16. Kontio, J., G. Getto, and D. Landes. *Experiences in improving risk management processes using the concepts of the Riskit method.* in *6th International Symposium on the Foundations of Software Engineering (FSE-6).* 1998.
17. Freedman, D.P. and G.M. Weinberg, *Handbook of Walkthroughs, Inspections, and Technical Reviews - Evaluating Programs.* Projects, and Products. 1982, Boston, Toronto: Little, Brown and Company.
18. ISERN, *Meeting of the International Software Engineering Research Network (ISERN) in Oulo, Finland, June 1999.,* . 1999.
19. Birk, A. and F. Kröschel. *A Knowledge Management Lifecycle for Experience Packages on Software Engineering Technologies.* in *Workshop on Learning Software Organizations.* 1999. Kaiserslautern, Germany.
20. Kontio, J., *Software Engineering Risk Management - A Method, Improvement Framework, and Empirical Evaluation,* in *Department of Computer Science and Engineering.* 2001, Helsinki University of Technology: Helsinki. p. 248.
21. Stamatis, D.H., *Failure Mode and Effect Analysis: FMEA from Theory to Execution.* 1995: Amer Society for Quality.

How to Effectively Promote the Software Process Improvement Activities in a Large-Scale Organization

Hideto Ogasawara, Atsushi Yamada, Takumi Kusanagi, and Mikako Arami

Corporate Research & Development Center, Toshiba Corporation,
1, Komukai Toshiba-cho, Saiwai-ku, Kawasaki 212-8582, Japan
{hideto.ogasawara,atsu.yamada,takumi.kusanagi,mikako.arami}
@toshiba.co.jp

Abstract. In effective promotion of SPI (Software Process Improvement) activities in a large-scale organization, it is necessary to establish an organizational structure and a deployment method for promotion, develop training courses and support tools, etc. In order to promote the SPI activities throughout Toshiba group, we organized an SPI promotion project in April 2000.This paper discusses the problems encountered in the promotion of SPI activities and presents the solution to those problems. Moreover, the actual results are explained. As a result, it was found that the solution we developed can be used to effectively promote SPI activities. Further, some development departments reached a higher maturity level more quickly than envisaged in the CMU/SEI maturity profile.

1 Introduction

In recent years, software is used increasingly in various domains. Consequently, the scale and complexity of software is increasing, and development organizations are becoming large.

In order to build in higher quality and to develop large-scale or complex software efficiently, it is necessary to implement the optimum software development process in a development organization. Indeed, the development process of software has become a focus of attention in recent years.

The Capability Maturity Model for Software (SW-CMM) is a model for organizational capability that provides guidance for establishing process improvement programs. Carnegie Mellon University's Software Engineering Institute (CMU/SEI) developed it, with industry, government and academic participation. The model consists of five levels of increasing maturity, with different Key Process Areas (KPA) at each level. Achieving higher levels of maturity implies successfully addressing these KPAs and using them in a process to meet schedule, cost, quality and functionality targets.

We have used SW-CMM as a road map for SPI. However, in order to improve a software development process efficiently, it is not necessarily sufficient just to introduce such an existing process improvement technique.

J. Kontio and R. Conradi (Eds.): ECSQ 2002, LNCS 2349, pp. 124–134, 2002.

Regarding the improvement of a software development process, the promotion system is an important factor in determining success or failure. In fact, process improvement changes the culture of a software development organization. Development organizations vary greatly in terms of culture, and it is seldom effective to apply a uniform process improvement technique as it is. So, it is necessary to tailor the existing process improvement technique for various organizations. For this reason, construction of the organizational promotion system is an important task.

This paper introduces the organizational promotion system concerning the software development process improvement activities implemented in Toshiba group.

2   Problems for the Promotion of SPI Activities

Within Toshiba group, process improvement centering on the ISO9000s quality system has been promoted. Toshiba group's experience of promotion of process improvement indicates that the organizational promotion system is subject to the following problems.

1. **The structure of promotion organization:** Considering the impact on the culture of the organization, an ad hoc promotion system for process improvement never functions effectively. A hierarchical management system is effective for management of a large organization. Additionally, it is necessary to build an organizational promotion system corresponding to each hierarchical section.
2. **Infrastructure for process improvement promotion:** Even if an organizational promotion system is established, SPI activity of each department cannot be promoted effectively without infrastructure. This infrastructure can supply the common information for SPI by means of a database. It is useful to achieve a common recognition of the importance of SPI and, on that basis, guide SPI activity effectively.
3. **Improvement of the ability for SPI:** In order to promote process improvement systematically, it is important to achieve a common, accurate recognition of the importance and content of process improvement. This ensures promotion of software process improvement. Moreover, by improving the skills of those people involved in SPI, SPI activities can be promoted effectively. For that purpose, it is effective to provide training courses for them.

3   Implementing an SPI Promotion Program at Toshiba

The purpose of software process improvement activities is to achieve the targeted QCD (Quality, Cost, Delivery) in software development, and establish an organizational culture conducive to continuous improvement. For this purpose, from April 2000, a project for promoting SPI activity throughout Toshiba group was launched. In this chapter, we explain the framework for promoting SPI activity in Toshiba group and introduce a solution to the problems identified in the preceding chapter.

3.1 The Framework for the Promotion of SPI Activities

We have used SW-CMM as a road map for SPI. The process assessment method is used to grasp the gap between SW-CMM and the process used in the organization. The improvement plan is made and performed based on the detected gap. This improvement cycle is crucially important for the effective conduct of SPI activities. For the improvement cycle, we modified the IDEAL model. IDEAL consists of 5 phases, namelyInitiating, Diagnosing, Establishing, Acting and Learning, and is a service mark of Carnegie Mellon University.

To promote SPI activities in Toshiba group, we proposed the framework shown in Fig. 1. The framework has the following some features.

1. Techniques, such as CMM and IDEAL, and methodology are not adopted as they are.
2. Techniques and methodologies are tailored for practical use by SEPG (Software Engineering Process Group) divided by class as process improvement promotion organization.
3. The service items and results for SPI are stored in the SPI database. SEPG can use the database easily.
4. Various training courses are developed and offered to SEPG members

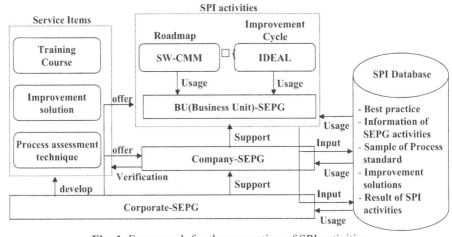

Fig. 1. Framework for the promotion of SPI activities

3.2 SEPG Divided Three Classes

SEPG is divided into three classes as shown in Fig. 1 for promoting the SPI activities. We have identified the process improvement activities which change the culture of an organization. In order to promote these changes, an adequate grasp of the present culture and flexible action are required. The software products developed by Toshiba group are numerous and diverse, ranging from large-scale software such as power plant control software to embedded software such as cellular phone. Moreover, within Toshiba group, culture varies among the many business units developing these products.

How to systematize an organization for promoting process improvement throughout a large organization such as Toshiba group is an important issue. Our solution was to organize three classes of SEPG. The three classes of SEPG are Corporate-SEPG, Company-SEPG, and BU(Business Unit)-SEPG. The purpose and role of each SEPG and the ability SEPG members are required to have are explained in the following.

BU-SEPG

Purpose	Improve the QCD(Quality, Cost, Delivery) of software development
	Establish the development process
Role	Promote the SPI activities
	Practice evaluation and improvement using the techniques and tools developed by Corporate-SEPG and Company-SEPG
Member	High motivation for improvement
	Assign a manager candidate as SEPG leader
	Involve the other affected group's members

Company-SEPG

Purpose	Promote the SPI activities in the company
Role	Make the strategy and plan for SPI activities according to the management strategy of the company
	Develop the methodology and tools in cooperation with Corporate-SEPG
	Support the SPI activities of BU-SEPG effectively and efficiently
	Verify the activities of BU-SEPG
Member	Promoter who can explain why SPI activities are necessary
	Consultant who can promote SPI activities of BU-SEPG
	Engineer who can maintain the infrastructure for information sharing and develop tools

Corporate-SEPG

Purpose	Promote the SPI activities throughout Toshiba group
Role	Make the strategy and plan for SPI activities according to the management strategy of Toshiba group
	Research new methods and tools for SPI
	Develop the methodology and tools in cooperation with Company-SEPG

	Support the SPI activities of Company-SEPG effectively and efficiently
	Verify the activities of Company-SEPG
Member	Promoter who can raise awareness of the importance of SPI activities
	Coordinator who can coordinate the plan and schedule for SPI between companies
	Consultant who can promote the SPI activities of BU-SEPG and Company-SEPG
	Specialist for specific process domain (software configuration management, peer review, etc.)
	Engineer who can maintain the infrastructure for information sharing and develop tools

3.3   Construction of Infrastructure for Information Sharing

As mentioned above, in order to promote process improvement activities by means of hierarchical SEPG, it is necessary to share information from various viewpoints about a software process improvement. Furthermore it is necessary to send the results of SPI activities to executives, managers and other personnel in a timely manner. The following two methods are prepared for information sharing.

Construction of SPI database: The information indicated in Table 1 is accumulated in the SPI database. It is shown at which phase of IDEAL this information can be used. People engaged in the promotion of process improvement activities can acquire the information they need from this database according to an activity situation. Using information and artifacts supplied through SPI Database, consistent quality of SPI activities can be maintained.

Table 1. Contents of SPI Database

Item	Contents
Best practice	Example of success in process improvement activities
SEPG activity situation	Activity situation of BU-SEPG
Sample	Process definition, template, checklist
Training	Training material for the promotion of SPI activity - SW-CMM, KPA Guide, IDEAL, etc.
Solutions	Solutions to improve specific process areas (see item 3.4.2, 3.4.3 for details)
Result of SPI activity	Quantified data "Person-hours of SEPG activity", "Effect of QCD", "Degree of employee satisfaction", "Sponsor's commitment", "Maturity level for each KPA"

Moreover, based on the SPI activity result of each SEPG, a software process improvement report is published periodically. The progress situation of the SPI activity, the level of maturity, the activity person-hours of SEPG, the effect on SPI activity, etc. are reported in this report. This information is utilized in order to secure the continuing commitment of executives and managers. Company-SEPG and BU-SEPGs can use the information in this report for the improvement of SPI activity.

SEPG workshop: Corporate-SEPG plans and holds a SEPG workshop every year. The workshop includes the following sessions: introduce of the latest topics, activity reports of SEPGs, keynote speech, and panel discussion. In the workshop, members of SEPGs can exchange information. We think this workshop is very useful for raising the motivation of SEPGs and accelerating SPI activity in Toshiba Corp.

3.4 Training and Solution for SPI Activities

In order to promote SPI activity effectively and efficiently, implementation of training and provision of the solution for diagnosis and improvement are important. In this section, we explain the outline of a training course and the solution for diagnosis and improvement.

3.4.1 Training Course

In order to promote SPI activity systematically, training corresponding to each class is important. Although SW-CMM shows the progression toward maturity as a road map, executives and managers sometimes often refer to "level acquisition". To prevent the incorrect usage of SW-CMM, training for executives and managers is particularly important. Also, training for SEPG and SQAG which promote SPI activity is required. We developed the training courses shown in Fig.2.

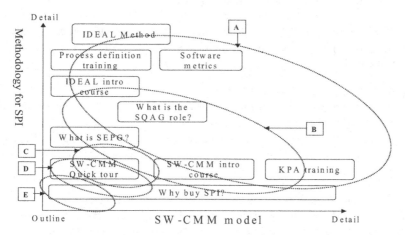

Fig. 2. Training course for the promotion of SPI activities

These training courses have been established and promoters of SPI activity can take a suitable training course. Training courses A-E listed in Fig. 2 are explained below.

1. Improvement in performance of BU-SEPG: *Training course A* is for SEPG leaders. This training course occupies about one week each month for four months. The purpose of training course A, which involves lectures and homework, is to teach each cycle of IDEAL in detail . SEPG leaders can acquire the skills the require for promoting process improvement activities efficiently and effectively. Corporate-SEPG offers this training course.

Training course B is for SEPG members. They need to understand the roles of SEPG and SQAG, the outline of the modified IDEAL and the contents of KPA, etc. Generally, this course is offered by Company-SEPG.

The members of Corporate-SEPG and Company-SEPG have to take this training course consisting of lectures.

2. Good understanding to the process improvement: There are training course for software engineers, managers and executives. The training courses are provided for the various categories of people, and their purposes are described below.

Software engineer (course C): Software engineers are trained to understand the outline of SPI activity. The training includes such topics as the importance of SPI, the roles of SEPG and SQAG, and the outline of SW-CMM.

Manager (course D): Managers who manage the software development are trained to understand the outline of SPI activity and the importance of sponsor commitment. The training includes such topics as the importance of organizational activity.

Executive (course E): Executives who manage the company's SPI activity are trained to understand the outline of SPI activity. The training includes such topics as investment and effect for SPI.

3.4.2 Tailoring for Process Assessment Technique

In the diagnostic phase of IDEAL, it is important to evaluate the process used and clarify the gap between it and the ideal process. We have prepared the following diagnostic methods.

1. The formal assessment method CBA-IPI: Toshiba has some lead assessors who are authorized to perform CMU/SEI assessment. We provide the CBA-IPI assessment method if necessary.

Usually, we use the methods to judge whether the organization achieved the target level or not after SPI activities. CBA-IPI means CMM Based Appraisal - Internal Process Improvement.

2. Mini-assessment method: The CBA-IPI assessment can evaluate problems of the process used exactly. However, this method is costly and time-consuming. So, we developed the CMM mini-assessment method based on CBA-IPI. This mini-assessment uses fixed script, Excel wall charts, customized questionnaires, etc. Using this method, an experienced assessor can evaluate the maturity level and grasp the problems quickly.

This method is used to secure the sponsor's commitment and accelerate improvement activities in the initial phase.

3. CMM questionnaire system: This is a questionnaire system for diagnosing maturity levels. There are four kinds of rating levels: Always, Mostly, Sometimes and Never. A key process maturity level was determined based on several questions.

This system is often used to disseminate the concepts and contents of SW-CMM.

4. The self-diagnostic method: SEPGs use this method to compare and diagnose each KP of SW-CMM and the process currently used. It is effective for promoting understanding of SW-CMM among SEPGs. However, the method is imprecise and the diagnostic result tends to be incorrect. We recommend this method to SEPGs in view of its educational value.

3.4.3 Improvement Solutions

Improvement solutions which can be used in the acting phase of IDEAL are offered together with tools and introductory procedures. These improvement solutions have achieved actual results within Toshiba group over several years. Consequently, development departments can easily introduce the improvement solutions. We have established the following improvement solutions.

1.   Program static analysis: The static analysis tools of a program can point out many problems which usually are found in the code review. These static analysis tools can analyze programs developed by C, C++, Java and Visual Basic. We have proposed a method for building in software quality using static analysis tools.

2.   Software configuration management: Generally, a software configuration management tool (SCM tool) has many functions and requires a special computer environment. So, it is difficult for developers to introduce SCM tools. To cope with this problem, we have promoted the services to establish an SCM environment and introduce SCM tools.

3. Defect management: Appropriate defect management is required in order to build in quality and project management. And, the defect information collected through the defect management can be used as the base data for post-project process and product improvement. In order to improve defect management, we have promoted a defect management tool that can define workflow.

4. Peer review and inspection: It is important to practice peer review and inspection so as to build in software quality from the early phases such as requirements analysis and design. Based on great experience of SPI activities at our company, we established a training course on peer review and inspection. Further, we have promoted improvement of the review process in development departments.

5. Estimation using Function Point: Recently, function point is used to estimate the scale of software in business application development departments. We have held a training course on function point and promoted activities to improve the estimation process.

4   The Actual Result of SPI Activities

We applied the SPI activities encompassing the training courses, the improvement solution, and the modified IDEAL model from April 2000 to December 2002. As a result of this application, it was judged that our SPI activities should be extended to the entire Toshiba group. From April 2002, we will promote SPI activities throughout Toshiba group. About 50 companies in Toshiba group are engaged in software development, providing large scope for promotion of SPI activities. In this chapter, we show the effect of the hierarchical SEPG and the situation regarding acceleration of SPI activities.

4.1   The Effectiveness of the Hierarchical SEPG

Figure 3 shows the numbers of BU-SEPGs and CBA-IPI assessments. Since the establishment of the framework shown in Fig.1, the number of BU-SEPGs has increased rapidly. This shows that the organization for a systematic process improvement has been built and SPI activity has been promoted.

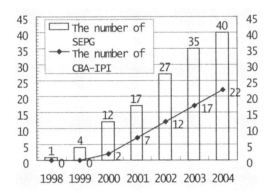

Fig. 3. The growing numbers of SEPGs

The key factor of success is to establish the hierarchical SEPG. It is particularly effective for Company-SEPG to support BU-SEPG in cooperation with Corporate-SEPG. The data after 2002 are predicted values. The number of SEPGs is predicted to increase rapidly. Although it is desirable that Corporate-SEPG and Company-SEPG provide consulting services to all BU-SEPGs, it is difficult to achieve in view of the resource constraints. To cope in CBA-IPI assessments with the rising number of SEPGs, it is important to improve the skills of SEPG leaders. The SEPG leader training course is expected to provide a sufficient number of leaders possessing the requisite skills. Those participating on a thorough SEPG leader training course can acquire the skills they need in order to promote SPI activities based on SW-CMM and the modified IDEAL model.

4.2 Acceleration of SPI Activities

The SPI activities based on the modified IDEAL and the provision of training courses on SW-CMM are connected with the acceleration of improvement activities. In the past 2 years, five development departments have conducted CBA-IPI assessment. The main focus of these assessments is SW-CMM level 2. It was confirmed that these 5 departments had reached SW-CMM level 2. The average period of time it took to reach level 2 was about 10 months, as shown in Fig. 4.

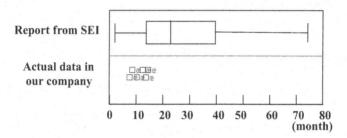

Fig. 4. Time required to reach level 2

According to the Maturity Profile periodically published by CMU/SEI, progressing from level 1 to level 2 takes 24 months on average. Thus, we have demonstrated that improvement activities can be carried out successfully in a short period of time.

Since these development departments used ISO9001 as the basis of their improvement activities, they enjoyed advantages of a stable process. Therefore, SEPG members were not familiar with SW-CMM, IDEAL, how to develop the process, etc. We think it is effective to provide training courses, the improvement solution, and consultancy for Corporate-SEPG and Company-SEPG.

5 Conclusion

We have proposed an SPI activity framework consisting of a road map, an improvement cycle, training courses, an improvement solution, and assessment techniques. We have applied the framework to actual SPI activities. The following summarizes the effectiveness of the framework.

1. We have confirmed the effectiveness of the framework. Through our SPI activities, the number of SEPGs is increasing rapidly. Some organizations have reached SW-CMM level 2 faster than the average reported by CMU/SEI. It was confirmed that our proposed framework can accelerate SPI activities.
2. We have confirmed the effectiveness of the improvement solution. The fault management tool has been introduced to, and utilized by about 20 sections in the past two years. This shows that the fault management process is established in the organization and is improving. Moreover, some organizations have established the review process by introducing review technology and program static analysis tools.

It was found that fault-prone areas can be detected and removed at an early stage by using review techniques and static analysis tools.

In order to accelerate this activity, it is important for executives and managers to have a correct understanding for SPI activity. We would like to stress that "acquiring a level does not lead to improvement in QCD", but carrying out SPI activity leads to improvement in QCD. Moreover, it is vitally important to improve the skills of SEPG leaders. From now on, the training courses for sponsors and SEPG leaders are to be improved, which is expected to lead to the effective and efficient promotion of SPI activity throughout Toshiba group.

References

1. J.Herbsleb, et al., : Software Quality and the Capability Maturity Model, CACM Vol.40, No.6, 1997, pp.30-40.
2. H.Ogasawara, et al., : Process Improvement Activities by High Quality Software Creation Support Virtual Center, The Second World Congress for Software Quality, 2000.
3. Sam Fogle, Carol Loulis, and Bill Neuendorf : The Benchmarking Process: One Team's Experience, IEEE Software, September / October 2001.

Consideration of EVMS Technique Application to Software Development

Yoshihiro Kitajima[1], Hitoshi Fuji[2], Seiichiro Satou[3], Hitoshi Ohsugi[4], Isao Gotou[5], and Hitoshi Oono[6]

[1]NTT Comware Corporation,
1-6 Nakase Mihama-ku Chiba-shi, Chiba-ken, 261-0023, Japan.
Tel:+81-43-211-3622
y.kitajima@nttcom.co.jp
[2]NTT Information Sharing Platform Laboratories, Japan,
[3] FUJITSU Ltd, Japan,
[4]Tokiomarine Systems Development Co. Ltd, Japan,
[5]INTEC Inc, Japan,
[6]Japan Novel Corporation, Japan

Abstract. Earned Value Management System (hereafter EVMS), as introduced in "A Guide to the Project Management Body of Knowledge" (commonly known as PMBOK Guide and published by the Project Management Institute (PMI))[1], has been employed as an essential technique in managing various project operations, especially in their progress management. In this article, we apply this technique on a trial basis to our software products, and discuss its advantages and disadvantages through analysis of our trial results. Based on these results, we propose some specific methods for improving the progress graphs required in managing a project in software development using EVMS. Furthermore, we weigh some considerations required in EVMS-based project planning and revising of processes and we also analyze how EVMS relates to the quality of software under development.

1 Introduction

1.1 Triggers of this Research

EVMS is a method for progress management using cost as its yardstick; the techniques it embodies have a long history. In recent years, it has been attracting more attention, as typified by its being adopted in PMBOK and also standardized under ANSI/EIA in 1998.

Along this line, we apply EVMS to the progress management of our software development project. Then, we extract several points requiring particular consideration in this software development, and propose some solutions to problems involved in EVMS-based software development projects.

J. Kontio and R. Conradi (Eds.): ECSQ 2002, LNCS 2349, pp. 135–145, 2002.

1.2   What Is EVMS (Earned Value Management System)?

The term "earned value" means a monetary representation of the volume of work expended in performing the project. EVMS is a management technique used for such management purposes as progress management. Figure1 shows an example of an EVMS application.

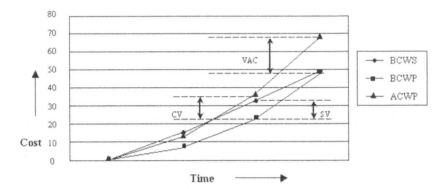

Fig. 1. Example of EVMS

The abbreviations used in the figure include (see PMBOK[1] in detail):
- BCWS (Budgeted Cost of Work Scheduled) = PV (planned value) or baseline
- BCWP (Budgeted Cost of Work Performed) = EV (earned value)
- ACWP (Actual Cost of Work Performed) = AC (actual cost) or actual expenses
- CV (Cost Variance): the monetary difference between the EV (BCWP) and AC (ACWP).

$$CV = BCWP.ACWP = EV.AC . \qquad (1)$$

- SV (Schedule Variance): the time progress expressed in the form of monetary difference between EV and PV.

$$SV = BCWP.BCWS = EV.PV . \qquad (2)$$

- VAC (Variance at Completion): the difference between the budget at completion and the estimate at completion

2   Application to Software Development Project – Case Studies

2.1 A Case Study of a Project to Expand the Functions
of an Existing Production Management System

In this project, our customer was responsible for the design process. Based on their design sheets, we completed the programming and subsequent stages. The overall development process required 10 person-months, from the programming to the System Integration Test (ST).

First, we prepared an Input Sheet as shown in Table 1. At the time of project planning, all work items were identified and the planned value (BCWS) for each work item was set and further allocated on a daily basis.

Table 1. Case Study (1) Input Sheet

Work Item		7/1	7/2	7/3	7/4	...	Total
Work . estimate person-hour 30hours Amount.180,000yen	Planned performance level (%)	25	25	25	25	...	100
	BCWS.thousand yen.	45	45	45	45	...	180
	Performance reached(%)	30	30	40	0	...	100
	BCWP.thousand yen.	54	54	72	0	...	180
:	:	:	:	:	:	:	:
ActualCost.expenses.	Worker A person-hours(H)	6.5	5.5	5.0	6.0	...	350
	Worker B person-hours(H)	8.0	7.5	9.0	6.0	...	550
	:	:	:	:	:	...	:
	Traveling expenses ,etc .thousand yen.	0	30	0	0	...	5700
Total estimate person-hour 1,070hours Amount.7,000,000yen	BCWS.thousand yen.	200	195	195	205	...	7,000
	Cumulative BCWS	5,141	5,336	5,531	5,736	...	7,000
	BCWP.thousand yen.	190	185	200	195	...	7,000
	Cumulative BCWP	4,955	5,140	5,340	5,535	...	7,000
	ACWP.thousand yen.	195	225	205	200	...	8,900
	Cumulative ACWP	5,315	5,540	5,745	5,945	...	8,900
	SchedulePerformance Index (SPI)	0.96	0.96	0.97	0.96	...	
	Schedule Variance (SV)	-186	-196	-191	-201	...	
	Cost Performance Index (CPI)	0.93	0.93	0.93	0.93	...	
	Cost Variance (CV)	-360	-400	-405	-410	...	

It was necessary to make some modifications to our original plan. That is, the design work of the project, conducted by our customer as mentioned earlier, was behind schedule. This prevented us from starting the design for other parts of the work, thus compelling us to change our original plan twice (see BCWS 1 through 3 of Fig. 2).

The project was on schedule, but its actual expenses exceeded the original plan to a great extent (see Fig. 2, BCWS and ACWP1). This was because there were some persons in charge whose individual unit prices were high yet, who performed far below our standard productivity. We could foresee this situation in the middle of our project, but we proceeded without providing any specific remedy for the situation, with hope that such workers would improve their skills and also because of difficulties involved in replacing these workers. Cost calculations that we conducted upon completion of the project in the assumption that these workers' productivity conformed to our standard (with less person-hours performed) yielded a cost roughly matching our original plan (see Fig. 2.: ACWP2).

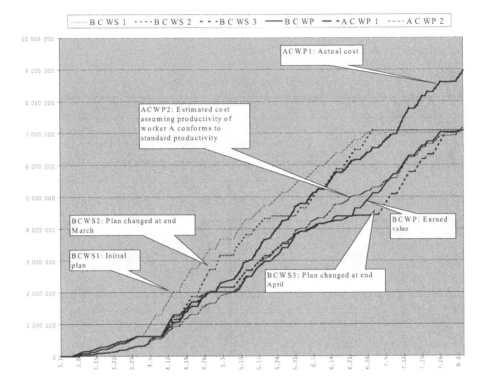

Fig. 2. Case Study (1) EVMS Graph

The abbreviations used in the Table include:

SPI (Schedule Performance Index): the ratio of the earned value (BCWP) to the baseline (BCWS).   SPI >1: progress ahead   SPI =1: on time   SPI <1: delay

CPI (Cost Performance Index): the ratio of the earned value (BCWP) to the actual cost (ACWP).   CPI >1: profit   CPI =1: as budgeted   CPI <1: loss

2.2   A Case Study of a Project to Develop a Packaged Software Product

The project introduced in this case study is a secondary development of a package software product using Visual Basic. The overall development process extended from the basic design to the verification at the user-site, with the development scale of about 15 person-months.

We started with the identification of work items. As shown in Table 2, the planned value (BCWS) for each work item as "estimated person-day (days) × standard unit price per day."

Regarding the performance, the earned value (BCWP) was set as "planned value (BCWS) × performance reached (%)." Here, with the view to determining the performance reached as exactly as possible, every work item was set to a fine measure, namely within five person-days. Besides, the cost (ACWP) was set as "performed person-day (days) × individual cost per day." During this development period, we calculated the planned value (BCWS), the earned value (BCWP), and the cost (ACWP) in units of weeks (see Annex-Figure 2: Case Study (2) EVMS Graph").

Table 2. Case Study (2) Input Sheet

Classi fi-cation	Work item	Person	Plan (person-day)	Perform ed (person-day)	Planned comple-tion	Performed completio n	BC WS	BC WP	AC W P	SP I	SV	CPI	CV
Test	Test 1	K	2	1.3	100	100	90	90	42	1.0	0	2.15	48
Test	Test 2	.	2	1.1	100	100	90	90	37	1.0	0	2.42	52
Test	Review 1	.	2	1.9	100	90	90	81	60	0.9	-9	1.34	19
Test	Review 2	.	1	3	100	100	45	45	13 5	1.0	0	0.33	-90

2.3   Advantages and Disadvantages – Case Studies

As a result of applying EVMS to two actual projects, we confirmed some advantages that EVMS delivered, as enumerated below:

- Since EVMS can represent the status of schedules and costs graphically as numeric values, it is very persuasive and also facilitates predictions for the future.
- EVMS facilitates ex-post analyses by use of data collected after the completion of a project.

At the same time, our analysis also identified some issues in applying EVMS to two software development projects, as shown below:

- It is impossible to weigh the earned values for those items not related to the work progress, such as traveling expenses and equipment renting expenses. (In this Case study, we set the traveling expense budget at 100%, and followed a method to let the actual expenses increase only if they exceeded the budget, while leaving the earned value intact as 100%).
- The EVMS approach gives rise to returns of the earned value, from such factors as reviews and software debugging. (In this Case study, we followed a method to proceed without decreasing the earned value even in the event of software bugs, while such debugging work was reflected only as an increase in the actual expenses).

3. Considerations in Applying EVMS to a Software Development Project

With respect to considerations required in applying EVMS that we identified in the two case studies above, we studied specific measures to cope with them, using the four dimensions as follows.

3.1 Planning Phase

A problem in the planning phase in applying EVMS lies in the difficulty of "converting the work details into a monetary value." This conversion work can be broadly divided into two types as follows:

• Setting the monetary value
• Assigning the monetary value to each work item

In our case studies, no notable difference was found between the planned values in the initial phase and the entire values at the final stage. This presumably is due to the fact that only the programming and subsequent processes were applied in the first case study and also because of the characteristics of being the secondary development in the second case study. Similarly, with other management techniques, these examples tell that more precise predictions and treatments become possible if work items involved are adequately identified. Besides, looking back these two cases, we can safely say that more accurate planning becomes possible by using per-worker productivity and unit prices. Since this is a management technique requiring conversion into the monetary values, it can be better to divide the work items and the unit price settings into the finest level possible.

Usually, software development projects involve returns of the work to the previous process for reworking or other purposes. In our case studies, we expressed the required reviews and defect-based rework in terms of an increase in the actual cost. In this case, the yield (BCWP) remains unchanged (no increase) while the actual cost (ACWP) increase, making it difficult to predict the future trends. Besides, there were virtually no changes in the specifications, so that no impact from such changes were seen in our case studies. Yet, it is necessary to estimate a certain level of returns due to possible changes in the specifications.

Leading a software development project to success requires proper assessment of its progress and its quality. Nevertheless, conventional project management techniques have conducted the progress assessment and the quality control independently from each other. To improve this situation, we propose a method for fusing these two evaluation processes, as follows:

There has been several research efforts conducted to date in relation to the quality costs of software products. According to Capers Jones, these quality costs are classified as prevention cost, inspection cost, and defect cost [2], represented as planned value (BCWS) in EVMS, as illustrated in Annex-Figure 1. The prevention cost is included in the development cost since it is consumed for prevention of any defects in the course of development. Next, we discuss the inspection cost (for testing and reviewing) and the defect cost.

1. Design process: The quality cost in the design process can be those costs coupled to the design review person-hour or person-day along with other costs required in predicting and modifying possible problems involved in design review. According to B. W. Boehm, the cost for the design process can be merely one tenth up to one half of the cost incurred in the test process [3]. This clearly tells us that quality built in upstream processes are essential from the perspective of cost management as well.

2. Test process: The test process is considered a process to remove defects. So that those costs incurred in carrying out all required tests are estimated as the inspection cost. In addition, it is also necessary to predict problems that could be detected and take into account any costs required in correcting them.

3.2   Identification of Expenses Involved

In an EVMS-based approach, all expenses involved in the project are summed up as actual cost (ACWP). Accordingly, expenses which do not contribute to the progress of the project, such as traveling expenses for meetings with the user and expenses for renting equipment, are also cumulated as the actual cost (ACWP). Nevertheless, since the determination of expenses in software development projects has conventionally been to use direct person-hour or person-day as the management standard, the progress of actual cost (ACWP) inevitably indicates a value that has no connection to the direct person-hour or person-day. This gives rise to a problem, in that using EVMS in managing the progress (the cost) makes the management more difficult. To mitigate this difficulty, we now propose a method in which ACWP is divided into two groups, one containing direct expenses and the other containing all other indirect expenses. That is, ACWP is managed under two different items; one called ACWP-PD (Actual Cost of Work Performed – Progress Dependent) and the other called ACWP-PI (Actual Cost of Work Performed – Progress Independent), respectively. This solution is illustrated in Annex-Figure 3.

In this new approach, ACWP-PD representing expenses related to direct expenses is expressed as a cumulative graph, similar to ACWP in the conventional EVMS, whereas ACWP-PI is added to the bottom of the graph every time indirect expenses, such as traveling, are incurred. This method enables an easy-to-follow visual representation of both those expenses that contribute to the progress and others that do not, from the viewpoint of making use of them in the progress (cost) management. Besides, this approach also makes it possible to view the actual cost (ACWP) in their true sense, as illustrated, thus in no way causing inconvenience when used as EVMS.

3.3   How to Reflect the Results of Quality Evaluations

In the software development, quality is the most important factor. When applying EVMS to software development, how to reflect the results of quality evaluations into the progress evaluation is an issue, because the software, a main product of software development, is invisible. Therefore, it is considered that how to visualize the progress of the development correctly is the most important point.

It is possible to understand the quality evaluation of software quantitatively can be understood from the result of reviews and tests. Thus, I would like to suppose the method to express the result of quality evaluation as a cost and reflect it into the earned value (BCWP) as shown in Annex-Figure 4. In this example, if the quality is better than the estimated planned value (BCWS) as a result of evaluating the quality in the review of design process, the earned value (BCWP) will rise and the schedule will advance. On the contrary, if the quality is worse than the estimated planned value

(BCWS) as a result of evaluating the quality in the review of programming process, the earned value (BCWP) will decline and the delay of schedule will arise. The details that the actual cost (ACWP) is exceeding the target after making up the delay to be in time for the delivery date can be grasped. In this way, more precise progress management is possible by applying EVMS considering the software quality.

3.4 When to Review the Plan

Software projects inevitably involve review of the original plan. Because software development involves diverse risks, and these risk factors often make the workload performance deviate from the original plan.

1) Reviewing methods (when changes in the specifications are finalized)

As shown in Annex-Figure 5, the changed value in the specifications should be reflected in the planned value (BCWS) when the specifications are finalized. The catch up angle α may be determined by connecting the earned value (BCWP) reviewed when the specifications are finalized with the final planned value (BCWS) following the review. Generally speaking, changes in the specifications cause the catch up angle α to grow extremely large, thus giving more significant impact on the progress of the project. Besides, more returns are produced as the project progresses, which also require substantial correction of costs. The remainder work volume divided by the remainder work period allows the Scheduled Performance Index (SPI) to be determined. Based on these values, progress management should be conducted so that the earned value (BCWP) can be reached with respect to the new planned value (BCWS). It is also necessary to continue managing the Cost Performance Index (CPI) and the Cost Variance (CV) in a manner to prevent the actual cost (ACWP) from exceeding the post-review final planned value (BCWS).

References

1. "A Guide to the Project Management Body of Knowledge", "PMBOK"is a trademark of the Project Management Institute Inc ,which is registered in the United States and other nations
2. Capers Jones, "Applied Software Management (2nd Edition)", KYORITSU SHUPPAN CO., LTD., 1998
3. B. W. Boehm, "Software Engineering Economics", 1981

Appendix: Tables and Figures

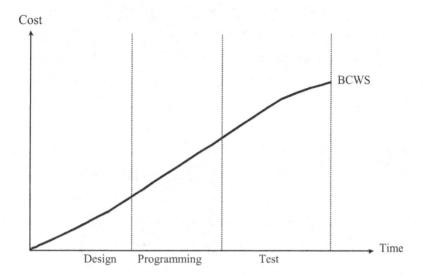

Annex -Figure 1 Embedding of Quality in Planning Phase. BCWS.

BCWS . Development cost + Inspection cost + Defect cost

Development cost: Costs required in creating the product
Inspection cost: Costs required in testing and reviews
Defect cost: Costs required in correcting defects

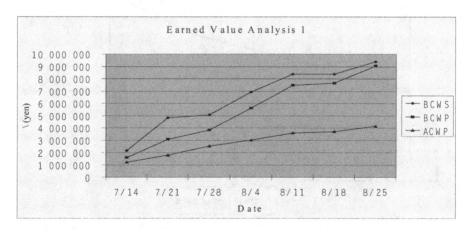

Annex-Figure 2 Case Study (2) EVMS Graph

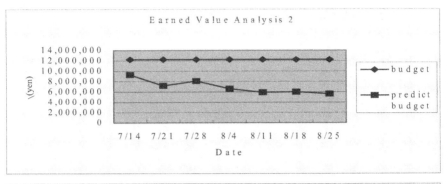

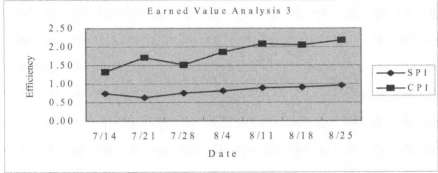

Annex-Figure 2 (continued)

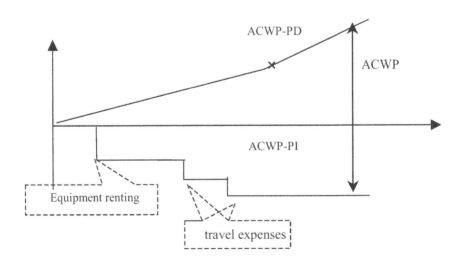

Annex -Figure 3 Proposed Method for Determining （ACWP-PD & ACWP-PI）

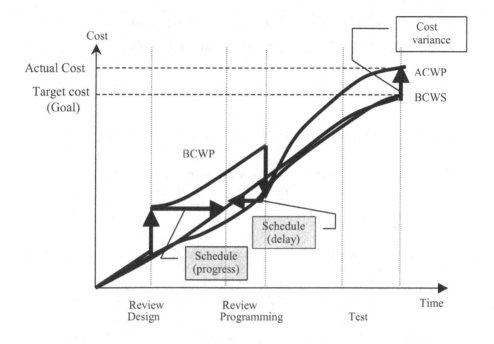

Annex -Figure 4 Application of EVMS Considering Quality

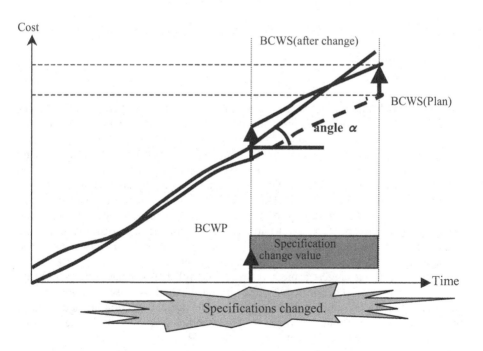

Annex -Figure 5 Review of Original Plan due to Change in Specifications

Performing Initial Risk Assessments in Software Acquisition Projects

Esa Rosendahl[1] and Ton Vullinghs[2]

[1]R&D-Ware Oy,
Rautakallionkatu 4 A 9, FIN-01360 Vantaa, Finland
ejrosend@surfeu.fi
www.rdware.com
[2]DaimlerChrysler AG, Research and Technology,
P.O. Box 2360, 89013 Ulm, Germany
ton.vullinghs@daimlerchrysler.com

Abstract. Managing the acquisition of large and complex software systems is a difficult task. Obviously, there are many sources for risks that may hazard the success of an acquisition project. In this paper we discuss a method for assessing a risk situation at a very early stage of a software (acquisition) project in a structured way. The method, called "FIRMA", helps to identify risk areas. Based on a derived risk-profile, the method proposes adjustments to the risk management process and the overall acquisition process. The method was applied in several projects at DaimlerChrysler, Nokia and Novo Group. In this paper we describe first results of the validation of our method. First experiences have shown that FIRMA is not only a helpful instrument to collect initial risks, but also facilitates the introduction of formal risk management.

1 Introduction

The importance of performing risk management in software projects has been well established and there is a wealth of information and experience available for performing risk management. Since the late 1980's, risk management has been an active topic in software development and management. Boehm [1] and Charette [2] introduced the basic concepts into this field, the SEI consolidated and packaged many practical techniques into a usable form [3] and industry has increasingly started applying risk management in practice. Also, many standards have begun to request risk management to be in place. However, most of the literature deals with risk management from the perspective of the developing organization, yet, an increasing amount of projects largely rely on partners and subcontractors to deliver important components of the software. The issues related to such *software acquisition* risk management are rarely addressed in the literature, though.

In this paper, we suggest a method that deals with risk management in software acquisition projects. The principal idea of our method is based on the use of situational factors to describe and analyze complexity and uncertainty factors in a project. This idea originates from the Euromethod [4] and its successor, the Information Services Procurement Library (ISPL) [5].

J. Kontio and R. Conradi (Eds.): ECSQ 2002, LNCS 2349, pp. 146–155, 2002.

The primary objective and contribution of this work was the development and validation of a systematic method for evaluating the risk situation at an early stage of a software acquisition project. This method is called FIRMA (Fast Initial Risk Management Assessment). More specific contributions in this work are 1) the use of a multi-layered risk factor taxonomy and its adaptation to the software acquisition domain, 2) the aggregation of a risk profile for the project, 3) the linking of possible risk events and corresponding controlling actions, and 4) the inclusion of suggestions and guidelines for customizing the risk management and software acquisition processes.

This paper is organized in the following way: In Section 2 we describe the context and motivation for our research. In Section 3 we describe our risk assessment methodology. In Chapter 4 we discuss the study that we have performed to validate our method. Our conclusions can be found in Chapter 5.

2   Context and Motivation

The development and deployment of mature software acquisition processes has become a critical business success factor for many traditional engineering companies. At DaimlerChrysler, for example, the greatest part of business and automotive software is developed in (often complex) acquisition projects. Typical activities performed by an acquiring organization are, among many more, requirements management, supplier selection, and supplier monitoring.

Many software acquisition projects seem to be high-risk by nature. Often, the acquiring organization is responsible for integrating and managing a large group of different suppliers. For this reason, risk management plays an important role in several software acquisition approaches (e.g., Euromethod or ISPL). Besides typical software development risks like creeping user requirements, missed schedules, and low user satisfaction there are many risks that are specific for acquisition projects. McConnell [10] lists some major risks of outsourcing the development (viz., transfer of expertise outside the organization; loss of control over feature development; compromise of confidential information; loss of progress visibility and control). Also Jones [6] lists several risks that are typical for an acquisition context (e.g., risks related to friction between clients and software contractors).

Experience has shown that formal risk management activities in software acquisition projects often start after the actual development work is already under way. At this stage, however, it is too late to influence several aspects that outline the overall risk environment of the project. At a very early stage of the project the degree of freedom in affecting the project risk environment and the project outcome is the greatest, while at the same time the uncertainty is the highest [11]. Therefore, it is important to identify risks as early as possible and to adjust the software acquisition strategy to manage those risks [12].

We propose introducing risk management early in project life cycle in requirements definition phase in the form of initial risk assessments. It should be noted that initial risk assessments do not replace a normal risk management process, instead, they provide the process with valuable input information. We have defined initial risk assessments as an activity requiring very little actual effort but still being able to produce valuable results.

Risks that are identified early in the project will serve as pointers to the specific high-risk areas of the project that need special attention during contract award and contract performance. Depending on those risky areas we can tailor the acquisition activities. In particular, we are able to tailor the overall risk management process. If the initial risk assessment already identifies many critical risks it is more likely that an extensive risk management will be necessary. If the assessment does not return any critical risk a "lightweight" risk management process probably will suffice.

3   The Risk Assessment Methodology

The overall structure of our assessment methodology is shown in Fig.1. The principle idea is to perform structured interviews. The procedure in this interview is guided by the structure of the software acquisition risk taxonomy (see Section 3.1).

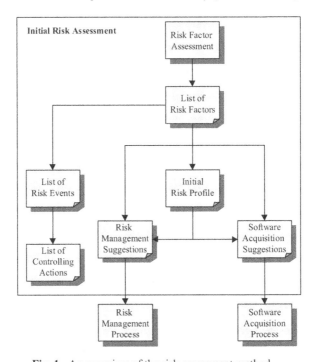

Fig. 1. An overview of the risk assessment method.

In the interview, project leaders and experts are asked to rank the criticality of their project. The outcome of the assessment is a list of top risk factors and an aggregated risk profile. For critical risk factors, we list typical risk events that might occur. To prevent those risks from happening, we suggest a list of related default controlling actions. The derived risk profile gives hints to particular high-risks areas in the overall risk domain. These areas should be paid special attention to during the acquisition life-cycle. In this way, the risk profile, together with the list of top risk factors, may serve to guide the overall acquisition and to determine the formality of the needed risk management (see Section 3.2).

3.1   A Taxonomy of Software Acquisition Risks

Risk taxonomies provide a systematic way to identify risks. Risk taxonomies, as for example the SEI software risk taxonomy [2], help to structure known software development risks from general classes to specific element attributes. In practice, a risk taxonomy may be used as a checklist for reviewing the project's critical success factors.

Table 1. The software acquisition risk taxonomy

Area	Category	Factor
Product	Uncertainty	quality of requirements
		novelty and specificity of system
		instability and novelty of target technology
		strategic importance
		dependency on other projects
	Complexity	size and complexity of the system
		size of distribution
Process	Acquisition	formality of acquisition process model
		enforcement of acquisition process model
	Management	maturity level of project management
		maturity level risk and quality management
	Support	maturity level of support processes
	Organization	maturity level of organizational processes
		effectiveness of the project organization

Area	Category	Factor
Resources	Human	technical skills of project personnel
		people skills and co-operation
		volitility of project participants
	Financial	adequacy of the budget
	Time	adequacy of the schedules
	Infrastructure	availability of infrastructure
Context	Corporate Context	instability caused by climate of change
		influence of politics
		management support
		instability caused by competitive pressure
	Project Context	instability of project portfolio/priorities
	Regulatory Context	instability caused by regulatory environment
	Location	geographical distribution of project personnel

Area	Category	Factor
Supplier	Process Maturity	number of suppliers
		coordination between suppliers
		maturity of supplier's project culture
		maturity of supplier's risk management
	Resources	suppliers skills
		suppliers resources
	Experience	results of previous co-operation with supplier
		suppliers experience with similar projects
Stakeholder	Customer	customer commitment
		customer experience
	User	end user involvement
		user experience and ability
	Sponsor	clarity of stakeholders roles

The core of the FIRMA method is also based on a taxonomy [8]. However, in contrast to the SEI and many other software development related risk taxonomy, our taxonomy is based on risk classes relevant to software acquisition projects. Table 1 shows the software acquisition risk taxonomy. The risk taxonomy has three levels. On level one, we define six risk areas. A risk area groups all risk factors that have their root cause in a common domain (e.g., supplier, product). The risk areas are subdivided into risk elements, which are in turn divided into risk factors. A risk factor is any characteristic that influences the overall riskiness of a project.

An endemic dilemma of devising any risk taxonomy is to be as general as possible, but not too general. Our risk taxonomy is deliberately kept as lean as possible. In particular on the level of risk factors we have verified the risk factors with our actual project experience.

3.2   The Risk Factor Assessment

The risk factor assessment is based on the risk taxonomy. For each risk factor we have defined a question. The interviewee or interviewees select the most appropriate answers to the questions. Based on these answers we derive an ordered list of risk factors. The following table (Table 2) shows a typical example of a risk factor related question (number of suppliers):

Table 2. An excerpt of the questionnaire

factor	question	answer	need for action
number of suppliers	what is the number of suppliers and other external parties in the project?	○ high ◉ moderate ○ low	○ high ○ moderate ◉ low

We use two attributes to rank a risk. The first attribute directly depends on the answer the interviewed person has given to the presented question. The answer either implies a high, moderate or low risk factor. The second attribute is called "need for action" and is a measure for the relevance of the risk factor (the number of suppliers could be high, but in the particular project, there is no reason to rank it as a potential risk). The scores for the two attributes are combined to calculate the overall risk value for the risk factor.

Associated with every risk factor are risk events that may be caused by these factors as well as possible controlling actions for these events. Associated with the factors are also suggestions and guidelines for the acquisition process of the project and especially risk management activities within it. An example for the risk events and controlling actions is given in Table 3.

Based on all derived risk factors a risk profile for the project is aggregated. The risk profile is utilized, when making decisions on the acquisition process and tailoring accompanying risk management activities. Figure 2 shows an example of such a risk profile.

Table 3. Risk events and the implications for the risk management and acquisition process

risk factor	risk event	controlling action	risk management implication	acquisition process implication
number of suppliers	coordination & communication overhead	install interface manager	involve supplier in risk management	use formal approach for development and quality monitoring

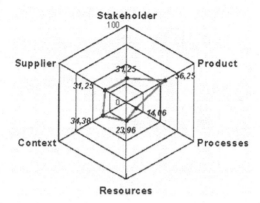

Fig. 2. An example of an aggregated risk profile. From this sample profile we may conclude that the risk management shall particularly focus on product related risks.

Along with the development of the assessment method, we have developed a simple tool to assist in performing the assessments. This tool automatically produces the risk profile and other relevant figures and sheets for the risk factors.

4   First Experiences

This chapter describes the objectives and results of the studies we have conducted at DaimlerChrysler, Nokia, and Novo Group in order to evaluate the FIRMA method.

4.1   The Study

The studies were conducted in five projects, three of them at DaimlerChrysler, one at Nokia, and one at Novo Group. The participants in the sessions conducted their analyses independently, without the participation of the authors or other facilitators.

The assessments returned interesting data on the riskiness of the different projects (Table 5 shows some numbers). In general, most of the risks were related to risk factors in the process or product area. However, analyzing the nature of the detected risk was not subject of our evaluation. The objective of our studies was two-fold. First, we wanted to find out, whether the FIRMA method is actually feasible to use in practice. Second, we wanted to gather experiences from the use of FIRMA so that we would be able to suggest improvements to it.

Based on the GQM statement (see Table 4), we created a standard questionnaire that was used to gather information from each of the assessments. The questionnaire collected information about the project, where the method was applied, hard data about the results of the assessment, and perceptions of the participants. The use of such standard questionnaire makes the results more reliable than would be, should they be based on simple subjective feedback.

Table 4. Goal Question Metric statement for FIRMA experiences

Analyze	The FIRMA method
In order to	Characterize and validate
With respect to	Effort to use, effectiveness and perceived benefits, suitability to the application domain, observed problems.
From perspective of	Method developer, assessor
In the context of	DaimlerChrysler, Nokia, and Novo group software acquisition projects
Because	To improve the method, to help deployment of the method and to improve the software process at the participating companies

The participants were given a short description of the method and asked to familiarize themselves with it. They were also given an MS Excel based tool for performing the analysis and instructions for using the tool.

4.2   Results of the Evaluation

Effort to use: A goal we had in mind when developing the method was to make it as easy to perform as possible. The questionnaire contains only 40 questions. The assessment does not require intensive preparation nor does it require much time. The average time that was needed to perform an assessment was close to two hours (see Table 5). Also the number of people participated in the assessment workshop was rather low (2.6 in average). All participants ranked the method as "easy to perform".

Table 5. Some facts about the application of FIRMA. The numbers refer to averages for the five assessments

time needed	1h 50min	*# participants*	2,6
# high risks	7	*# high risk areas*	0,4
# medium risks	15	*# medium risk areas*	4
#low risks	18	*# low risk areas*	1,6

Effectiveness and perceived benefits: To measure the perceived benefits of the method, we analyzed the detected risks and asked whether the proposed measures or process adaptations would be implemented. In general the method did not reveal surprising new risks. However, the method helped to structure and classify the potential risks and gave, according to the interviewed project leaders, a realistic view on the actual state of the project. The aggregated risk profile, which gives an overview of the project areas with highest risk, was also found very useful. At NovoGroup, participants found this "big picture" of risks much more beneficial than concentrating on individual risks. Somewhat surprising to us was that the output preferred by all participants was a simple graph showing the risk levels of all the questions in different colors (see Fig. 3). It was generally viewed as giving a good overview of the actual risk situation in the projects.

The proposed controlling actions, although rather high-level, are useful. In every study, one or more controlling actions were implemented. In one project, for example, the proposals for controlling actions led to extending existing quality management programs. In one assessment, the project leader was rather enthusiastic about the risk profile. He decided to let his co-project leaders do the same assessment independently, and afterwards compare the different profiles. Comparing the profiles would illustrate whether the co-project leaders share his vision on the risk status of the project.

Stakeholder	Product	Processes	Resources	Context	Supplier
2	9	1	1	6	4
3	2	1	2	2	2
4	2	2	2	6	9
1	9	4	2	2	1
9	9	1	4	6	6
	6	6	4	2	3
	6	1		6	1
					4

Fig. 3. An example risk overview table. The criticality of each risk factor is expressed by a corresponding color; green (dark gray) for low risk, yellow (bright gray) for medium risk and red (medium grey) for high risk. The numbers refer to calculated risk values.

Suitability to the application domain: The domain in which the method was applied was quite diverse. At DaimlerChrysler, projects were related to the acquisition of electronic control units and in-car entertainment systems. In particular for embedded systems the interpretation of questions was sometimes difficult (who is the user? what does end-user involvement mean?). In general, interpretation and translation of risk factors to the problem domains was necessary for almost every question. Participants did however not rate this as a problematic factor.

At Nokia Networks, the method was applied in a software acquisition project, which was a part of a program that developed hardware and software for a part of mobile communication network. During the assessment some of the terminology in the questionnaire raised additional discussion, but all in all, the method seemed to suit this domain very well. The participants were also interested in taking FIRMA for continuous use.

The study at Novo Group differed from the other studies in a sense that this was not an acquisition project; the analysis was performed by the delivering organization, instead of the acquiring one. This meant that the questions concerning the risk area supplier were left out of the analysis. The purpose of including this project as one of our studies was to evaluate, whether the FIRMA method would be feasible, when used by the developing organization. The participants at this study had trouble answering some of the questions due to different project domain, but they found the assessment as a smart way of tackling risks in projects. The use of the assessment also led to changes in a way they handle risks in their future projects – they decided to adopt some aspects of the FIRMA to their current procedures.

Observed Problems: Besides some difficulties that were faced with the interpretation of the risk factors, most comments considered the granularity of the improvement and adaptation suggestion. In general, the people that were interviewed were responsible for coordinating the development, not for coordinating the contract performance. These people have hardly any influence on the adaptation of the acquisition process. Therefore, suggestions like "formalize the approach for quality monitoring" are difficult to interpret and even more difficult to implement.

Several participants commented that the assessment method should pay more attention to risk factors at the supplier's side. In particular questions regarding process and resources are understated. In a next version of the assessment method we will probably include some more questions on this topic.

5   Conclusions

We have presented a lean method for assessing risks in software acquisition projects, including its validation. Based on the improvement suggestions that we derived from the studies, we will further refine and improve our method. The studies have shown that the method is an effective and easy to handle instrument to get a snapshot of the actual risk state of an acquisition project in its early phase. Compared to other risk management assessment methods we think that simplicity is one of our strengths. A further difference to other assessments methods is that the assessment is performed only once. It is not an instrument for continuous risk management. However, as also some of the participants in the study stated, the method can easily be adapted to support a continuous risk management process.

We found out that in particular in those areas where no tradition of a (formal) project risk management exists, FIRMA may help to improve their "risk culture". In one project, the outcomes of FIRMA directly served as a motivator for the installation of a risk and quality management program.

Besides the above-sketched studies, we found some other areas of application for FIRMA as well. In an organizational wide initiative for process improvement at DaimlerChrysler's central IT division, a large and diverse number of software acquisition projects committed themselves to introduce software risk management in their projects. Here, the intensity of the followed risk management approach (no risk management, lightweight risk management, formal risk management) depends on the criticality of the project. In these projects, an adapted version of FIRMA will be used to assess their criticality level.

There are many factors that contribute to the success of a risk management process introduction [9]. Besides organizational and individual characteristics that mainly relate to the risk management culture of an organization, direct visibility of the benefits of risk management has a high impact on its acceptance. It is our hope that FIRMA will help to increase this visibility and enables a better acceptance of risk management practices.

References

1.   Boehm, B., Tutorial: Software Risk Management, IEEE Computer Society Press, 1989.
2.   Charette, R., Software Engineering Risk Analysis and Management, McGraw-Hill, New York, 1989.

3. Dorofee, A. J., Walker, J. A., Alberts, C. J., Higuera, R. P., Murray, T. J., & Williams, R. C. , Continuous Risk Management Guidebook, Software Engineering Institute, Pittsburgh, PA, 1996.
4. Euromethod, http://www.fast.de/Euromethod/, 1996.
5. Information Services Procurement Library, Managing Risks and Planning Deliveries, tenHagenStam, The Netherlands.
6. Jones, C., Assessment and Control of Software Risks, Yourdon Press Computing Series, 1994.
7. Kontio, J., Software Engineering Risk Management: A Method, Improvement Framework, and Empirical Evaluation, The Center for Excellence, Helsinki, Finland, 2001.
8. Lyytinen, K., A Source Based Questionnaire of Main Software Risks, Technical Report DaimlerChrysler, Ulm, Germany, 2000.
9. Lyytinen, K., Getto, G., Vullinghs, T., Success Factors for Managing Risk Management in Complex Software Projects, Technical Report DaimlerChrysler, Ulm, Germany, 2000.
10. McConnell, S., Rapdi Development, Microsoft Press, 1996.
11. Pitkänen, P. 1999, Project Risk Management Applications in Industry, Project Management Association Finland. Helsinki, Finland.
12. Software Engineering Institute. *Software Acquisition Capability Maturity Model*, Version 1.02, CMU/SEI-99-tr002, Jack Cooper and Metthew Fisher and S.Wayne Sherer editors, 2001.

UML Developments:
Cost Estimation from Requirements

Philippe Larvet[1], Frédérique Vallée[2]

[1] Alcatel CIT,MDL, 10 rue Latécoère, BP 57,
78141 Vélizy-Villacoublay Cedex, France
Philippe.Larvet@alcatel.fr
[2] Mathix, 19 rue du Banquier,
75013 Paris, France
frederique.vallee@mathix.fr

Abstract. This paper presents the result of a model developed by Alcatel CIT to be able to predict, early in the life cycle, the development cost of UML projects. It demonstrates that textual metrics extracted from the requirements document are able to provide a rather precise information of the total development cost of a UML project.

1 Introduction

Being able to estimate accurately the cost of software development early in the life cycle is both an important and a difficult issue. Management can use cost estimation at different level, for example to set up a project proposal or to control the development process more efficiently. Consequently, a lot of effort has been dedicated since years to cost estimation ([1], [2], [3]).

In the usual process of cost modeling, one important thing is to have historical project data on which the model is constructed and validated. The useful data consist generally in a measure of size, whether evaluated in terms of LOC or of functional size measure, and a number of productivity characteristics that are dealing with the project and the process.

For Alcatel, in the precise case of UML[4] object-oriented software development projects, the need was to be able to master the cost aspect the earliest as possible, i.e. as soon as the text of requirements is available. Relevant work already exists in the area ([5], [6], [7]) but most of it is based upon metrics based on the UML models that are available too late to fulfill the need of Alcatel. Therefore Alcatel has undertaken a study with the Consultant Company Mathix, in order to develop an adequate cost estimation model.

To reach this objective, Alcatel and Mathix have decided to build a model that shall be able to give directly a good initial estimation of the total development cost. The model construction should be based on a sample of thirty-three UML projects, real industrial projects, already done.

J. Kontio and R. Conradi (Eds.): ECSQ 2002, LNCS 2349, pp. 156–164, 2002.
© Springer-Verlag Berlin Heidelberg 2002

The process followed to build this model is constituted of 4-main steps:

- refinement of the cost variable to be evaluated ;
- definition of the well-known, potentially useful, project characteristics ;
- gathering of the data ;
- data analysis and cost model building.

Remark 1. The model built in this study is mainly pragmatic and come from lessons learned. Consequently, it is specific to the scope of this work. Especially the incredibly low variance in the data is likely due to the fact that the projects on which the modeling is based were all of the same nature and were developed with similar techniques and skills.

This paper presents the modeling process and the results obtained:

- Section 2 defines the cost variable to be modeled ;
- Section 3 describes which explicative project characteristics have been selected to enter into the model construction ;
- Section 4 shows the available data that have been used as reference ;
- Section 5 gives the formulas obtained with their performances of prediction on the reference sample.

2   Refinement of the Cost Variable

The cost variable targeted is the Total Development Cost. In the Alcatel historical database, this cost was asked to be decomposed into 5 partial costs as follows :

$$\text{Total Development Cost} = \text{Specification Cost} + \text{Design Cost} + \text{Coding Cost} + \text{Documentation Cost} + \text{Management Cost.} \qquad (1)$$

In formula (1), the verification, validation and testing costs are distributed between specification, design and coding.

Our feeling was that these partial costs were not independent and that the Coding Cost was probably correlated to the Total Development Cost. This feeling has been verified through a graphical analysis of the distribution of the ratio: Coding Cost / Total Development Cost on our modeling sample.

Figure 1 gives the distribution of this ratio for the 22 projects of the historical database on which the cost decomposition was given.

This analysis allowed us to assert that it was possible to calculate the Total Development Cost from the Coding Cost, by using the following formula :

$$\text{Total Development Cost} = \text{Coding Cost} / 17\% \qquad (2)$$

Remark 2. When used on the reference sample, the average error provided by this formula is 0.9%. Let's notice that for those that are only interested by the coding cost evaluation, this formula can be skipped and its error too !

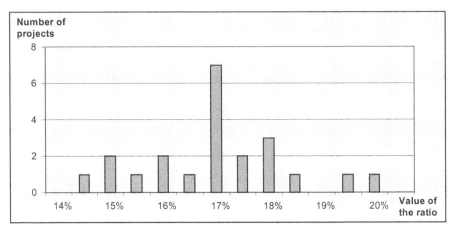

Fig. 1. Distribution of the ratio: Coding Cost / Total Development Cost

3   Definition of the Project Characteristics

3.1 Size Evaluation

As we have said in the introduction, most of the cost models use as an entry variable a characteristic of size: LOC, function points, etc. In our particular case, we have thought that the number of domain classes (" business classes ") could be a good representation of size for the considered UML projects.

Unfortunately, this size characteristic is not known at the stage at which we would like to apply the model, i. e. as soon as the requirements are available. To bypass this problem, we needed to define an estimator based on the information available at this stage, mainly the text of requirements.

To reach that, we did choose a set of textual metrics that could be good predictors. This set is constituted of 4 distinct metrics named TNW, NKW, AUTO and MANU, that are defined hereafter:

- TNW = total number of words in the original requirements document ;

- NKW = number of kept words, after a first analysis of the words, and elimination of non-significant words (pronouns, articles, prepositions, adverbs, etc) ;

- AUTO = number of " candidate " classes, automatically calculated by a linguistic analyser ;

- MANU = number of candidate classes, manually revised, after reading and correcting the result of the automatic evaluation.

The candidate classes are extracted by the following way:

– a first and very basic level of text analysis allows to extract all the nouns from the text ;

– then, a specific filter is applied on this list, in order to eliminate three kinds of "non-candidate classes":

  – the nouns that describe low level data, properties or attributes (nouns like : number, average, amount, number, age, value, etc.) ;

  – the nouns that hide an activity or action (like : treatment, distribution, test, management, validation, calculation, etc.) ;

  – the "hollow" nouns, expressing very common topics (like : action, operation, data, information, thing, structure, system, etc.).

This filter is made of three main lists, that have been built little by little, by including plenty of words directly coming from the analysis results of many technical and specification documents, inside the scope of Alcatel's projects.

After applying this filter, the result is a list of acceptable "candidates" to be considered as "classes".

3.2 Other Metrics Candidate

We have introduced other characteristics into the model by thinking at the other project properties that might have some influence on the final Coding Cost.

For that 6 project attributes were selected and are listed below:

– number of functions to be developed ;

– number of requirements to cover ;

– number of 1st level UML use cases (non split use cases) ;

– reuse rate ;

– language (C++, Java or other) ;

– development type of lifecycle (waterfall, iterative, spiral, Y lifecycle [8], etc.).

Remark 3. The 4 first metrics are quantitative metrics, but the 2 last one are qualitative metrics.

4   Available Data

The difficulty was that the projects historical database was incomplete. Metrics available for the projects of Company A (12 projects) were not available for the projects of company B and C (21 projects) and vice versa.

The available data, concerning the textual metrics to be used for size evaluation, are presented in Table1.

As can be seen in Table 1, among 33 projects available in the historical database, only 12 projects had their requirements measured and for only 5 of them, we had the value of the number of manually revised candidate classes (MANU).

Table 1. Known values of textual metrics on the sample

Project	TNW	NKW	AUTO	MANU	Real number of classes
Project 1 Company A	380	77	33		27
Project 2 Company A	903	163	98		43
Project 3 Company A	3179	323	151		67
Project 4 Company A	2440	547	236		102
Project 5 Company A	2448	406	243		103
Project 6 Company A	4434	537	371	223	80
Project 7 Company A	4075	646	385		92
Project 8 Company A	3839	701	400		192
Project 9 Company A	13528	707	443	262	82
Project 10 Company A	6311	753	527	318	120
Project 11 Company A	16201	1542	1072	467	233
Project 12 Company A	49246	2981	2135	720	300

The available data for this study, concerning the other metrics candidate, are presented in Table 2.

Remark 4. In Table 2, **Name** is the name of the project, **Fun.** is the number of functions to be developed , **Req.** is the number of requirements to cover, **UC** is the number of first level UML Use Cases, **Reu.** is the reuse rate, **Lang.** is the language, **LC** is the type of life cycle, **Dom.** is the number of domain classes , Cost is the Coding Cost (in man days).

Remark 5. The 4 first metrics are quantitative metrics, but the 2 last one are qualitative metrics.

As can be seen in Table 2, among 33 projects available in the historical database, the metrics were known on only 21   projects (only 14 projects if the number of requirements covered is used)).

5   Modeled Results

The fact that different data were available from Company A on one hand and Companies B and C on the other hand did force us to build two models (or one "two steps" model).

Table 2. Known values of other metrics candidate on the sample

Name	Fun.	Req.	UC	Reu.	Lang.	LC	Dom.	Cost
Proj. 1 Comp. B	25	72	52	15%	C/C++	V	125	212
Proj. 2 Comp. B	37	145	75	25%	C/C++	V	240	420
Proj. 3 Comp. B	75	280	90	40%	C++	Y	700	1240
Proj. 4 Comp. B	18	60	27	12%	C++	Y	121	245
Proj. 5 Comp. B	20	47	32	20%	Java	iterative	67	97
Proj. 6 Comp. B	38	75	82	12%	C++	V	325	712
Proj. 7 Comp. B	15	67	55	15%	C/C++	Y	215	380
Proj. 8 Comp. B	140	760	225	10%	C/C++	V	1850	3400
Proj. 9 Comp. B	70	420	420	25%	C/C++	V	435	720
Proj. 10 Comp. B	45	92	67	40%	C++	Y	90	150
Proj. 11 Comp. B	150	625	280	8%	C++	Y	560	1025
Proj. 12 Comp. B	70	320	120	10%	C++	iterative	440	780
Proj. 1 Comp. C	65		27	5%	C/C++	V	65	121
Proj. 2 Comp. C	75		32	10%	C++	Y	70	125
Proj. 3 Comp. C	125		50	10%	C++	V	280	465
Proj. 4 Comp. C	25		12	15%	Java	iterative	27	42
Proj. 5 Comp. C	20	80	32	20%	Java	iterative	65	72
Proj. 6 Comp. C	360		450	7%	C/C++	V	850	1680
Proj. 7 Comp. C	250	70	135	12%	C/C++	Y	620	980
Proj. 8 Comp. C	190		285	5%	C++	iterative	780	1750
Proj. 9 Comp. C	20		20	15%	Java	itératif	42	65

5.1   First Model

The first model aims to express the number of domain classes (" business classes ")
directly from the textual linguistic metrics. This model is based on data in Table 1.
Regression techniques [9] have been used for that and, as shown in figure 2, finally
the simple logarithmic regression using the variable AUTO did provide the best
estimation.

The obtained formula is:

$$\text{Number of Domain Classes} = 3.42 * \text{AUTO}^{0.584} \qquad (3)$$

Remark 6. Used on the available sample, this formula provides an average error of
18.9%.

5.2   Second Model

The second model aims to get the Coding Cost from the selected characteristics on the
projects: size (in number of Domain Classes) plus other selected characteristics. This
model is based on data in Table 1.

Once again, the regression techniques have been used and this time the simple linear regression using variable Number of Domain Classes has provided good results. This can be seen on figure 3 hereafter.

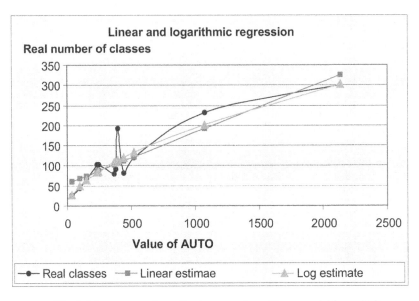

Fig. 2. Linear versus logarithmic regression with one variable: AUTO

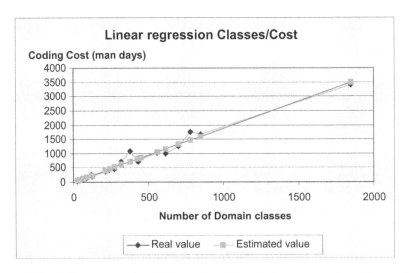

Fig. 3. Linear regression of the number of domain classes versus the coding cost

Remark 7. It was vesry surprising that the other characteristics candidate did not provide significant difference on the cost estimation. This could be due here to the very little size of the sample that could have hidden the influence of these variables (if there is one). At the moment, the hypothesis of such an influence is not rejected and we wait for a bigger sample to look at it again.

The obtained formula is:

Coding Cost (man days) = 1.88 * Number of Domain Classes + 2.02   **(4)**

Remark 8. Used on the available sample, this formula provides an average error of 15.7%.

6   Conclusion

Considering the little size of the sample, these first results are heartening. Some UML projects in Alcatel are willing to use and test them on the field.

In any case, this study was very interesting because the obtained results allowed us to validate or invalidate our initial feelings about what were the main factors impacting the cost of software development. The main learned lessons can be summarized as follows:

a) the number of domain classes has effectively a major impact on the coding cost;

b) it is possible to quantify the complexity of a project through simple linguistic metrics that are directly issued from the requirements;

c) it has not been demonstrated that other project characteristics, such as development cycle, language or reuse rate, have a subsequent impact on the development cost (and this point was a surprise for us);

d) simple statistical tools are very efficient as soon as the metrics are relevant and the problem is well decomposed.

In the future, the two regression-obtained models must be refined with:

− new metrics and characteristics,

− a broader sample,

− other statistics modeling techniques,in order to reduce the global error rate.

These points are open ones for the continuation of the study described in this paper.

References

1.   A. Albrecht and J. Gaffney - Software Function, Source Lines of Code and Development Effort Prediction - IEEE Tran. Software Eng., June 1983
2.   B. Boehm - Software Engineering Economics - Prentice Hall, 1981
3.   J. Printz and N. Trèves - Coût et durée des projets informatiques - Hermes Science, 2001

4. G. Booch, J. Rumbaugh and I. Jacobson - The UML User Guide - Addison Wesley Longman Inc., 1999
5. T. Fetcke, A. Abran and T. H. Nguyen - Mapping the OO-Jacobson Aprroach into Function Point Analysis - Proceddings of Tools USA, 1997
6. S. Labyad, M. Frappier and R. St-Denis - Calcul des points de fonction à partir du diagramme de cas d'utilisation de la notation UML - International Workshop on Software Measurement, Sept 1999
7. G. Caldiera, C. Lokan, G. Antoniol, R. Fiutem, S. Curtis, G. La Commare and E. Mambella - Definition and Experimental Evaluation of Function Points for Object-Oriented Systems, FPA, 2001
8. P. Roques and F. Vallée - UML en action - Eyrolles Technologies Objet, 2000G.
9. Saporta - Probabilités, Analyse des données et statistique - Editions Technip, 1990

The Personal Software Process in Practice: Experience in Two Cases over Five Years

Georg Grütter[1] and Stefan Ferber[2]

[1] Line Information GmbH, Garbershoff 4, 21218 Helmstorf,
`GruetterAtWork@gmx.de`
[2] Robert Bosch GmbH, Corporate Research and Development,
Eschborner Landstraße 130–132, D-60489 Frankfurt, Germany,
`Stefan.Ferber@de.bosch.com`

Abstract. The Personal Software Process (PSP) started in 1995 and promised to improve individual software engineering practice. PSP addresses in particular the software quality in terms of defect densities and the process quality in terms of defect prevention (yield) and predictability of development time and size of the software products.

This experience report of two software developers applying the PSP over five years first in an academic setting and later over three years in industrial software development shows that (1) PSP is an appropriate method to understand your software development process and its capabilities, (2) PSP makes it easy to identify areas of improvements in the process, and (3) PSP allows to do impressively accurate time, size, and defect estimates.

The main drawback of PSP is its restricted applicapability in todays software development community. The challenging task to use PSP in your daily work requires a huge amount of discipline.

1 Introduction

1.1 The Personal Software Process

The Personal Software Process (PSP) was invented by Watts S. Humphrey in 1995 at the SEI, Pittsburgh. Being involved in the development of the Capability Maturity Model (CMM), Humphrey recognized that it provided almost no support for the work of individual software engineers. As a result, he devised the PSP based on the practices of the CMM relevant for the work of individual software engineers. These practices were appropriated and substantiated further to provide the intended guidance for individual software development. The PSP is similar to the CMM in that it does not propose a static set of practices. Instead, it focuses on the empirically based continuous improvement of the software development process.

1.2 Environment of the Experience

Both authors participated in a PSP course during their study at the University of Karlsruhe, Germany in 1996. The success of this course convinced both authors to continue

J. Kontio and R. Conradi (Eds.): ECSQ 2002, LNCS 2349, pp. 165–174, 2002.

using the PSP. Though the process improvements in the PSP course were not statistically significant, we felt that our product quality had increased. The data of the PSP course is not covered in this paper.

The PSP data published in this paper was gathered in both cases while developing software as researchers for the DaimlerChrysler research facility in Ulm, Germany. Having worked in standard industrial settings, too, we feel that the differences for individual software development are marginal and have no impact on the external validity of our observations.

After several years of successfully using the PSP in academic and semi-professional settings the main objectives in the first real world software development job were: (1) establishing PSP in the daily work, (2) increase product quality by establishing code reviews, test procedures, and sound design, and (3) increase predictability with the Proxy Based Estimating (PROBE) method.

1.3 Context for Case 1

The data of this case was gathered during the development of a new Workflow Management System and covers two years of continuous software development. The system was built as a pure Java Application and designed using object oriented analysis and design. The implementation took place on both, Unix and PC platforms using IBM VisualAge for Java.

The development team comprised five software engineers and students at its peak. The PSP data of this case covers the development process of Georg Grütter, who was the only software engineer to use the PSP in this project. He had already used the PSP in a semi-professional setting for 2 years.

1.4 Context for Case 2

This case covers Stefan Ferber's software development for a 3D-optical measurement system. This system was designed in object oriented technology and was realized mainly in C++. Design was done on paper using UML notation and cross checked in informal peer reviews. The implementation took place in Visual C++ on a PC platform and sometimes on a SGI platform with standard Unix tools. Testing used tools for code integrity checking and automated GUI test tools.

Though the software development took place in a group of 5 to 10 software engineers and students, most development tasks were assigned to individual work. The PSP data covers only one software developer in this group.

2 Understanding Your Personal Software Process

2.1 Setting the Baseline

Just understanding your own process is highly informative and might result in changes in your process that you did not really plan. But for long term improvements one needs a more systematic approach — a software process improvement process.

In the "real world" many things are different from the PSP course as described in the PSP book [9]. You have to adapt the process even for setting the baseline. The first improvement in both cases was to use UML for design purposes instead of the non-standard formal specifications introduced in the PSP. Furthermore, design pattern considerations were an integral part of the design process. Time and defect logging were carried out with a text editor and a slightly changed version of the "evalpsp" log evaluation perl script by Oliver Gramberg. It largely automated the post mortem task. Planning with the PROBE method for a new project was automated with MS Excel to a large extent. Analyzing data across several projects was facilitated by many charts and regression calculations in several Excel spreadsheets, which also served as the database for historical project and product data.

In case 1, a version of the iterative PSP 3 was used initially. Process changes covered only minor process aspects and were not based on a detailed process analysis. The process was extended after a year with unit test automation using a tool developed by the author. The calculation of "New and Changed LOC" was also automated after 14 months.

The PSP2.1 process definition used in case 2 was extended with a phase called "after development" to cover all activities that happened after the software release. This phase is treated like another test phase. There can be none or many after development phases for one project. As there was no personal historical data available for C++ development, the categories and size base data for the PROBE method were taken from table 5.7 on page 117 of the PSP book [9]. LOC counting was carried out using Sven Braun's personal C++ counter. The process, the standards and the tools changed only slightly over the time for case 2.

2.2   Planning with the PROBE Method

The PSP introduces an estimation method called Proxy Based Estimating (PROBE). The PROBE method is an empirical method which combines parts of well established estimation practices, such as using object types (Function Point Analysis), class based estimation (Standard Components), class size categories (Fuzzy Logic) and correctional measures (Delphi).

Kemerer reports in [16], that the median time estimation error for non-model-based estimation processes varies between 85% and 610% and between 50% and 100% for estimation processes based on empirical models. The PROBE method was used with differing success in our cases. However, the median estimation error was even better than 50% in both cases.

Case 1 used a version of the PROBE method which was based only on one size category instead of the 5 proposed by the PSP. With the only outlier eliminated (project 7), the median time estimating error was good (44%). However, the fluctuations of estimation errors were quite high (standard deviation = 60%). This is obvious also in figure 1 and table 3. These fluctuations are a consequence of the simplicity of the estimation model, which did not sufficiently take the variations in product complexity into account and hence in productivity represented by the size categories used by the PROBE method. This hypothesis is supported by the fact, that the fluctuations increased further after the introduction of automated test — another level of complexity, to which

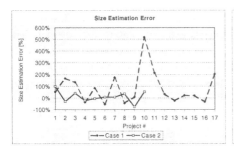 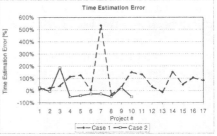

Fig. 1. Case 1 and 2: Size and Time estimation error show high fluctuation in case 1 and are much smaller in case 2

Table 1. Case 2: The linear regression $y = b_1x + b_0$ with correlation r and significance t has odd values for b_0 and b_1 but very good correlation and significance

Project	Projected (P) [LOC]	Total N&C [LOC]	Time Total [Min]	Parameter	Total N&C [LOC]	Time Total [Min]
DB001	396	967	4512	b_0	-65.32	-56.14
DB002	31	57	446	b_1	2.87	7.95
DB003	130	269	1239	r	0.97821	0.88267
DB004	72	114	380	r^2	0.95689	0.77910
DB005	181	390	1134	t	0.00003	0.00369
DB006	335	864	2549			
DB007	517	1421	3663			
DB009	297	1022	1205			

the simple estimation process was initially poorly adapted. As can be seen in case 2, a more elaborate estimation method based on the full range of size categories can yield a much more stable estimation process.

Time and size planning is the major success in the PSP of case 2. As the base data for the PROBE method were taken from someone else, the input to PROBE is not the real estimation for method sizes. This is evident in the strange values for b_0 and b_1. As there were not enough C++ programs available to produce better data, it was used throughout the projects. Because the regression takes care of a linear fit to the real personal method sizes, this does not influence the accuracy of the planing estimates (see figure 2, figure 1, table 1, and table 3). Correlation and significance is high and serves as an excellence base for planning purposes.

Furthermore, planning the number of defects turned out to be very useful. With the help of the historical data and the correlation shown in figure 3 the number of defects which were still in could be estimated. This data can be used to control the intensity of reviews and tests.

2.3   Identifying Areas of Improvement

In case 1, the software product was built from scratch. As the product grew in size and complexity, the effort for continuous and manual re-testing the complete system during

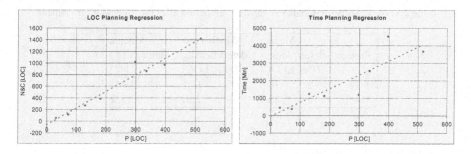

Fig. 2. Case 2: Correlation of "projected lines of code" P [LOC] with size and time is high and significant. The size is measured in "New and Changed lines of code" N&C [LOC] and time in overall development time in minutes. Refer to table 1 for the data

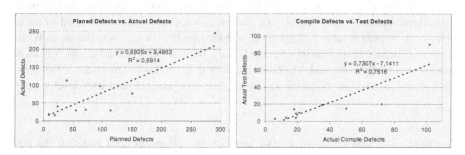

Fig. 3. Case 2: Planning Defects before and during development can be done quite well. This helps to direct efforts in review and testing

integration of new components increased heavily and clearly had to be reduced. Another area of improvement for case 1 is the high fluctuation of the time estimation accuracy. This problem has not been addressed yet. Furthermore, the estimation process generally tended to produce underestimates instead of balancing over- and underestimates. An analysis of A/FR Ratio vs. Yield and vs. Test Defect density indicates, that even a small increase of development time spent in case 1 for appraisal will lead to a dramatic increase in yield and decrease in test defect density. Clearly, the intensity of design and code reviews could and should be increased.

Case 2 did not start active improvements though defect densities and yield were known not to be sufficient.

2.4   Improving the Process

The major improvement in case 1 after a year of development was the introduction of automated tests in project 10. The author developed a tool, which generated test code from a custom test description language. The estimation process was adapted in project 12 to take the sizes of generated code into account.

Furthermore, the review checklists were adapted continuously. This improvement probably helped to find defects faster.

Table 2. Case 1: Software Quality Measures before and after the process improvement

Project	Median defect density [Def/KLOC]	Median test defect density [Def/KLOC]	Median Failure COQ [%]
1 - 9	38.5	11.5	15.8 %
10 - 17	23.7	21.0	13.5 %

2.5　Observing Improvements

Software Quality The initial goal of reducing the time spent for integration testing was reached in case 1. While this measure was already quite low — spending 50% or more of the development time in test is quite common — it could still be improved by about 14% as can be seen in table 2. The overall software quality stayed about the same. While the overall defect density dropped considerably, the test defect density, which is more important, actually increased. The latter fact hinted at a better testing process. However, this hypothesis could not be confirmed by an analysis of errors found after development.

Planning. The first observation after introducing automated tests was that the size estimation error reached the highest values in projects 10 and 11. This was due to the fact, that the amount of generated test code was not known and therefore not reflected by the size estimate. The impact of this shortcoming was predictably less strong on the time estimation error. This is because the productivity for generating test code is much higher than manually writing the code being tested.

As can be seen from table 3, the median size estimation error decreased while the median time estimation error actually increased. The observations show that while sizes could be predicted well, the productivity for designing and implementing tests could not.

The process therefore now incorporates test design and test implementation time measured in a more elaborate estimation process for the future.

In case 2 only slight improvement of defect densities and productivity over time were observed in figure 4 while the process was kept stable. The slight improvement can be explained with the gain of experience in the problem domain and with the programming language C++.

Table 3. Size and Time estimation error, Case 1 left: before and after the process improvement, Case 2 right: in a stable process

Project	Median size estimating error	Median time estimating error
1 – 9	52.2 %	30.5 %
12 – 17	21.3 %	65.8 %

Median size estimating error	Median time estimating error
9%	-27%

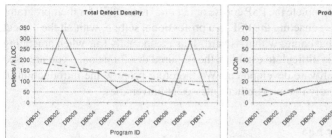
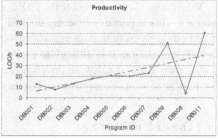

Fig. 4. Case 2: Slight improvement of defect densities and productivity which is due to more experience

3 Lessons Learned

3.1 Need for Process Improvement

Both authors experienced that measuring by itself and thus learning about "ones" own process yields satisfaction. All the more so when improvements can be observed as it was the case for us. With this satisfaction we failed to notice the necessity of improving the process itself. There is empirical evidence that measuring by itself can help to improve performance on a small scale [7,20]. However, major, sustained and faster improvements are usually only possible by improving the software development process itself.

To improve process and product quality substantially, one needs to adopt new methods, technologies or tools. Just observing your process is not sufficient. We think that peers are required for objective process improvements.

3.2 Process Discipline Required

Even though the german culture is said to place a high value on formality and discipline, we doubt the the PSP is more appropriate for german software engineers than it is for software engineers from other cultures. The problem is not the associated time for conducting PSP during daily work (see figure 5).

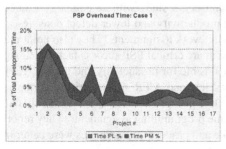
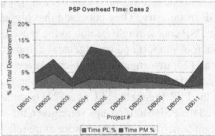

Fig. 5. Case 1 and Case 2: Not much overhead in time (only discipline required) if your tools allow a fast planning phase (PL) and post mortem phase (PM)

Most people fail to complete the PSP course or later fail to use PSP for their programming job. This is because enacting the PSP in a professional setting, with all the project and schedule pressure that comes with it, is hard. This is especially true when practicing the PSP in isolation. It is difficult to establish the required discipline once you are used to your own style of software development. We therefore propose the introduction of PSP in high school or early in undergraduate classes at universities.

3.3   The Risk to Your Ego

The PSP is not at all a continuous success story. The PSP measuring makes it hard to fool oneself. We did encounter setbacks from time to time. While some of them were true setbacks, others can be explained by mere statistical fluctuation. Our conviction helped us to view these setbacks as encouragements to improve rather than as discouragements. PSP will show you the limits of your performance. We believe that one who cannot objectively face his own limitations and the fact that there are others who are more capable, will probably not be able to keep up the discipline required by the PSP.

4   Related Work

PSP is the CMM approach scaled down to the individual engineer. CMM is described in detail by Paulk et al. [19] and Clark [2] reports 4–11% development effort reduction for every CMM level improvement.

The fundamentals of the PSP are laid out in "the book" [9]. Introductions are also available by Humphrey in [10,11]. The team software process scaled up PSP for software development groups [12]. There is a special issue of IEEE Software on Software Estimation and the PSP with an overview of its articles [1,13]. Humphrey [13] describes the current status of PSP in academia and industry.

There are several studies based on the PSP course in universities or companies. Humphrey [10] evaluates the PSP course data of 104 engineers. He reports improvements of average defect levels and more accurate size and time estimates. Hayes and Over [8] describe improvements observed while introducing the PSP based on the ten PSP course assignments with 298 engineers. They report much more reliable time and size estimates, better product quality in terms of test defect density and higher yield. Productivity did not change significantly. Emam et al. [3] published a study with 28 engineers trained PSP in industry. They conclude that higher productivity and lower defect densities in the PSP course might be due to the reuse in the work assignments. They also point out that tool support and management commitment are critical PSP success factors. Zhong et al. [22] investigated variables that are responsible for productivity and quality. They used data from 53 students and showed that Yield and A/FR are two critical variables in the PSP. Prechelt and Unger [21] compare two groups of students, of which only one used the PSP. Both groups were given the same programming assignments. They report slight benefits as programs were more reliable and productivity estimates were better in the PSP group.

The problems of introducing PSP in industry are covered by Morisio [18]. He reports only limited benefits in this case study. PSP is a profound change in people's behavior.

This was analyzed as an example of innovations in IT organizations by Green and Hevner [6]. Studies that took place in industrial settings, like our two cases did, have already been published. Ferguson et al. [5] is the first empirical study with three cases in industry[1]. They conclude that PSP effectiveness depends on the proper training. The data they provide hints at better planing capabilities, shorter development time, and higher quality in terms of defects. Kamatar and Hayes [15] describe the transfer of the PSP from the course to the daily software development job for one engineer. They show that planning accuracy has improved and only few defects were found during system integration test. Johnson et al. [14] compare several estimation methods and conclude in an academic experiment that empirically guided guesses are the best estimates (they call it "guestimates").

5 Conclusion

Software development is a highly creative task, which is different for every project and changes over time. However, we see that our personal process is stable and well predictable. The PSP enables us to spend more time in creative tasks, like design, and less time in annoying ones, like debugging and testing. Furthermore, the PSP does not cause mentionable costs. Therefore, we will continue to use the PSP in our daily work.

We think that the reputation of our profession rides on our ability to mature from an applied art to a true engineering discipline. Having achieved this on a personal level on the one hand reduces the burden somewhat. On the other hand it also motivates us to act as role models and try to convince others of the usefulness of the PSP.

However, we doubt that the PSP will solve the software crisis dilemma as the required process discipline is simply not available in todays software development community.

References

1. Barry W. Boehm and Richard E. Fairley. Software estimation perspectives. *IEEE Software*, 17(6):22–26, November/December 2000.
2. Bradford K. Clark. Quantifying the effects of process improvement on effort. *IEEE Software*, 17(6):65–70, November/December 2000.
3. K. El Emam, B. Shostak, and N. H. Madjavji. Implementing concepts from the personal sofware process in an industrial setting. In *Proceedings of the 4th International Conference on the Sofware Process*, pages 117–130, Los Alamitos, CA, 1996. IEEE CS Press.
4. Norman E. Fenton. *Software metrics: A rigorous approach.* Chapman & Hall, London, 1992.
5. Pat Ferguson, Watts S. Humphrey, Soheil Khajenoori, Susan Macke, and Annette Atvya. Results of applying the personal software process. *IEEE Computer*, 30(5):24–31, May 1997.
6. Gina C. Green and Alan R. Hevner. The successful diffusion of innovations: Guidance for software development organizations. *IEEE Software*, 17(6):96–103, November/December 2000.
7. Georg Grütter. Validation einer Methode zur Defektdatensammlung und Defektdatenvermei- dung. Master's thesis, Universität Karlsruhe (TH), Karlsruhe, 1998.

---

[1] One of these cases is published here as well [17].

8. W. Hayes and J. W. Over. The Personal Software Process (PSP): An empirical study of the impact of PSP on individual engineers. Technical Report CMU/SEI-97-001, Software Engineering Institute (SEI), Pittsburgh, PL, December 1997.

9. Watts S. Humphrey. *A discipline for software engineering*. Addison-Wesley, Reading, MA, 1995.

10. Watts S. Humphrey. Using a defined and measured Personal Software Process. *IEEE Software*, 13(3):77–88, May 1996.

11. Watts S. Humphrey. *Introduction to the Personal Software Process*. Addison-Wesley, Reading, MA, 1997.

12. Watts S. Humphrey. *Introduction to the Team Software Process*. Addison-Wesley, Reading, MA, 2000.

13. Watts S. Humphrey. The personal software process: Status and trends. *IEEE Software*, 17(6):71–75, November/December 2000.

14. Philip M. Johnson, Carleton A. Moore, Joseph A. Dane, and Robert S. Brewer. Empirically guided software effort guesstimation. *IEEE Software*, 17(6):51–56, November/December 2000.

15. Jagadish Kamatar and Will Hayes. An experience report on the Personal Software Process. *IEEE Software*, 17(6):85–89, November/December 2000.

16. Chris F. Kemerer. An empirical validation of software cost estimation models. *Communications of the ACM*, 30(5):416–429, May 1987.

17. S. Macke, S. Khajenoori, J. New, I. Hirmanpour, J. Coxon, and R. Rockwell. Personal software process at motorola paging products group. In *Proceedings of the Software Engineering Process Group Conference*, 1996.

18. Maurizio Morisio. Applying the PSP in industry. *IEEE Software*, 17(6):90–95, November/December 2000.

19. M. C. Paulk. *The Capability Maturity Model: Guidelines for Improving the Software Process*. Addison-Wesley, Reading, MA, 1995.

20. Lutz Prechelt. Accelerating learning from experience: Avoiding defects faster. *IEEE Software*, to appear in 2002.

21. Lutz Prechelt and Barbara Unger. An experiment measuring the effects of Personal Software Process (PSP) training. *IEEE Transactions on Software Engineering*, 27(5):465–472, 2001.

22. Xiaoming Zhong, Nazim H. Madhavji, and Khaled El Emam. Critical factors affecting personal software processes. *IEEE Software*, 17(6):76–83, November/December 2000.

Personal Software Process: Classroom Experiences from Finland

Pekka Abrahamsson[1] and Karlheinz Kautz[2]

[1] VTT Electronics, P.O.Box 1100, FIN-90571 Oulu, Finland
Pekka.Abrahamsson@vtt.fi
[2] Department of Informatics, Copenhagen Business School, Howitzvej 60, 3.,
DK-2000 Frederiksberg, Denmark
Karl.Kautz@cbs.dk

Abstract. The personal software process (PSP^{SM}) method was introduced a little less than a decade ago with high expectations. Still, only a limited number of experience reports have been published. This paper reports results from the University of Oulu in Finland, where PSP is a mandatory course for students majoring in software engineering. The results do not indicate a significant improvement in size or effort estimation skills, but the defects found in the unit test phase were decreased by a factor of 4.2. Students however did not plan on using the PSP skills in industry. It is suggested that course assignments are tailored to local context, and a stronger emphasis is placed on the concept and classification of defects. Software industry should in turn develop capabilities for using the PSP trained engineers. These and other implications are discussed.

1 Introduction

The personal software process (PSP) is an accepted method for improving software processes at personal level [1]. However, only a limited number of the research efforts concerning the PSP are documented. In fact, a database search into the INSPEC information repository discovered 69 PSP related publications from the years 1994-2001. Only one of these [i.e., 2] reported experiences from Northern Europe. This is the starting point for our work.

There are some results from practitioners using the PSP in their daily work [3-5]. The majority of results are, however, provided from PSP courses and classes [e.g., 6, 7-9]. While one might argue that classroom experiences are of limited value, research [10, 11] has shown that students are valid representatives for practitioners in industry. This work we present here is based on classroom experiences, which we thus believe gives valuable insights into the effect of the PSP in general.

The University of Oulu in Finland is now offering a full PSP course to its students. The PSP course is mandatory for all students majoring in software engineering. This paper reports results from the first course held in 2000-2001 in terms of effort and size estimation improvement as well as the improvement in product quality. Also, students' reactions to the PSP method are described. Results show that while no

J. Kontio and R. Conradi (Eds.): ECSQ 2002, LNCS 2349, pp. 175–185, 2002.
© Springer-Verlag Berlin Heidelberg 2002

significant improvement was identified in size and effort estimation, product quality in terms of defects found in the unit test improved by a factor of 4.2. Students faced problems with mathematically oriented contents of the programming assignments but appreciated the ability to track personal data. However, beyond a few items of PSP method, students did not plan on continue using the method as taught. These results are discussed and future changes to the course are outlined.

The paper is organised as follows. The following section provides an overview of the PSP method. This is followed by an introduction to the course setting. Course results are presented in section 4 and discussed subsequently in section 5. The paper is concluded with final remarks.

2. Overview of the PSP

The PSP was developed by Watts Humphrey [12] to extend the improvement process from an organisation or a project to an individual software engineer. The underlying principle in PSP states that every engineer should do quality work. A high level of quality is achieved through the disciplined utilisation of sound software engineering principles. These principles include a strong focus on the measurement of individual performance. The aim of the PSP is thus to enable software engineers to control and manage their software products as well as to improve their predictability and quality. This is achieved through the gradual introduction of new elements into the baseline personal process in a series of 7-10 small programming tasks.

The progression of PSP is shown in Figure 1. A student entering a PSP course starts with PSP0, that is, their current process enhanced with time and defect tracking

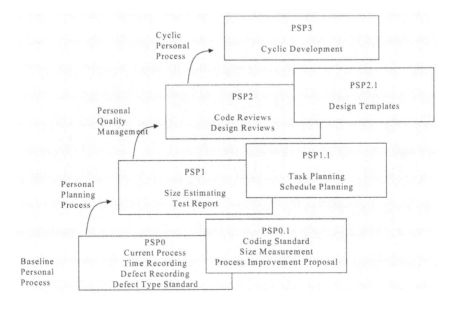

Figure 1. The PSP process development

instruments. PSP0.1 extends the personal baseline process to include a systematised coding standard, software size measurement in terms of logical lines of code (LOC) and a personal process improvement proposal mechanism. PSP1 augments the initial process to include the size estimation and a test report practices. PSP1.1 extends the personal planning process to involve a resource planning mechanism. At this level the students become aware of the relationship between program size and use of resources. The size and effort estimations are performed using a Proxy Based Estimation (PROBE) method, where students systematically use the historical data they have collected from the programming exercises.

At PSP2 level the focus is directed towards personal quality management through the introduction of code and design review practices. Students develop their personal defect and design review checklists, based on their historical defect data. PSP2.1 extends the process to include design specifications and analyses. Finally, PSP3 scales up the process from a single module development to larger scale projects. As an outcome, the project is divided in a series of smaller sub projects that are then incrementally implemented.

3. Course Setting

As the students' academic year at the Univ. of Oulu is divided into three 10-week periods, this sets some constraints on the length of the course. As a consequence the course was divided in 9 weekly held 2-4 hour lectures, 7 programming exercises, 2 reporting (mid-term and final) assignments and an exam. Humphrey's [12] book was used as the course book. The goal of the course was that students would reach the PSP 2 level.

Out of 31 students enrolling to the course, 20 finished the course with a pass grade. Thus, the drop out rate was 35%. Students were credited for the workload equalling 160 direct hours for the whole course. Course participants were predominantly fourth year students with at least two years of experience in programming. In fact, most of the students - i.e., 68% - were working in software organisations part-time or even as a full-time employee. While no specific programming language was enforced, students used a language they felt most comfortable with. As a consequence Java and C++ were dominantly used.

Students were given 6 calendar days to complete each assignment. In order to facilitate the data collection process, only electronic documents were used. However, automated data collection tools were not used. Thus, students kept manually – i.e. in a spreadsheet – track of time and defects.

4. Course Results

We will explore the results from the course in terms of effort estimation accuracy, size estimation accuracy and product quality in terms of defects found in the unit test. It has been widely claimed that effort and size estimation accuracy should improve significantly, while defects found in the unit test should lower towards the final programming assignments. Disney and Johnson [13, 14] have found that the data collected from the PSP course is often error prone and should not be used as a sole indicator of success or failure. Thus, we do not claim that the results presented here point in either direction but that they work as a basis for subsequent discussion.

4.1. Size Estimation

In the PSP method, size estimation is performed in order to arrive at close to accurate effort estimates. The size measure that is used is lines of code. PSP research has repeatedly demonstrated that LOC correlate reasonably well with the development effort. Future estimates are based on the students' personal data that they have collected from the previous assignments. Thus, this indicates that the size estimates may vary largely in programs 2-3 (note that in program 1 no size estimation was performed) but that this estimating error % variation would diminish to around a 25% error margin or even less as recent studies [e.g., 15] have shown. A box plot[1] diagram of the distribution of size estimating accuracy is shown in Figure 2.

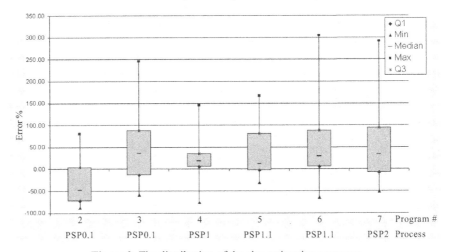

Figure 2. The distribution of the size estimation accuracy

A close look at the median values indicates that while students initially overestimated their work, their estimation bias trend stabilised to a varying degree of underestimation. When the differences between the minimum and the maximum values are studied, the variation does not diminish but gets larger toward the final program. Figure 2 leads one to suspect that no significant improvements were

---

[1] A box plot diagram visualises the 5 number summary of a data set. Median (a line in the shaded area) value indicates that 50% of data points are below and 50% are above the line. Q1 (first or lower quartile) shows the median of the lower 50% of data points. Q3 (third or upper quartile) shows the median of upper 50% of data points. The minimum value indicates the lowest and the maximum the highest values in the respective data sets.

achieved in improving the size estimation accuracy. Table 1 groups the data points according to the PSP level practised and the estimation accuracy range. The goal set for the course was to achieve an estimation margin of 5%, which is the highlighted row in Table 1.

Table 1. The development of the size estimation accuracy

Estimation Accuracy Range %	PSP0	PSP1	PSP2
< 5	0%	12%	11%
0-25	19%	45%	32%
26-50	30%	16%	21%
51-75	19%	16%	11%
76-100	24%	7%	11%
> 100	8%	17%	26%

This data shows that 32% of students were able to estimate program # 7 at PSP2 level within the 25% error margin. Only 11% achieved the course target, i.e., a 5% error margin level. Moreover, the percentage of students having an error margin over 100% increased to 26%.

4.2. Effort Estimation

PSP uses size estimates as the basis for deriving the effort estimate. While students experienced trouble in stabilising the size estimates to a certain level of accuracy, a similar trend was identifiable with the effort estimates (Figure 3). The median value approached zero but the difference between minimum and maximum estimates grew larger.

Classroom reports generally indicate a significant improvement in the effort estimation accuracy. However, as Table 2 indicates, only 45% of students were able to achieve a 25% effort estimation error margin. 10% of students achieved the 5% error margin, which was the goal set for the course. Similarly 10% of students were not able to estimate the effort expenditure within a 100% error margin. While no clear improvement was achieved in this regard, reasons for this marginal achievement may be manifold and are discussed later in detail.

Table 2. The development of the effort estimation accuracy

Estimation Accuracy Range %	PSP0	PSP1	PSP2
< 5	11%	5%	10%
0-25	53%	38%	45%
26-50	19%	29%	30%
51-75	14%	12%	15%
56-100	7%	3%	0%
> 100	7%	17%	10%

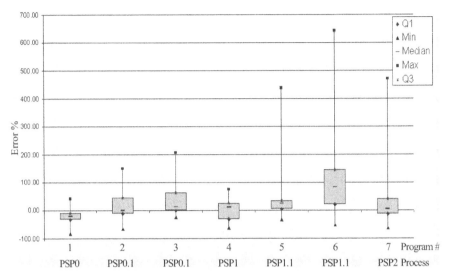

Figure 3. The distribution of the effort estimation accuracy

4.3. Product Quality

One of the fundamental skills that the PSP course attempts to teach is the ability to catch and correct defects as early as possible. Design and code reviews are the techniques that PSP method incorporates into students' process. As a consequence, defects found in compile and unit test should be reduced. This in turn should indicate increased product quality, since PSP research has shown that the number of defects found in unit test correlates to the number of defects found in later testing phases. Figure 4 shows that the median was reduced from 27 (PSP0 level, programs 1-3) to 6 (PSP2 level) defects found per thousand lines of code (KLOC) thus indicating an improvement of factor 4.2.

The single most effective improvement in the defect tracking practice is the introduction of design and code reviews in the PSP2 level as the data shows in Table 3. The compile phase is the main error removal mechanism when the students enter the course and only after the reviews are taken into use does this mechanism change. The types of defects caught in the code review were function (28%), variable assignment (30%) and syntax (38%) related. The majority of defect types caught in design review (54%) were function defects, which includes the logical defects.

4.4. Student Reactions

Students were asked to evaluate the current PSP process after each programming assignment in terms of positive and negative findings. In the early assignments, students generally appreciated the ability to explain how the effort used is distributed over different software development phases. Criticism was directed towards the problems to be solved – i.e. too mathematical, the amount of paperwork as well as the lack of automated data collection tools. Also, some confusion about the course intentions were identified, as the following extract demonstrates:

"There's one thing about the PSP that I really can't understand. PSP is meant to make the software developers more efficient and I can't help noticing that I'm spending app. 25 % of my time filling out documents that are PSP related! I understand that the PSP is a long term goal, but I'd sure like to see some hard evidence about the benefits of the PSP."

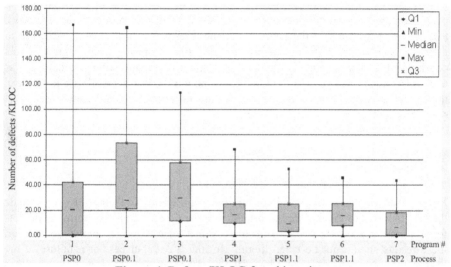

Figure 4. Defects/KLOC found in unit test

Table 3. The total number of defects removed

	Plan	Design	Design review	Code	Code review	Compile	Test
PSP0	0	1	-	29	-	104	69
PSP1	0	0	-	16	-	106	40
PSP2	0	3	14	15	56	37	29

Indeed, the effort distribution among different phases changed significantly over the PSP phases. While the effort spent for the coding phase decreased from 40% to 24%, the effort spent in the planning phase increased from 4% to 26%.

When work efficiency is made explicit, it has been shown that the PSP method does not increase or decrease an engineer's productivity, even though several new elements are introduced into the practice. The data (the median varied between 18 to 26 LOC/hour) collected in the course supported this argument. In the later assignments, students gradually became aware of the true effort required to complete the course and strong statements were made about its feasibility.

Also, increasing dissatisfaction concerning the content of the programming assignments, which in most cases was to implement a mathematical equation as the course book [12] suggests. However, those students that were able to collect data on their assignments systematically appreciated the strong evidence that they can base their estimates on.

Moreover, since many of the students were actively working alongside in software companies, they found it useful to try to relate their experiences to company's practice. As a result students reported that in some companies coding practice standard was redefined based on their suggestions. Other concrete practice transfers were related to the use of design and code review checklists. In the final course evaluation the students did not consider, however, using PSP processes in their work that they had tried out in the course. Students claimed to lack the infrastructure in their work to support the kind of practice that PSP proposes. Their argument was confirmed by interviewing the students by email 12 months after the course was ended. However, students reported that even though the PSP methods are not in use, the course substantially contributed to their general knowledge and understanding of software engineering at a personal level.

5. Discussion

Results indicate that students did not improve significantly in their ability to estimate the program size or the required effort, but that the product quality in terms of defects found in the unit test showed a major improvement. However, as emphasised earlier, these results should not be taken literally to indicate the success or a failure of the PSP method. Moreover, the purpose of the course is not to test the method *per se* but to allow students to explore its possibilities. In what follows, the implications of these results are discussed.

To us the results indicate several improvement opportunities for the software engineering course curriculum, as well as some suggestions regarding industrial practice. While all students were fourth or fifth year students, there was a great variety in their basic programming abilities as well as in their ability to produce a module level program designs. The ability to produce programs should be possessed by everyone who graduates from university with a degree in software engineering. While steps in this direction have been taken, the results from this course indicate a need for stronger emphasis on basic programming ability, since it is inherently central to any software engineering activity.

Secondly, the concept of a defect was unmistakably vague for many students entering the PSP course. Defect data provides the fundamental basis for software quality management. However, while the course provides tools to meaningfully collect, analyse and use defect data as a basis for personal improvements, students face difficulties in keeping up with the rigorous tracking practice if they are not carefully followed up. The very concept of a defect was not adequately addressed at the beginning of the course and this led to difficulties in that the tracking practice varied between each student. Moreover, when data from an individual student is carefully analysed over a set of assignments, it can be found that the defect tracking practice is not consistent but varies, depending on factors such as deadline pressure for example. Studies have shown that background experience does not affect the number of defects found or the overall defect density [16]. While our data supports these findings, the quality of the work being done is jeopardised if the concept and classification of a defect is not clear.

Thirdly, the level of knowledge required to understand the statistical data manipulations was underestimated. Students thus encountered problems in just understanding the content of the assignment since the lectures were targeted towards exploring the process aspects of the PSP method. This partly explains the continuing variation in the size and effort estimates. The role of statistics and mathematics in software engineering education has been reduced in recent years to a few isolated courses. As shown earlier, students' reactions towards dealing with statistics was even hostile. As a result, we do not however suggest that more emphasis should be directed towards the statistics but on the way the PSP method is being taught in universities where statistics and mathematics do not play a major role in the software engineering curriculum. This points in a direction where the contents of programming assignments need to be tailored and the statistical data treatment taught explicitly, including its advantages and disadvantages. Actual calculations that involve data treatment such as linear regression can be calculated using freely available tool packages.

Adopting the PSP method to course curriculum as a mandatory course in software engineering major sends a strong signal to the industry that process control and improvement abilities are being focused on. However, while these abilities are now being systematically taught, the software industry needs to develop its capabilities for using these PSP trained engineers. This requires top and middle management training in PSP. One major finding in the use of PSP in an industrial setting [e.g., 4, 17] has been that without ongoing support from the organisation, a single engineer finds it difficult to continue applying disciplined practices. Moreover, organisations need not adopt the PSP as it is defined, but can tailor it to the individual organisation's specific needs.

The positive post-course feedback from students indicates that the inclusion of PSP in the software engineering course curriculum might contribute to the much-needed development of professionalism within the field.

6. Conclusion

While the personal software process method was introduced a little less than a decade ago, only a limited number of experience reports have been published. This paper contributed to the body of knowledge within this area by reporting classroom experiences from the first PSP course at the Univ. of Oulu. While results did not indicate a significant improvement in size or effort estimation, the defects found in the unit test phase were reduced by a factor of 4.2. Students did not plan to use PSP skills as taught in industry. They argued that they lack the infrastructure to support such an effort. Based on these experiences the PSP course will be further developed and held at Copenhagen Business School, Denmark. Convinced of the benefits, the University of Oulu continues to deliver a PSP course on a yearly basis.

Acknowledgements

The authors would like to thank the students participating in the PSP course for their effort in collecting the PSP data and for their valuable comments throughout the course, and Dr. Juhani Warsta and Phil. Lic. Antti Juustila at the University of Oulu and the three anonymous reviewers for their insightful comments on the early version of the paper.

References

1.   Zahran, S., Software process improvement: practical guidelines for business success. SEI series in software engineering. Reading, Mass.: Addison-Wesley Pub. Co. (1998)
2.   Runeson, P. Experience from Teaching PSP for Freshmen. in 14th Conference on Software Engineering Education & Training (CSEE&T). Charlotte, NC: IEEE Comput. Soc, Los Alamitos, CA, USA (2001) 98-107
3.   El Emam, K., B. Shostak, and N.H. Madhavji. Implementing concepts from the personal software process in an industrial setting. in Fourth International Conference on the Software Process (ICSP '96). Brighton, UK (1996) 117-130
4.   Morisio, M., Applying the PSP in industry. IEEE Software 17 (2000) 90-95
5.   Kamatar, J. and W. Hayes, An experience report on the personal software process. IEEE Software 17 (2000) 85-89
6.   Lisack, S.K. The Personal Software Process in the Classroom: Student Reactions (an Experience Report). in Thirteenth Conference on Software Engineering Education & Training (CSEE&T). Austin, Texas (2000)
7.   Hayes, W. and J.W. Over, The Personal Software Process (PSP): An Empirical Study of the Impact of PSP on Individual Engineers. Software Engineering Institute. (1997)
8.   Zhong, X., N.H. Madhavji, and K.E. Emam, Critical factors affecting personal software processes. IEEE Software 17 (2000) 76-83
9.   Carrington, D., B. McEniery, and D. Johnston, PSP in the large class. Forum for Advancing Software engineering Education (FASE) 11 (2001) 81-88
10.   Höst, M., B. Regnell, and C. Wohlin, Using students as subjects - a comparative study of student and professionals in lead-time impact assessment. Empirical Software Engineering 5 (2000) 201-214
11.   Jørgensen, M. and D.I.K. Sjøberg, Software process improvement and human judgement heuristics. Scandinavian Journal of Information Systems 13 (2001) 99-122
12.   Humphrey, W.S., A discipline for software engineering: Addison Wesley Longman, Inc. (1995)
13.   Disney, A. and P. Johnson. Investigating data quality problems in the PSP. in SIGSOFT'98 (1998) 143-152
14.   Johnson, P.M., The personal software process: A cautionary case study. IEEE Software 15 (1998) 85-88
15.   Hayes, W. Using a personal software process to improve performance. in 5th International Symposium on Software Metrics. Bethesda, Maryland (1998)

16. Wohlin, C. and A. Wesslén. Understanding Software Defect Detection in the Personal Software Process. in Proceedings IEEE 9th International Symposium on Software Reliability Engineering. Paderborn, Germany (1998) 49-58
17. Cannon, R.L. Putting the Personal Software Process Into Practice. in Proceedings of the 12th Conference on Software Engineering Education and Training (1998) 34-37

GARP – The Evolution
of a Software Acquisition Process Model

Thomas Gantner[1] and Tobias Häberlein[2]

[1] DaimlerChrysler, Research and Technology, Ulm
Thomas.Gantner@DaimlerChrysler.com
[2] University of Ulm, Faculty of Computer Science, Department of Software Methodology
Tobias.Haeberlein@informatik.uni-ulm.de

Abstract. At DaimlerChrysler, the greatest part of the business and automotive software is provided by suppliers, often developed in complex software acquisition projects. Therefore, the development of a mature software acquisition process is essential for business success. One task of the DaimlerChrysler software process research department is the evaluation, customisation, and implementation of methods and techniques for software acquisition. This paper gives an overview of software acquisition process activities that were performed at this department. We developed a comprehensive lifecycle oriented model of a software acquisition reference process. The sub-steps of this process model are further explained by best practices. Furthermore, we describe how we used this acquisition process reference model for improving software acquisition activities at DaimlerChrysler.

1   Introduction

Software acquisition and supplier management are a critical issue for many enterprises world-wide. Software acquisition is concerned with the provision of an organisation's need for software. Supplier management applies to management tasks while dealing with suppliers or subcontractors. Their impact on business processes is increasing dramatically. Software investments may result in essential productivity and customer benefits as well as in strategic advantages. Following a systematic approach for software acquisition and supplier management might help to increase the benefits on these investments.

DaimlerChrysler is purchasing more and more software products. Software acquisition and supplier management are major issues. Professional management of a customer-supplier-relationship sets a number of prerequisites such as requirements management, risk management, establishing communication, managing legal aspects as well as controlling ambitions and costs. To avoid failure of a software acquisition, a strategy for procuring software needs to be in place. The elements of such a software acquisition strategy should consist of defined processes based on best practices for each phase of the acquisition lifecycle. As a software acquisition can be a complex task, the requirement to have a comprehensive hierarchical lifecycle model of a

J. Kontio and R. Conradi (Eds.): ECSQ 2002, LNCS 2349, pp. 186–196, 2002.

software acquisition arises. Hierarchical lifecycle model means that firstly the processes of the model are temporally ordered and secondly that processes may have sub-processes and they again may have sub-processes. Another benefit of using a hierarchical lifecycle model is that it provides an *explicit* guidance for our company's internal customers by defining a temporally ordered representation of all relevant activities during software acquisition that can be used a sa work sequence.

The following section gives a more detailed motivation for the work conducted and describes some approaches that greatly influenced the achieved results. In section 3 the structure of the defined software acquisition process model and the relationship between the process steps and associated best practices is explained. How we actually use the defined acquisition process model is covered in section 4. Section 5 concludes the paper with some remarks concerning further work.

2   Our Need for a New Acquisition Process Model

Before we started to develop a software acquisition reference model we did a comprehensive survey to identify already existing software acquisition process models that might fit our needs. Some of the identified approaches which have a main influence on our reference model are shortly described below. A more detailed description of the results of our survey can be found elsewhere [3,4].

2.1   Existings Software-Acquisition Process Models with a Main Influence

The approaches that strongly influenced our activities are:
– **HBSG**, a DaimlerChrysler internal handbook for project and quality management for the development of software systems. As this handbook addresses software projects in general, it is not especially intended to cover software acquisition. But as the described processes have a strong work sequence character, the intended software acquisition reference model should possess this requirement, too.
– **SA-CMM** [16], SEI's capability maturity model for software acquisition is similar in structure to the well-known SW-CMM. It is a process framework that identifies important key process areas for software acquisition.
– **ISPL [8]** (the predecessor is called Euromethod) is an acquisition lifecycle oriented set of best practices for the management of acquisition projects.
– **PULSE** [13] is a methodology for assessment of software acquisition activities. It has similar goals as the SA-CMM. It contains a comprehensive process framework for software acquisition, that classifies the relevant sub-processes into four process categories.

2.2   Why All This Is Still Not Enough

As stated in the introduction, our goal at DaimlerChrysler is to have an acquisition model that consists of defined, hierarchically and temporally ordered processes in the sense of a work sequence based on best practices for each phase of the acquisition lifecycle. None of the described approaches above completely fulfils this requirement. SA-CMM and PULSE are comprehensive process frameworks for software acquisition, but they don't explicitly combine the contained sub-processes into a work sequence. HBSG is lifecycle oriented, but concerning software acquisition it is not as comprehensive as for example SA-CMM or PULSE. ISPL has a work sequence character and it also comprises best practices. Therefore, it is close to our requirement and can be seen as a backbone for our process reference model, but for our needs – building a ready to use cookbook for software acquisition as far as possible - some activities are described on a too abstract level, e.g. the sub-process of monitoring suppliers.

3   Building GARP (Generic Acquisition Reference Process)

This section describes how we achieved our goal: The development of a comprehensive process reference model for software acquisition by combining the strengths of existing approaches in a coherent way.

3.1   The Process Framework

As a first step towards an adapted software acquisition process model we analysed the way software acquisition is currently done at DaimlerChrysler. Coherently merging these results with the ideas from Euromethod, a predecessor of ISPL, we developed a first version of a hierarchical lifecycle model. Since a main goal was to make the model comprehensive we supplemented GARP with aspects from PULSE, SA-CMM, FAA-iCMM [2] and IEEE Std. 1062 [7].

GARP's processes cover the whole spectrum of acquisition activities beginning from defining the acquisition's goals through defining the technical requirements, acquisition project planning, tendering (which is GARP's most detailed part) driving the actual procurement process (which for example comprises process steps for joint risk management, joint reviews, joint configuration management) to activities like acquisition acceptance, transitioning the acquired system to support and maintenance and reviewing the completed project.

GARP's processes are mainly sequentially organised, but some activities may run in parallel. Examples for this can be seen in the left part of figure 1. Also shown in figure 1 is that we use links to connect processes with their respective sub-processes.

We incorporated the whole spectrum of management processes (although a lifecycle model is not fully capable of expressing their continuous dynamics). Basically we integrated the management processes into GARP by splitting them into a planning process in the initiation phase and a corresponding process performing the management activities in GARP's "Driving the Procurement" part. For example, quality management is represented in GARP through the "Define Quality Management Process" and "Define Project Quality Plan" processes in the initiation phase and the "Quality Management" process in the "Driving the Procurement" phase.

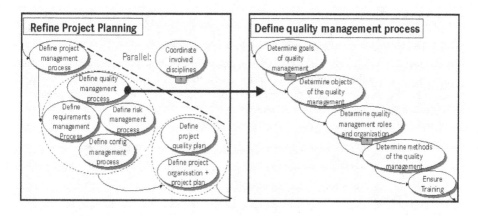

Fig. 1. Two sample pages of GARP's process level graphical presentation. In the right page, all processes are sequentially ordered. The left page shows parallel processes grouped in a dashed oval. Associated with the oval "define quality management process" is a hyperlink to the corresponding refinement. Some processes have a "?"-tag. These are hyperlinks to more detailed information about the respective process

3.2   The Best Practice Framework

A model that says what should be done in what order is a useful tool in assessing running acquisition projects and in determining processes to be improved. But in order to provide the projects with suggestions on *how* to do it better, it was inevitable to get more concrete. We decided to enrich GARP with best practices from popular software acquisition guides (see also figure 2).

To sketch the diversity of the different sources and the resulting difficulty of integrating them into GARP in a coherent manner, we give a short description of a few best practice guides:

- **Schreiber** [15]: This is a compact guide (only available in German) which gives orientation in procuring software. The whole approach is document oriented. For example, a specification document template is provided to guide the tendering process and an evaluation document template is provided to guide the evaluation process.
- **The SPMN Guide to Software Acquisition Best Practices** [17]: The guidebook's mission is to help managers of large-scale software acquisition projects by identifying best management practices and lessons learned. The approach here is activity oriented.
- **The Procurement Forum** [12]: This is a forum for procuring companies to discuss and exchange experience and learning in improving acquisition projects and to solve procurement-related problems. The direct source of best practice information provided here is worth a lot.
- **IEEE Std 1062** [7] This standard describes a set of quality practices that can be selected and applied during one or more steps in a software acquisition process.

– **ECSS** [1]: This is short for "European Cooperation for Space Standardization". It also denotes a set of standards which are intended for use in management, development, and quality control of space software projects.
– **Validate** [10]: This is – like GARP – a collection of best practices from different sources. The authors studied procurements conducted by many organizations and analyzed the impact of best practices. Validate claims to show which best practices really work and which are less efficient.

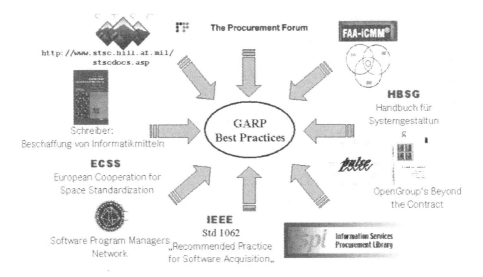

Fig. 2. (Some of the) sources we used as best practice inputs for GARP. Thus GARP can also serve as a guidance on how to perform specific processes

The graphical representation of GARP supports hyperlinks and so it is obvious to link GARP's processes (typically those on the lowest process level) to a corresponding set of best practices. In doing this we were faced with two main problems: the heterogeneity of the best practice sources firstly in terms of the level of abstraction (e.g. ISPL provides quite abstract material whereas Schreiber gets very concrete) and secondly, in terms of the kind of information provided (e.g. Schreiber gives document templates whereas SPMN is based on tips and hints).

Structuring Best Practice Sources. To keep GARP maintainable, all best practices should be traceable to their sources. In addition to linking each best practice information with its corresponding source we chose to structure the sources itself in order to cope with their diversity.

Thus we decided to record the following two criteria (see also Figure 3) for each source in a sub-process's best practice collection:

1. **Level of coverage**: This criterion indicates how broadly the respective area is covered. Sources with a high degree of broadness could be used as a guideline to check if all important aspects of a sub-process are accounted for.
2. **Level of detail**: This criterion indicates the level of detail and the depth of treatment of the respective best practices. A high degree of detailing entails directly implementable best practices whereas a low degree of detailing means that one has to instantiate the probably more abstract material.

Figure 3 is an extract of GARP showing the graphical representation of this structuring.

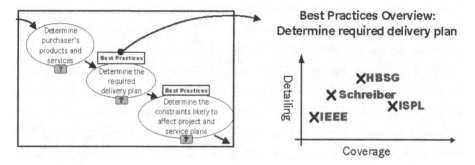

Fig. 3. An extract of GARP that shows how processes and best practice sources are linked. The sources are points in a coordinate system, where the x-axis represents the degree of broadness and the y-axis the degree of detailing of the respective information

Structuring Best Practices. To deal with the above mentioned disparity in the kind of information provided by the best practice sources, we decided to organize the best practice material (of each GARP sub-process) into three *information kinds*:

- **Document Template:** It consists of a proposal for the structure of the deliverable, usually in form of a table of contents, which should be developed in the context of the respective GARP sub-process.
- **Detailed Procedure:** It provides a "mini process" describing the concrete implementation of the respective sub-process.
- **Tips, Hints and Dont's:** This is probably the most common form of best practice information. Suggestions are given what – from experience – should be done or what should be avoided.

Managing the best practice disparity in the level of abstraction turned out to be more difficult. We tried to deal with that by creating a "coherent view" of the best practices in each information kind category. This concretely means that firstly best practices from different sources in one information kind category should be kept free of redundancy and secondly, if specific information is available in different levels of abstraction, preference is given to those with the lowest level (i.e., those which are most easy to implement).

In order to get the big picture of how best practice information is organized in GARP, figure 4 shows the structure of GARP's best practice framework.

Clicking on the links in this best practice overview's coordinate system (arrow 1) leads to detailed information where exactly in the source the respective information can be found and to details about the source itself (arrow 3). Following the "coherent view"-link under the coordinate system (arrow 2) leads to an information-kinds list. From here, the best practices themselves can be accessed by following the "document template" (arrow 4), "tips, hints and dont's" (arrow 5) or "detailed procedure" (arrow 6) links.

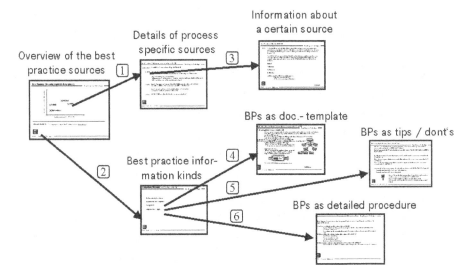

Fig. 4. The structure of GARP's best practice framework is shown for one sub-process. The numbered arrows denote hyperlinks from some text/graphic of one page to another page

Despite its elaborate design, GARP's usability has some limits. These are discussed in section 5.

4   Using GARP

4.1   The Improvement Cycle

The goal of our activities is to establish a continuous improvement process for the software acquisition activities of our internal customers. GARP and the GARP based assessment method SAM [5] are important inputs for an improvement cycle which is shown graphically in figure 5. Process assessment provides the means of characterizing the current practice within an organizational unit in terms of capability of the selected processes and reveals weaknesses.

SAM differentiates two types of process assessments: a "light assessment", which comprises a well prepared self-assessment workshop and a "full assessment", which contains most of the steps of the PULSE assessment process. Together with the assessment data, GARP's process framework is used to define improvements in the assessed process. Suggestions in GARP's best practice framework can give significant input in how the respective improvements could be implemented. Figure 5 also shows this correlation.

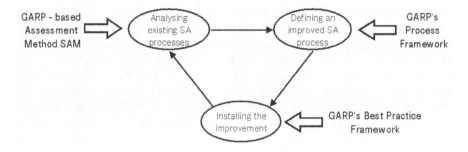

Fig. 5. GARP supports the software acquisition improvement cycle

4.2 GARP and Assessments: Examples

In a software acquisition assessment in a department of the passenger car development business unit the need for defining an acquisition strategy was identified as one important improvement activity.

GARP, influenced by ISPL, suggests to conduct an early risk analysis, even before the preparation of the request for proposal is conducted. The derived risk profile of the planned project is then used to fix the acquisition strategy (type and formality of monitoring activities, contractual aspects, density of milestones and so on). This concept of an early and fast risk analysis for a planned project is further developed as a stand alone method [14], but of course the link to this concept still is part of the relevant sub-processes of GARP.

In another department of the passenger car development business unit a software acquisition process assessment revealed that the quality assurance concerning system requirements documents was weak. We developed for our customer a specific review process which had to consider that 20 documents had to be reviewed in a very short time (two weeks) and that the potential reviewers all worked in a open-plan office and therefore couldn't thoroughly read a document at their workplace. Now, the defined review process concept can be plugged into GARP as a further best practice that may be used in future by other development projects with similar constraints, too.

4.3 Further Applications of GARP

In addition to the use of GARP in the context of an acquisition process assessment as a source of best practices for achieving intended improvements, GARP proved worthwhile in other contexts, too.

GARP as a Checklist for Existing Acquisition Concepts. At the passenger car development business unit a concept for the management of software suppliers (called SLIM) was analysed. The main areas covered in SLIM are monitoring software technologies and trends, scanning potential software suppliers, bidding, and contracting aspects. The analysis was conducted in the following way: for the topics covered in SLIM it was checked if related sub-processes in GARP and/or the best practices associated with these sub-processes could lead to an improvement of SLIM.

According to GARP the aspect of how the procurer and the supplier should cooperate during the project (e.g., common risk and problem management or common procedure when contractual aspects should be changed during the project) is not completely covered in the bidding procedure of SLIM. So the best practices in GARP related to the sub-process "Preparation of a Request for Proposal" could give helpful hints, how to enhance the SLIM concept in this aspect, especially as aspects related to requests for proposal as a key document for acquisition is treated very thoroughly in GARP.

GARP as Training and Guiding Material. The lifecycle orientation of GARP, its comprehensiveness, the association of best practices to the sub-processes, and the easy accessibility from the technical and the structural viewpoint convinced the management of a purchasing department of DaimlerChrysler in India to use GARP as a guide for the acquisition of software especially for new members in their group. As a pilot application one member of their group is introduced to GARP. Afterwards this person shall use the concepts of GARP, coached and supported by us, if necessary. As this is an ongoing activity at the moment, it is too early, to report on experiences.

5   Conclusions and Future Work

This paper described the need for a software acquisition process model tailored to our requirements. The construction process and structuring principles of such a process model were presented and we showed the use and usefulness of the model. We think the ideas and the approach for the development of the process model could be valuable for other organizations who want to fix their own principles of software acquisition.

So far, GARP is a helpful tool for supporting specialists in process improvement. However, two things may prevent GARP from specially being an educational facility. Firstly, as our process model is *very* comprehensive novices get easily lost in details. Secondly, since it is a lifecycle model, it is neither fully capable of expressing the continuous dynamics of all the management processes, nor is it made for giving a grasp of how in detail the actual management of an acquisition process should work.

Thus, in addition to further refining GARP itself, we search for alternative representations of the information contained in GARP to make it more suitable for educational purposes. A GARP based interactive simulation of an acquisition project, with one person taking the role of the project manager, is an interesting (and challenging!) possibility to impart GARP's knowledge playfully and we are currently investigating this possibility and the respective literature [6,11]. Similar research projects [9] showed that this approach could be valuable in training project managers. The underlying principles of the commercial game SimCity strongly resemble these ideas. This demonstrates the entertaining potential of such a simulation.

Another option we are probably investigating in is a GARP based catalog of project situation patterns. Here, GARP's information is represented through a mapping of specific (patterns of) frequently recurring acquisition project constellations to a configuration of best practices which should be applied in the respective project constellation to achieve improvements. Clearly such a mapping only could be designed empirically after gaining a sufficient amount of experience with GARP.

References

1. European Cooperation for Space Standardization (ECSS): *Space Engineering, Software*, ESA Publications Division ESTEC, P.O. Box 299, 2200 AG Noordwijk, The Netherlands, 1998.
2. The Federal Aviation Administration: *Integrated Capability Maturity Model*. http://www.faa.gov/aio/icmm/FAA.htm
3. Getto, G.: Evaluation von Prozessen und Methoden für Softwarebeschaffung und Management von Auftragnehmern, *In Proceedings of the 4th Kongress Software Qualitätsmanagement "Made in Germany"* (SQM1999), 1999
4. Getto, G., Gantner T.: Software Acquisition Processes at DaimlerChrysler AG: Research Activities for Improvement, *In Proceedings of the European Conference on Software Process Improvement* (SPI99), 1999
5. Getto, G., Gantner, T., Vullinghs, T.: Software Acquisition: Experiences with Models and Methods. In *EuroSPI*, 2000.
6. Nigel Gilbert and Klaus G. Troitzsch. *Simulation for the social scientist*. Open University Press – Buckingham – Philadelphia, 1999.
7. IEEE Standards Association. *IEEE 1062: IEEE Recommended Practice for Software Acquisition*, 1993.
8. ISPL: *Information Service Procurement Library. Managing Acquisition Processes*, 1999.
9. Ludewig, J.; Deininger, M.: *Teaching software project management by simulation: The SESAM project*. In Irish Quality Association (ed.), *5th European Conference on Software Quality*, pages 417 – 426, Dublin, 1996.
10. The Opengroup: *Beyond the Contract: An Analysis of the business impact of IT procurement best practices*, ISBN 1-85912-281-7. 1999.
11. Pidd, M. *Computer Simulation in Management Science*, Wiley, Chichester, 1984.
12. The Procurement Forum, Rond Point Schuman 6, B1040 Brussels, Belgium, http://www.procurementforum.org
13. PULSE: *A Methodology for Assessment and Benchmarking of Procurement Processes*. http://www.ispo.cec.be/sprites2/fi-pulse.htm
14. Esa Rosendahl, Ton Vullinghs: *Performing Initial Risk Assessment in Software Acquisition Projects*, to be published at the 7th European Conference on Software Quality, Helsinki, 2002.
15. J. Schreiber. *Beschaffung von Informatikmitteln. Pflichtenheft, Evaluation, Entscheidung*. Paul Haupt Verlag, 2000.

16. Software Engineering Institute. *Software Acquisition Capability Maturity Model*, Version 1.02, CMU/SEI-99-tr002, Jack Cooper and Metthew Fisher and S.Wayne Sherer editors, 2001.
17. Software Program Managers Network. *Program Managers Guide to Software Acquisition.* http://www.spmn.com/pdf_download.html

Cooperation and Competition with Partner Companies: Practices for Quality Control through Competition among Teams

Yasuko Okazaki

Software Development Laboratory, IBM Japan, Ltd.
Shimotsuruma 1623-14, Yamato-shi, Kanagawa-ken 242-8502, Japan
yokazaki@jp.ibm.com

Abstract. We have been cooperating with remote partner companies and managing software quality with a cross-company team organization, competitions among sub-teams, postmortem analysis, and an experience repository. The practices have built good relationships with partner companies, motivated the engineers, and established a quality control process for developing highly reliable software. No more than two field defects for any product have been reported for the last 24 months. This paper describes how our practices improved our processes and the quality of the products.

1 Background

Since the computer industry is growing so fast, user requirements are getting more and more complex and diversified. On the other hand, we suppliers are asked to capture the users' requirements precisely and continuously reduce our development costs.

In these circumstances, we have seen increasing involvement of partner companies (vendors) in our projects. We have been working with some partner companies in remote locations in Japan, and anticipate the trend will continue. There are reasons that we need their cooperation, for example, in a case where a partner knows customer needs better than we do, because the company has a long-term relationship with the client. Though we sometimes need their cooperation and support during the peak time of a project, the primary reason is cost reduction. Smaller companies have less overhead than bigger companies. Their costs are, therefore, usually lower than ours.

Cooperation with a partner company is difficult because of the differences in cultures and locations between the two companies. In the early '90s, we faced the following difficulties in our joint effort with partner companies.

The firsts one is "Communication". Engineers of our company often complained about the outputs from the partner companies. On the other hand, we were not really concerned about any complaints the engineers of the partner companies might have about our development process. We divided project members up based on the company, clarifying the responsibilities of each company. But this seemed to cause feuds between the two sides. We needed a new type of team organization.

J. Kontio and R. Conradi (Eds.): ECSQ 2002, LNCS 2349, pp. 197–206, 2002.

Next one is "Phase exit criteria". Though we had to improve our products' quality year by year, we did not have well-defined reliability criteria for accepting intermediate products from partner companies. We had been measuring a set of metrics, e.g., the number of defects and the number of test cases written for each product. Although we were satisfied simply by the measuring, we did not effectively utilize the data collected in a project or in a department. We did not analyze defects qualitatively, we did not have well-defined defect classification categories in common, we did not share project data or development procedures within our department, and we did not even know the average number of defects for our department. We also did not have a defect database that could be accessed by both companies.

This paper describes our practices that have solved the two problems and how these practices have contributed to our development process improvement.

2   Our Practices

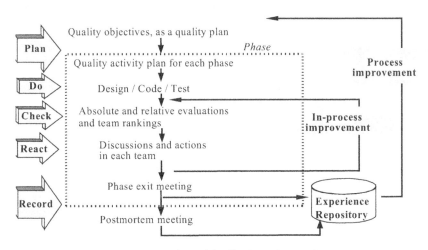

Fig. 1. Overview of Quality Improvement Process

Figure 1 shows an overview of the quality improvement process. In the Plan Stage, we first define quality objectives and activities to achieve them. In the Do Stage, we perform the design, coding or testing, by splitting the entire project team into sub-teams. In the Check Stage, an assurance expert evaluates the outputs of all sub-teams, and prepares the analysis results consisting of a summary and quality ratings of the sub-teams' outcomes, and feeds them back to each sub-team. If the sub-team decides that any remedial actions are required on the basis of the qualitative defects analysis, they define an action plan and execute it in the React Stage. Then, we move on to the Record Stage. We hold a phase exit meeting, and share and consolidate our software quality assessment, producing a "Quality Certification Report" which includes all measured data from each phase. Then we move on to the next phase and repeat the cycle. Finally, soon after a product is released, we hold a face-to-face meeting, the postmortem meeting. All project members from both companies attend the meeting to discuss strengths and weaknesses of the processes used during the project. Although the discussion themes of the meeting are defined as communications, management, tools, environment, education, product, morale, manuals, development process, root cause analysis of high severity defects, etc., the discussion process is actually flexible. We collect the individual analysis results and discuss what we have learned from the project. The results are summarized as a "Postmortem Report" and stored in the repository for process improvements.

Our team operation involves the following key elements, "Cross-company team organization", "Competition among sub-teams", "A development experience repository", and "Postmortem meetings", and the following subsections give detailed descriptions.

2.1 Cross-Company Team Organization

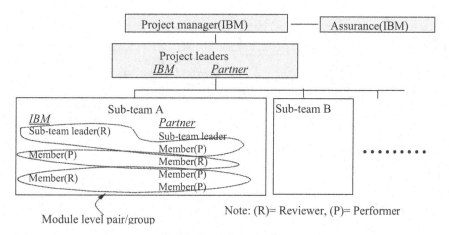

Fig. 2. Team Organization

The cross-company team organization is shown in Figure 2. Each sub-team has responsibility for some functions or components, such as database access, a message reader, common modules, archives, or the main controller.

Each sub-team member from IBM has one or more designated partners from the partner company, and has responsibility for some modules. Though such a module level pair (or group) does not actually share a terminal as in Pair Programming for the XP (eXtreme Programming) Method[2], because the partner companies are in remote locations in Japan, they review the designs and code for their areas of responsibility with each other, usually displaying the same screens while talking over the phone. They also communicate with e-mail daily, and have a televised meeting monthly. One of the partners takes the role of the presenter while the other partner is the reviewer. Though a partner from IBM in most cases takes the reviewer's role, there are cases where a non-IBM partner takes the reviewer's role if it is appropriate. We do not require that an IBM employee should take the reviewer's role. We do, however, believe the double-checking is always necessary to achieve high reliability.

After the high level design is complete, we form new teams consisting of different sub-teams and pairings for the next phases. The purpose of this reforming is to reduce interface errors between the components. Though the purpose of this approach is similar to the Collective Ownership in XP method, we do the following to improve the effects of dynamic member shuffling:

● We do not change all of the members. At least the sub-team leaders in each sub-team remained in place to explain the detailed design to new sub-team members.
● We created a design standard which defines the design document format and its required content. The standard helped every engineer to read the design documents for their new responsible area.

2.2   Competitions among Sub-teams

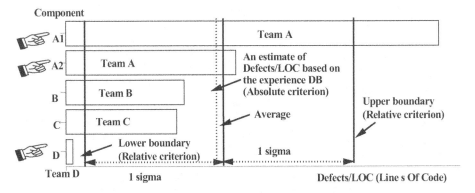

Fig. 3. An Example of the Error-Prone Component Analysis in the Function Test Phase

We evaluate each sub-team's performance by comparing the results of the sub-teams. Figure 3 shows an example of the sub-team evaluation, using the Defects/LOC (the number of defects per line of code) metric. In this example case, both components A1 and A2 were developed by sub-team A, and component B was developed by sub-team B. The chart suggests that component A1, A2, and D are error-prone components. Based on comparisons relative to the norms, any component that exceeds the upper bound, A1 here, is very likely to be an error-prone component. The relatively large number of detected errors suggests that the code was poorly written. On the other hand, a component under the lower bound, such as D, is also suspected to be potentially error-prone, because the very small number of detected errors may suggest inadequate testing for the particular component. Judging only by the absolute numbers, the components that exceed the anticipated Defects/LOC criterion, namely A1 and A2, are possibly error-prone.

The error-prone components analysis utilizes other metrics: e.g., Test Cases/LOC (the number of test cases per line of code), the number of defects not covered by the planned test cases, the number of high severity defects reported, and the number of defects that should have been detected in previous phases. We feed the results back to all sub-teams. The sub-teams that are responsible for the error-prone components, sub-teams A and D in the example, have to discuss the situation and perform a qualitative analysis of the defects. The qualitative analysis method, the ODC method[5], suggests expected changes of the defect type distribution for each phase based on statistical project studies (Figure 4 left). If the defect type distribution for components A1, A2, or D is significantly different from the profile expected, it suggests that the responsible sub-team has done something inappropriate prior to that point, so that they have to prepare and execute an action plan. The right chart of Figure 4 suggests that the Function Test of the component A1 is not sufficient. The evaluation-action cycle continues until there are no suspicious areas.

When all prepared actions have been performed, the phase exit decision meeting is held by all sub-team leaders. All sub-team leaders have to present the results for their areas of responsibility to the other sub-team leaders. Starting with the evaluation results, they include in-depth analysis results prepared by the sub-teams, summarize the sub-teams' decisions and actions, and present their conclusions. If a sub-team leader did not complete the appropriate actions before the meeting, his or her team's output is rejected at the meeting. Therefore, all sub-team leaders are strongly motivated to complete all remedial actions on a timely basis.

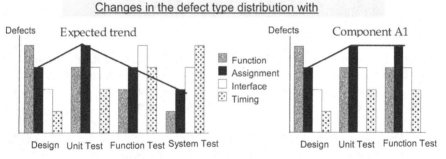

Fig. 4. An Example of Qualitative Analysis based on the ODC Method

2.3 Development Experience Repository

The experience repository consists of two parts.

The first part is used to track the status of all projects in our Laboratory. This part stores the project summary data such as the current development phase, the key dates, the manager's name, and the change history. The repository system sends a monthly update request notice to all project managers.

The second part is unique to our department, and is used as a knowledge database. This part stores the key project documents such as the final development plan with the actual results, the phase exit reports with their planned results and actual results for each phase, and the postmortem report, which is a treasure house of improvement ideas. These documents show who attended each design review, the time required for each design review, the number of test cases, the lines of code produced, person-months for each activity, the number of defects detected in each phase, the estimated number of defects after release, the changes in the defect type distribution for each phase, comments on the project process, and actions on the comments, etc., both planned and actual, concerning each phase.

The data in the repository helps new projects make planning commitments and estimates, such as schedules, the number of defects, the number of test cases, the program size, and person-months. The planned figures also become the exit criteria for each phase and also become one of the acceptance criteria for the results of the partner companies. The Defects/LOC in Figure 3 is an example used as an absolute criterion.

Basili et al.[1] performed data analysis through Understanding-Assessing/Refining-Packaging steps, mainly to evaluate new technologies such as the Cleanroom[11], or Ada/OOD (object oriented development), but they did not emphasize productivity improvement. We utilize the above data for productivity improvements, too, by doing task investigations. Every day, everyone recorded all of their activities and the hours spent, and we used these records for our research. For example, we optimized the number of attendees at group design reviews, developed auto-test execution tools, and reduced travel, etc. The resources of our research was much more limited, and we focused on hints and tips about data evaluation, like Landes el al.[9]. We also focused on In-process improvement.

2.4 Postmortem Meetings

As Humphrey wrote[7], engineers themselves know the parts of their processes that should be improved. On the basis of analysis of the postmortem data in the repository, we have introduced a competitive sub-team organization approach. We have received the following process change requests from the postmortem meetings, and have taken actions to implement them.

- During the team reassignments, the sub-team leader should stay in the original sub-team. (We now do this. Before that, we reassigned all team members.)
- A project database should be accessible by both companies. (We developed a Lotus Notes database to store defects.)
- When we adopt a new methodology, training should be provided for all members, and the team members need to be encouraged repeatedly by being reminded of the results and effectiveness during these projects.

3   Effectiveness

Our projects have consistently met our schedule commitments. The partner companies and IBM maintain good relationships and a sense of solidarity, because we all work as a single team. All sub-team members are motivated to accomplish their goals, because all sub-teams are competing on quality, and everyone has the chance to speak up at the postmortem meeting.

Figure 5 summarizes the trends of comments at the postmortem meetings. As described in the background, in 1991, we had to improve communications, relationships with the partner companies, and so on. In 1998, our areas of weakness had shifted to the development process. In 2000, most of the comments were related to project management, the environment (such as tools and test system configurations), and training. This means that we have been improving our process and solved the problems addressed, such as the comments that addressed communications. The dynamic member shuffling seemed to reduce the "communication" comments, and the team organization seemed to reduce the "relationship with a partner company" comments.

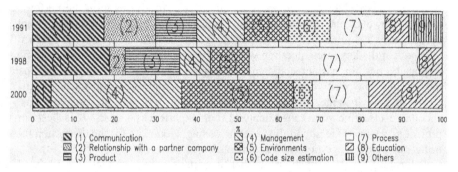

Fig. 5. Comments at Postmortem Meeting (Total)

All of our software products have been well accepted by the Japanese banking industry, the business area of these customers. The number of field defects reported within the last 24 months is less than two for each of these products, which is less than half of our previous defect level. The average testing effectiveness ratio in the U.S. is reported as approximately 80%[8], while our average is now 97.1%. This is because of the low ratio of undetected defects (the defect leak ratio) in each development phase. Figure 6 shows the defect leak ratio of the in-process phases. Most defects were detected within the same phase where they were produced. Historical data in our repository was useful for defining phase exit criteria.

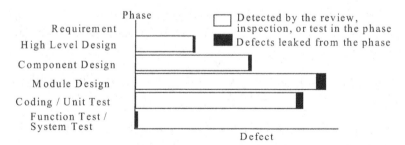

Fig. 6. Effectiveness Ratio of In-process Improvement

4 Lessons Learned

The cross-company team organization encouraged the teamwork of each pair (or group), and the fence or barrier between the partner companies and IBM has almost disappeared, as we hoped. On the other hand, double-checking sometimes makes the presenters slightly too relaxed. The presenters sometimes rely on the reviewers more than they should.

Competition among sub-teams creates a certain level of psychological tension for all project members, and the practice helps motivate all project members. The bug density often depends on the complexity of the function to be implemented, and the sub-team responsible for a complex module has a disadvantage in the performance ranking. However, the responsible members did not complain about this disadvantage, because they had pride that they were in charge of the difficult area of the product. We learned that the key to cooperation with a partner company is not a strict definition of responsibilities for partner companies, but good teamwork and employees' positive motivations. The positive motivations also helped to improve our products quality.

We believe postmortem meetings would work well for all organizations. To encourage effective root cause analysis, our experiences suggest it is best for the project manager not to attend this meeting. Using a template for the discussion themes brings out many suggestions and comments.

Fukuyama et al. said about another important aspect in their paper that "[An unsolved problem was how to] establish the security policy to protect private information disclosed on the Internet" [6]. As O'Hara and Ohba said in their paper, "Two groups that are to collaborate effectively may need to permit each to access data behind the other's corporate firewall."[10]. We also faced this problem. When we worked together with other IBM Laboratories in other countries, we sometimes faced difficulties such as different time zones, different languages, and distances. However they could be managed. But even if we trust our partner companies, we could not ignore the corporate security regulations, that "non-IBM people are not allowed to access IBM's internal network". To deal with the regulation, we set up a direct line between the companies, assigned a data entry clerk, or asked for help from the nearest IBM Laboratory, etc. We are waiting for highly trustworthy network technology to become more available.

The historical data in the experience repository enabled IBM to discuss the acceptance criteria with the partner company logically. We no longer quietly complain about the outputs form the partner companies, as was the situation in the early 90s. On the other hand, repository data maintenance was difficult. At first, each development manager had the responsibility for storing the data, but they often forget to do it. Therefore, the quality assurance group had the responsibility for gathering and maintaining the data.

On the basis of analysis of the repository data, we have developed the following rules, and most of them can be applied to all kinds of projects:
- One person alone, without impact on review quality, can do design reviews for simple macros. On the other hand, 4 or 5 persons have to participate in design reviews for shared modules.

- Defects/LOC can be a criterion for the design exit decision. We have analyzed the component history data, and found that components for which defects were thoroughly detected and removed during the design review contain a smaller number of defects to be detected in the test phases. On the basis of analysis of the data, we are convinced that we can use nn Defects/LOC metric as a criterion for the design exit decision and as one of the acceptance criteria for the partner companies. (The value of nn represents a constant based on our experiences.)

- Workload estimation based on the LOC metric is still valid for middleware software, whether it runs on mainframes or workstations. The high correlation coefficient, over 0.91, between Person-months and LOC supports this conclusion.

- As reported elsewhere[3][4], ODC was effective for in-process improvement. ODC has been well accepted by our product development staff and our partner companies since we introduced it in 1995, because it is easy to understand and reasonable. And we noticed the following points:

  - To ODC beginners, every defect looks like an assignment defect. Therefore ODC training is required.

  - Successive releases usually have very similar categorical defect ratios.

  - The ODC data of each organization helps the organization to perform more detailed defect analysis than the traditional ODC analysis. Correlation lines between defects in the Function Test and defects in the Product Verification Test were derived for each defect type from our practices, and the lines allow us to judge if we have or have not sufficiently detected each defect.

5 Summary and Plans for the Future

Our process history is summarized in Figure 7 on the following page.

We have been improving team operations and quality control processes, and have extended the scope from one project to the entire department.

In 2001, special task groups (such as the quality group, the project management group, the skills group, and the tools and reuse group) were established throughout our laboratory. Each group consists of experts selected from each department. For example, the quality group focuses on the process and project data sharing, common issue resolution, and partner company selection (assessment). Our focus for partner companies is shifting from "how to cooperate" to "with which company or country should we cooperate". An international search to find new partners has already started, considering cost, past records, and reputation.

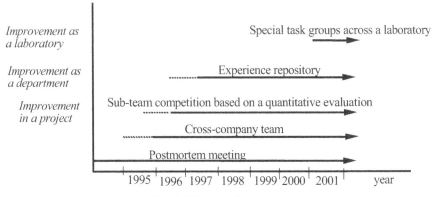

Fig. 7. History of our Innovation

References

1. Victor Basili et al.: The Software Engineering Laboratory–An Operational Software Experience Factory, 14th International Conference on Software Engineering (1992) 370-381
2. Kent Beck: Extreme Programming Explained-Embrace Change, Addison-Wesley Publishing Company (1999)
3. Inderpal Bhandari et al.: In-process improvement through defect data interpretation, IBM Systems Journal Vol. 33. No. 1 (1994) 182-214
4. M. Butcher et al.: Improving software testing via ODC: Three case studies, IBM Systems Journal Vol. 41. No. 1 (2002) 31-44
5. Ram Chillarege et al.: Orthogonal Defect Classification-A Concept for In-Process Measurements, IEEE Transaction on Software Engineering Vol. 18 (1992) 943-956
6. Shunichi Fukuyama, Mitsuru Ohba, Motomu Koumura and Wataru Kuno: An experiment on the procurement process for open and global software services on the Internet: Software CALS experiment in Japan, Sixth European Conference on Software Quality (1999) 45-55
7. Watts S. Humphrey: A Discipline for Software Engineering, Addison-Wesley Publishing Company (1995)
8. Caper Jones: Software Quality-Analysis and Guidelines for Success, International Thomson Publishing Inc. (1996)
9. D. Landes et al.: Organizational Learning and Experience Documentation in Industrial Software Projects, The 1st Interdisciplinary Workshop on Building, Maintaining, and Using Organizational Memories (1998) 47-63
10. Almerin O'Hara and Mitsuru Ohba: Quality throughout Collaboration and Competition, The Second World Congress for Software Quality (2000) 471-476
11. H. D. Mills et al.: Cleanroom Software Engineering, IEEE Software (1987) 19-25

Cooperate or Conquer?
A Danish Survey of the Customer-Supplier Relationship

Robert Olesen and Jørn Johansen

DELTA, Venlighedsvej 4, DK-2970 Hørsholm, Denmark
{ro,joj}@delta.dk

Abstract. In order to gain more information about the maturity of software customers, as well as the customer-supplier relationship in general, a Danish national survey was carried out by DELTA[1] and Ingeniøren[2] during the summer of 2001. The survey was based on a part of the BOOTSTRAP process model. It took the form of a self-assessment, allowing the calculation of maturity levels for individual processes for the respondents. The results show a lack of cooperation between customer and supplier as well as a comparatively low maturity of the customers. ISO 9001 certification was found to increase maturity, but in general the respondents' focus on work processes is quite low.

1 Introduction

Over the last years there have been several recent examples of large failed IT projects in Denmark. The suppliers often gets the majority of the blame for the problems; typically because they failed to deliver on time and/or delivered a product with serious quality problems.

The craft of software development is roughly 50 years old, and it is obvious that it has not matured yet. Many software suppliers still have much to learn. There are two parties to a software contract, however, the supplier and the customer.

Over the last decade, many software suppliers have responded to the different maturity models, e.g. CMM and BOOTSTRAP, and have embarked on a program to develop the way they produce software. DELTA has performed more than 50 BOOTSTRAP assessments over the last six years, mostly in Denmark. There exists a considerable amount of knowledge about the maturity of the software suppliers in general. However, very little knowledge exists on the maturity of customers.

There are a number of maturity models that can be used by software customers. For example, SA-CMM [1] and the PULSE project [2] are dedicated towards this area. SPICE [3] and BOOTSTRAP (www.bootstrap-institute.com) also contain several processes pertaining to this area. Very few customers are using these models

---

[1] DELTA Danish Electronics, Light & Acoustics is an independent, self-governing organisation emphasizing certification, consultancy and implementation of new technology.

[2] Ingeniøren is a Danish information communicator in the field of technology and natural science.

J. Kontio and R. Conradi (Eds.): ECSQ 2002, LNCS 2349, pp. 207–216, 2002.

and, as far as the authors are aware, no maturity assessments of software customers have yet been performed in Denmark.

This paper presents the results from a survey performed by DELTA in cooperation with the Danish magazine Ingeniøren. Previous experience suggests that customers tend to entrench themselves behind a barrier of legal issues while suppliers strive to protect their own business, resulting in a lack of cooperation. This is largely confirmed by the survey.

2   The Survey

The goal of this survey has been to map the maturity of software customers as well as of suppliers, and in particular their cooperation.

The survey was performed during the summer of 2001 by DELTA in co-operation with the Danish magazine Ingeniøren. An extensive questionnaire was sent to app. 1300 recipients (public institutions and private companies) in Denmark. The result is documented in a report [4] in Danish. A conference on the topic was planned, but it had to be cancelled because of lack of interest. This is in itself an interesting observation.

2.1   Method

BOOTSTRAP version 3.2 was chosen as a reference model, partly because DELTA has a great deal of experience with this maturity model, and partly because it has several processes covering the customer-supplier relationship.

A questionnaire was prepared, with questions covering 8 of the processes in the BOOTSTRAP process model. The questions and possible answers were formulated in such a way that the answer allowed the calculation of a maturity level for each process according to the algorithm used in BOOTSTRAP. The maturity level of the process was assessed through four questions for each process.

This questionnaire was sent to app. 1300 public institutions and private companies, and was in addition available on the internet.

The respondents in effect performed a self-assessment when answering the questionnaire. This was naturally not as accurate as a full assessment could be, or as a guided self-assessment, because most of the respondents can be assumed to have little knowledge of and experience with the concept of process maturity. The supplied information is still valuable, however. The answers from suppliers have been evaluated against a benchmark of actual assessments, as will be seen later.

It is important to note that this survey only asks for the respondents' opinion of their own work, not for their opinion of the performance of others.

In addition to the process evaluation, the questionnaire classified the respondents' institution/company according to type, size and role (customer or supplier) and they were asked if they had an ISO 9001 certificate and/or had been through a maturity assessment.

2.2   The Use of BOOTSTRAP

BOOTSTRAP is a licensed method, maintained by The BOOTSTRAP Institute.

The BOOTSTRAP Version 3.2 maturity model is SPICE compliant. BOOTSTRAP contains 42 process areas, slightly more than SPICE. Of these process areas, 8 were selected for this survey.

Table 1. The BOOTSTRAP processes included in the questionnaire

BOOTSTRAP Process	Answered by
CUS.1 Acquisition	Customers
CUS.2 Customer Need Management	Customers and Suppliers
CUS.3 Supply	Suppliers
CUS.4 Software Operation	Customers and Suppliers
CUS.5 Customer Support	Customers and Suppliers
ENG.9 Maintenance	Customers and Suppliers
MAN.4 Subcontractor Management	Customers and Suppliers
SUP.6 Joint Review	Customers and Suppliers

Table 1 lists the selected processes and who is expected to answer the questions for each process. Respondents only answered the questions for a process if their company had responsibility for performing the process.

More processes could have been selected, e.g. Project Management, but it was decided to keep the questionnaire at a reasonable size. Even with these 8 processes, it became quite large.

The questions to each process were formulated based on the definition of each process in BOOTSTRAP, i.e. the base practices of each process. Each question was related to the performance of a part of the process, and was rated on a scale from 1 (not or almost not performed) to 4 (fully or almost fully performed). The respondent was allowed to classify some of these activities as irrelevant and thus not rate them.

Table 2. BOOTSTRAP maturity criteria for level 2 and 3

Maturity level	Maturity Attribute	Criterion
2	Performance Management	Is the performance of the process planned and tracked?
	Work Product Management	Do the work products meet their quality requirements?
3	Process Definition	Are tailored versions of standardized process definitions used?
	Ressource Availability	Are all resources needed to perform the process available?

As BOOTSTRAP is a continuous maturity model, the maturity of the processes is measured independently of each other. Based on previous experience, it was assumed that the vast majority of the respondents would be at a maturity level lower than 4, so there was no need to ask for information about level 4 and 5. The maturity criteria for level 2 and 3 are listed in Table 2.

The questionnaire contained four questions for each process, designed to measure the conformance with the maturity criteria for level 2 and 3. Each of these was rated on the same scale as the other questions (1 to 4), but unlike the process questions they all had to be answered.

2.3 Response

80 replies were received. This is less than expected, but still enough to warrant a number of conclusions. The low rate of reply can be due to the size of the questionnaire, but may also express a lack of interest in process improvement among software customers.

2.4 Statistical Analysis

The analysis of the results involved performing a large number of statistical tests. All the performed tests were Chi-square tests for homogeneity of two or more distributions. These were typically distributions of the answers on the scale from 1 to 4, or of the maturity grouping shown in Table 3.

Table 3. Classification of process maturity results

Maturity level	Interpretation
< 1	The process is not performed fully
1	The process is performed and fulfils its purpose
2	The process and its products are managed
3+	The process is standardized and the necessary resources are available

In some cases averages have been used to visualize the results, because they convey the information in a simpler and more intuitive way, but the conclusions are in all cases based on homogeneity tests for the underlying distributions.

Even though the number of responses were less than expected, a number of differences with a significance level less than 0.001 could still be found. This level was chosen because of the number of tests carried out. All the differences reported here adhere to this significance level.

2.5 Benchmark

One third of the replies came from software suppliers. DELTA has performed more than 50 assessments of software suppliers, and thus a comparison could be made between the results obtained by professional assessments and the results obtained from this questionnaire.

The benchmark in Fig. 1 shows a clear difference in the distribution of the maturity. The BOOTSTRAP benchmark has a top at level 2, while the survey results show a bimodal distribution with a dip at level 2. This can probably be explained by the lack of professional qualification of the respondents regarding process maturity. It is easier to evaluate one's own company as either good or bad than as average.

It is worth noting that the averages of the two distributions are almost identical (1.95 for the survey and 2.02 for the benchmark). The average level of the replies is therefore satisfactory, even though the variation is greater than it should have been.

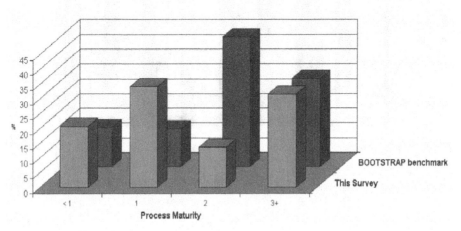

Fig. 1. Benchmark for private companies supplying software

3   Analysis

Based on this analysis of the results as well as the previous experience of the authors, the following major conclusions could be drawn.

3.1   Customers Are Less Mature than Suppliers

Roughly one third of the respondents were suppliers, and one third of the customers came from the public sector.

Fig. 2 shows the average maturity over all replies for the different processes, classified according to the role of the respondent. From this it can be seen that suppliers in general are rated as more mature than customers. The difference in maturity distribution is significant over all the processes.

There is also an indication in the survey that public customers are more mature than private customers, but this difference is only marginally significant (the significance level is 0.01).

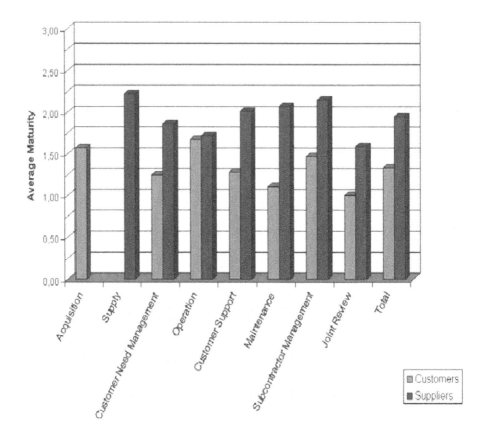

Fig. 2. Comparison between Customers and Suppliers

3.2 ISO Certification Increases Maturity

30% of the responding private companies are ISO 9001 certified.

Fig. 3 shows the maturity distributions with and without ISO certification. The two distributions are significantly different. ISO certification obviously does not guarantee high maturity, but the data show a clear tendency that ISO 9001 certification increases the maturity level.

The maturity attributes (see Table 2) are also affected by ISO 9001 certification. When comparing the score of the maturity attributes with and without ISO 9001 certification, there is a general tendency that the score is better with ISO 9001 certification, but only the scores for process definition and work product management are significantly higher. This is not surprising, as ISO certification emphasizes process definition and quality assurance and work product management, as it is defined in BOOTSTRAP, correlates heavily with quality assurance.

This observation matches DELTA's previous experience on this subject, see also [5].

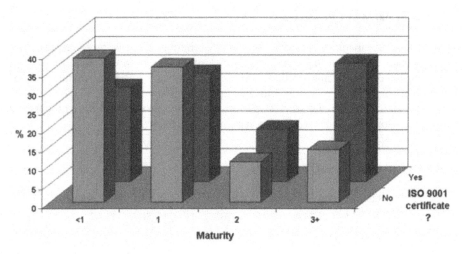

Fig. 3. The Effect of ISO 9001 Certification on Maturity Score

3.3 Lack of Cooperation

The two processes with the lowest maturity rating are those, of the selected processes, where BOOTSTRAP emphasizes cooperation most. The maturity distribution for these processes is shown in Fig. 4.

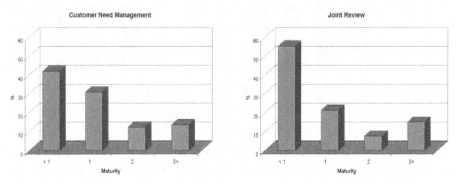

Fig. 4. Maturity distributions for Customer Need Management and Joint Review

In both cases, a large number of respondents do not fully perform the process.

In the case of Customer Need management, the problem mainly lies in establishing a baseline as well as in change management.

For Joint Review, all base practices have a very low performance rating, but the performance of joint assessments is, in particular, lacking. This is perhaps not surprising, as understanding of the need for such an activity typically increases with maturity.

3.4 Informal Work Processes

Of the four maturity criteria, Process Definition clearly received the lowest performance score on the scale used from 1 to 4. This is further exacerbated by the fact that those companies with an ISO 9001 certificate rated this maturity criterion relatively high, leaving the rest with a comparatively low score.

This indicates that the work is performed on the basis of informal processes and that consciousness about work processes in general is low.

3.5 Day-to-Day Work Has Priority

Fig. 5 shows the average maturity over all replies for the different processes.

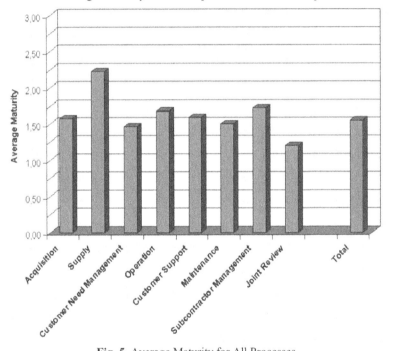

Fig. 5. Average Maturity for All Processes

The strong processes are those, which are needed to make the wheels turn, that is Supply and Operation as well as Customer Support and Maintenance, while the "extra" processes Customer Need Management and Joint Review score less. This indicates that day-to-day problems have priority over improvements and preventive actions.

The high score for Subcontractor Management does not quite match this pattern, and does not in fact correspond well with the experiences from assessments performed by DELTA.

4 Recommendations

Based on the authors past experiences and the results documented above, a number of recommendations can be made. The most important recommendations are listed below.

4.1 Improve Cooperation

Customers and suppliers should cooperate to a much higher degree. System development is in reality a joint venture and joint responsibility; it is not an off-the-shelf purchase, and it is typically characterized by changing requirements and a changing environment.

In terms of the BOOTSTRAP process model, the main focus should be on the Joint Review process, which will allow the two parties to align their experiences and expectations as the project unfolds. The project should have formalized meetings both at a managerial and technical level.

It is often advantageous to involve the customer in the project in order to ensure as early as possible that the product will fulfil the real needs of the customer (which are usually different from the needs perceived at the start of the project). Many iterative software development methods emphasize a high degree of customer involvement [6], but also in waterfall development reviews by the customer of e.g. prototypes can be used with effect.

The main hurdle is not the availability of methods, but rather the will to use them. That is the willingness of the customer to risk assuming responsibility for the end product and the willingness of the supplier to risk exposing his business to the customer.

Finally, a high degree of creativity is needed in order to facilitate cooperation when using public tenders.

4.2 Improve Customer Need Management

Arguments and accusations about mismanagement of requirements are typical when a project goes wrong. It is very important to strengthen this process, in particular to make sure that a baseline of requirements is created and that changes to this baseline are managed.

A well-defined baseline of requirements, approved and understood by both parties, will provide a sound basis for creating a quality product. And efficient change management with a clear delineation of responsibilities will help guide the product towards fulfilling the actual needs of the customer.

4.3 Increase Maturity

Last, but not least, the maturity of the customer-supplier related processes should be improved in general. There is in particular a need for an increased understanding of the value and use of process descriptions.

This is true for both customers and suppliers, but it is felt by the authors that the customers in particular may not have realized the full implications of the problem.

An increase in maturity can also be expected to increase the awareness about the need for cooperation.

5 Conclusion

A Danish national survey of the customer-supplier relationship was performed in the summer of 2001. The survey was based on parts of the BOOTSTRAP process model. The questionnaire took the form of a self-assessment and the results allowed calculation of maturity levels for the selected processes. 1300 questionnaires were distributed and 80 replies were received.

An analysis of the results shows mainly that customers were less mature than suppliers, that cooperation was lacking, that there was a general lack of process thinking and that day-to-day work had priority. It was also clear that ISO 9001 certification has a positive effect on the maturity level.

In order to overcome these problems, the authors recommend mainly that an effort is spent to increase maturity in this field and prioritize cooperation. This applies to both customers and suppliers.

There is a need to gather further information about the state of the customer-supplier relationship, as well as for making customers aware of the need for and the potential benefits of process improvement. One way of doing this could be to conduct an extended survey in the form of a series of small, focused professional assessments of software customers.

References

1   Cooper, J., Fisher, M: & Sherer, M.: *Software Acquisition Capability Maturity Model (SA-CMM) Version 1.02*, Technical Report CMU/SEI –99-TR-002.
2   Wang, Y: *A Recent Extension of ISP 15504 to IT Acquisition processes*, Proceedings of EUROSPI 2000, pp. 1-2 to 1-13.
3   ISO/IEC 15504 Information Technology. Software process Assessment Part 1-9, 1999.
4   J. Johansen & R. Olesen: *Analyse af Kunde-Leverandør Processen*, DELTA Report 265, October 2001
5   Johansen, J., Jonassen Hass, A. M. & Pries-Heje, J: *Taking the Temperature on Danish Software Quality.* pp 46-60 of Wieczorek, M. & Meyerhoff, D. (eds.): *Software Quality*, Springer-Verlag 2001, ISBN 3-540-41441-X
6   Korsaa, M., Olesen, R. & Vinter, O: *Iterative Software Development – A Practical View*, DF-16, Datateknisk Forum – available from the secretariat at DELTA

Introduction of the Software Configuration Management Team and Defect Tracking System for Global Distributed Development

Shinji Fukui

OMRON Corporation, Industrial Automation Company FA Systems Division Headquarters,
66 Matsumoto Mishima Shizuoka, Japan
shinji_fukui@omron.co.jp

Abstract. This article explains an experience of introducing a Software Configuration Management Team and Defect Tracking System for a global distributed development. A Software Configuration Management Team was set up at one site and included the responsibility of representing the other site for defect fixing prioritization. The Defect Tracking System could include descriptions in both English and Japanese and could replicate the contents between the two sites. The Software Configuration Management Team monitored metrics and identified the fundamental communication problems between the two sites, and improved the system to solve the problems. As a result of this, the ratio of the number of newly introduced defects by modification for defect removal was reduced to one-third of the ratio at the starting point of testing.

1 Introduction

OMRON Corporation, for which the author is employed, has five development centers in the world; the headquarters (Japan) and four overseas sites. Recently, global development is increasing especially for application software. We also decided to develop a global product to be sold all over the world which required global distributed development in collaboration with the headquarters and a development center in Europe. The size of the software was about 1 MLOC.

In global distributed development, project management becomes more difficult compared with domestic projects due to communication problems between the two sites. The precedent for this global project management was shown in the Global Software Development: Managing Virtual Teams and Environment [1]. In this project, we introduced a Software Configuration Management Team and a Defect Tracking System in order to enhance the Software Configuration Management (SCM) which is the key item for project management. We also continuously improved the SCM System during the project by monitoring and analyzing metrics. These efforts made it possible for us to overcome the fundamental communication problems and reduce the ratio of the number of newly introduced defects resulting from modification for defect removal to one-third of the ratio at the starting point of the testing.

J. Kontio and R. Conradi (Eds.): ECSQ 2002, LNCS 2349, pp. 217–225, 2002.

This article discusses what the fundamental communication problems were in defect tracking for global distributed development, and how the SCM team solved the problems.

2 Background

2.1 Project Organization

Fig. 1. shows the Project Organization Chart of this development project. The headquarters (Japan) and the development center in Europe were respectively positioned as Customer and Supplier. The relationship between Customer and Supplier is set by the ISO/IEC 12207 [2]. The Customer (Japan) took charge of Marketing, Requirement Specifications and Acceptance Testing, and the Supplier (Development center in Europe) took charge of Design, Implementation and Testing in this development.

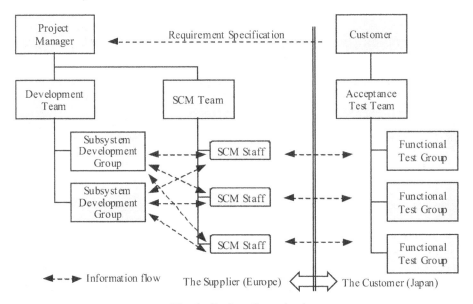

Fig. 1. Project Organization

2.2 Project Challenges

Since the Supplier had a lot of experience of similar size projects, there was no problem between the Customer and the Supplier regarding functional, performance, operability, schedule and cost requirement in this project. Therefore, both the Customer and the Supplier focussed on the following quality requirements at the requirement discussion and the acceptance of the product:

- Clear definition of the quality requirements based on ISO 9126 [3] in the Requirement Specification Document
- Sufficient Acceptance Testing schedule in the Project Plan
- Assignment of testing engineers experienced in global application development to the Acceptance Testing task

Considering the development size of the target system, one thousand or more defect reports were expected in the Acceptance Testing, including improvement suggestion and duplicated reports. Therefore, the project challenges were how to communicate accurately and quickly between the Customer (in Japan) and the Supplier (in Europe) in terms of defect information and how to track the modifications resulting from the defects at the both site.

3 Introduction of SCM and Its Results

3.1 SCM Team

In order to solve the communication issues, delegates from the Customer were assigned to the SCM team, which was located at the Supplier's site. SCM detail is set by the IEEE Std. 828 [4] and IEEE Std. 1042 [5]. For this project, in the project organization chart of Fig. 1, the persons in charge of SCM were assigned per function so that communication between Europe and Japan could be as simple and easy as possible.

The responsibilities of the Software Configuration Management Team were as follows:

- Development and maintenance of the defect tracking system
- Inspection and review of items in the defect tracking system
- Coordination of the prioritization of defect fixing
- Release of modified software and tracking of verification of modification results

For smooth introduction of the SCM team, an SCM plan document was prepared based on IEEE Std. 828 [3] and the activities were started after review by the Project Manager and Group Leaders.

3.2 Defect Tracking System

In this project, a commercial database software package was used to develop a new defect tracking system. Besides the basic functions of the conventional defect tracking system, all the fields were modified so that both Japanese and English descriptions could be contained and a new field was added for the translation status so that the translator could control the translation status. Database replication was used via the company Intranet for sharing information between Europe and Japan.

3.3 Results after the Introduction of SCM

Fig. 2. shows the ratio of the time duration from finding a defect to reporting it to the Subsystem Development Group. More than 80% of defects were reported to the developers within 10 days of being found. In this 10 days, the checking and translation of a defect report was done and the information was sent from Japan to Europe by the Acceptance Testing Team, the contents are checked by the SCM team, and the priority order decided by the Development Team with coordination of SCM team. The other 20% of defects were lower priority and had unclear points in the reports, so it took time for communication between the SCM team and the Acceptance Testing team.

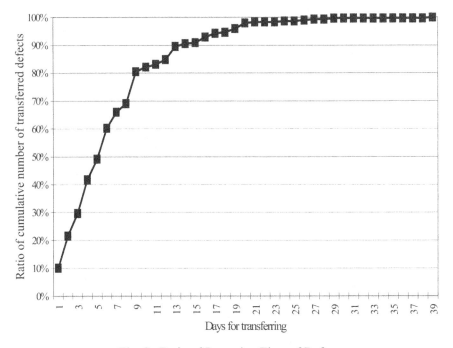

Fig. 2. Ratio of Reporting Time of Defects

4   Improvement of SCM and Its Results

4.1   Metrics Collection

Metrics on Software problems and Defects was reported by the CMU/SEI-92-TR-22 [6]. In this project, the SCM team collected and analyzed the following metrics to monitor the problems in the Acceptance Testing phase. The name, type, and definition of each metric were newly provided for this project. Data was collected and analyzed every other week, when the software of a modified version was released.

- Masking Defect Rate
  Purpose: To check that the order of defect fixing has been correctly prioritized and informed, and that the defects have then been modified according to the specified priority order
  Formula: The number of masking defects / The number of found defects * 100 (%)
  Definition: The ratio of the defects which cause partial malfunction that masks more than ten test cases, among the found defects
- Modification-failed Defect Rate
  Purpose: To check that the contents of a defect report have been correctly informed and the software has been correctly modified
  Formula: The number of modification-failed defects / The number of modified defects * 100 (%)
  Definition: The ratio of the defects that have a partial or entire error in modification within the defect report, among the modified defects
- Secondary Defect Rate
  Purpose: To check that the contents of a defect report have been correctly informed and the software has been correctly modified according to the contents
                 To check that the modification description has been correctly informed and the scope influenced by the modification has been tested.
  Formula: The number of secondary defects / The number of modified defects X 100 (%)
  Definition: The ratio of the defects newly introduced by modification for other defect removal, among the modified defects

4.2 Problem Analysis

As a result of checking the tendency of these metrics after a quarter of the Acceptance Testing had ended, the Masking Defect Rate decreased as expected, and it turned out that the decision and communication of the priority order of defect fixing had made good progress.

However, the Modification-failed Defect Rate and Secondary Defect Rate were still high and some problems were expected. Also, talking with the development team and testing team, the SCM team felt there was a credibility gap rising between the two teams. For instance, the development team felt the test contents were over ramified, and the testing team complained that defects had not been modified at stated in a newly released version.

As a result of analysis by the SCM team, the following two causes were identified:

(1) Insufficient Information for Analysis of the Scope of the Defect
Since defect fixing is an instance of software change, it is necessary to sufficiently analyze the scope influenced by the changes. In this project, the development team was in charge of this analysis, however, because of insufficient information from the

testers, the analysis was incorrect for some defects. Table 1. shows the information that needed to be provided from the testers to the developers, in addition to information such as "defect symptom" and "steps to reproduce" that had been described in the defect reports so far.

Table 1. Information Necessary for the Analysis of Influenced Scope

Information	Reason for Necessity
Function / use-case Running incorrectly	− To identify the cause of a defect − To identify all causes if many
Function / use-case Running correctly	− To verify that the identified cause is correct − To decide the method of software change that does not affect the correct functions

In domestic development within Japan, testers and developers were in the same location and this type of information was communicated informally. Therefore the problems rarely came to the surface. On the other hand, in the global distributed development, it was important to make a formal process to ensure that the testers needed to provide the necessary information for analyzing the influenced scope.

(2) Decline in the Sense of 'Teamwork'

The credibility gap between the developers and testers rose because of misunderstanding, for instance, the developers considered the quality and volume of defects were not so serious in the early stage of the acceptance testing, or they lacked the information for analyzing the influenced scope as mentioned previously. However, the cause was the decline of the sense of working as a team on the same project.

In a global distributed development project, compared to a domestic development project, the system to be developed is for end-users all over the world, so it takes time to get information into the project from the end-users and the interactive conversation within the project is limited. These information gaps decreased the consciousness of satisfying requirements from end-users, which was the final aim of the project, and decreased a sense of belonging to the same project team.

4.3 System Improvement

As counter-measures, the SCM team improved the System as follows.
(1) Analysis of Influenced Scope

A new responsibility that the tester should provide the information in Table 1. above was formally added to the SCM plan.
(2) Addition of User's Viewpoint

The end-users' viewpoints were added to the defect tracking system per defect so that the information distance between the end-users and the developers could be shortened. To be more specific, besides the existing "Defect Symptom" and "Steps to Reproduce", "Issue for the User" was added to describe the end-user's problems that a defect would cause. It describes operations disabled by a defect in the use case of an end-user's system and how the system use become difficult as a result.

(3) Improvement of the Defect Tracking System
The defect tracking system was improved to include (1) and (2) above. The class diagram of Fig. 3. shows the relationship between Viewpoint, Project Information and Defect Report. Not only the point of view from the requirement specification sheet but also that from end-users, which is the background of the requirement specification sheet, was added to each defect report. It did not bring a defect report to a close as merely a software problem indication, but expanded a defect report to a communication tool for discussing the end-user's profile such as level or background.

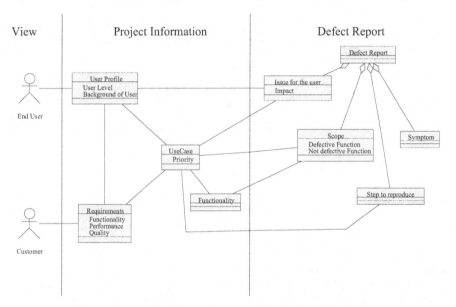

Fig. 3. Class Diagram of Improved Defect Tracking System

(4) Review by SCM Team
    The SCM team in turn reviewed the contents of the newly mentioned "Analysis of influenced scope" and "Issue for the User" and provided the feedback after listening to the opinions from both testers and developers to make the descriptions appropriate.

4.4 Improvement Results

The testers' information on the analysis of the influenced range was very valuable and useful to the developers. Moreover, the information on issues for the user had been adequately discussed at the time of requirement analysis and the result was described in the requirement specification document or use-case document, but the discussion itself had not always been recorded. So the testers reviewed the use-case per defect, and the developers were able to fully realize the use-case mentioned in each defect report when executing defect fixing. These methods were very effective in shortening the information gap between the project team and the end-users.

As a result of these improvements, a sense of 'Teamwork' increased again, and also the ratio of modification-failed defects and the ratio of secondary defects decreased as originally expected. Fig. 4. shows changes of each metric over time.

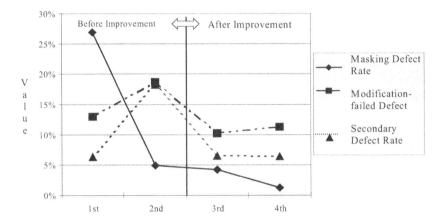

Fig. 4. Transition of Management Metrics

5 Conclusion

I evaluate these activities as successful on the bases of the metrics.

And also, the results of this project "Tester's participation in analysis of influenced scope" and "Addition of user's issues to defect reports" are adaptable and effective to non-distributed development as well as global distributed environment. In particular I believe that "Issues for the User" holds promise of future expansion as a technology for guiding a project to the user's side in the early stage, by applying it to the project analysis and design phase such as review of a Requirement Specification and use-cases and by forming it into a database.

Moreover, needless to say, clear documentation of the commitment (responsibility) of each team in a project is important since direct communication is difficult due to the time and language differences in the global distributed development environment. However, in the limited information environment, a minor misunderstanding easily destroys the relationship of trust within a project and de-motivates the project team. In the project reported in this article, the role of the SCM team as coordinator between developers and testers was very important in solving these problems. About 10% of the entire manpower were assigned to the SCM team in this project, and in my opinion, it was consequently the best allocation.

References

1. Dale Walter Karolak, Global Software Development: Managing Virtual Team and Environment, IEEE Computer Society Press, 1998
2. ISO/IEC 12207-1998: Information technology -- Software life cycle processes

3. ISO 9126: "Software product evaluation - Quality characteristics and guideline for their use", ISO/IEC 9126-1:2001, Software Engineering - Product quality - Part 1:Quality Model
4. IEEE Std.828-1998: IEEE Software Standard for Software Configuration Management Plans
5. IEEE Std.1042-1987: IEEE Guide to Software Configuration Management
6. William A. Florac, Software Quality Measurement: A Framework for Counting Problems and Defects, Technical Report CMU/SEI-92-TR-22

Software Development Bug Tracking:
"Tool Isn't User Friendly"
or "User Isn't Process Friendly"

Leah Goldin[1] and Lilach Rochell[2]

[1] Jerusalem College of Engineering, Software Engineering, P.O.B 3566,
91035 Jerusalem, Israel
L_goldin@computer.org
[2] NICE Systems Ltd., CEM, P.O.B 690,
43107 Ra'anana, Israel
Lilach.rochell@nice.com

Abstract. In this article we describe the implementation of software development bug tracking via WebPT/Continuus, in a development organization of about 200 developers, testers and managers of various ranks. We emphasize the interplay of technology, procedures and human nature, and describe our experiences and lessons on how this interplay affects the continuous quality improvement process. Often times, the implementer hears complaints about the tool not being user-friendly. In some cases, the implementer – committed to the tool – will perceive this as a case of a user being not process-friendly. Both responses may have a high emotional content. Who is right?

1 Introduction

Today's improvement of software development processes is heavily dependent on supporting CASE tools, which contain the knowledge about the developed products along with process knowledge used to track and verify the process itself. The commercial of-the-shelf (COTS) tools are usually customized to fit the local environment and process. Such customization includes modifying statuses, per-missions, etc.

By using the implemented tools for Bug Tracking (BT); the software development team reflects the realities of its processes and products into the tool content. The tool's users, therefore, are a key factor in successful process implementation. This is yet another special case of the truism that quality derives from the human factor.

1.1 Scope

About two years ago, the company decided to strive for development process improvement, and set a goal of achieving CMM level 2 [1]. Specifically, software

J. Kontio and R. Conradi (Eds.): ECSQ 2002, LNCS 2349, pp. 226–235, 2002.

development BT was the first initiative as part of the organizational Software Configuration Management process (SCM). Among other things, this was called for by the increasing size of the R&D department (about 250 people); and increasing complexity of product releases caused by combination of generic and customer specific versions. Continuus + WebPT [2] tools were purchased to support the company's SCM process along with BT, and a CM Manager was hired.

1.2 Motivation

The importance of BT is obvious. Once a software product is released to customers, all organizations adhere to some process of managing customers problems for the ultimate purpose of customer satisfaction.

However, it is more challenging to start tracking bugs during the software development phases, since Software Engineers are not so cooperative in tracking down their faults. It threatens both their creativity and professional ego.

The company is a product-based company, meaning that it produces modular qualified products that are sold to different customers with different needs assembled as different solutions. Since the products are generic, and declared as general available – GA, a great emphasis is given to their quality. Thus, Intensive testing and controlled BT come into play starting at the early software development phases, much before the product is released as GA.

1.3 Brief Review of Bug Tracking Methods and Tools

Bug reporting and tracking is an integral process in software development and maintenance. When performed correctly, it facilitates follow-up to completion of all software corrections, and accurate reporting on the status of the software product quality

A software bug or defect report is a perceived problem with the software product. Each problem report must be evaluated to determine 1) if there is an underlying software defect, and if so, 2) if, how and when to correct that defect. There are a variety of commercial tools that support software BT process, including ClearQuest [3], WebPT [2], MetaQuest [4].

Early work reported on bug or defect tracking mainly focus on measuring defects and collecting defect statistics as a criterion for software quality. Many organizations want to have an estimation of the number of defects in software systems, before they are deployed, so the delivered quality and maintenance effort are predictable. Fenton and Neil [5] provide a critical review of the large literature and the state-of-the-art of the numerous software metrics and statistical models have been developed.

More recently, the software engineering community has been paying attention to the development process [1], and specifically the BT process as a driver of software process improvement [6]. Monterio et al [7] describe an empirical software engineering pilot project using a software defect reporting and tracking system SofTrack, that help software managers to better understand, control and ultimately improve the software process. Wohlin and Wesslen [8] present a study of software defect detection that provides valuable insight into software defect detection in relation to the Personal Software Process (PSP). The results are interesting both for the PSP, and for understanding software defect detection itself for the sake of improving the reliability of software. Thomas et al [9] advocates more research into the human side of software quality management. They draw together two separate threads of research: software quality management, and the motivation of software developers.

1.4 Outline of the Paper

Once the software development BT scope, motivation and review have been presented above, the rest of the paper describes the BT process that was chosen, and analyses experience gained from implementing both the BT process and tool.

Section 2 gives the definition of the company's BT process, including the life cycle flow and roles granting at each transition within the "bug's life". Section 3 describes the BT process establishment at the company. Section 4 considers the evaluation of the BT process improvement and progress in various dimensions, i.e., tool usage issues, role's granting complexity, organizational hierarchy involvement, etc. Section 5 analyses the success factors of the BT process implementation and improvement, i.e., organization expectation, managerial culture, accountability, etc. Section 6 provides results obtained from this BT process implementation along with some lessons learned. Finally Section 7 and 8 summarize and describe future work respectively.

2 Bug Tracking Process

2.1 Bug Tracking Flow – "A Bug's Life"

WebPT BT tool uses a role-based security system, in which transitions (promotion) of bugs are allowed according to a user's role. In a classic bug life cycle, a tester identifies a bug and reports it through WebPT (entered status). The Testing Team Leader (TL) verifies the bug, and transits it into an in_review status. It is important that the verifier is highly qualified for few reasons: bugs' 'quality of details and depth is increased, "false-alarm" bugs do not arrive to developers, and it promotes accumulating knowledge within the testing group.

The Development TL assigns the bug to one of the developers, and transits it to *assigned* status. Since the Development TL is the person responsible for planning and allocating tasks, and has a wide view of all factors, she is the one to allocate development resources for the bug fixing. Upon fixing the bug and unit-testing it, the developer transits the bug into a *resolved* status. After the original finder-tester re-tests the bug fix, to ensure its complete fix, the Testing TL brings the bug life to its end by transiting it to a *concluded* status.

Of course, many other routes are possible in a bug life, such as rejecting it, from various stages, marking it as duplicate of other bugs, sending it to re-work by the developer, or requesting re-considering its assignments, etc. (Figure 1).

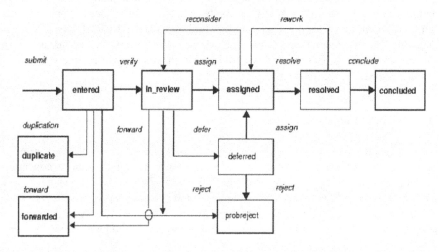

Fig. 1: Bug life cycle

2.2 Bug Tracking Roles Granting

The consideration of 'whom to grant which roles' raises two issues. First, it is subject to many group-specific variants and preferences. Crystallizing these decisions also raised many oppositions and disagreements within the group/teams involved. A second and interesting issue: Identifying clear ownership of bugs in certain statuses revealed situations in which managerial responsibilities of bugs were sometimes vague, ambiguous, or shared between two different position-holders (This will be further discussed later at the process improvement section).

We have tried to both fit the solution to the specific team while keeping 'correct' concepts and methods.

3 Bug Tracking Process Establishment

The definition of the company's BT process went through several stages, aiming towards minimizing resistance while achieving a full consensus.

First stage was setting a 'Testing Forum' that through brainstorming and discussion gathered preliminary requirement definitions of the desired BT process and tool. Second stage was "thinking" meetings of each group representatives, to identify specific R&D group needs prior to implementation. Last stage and most important, not to say vital to the process, was achieving a level of involvement from the relevant senior management (R&D VP & R&D Development Director). This also includes ensuring their commitment to implement the system in the R&D department.

4 Process Improvement

The most interesting observation of the BT tool implementation was to see the learning curve happening in real-time, both from tool and process views. The main issue was that this was the first Support tool introduced to R&D department for managing development bugs. Thus, the whole organization was taking a big step forward in the BT process visibility and decision-making. It was an interesting lesson to track progress stage by stage:

4.1 Technical Tool-Use Issues

In this stage we saw users' common learning issues, problems caused by misconception of the tool, or even more commonly, trying to impose conceptions developed using other tools, on Continuus/ WebPT. This is also the stage in which users reveal the most emotional antagonism. At the company, specifically, in this stage we had a major upgrade of Continuus software, which was a 'road-bump' in the adoption process. This kind of setback should be expected, and handled with patience.

4.2 Progression in the Horizontal Axis - Bug Status Transition

In this stage we saw the progression of the tool's penetration into the live texture of the working R&D department. People who at that time were involved in promoting bugs to their next status achieved the most progress.
1. After the 1/1/2000 deadline, in which bugs were treated only within Continuus/WebPT, the first roles that had to deal with the WebPT were the testers, who had to either gather all bugs (from isolated Excel sheets, for example) or accumulate all their knowledge of bugs into the WebPT records. After this stage was over (and we learned how to automate it), bugs were 'stacked' at the *entered* stage.
2. The Testing Team Leaders (TLs) had to first set a policy of verifying bugs and then learn how to do it technically with the WebPT. The bug verification activity was a totally new and was accompanied by some change resistance, mainly in groups with highest number of bugs (!), complaining that it is "time consuming". Those groups only later appreciated the benefit of the verification "filter" when it helped them to prevent "false alarm" bug from arriving to the developers and waste their time.
3. Similarly, Development TLs needed then to realize their mechanism of assigning bug's tasks (changes) to their staff, and then to learn how to do it via the WebPT tool (transition bugs into *assigned* status). They also needed to audit their ways of monitoring their staff's work, and use Continuus/WebPT.
4. Developers, then, needed to take responsibilities of their bug fixes by transiting bugs into *resolved* status. Developers had to get used to the fact that from now on, there is a 'stamp' of their name (and accountability) on each source change they make, or any bug transition.

5. Finally, the Testing group had to put the final stamp of bug fix approval by transition bugs into *concluded* status. Bugs were "stuck" in *resolved* state, meaning they were not transited to the *concluded* state, if they could not be reproduced. This raised another question concerning the development life cycle: Making sure bugs (and bug fixes) are reproducible.

4.3   Progression in the Vertical Axis - Hierarchal Organization

We could also identify progression in another dimension: the managerial responsibility hierarchy. At first, the quick learners were the 'production workers' (Developers and Testers), which were doing 'the real work', meaning reporting bugs, and producing them. They struggled with the tool, learned it, raised real questions of working policies with the tool, and suggested valuable directions.

Then, the managerial level, Development and Testing TLs, had to deal with the bug content via the WebPT tool reports. They learned to plan (according to bugs found) and supervise the work through the tool, evaluate its quality, re-plan work plans, etc. In their turn they also revealed other sides of the tools possibilities, like ease of use of certain actions, co-operability between teams, etc.

Group Managers were next in line to realize the tool place in their ~30 workers' group. They discovered the 'polling' concept of the tool; demanded more extended reports; sought for mails triggered automatically (like mail announcing all 'show stopper' bugs to all TLs, etc).

Other roles' holders, organization-wide, discovered their interests as well: Project Mangers learned to produce sophisticated reports of the release status and bugs overall behavior. The R&D Software Director found the tool useful in evaluating many things, from specific person's performance to inter group productivity comparison. The VP R&D could use Continuus/WebPT to have 'just-in-time' reports produced for him (using pre-defined queries on an intranet site, accessible from anywhere).

4.4   Progression in the Depth Axis – Emotionally Dealing with the Process

In the first stage of software BT implementation, can be characterized as the Euphoria Stage, everybody involved has a fantasy vision of how it can solve practically everything. Then, the tool merely reflects the reality, which is (in some areas) not so glamorous. Reality, that is, obviously, Bugs' situation, but also and even more important, reflects the decisions making mechanism and culture of what, when, by whom and how to fix a bug, for better and for worth. Some people slip into denial status. Others use it to improve the process.

As responsibilities vs. activities balance, (i.e. bug verification, work assignment, bug conclusion), becomes transparent, some groups tend to 'roll responsibility down', while others tend to centralize it. Perhaps, the best-fit solution is somewhere in the middle?

As 'tool-is-a-tool-is-a-tool', some groups tend to find creative solutions, which promote them into a more mature stage. Others complain about the tool: "till these flaws are fixed, this tool is unworkable". Other wonder: "How did we ever managed to work before?"

Even after a very successful initial implementation, improvement tends to arrive into a *stagnated stage*. Does the fact that our quality assurance isn't so sure is due to our process that need improvements, and the tool should be updated accordingly? Or, perhaps, is it because the QA system could be of a better quality? In other words, does the tool limit us, or our process maturity limits the tool usage?

Recognizing and being aware of this emotional factor, can substantially help the implementer to ease and resolve conflicts, and to provide more solid support to the people and the organization throughout the process of coping with the change.

5 Analysis and Discussion

5.1 Conciliating the Expectations of Company, Employee and Tools

When implementing a development process-supporting tool in a company, there is a need to walk on a thin line. On one side, there is a need to ease people's minds; to tell them that the tool's purpose is to serve them: To make their work easier, i.e., more automated, less error prone, and richer in functionalities. Additionally, the tool can and should match the company's way of doing things, and should be tailored to the company's policies, procedures, processes and temperament. On the other hand, and contradicting (or not), during implementation we suggested to people, to also examine all those factors, and if there's anything they have always wanted to change, or if they have a 'vision' – now is the time to try to implement it, as this is a chance for house cleanup and renewing.

5.2 Group Managerial Culture

Tool's implementers need to quickly identify different 'styles' of working groups, and to adjust the implementation itself to the group's 'culture'. Some groups are very hierarchal. Usually, there is one (very talented) contact person, who addresses all the issues; sets the guidelines, tests it and then pass the knowledge to the group. In this kind of group, implementation is slow but safe, easy, and invokes less resistance. The weakness, though, is that the solution reflects one person's way of dealing with problems and issues, which might be limited or biased.

On the other hand, other groups are more individualistic in spirit. Here, implementers will find all kinds of resistance/feedbacks from virtually everybody. In such a group, the result may be creative and sophisticated, but there will be numerous deadline-threating obstacles on the way, technical and emotional.

None-the-less, the organizational policy of assuring quality, requires all the R&D group to comply, even if it does not always fits their personal view. Thus, one should keep a delicate balance of fulfilling all the R&D Managers touch & feel "dreams" of bug management, while helping the R&D staff towards fruitful acceptance of the organization policy.

5.3 Accountability

Managing the BT via the tool exposed some real issues concerning accountability: identifying precisely whose bug it is, who is responsible for fixing it, and who is holding it, thus "causing" delay of the product release. The managerial visibility via WebPT tool support has sharpened accountability issues, which in turn assisted in improving the BT process (and the product quality).

In the past, before the WebPT, Testers were used to talk directly with the developers, "mentioning" the existence of a bug and "agreeing" to fix it. This way of managing bug fixes led to uncertainty in tracking the bug status, the actually fix of the bug, and amorphous planning and tracking of the R&D work for the next product release. Also, by implementing this structural tool, TLs had to assume responsibility both for planning the work and (by verifying it) to its quality.

5.4 Tool vs. Style

It is long known in music that there are two-way influences between the style's idioms and the instruments' evolution. Very briefly, the ideals of the current style had a great effect on the design and progression of the musical instruments. At the same time, instrument limitations or new technological improvements led to tremendous changes in the style's ideals. Making the implied analogy, we, as process change agents, can use this understating to strengthen the implementation progress. In the beginning, the current style of doing things will affect the desired design of the tool. We should be (and almost could not escape) obeying that. But in turn, the tool's technological functionality will eventually lead to change of concept in regard to the ways things should be done. This human-nature-pendulum does happen, and we might as well be aware of it and harness it to our aim.

6   Results and Lessons Learned

A year after the BT process and tool were used, significant quality improvement both in software and process was proved. Comparing version X of software that was released before the BT process was implemented, and version Y that was released a year after the controlled BT process and tool were used revealed the following data:

1. 'Known bugs' at release time were reduced by 60%!
2. 'Known bugs' severities profile has improved; 80% less 'Severe' bugs'.
3. The amount of bugs arrived from customers after release decreased by 50%.
4. Other lessons learned about quality factors were observed, but not measured:
5. Mangers benefited from the ability to monitor and follow up work plan and bug statuses, on 'real time' basis.

6. In order to be declared as 'concluded', bug fixes had had to be tested systematically on all operating systems, languages, configurations, etc.
7. Response time to customers' reported problem reduced significantly.
8. R&D department involvement in customers' bug situation, strengthen the relation between R&D personnel and customers.
9. Due to increased awareness of bugs, reported and approved bugs were 'copied' to future releases development streams, and therefore were reported, fixed and tested before products arrived to customers.

7 Summary

In this article, we try to present new angle of looking at the known fact– the human factor is #1, which delineates a triangle with the vertices held by Procedures, People, and Tools. Each side of the triangle represents a bi-directional interaction. Conflicts might be well disguised, i.e., People-Procedure sourced conflict may convincingly looks like a Tool-People disagreement, etc. Aware implementers might choose to solve the problem by a work around (such as technical solution to a Human-Procedure difficulty), but true identification might lead to better conflicts managing.

For example, if People-Tool friction is revealed, it might be wiser not to attempt to judge who is right, i.e., the tool or the human. If we are pre-supposing that the problem is in the People-Tools interaction, and is thus mainly technical- such a technical problem can be addressed either by improving the tools, or by training the users. However, this disagreement may not technical at all. In that case we'd really identify the problem on the People-Procedures interaction – what the user is actually saying, "the tool is forcing me to perform a procedure I do not like". If so, technical solutions might not fail, but one must realize that the problem is in the tougher realm of creating human-friendly processes and training process-friendly humans. The good news is that the tool has already delivered a major benefit in unearthing this conflict. Further good news: It's quite likely that the tool can effectively implement the solution, once found.

8 Future Work

Implementing the software development BT process via the WebPT tool in the software R&D department was a huge step forward, which enabled clear visibility of the software quality, and improved the planning and estimating the R&D maintenance effort internally.

Future work is planned to improve the interfaces of the software development BT to the other departments, such as Customer Services (CS) and Operations. CS have their own infrastructure for accumulating customer cases, i.e., problems, complaints, enhancements, etc. These customer cases have to be analyzed and mapped, many to many, to the software development BT process and repository. So, future work will focus on first defining the process interfaces between CS and R&D wrt problems and bugs management, and then integrate the relevant supporting tools. Operations department is responsible for installing and testing (ATP) the software before shipping the product to the customer. Thus, it identifies problems that have to be reported to the R&D department, no matter if the product is corrected before shipment or not. Again, future work will initially focus on defining the process interfaces between Operations and R&D wrt problems management, and then move to integrating relevant supporting tools.

Another work is planned to improve the fault analysis process, in order to help both CS and R&D to better identify the software problem source for each of the reported customer cases. This can tremendously improve the response to customer cases as to known software bugs, and enable more efficient bug fixes, which will provide better product quality.

References

1. Paulk M.C., Weber C.V, Garcia S.M., Chrissis M., Bush M.: Capability Maturity Model (CMM), CMU/SEI-93-TR-25, Carnegie Mellon University, Feb. 1993.
2. Continuus/CM: Problem tracking and Task Reference, PTTR-041-011, 1999
3. Rational: ClearQuest, http://www.rational.com/products/clearquest/index.jsp
4. MetaQuest : http://www.metaquest.com
5. Fenton, N.E., Neil, M.: A critique of software defect prediction models, IEEE Transactions on Software Engineering, Vol.25 Issue 5 (1999) 675 - 689
6. McConnell, S: Gauging software readiness with defect tracking, IEEE Software, Vol. 14 Issue 3 (1997) 136, 135
7. Monteiro, A., Almeida, A.B., Goulao, M., Abreu, F.B., Sousa, P.: A software defect report and tracking system in an intranet, The Third European Conference on Software Maintenance and Reengineering Proceedings, Amsterdam Netherlands (1999) 198 – 201
8. Wohlin, C., Wesslen, A.: Understanding software defect detection in the Personal Software Process, The Ninth International Symposium on Software Reliability Engineering Proceedings, 1998. Paderborn Germany (1998) 49 – 58
9. Thomas, S.A., Hurley, S.F., Barnes, D.J.: Looking for the human factors in software quality management, International Conference on Software Engineering: Education and Practice Proceedings (1996) 474 – 480

I-P-O/Multilateral Design Quality Evaluation Methods: Process Improvements and Effects

Nobuyuki Hashino, Satoshi Kurokawa, Mamoru Wakaki, and Junji Nakasone

NTT Comware Corporation, System Integration Headquarters, Sumitomo Fudosan Korakuen Bldg., 1-4-1 Koishikawa, Bunkyo-ku, Tokyo, Japan 112-0002

Abstract. The generally-used method of assuring design quality is to conduct quality evaluations when the process has been completed, to discover and solve any remaining problems.

However, the conventional evaluation method entails the following two problems: (1) Problems can be overlooked since the points covered by the evaluations aren't comprehensive, and (2) evaluations are conducted by the same designers that created the process, so lack objectivity and aren't done properly. To solve problem (1), we have proposed a comprehensive evaluation method that focuses on the design's input, process and output (I-P-O). To solve problem (2), we have proposed an evaluation method carried out from a multilateral, objective standpoint by using the designer of the process under evaluation as well as other employees. The use of these solutions has enabled us to discover problems early, and improve the work flow so that errors aren't conveyed to downstream processes.

1 Introduction

This paper has been written by members of NTT Comware Corporation, a company of 9,000 employees. NTT Comware spun off from NTT's System Development Operations Division in 1997, and continues to work mainly in system development and operations for NTT Group companies. (NTT is the largest communications carrier in Japan.) NTT Comware has a wealth of experience in areas such as small-scale client-server systems, mission-critical mainframe systems and telephone exchange software. This report has been written based on our experience developing a customer management/fee calculation system for the telecom industry.

The major characteristics of this project were: (1) the system was an ultra-large-scale system with multiple mailing lists, (2) development was relatively short-term (just over two years), and (3) the system included billing functions, so needed a high degree of reliability.

While NTT Comware had developed large-scale systems in the past, the project referred to in this report was the development of an ultra-large-scale system double the size of the largest system NTT Comware had ever developed (points (1) and (2)).

J. Kontio and R. Conradi (Eds.): ECSQ 2002, LNCS 2349, pp. 236–245, 2002.

Despite the large system size, development had to be completed in just over two years.

Although this demanding schedule entailed a risk we had never before undertaken, we achieved cutover on schedule. Various approaches were used in system development. To ensure the high reliability ultimately demanded (point (3)), we focused on the optimum use of quality evaluations to discover and solve problems in the upstream process of external design. This report discusses the problems with the conventional evaluation method, the evaluation methods we used, and the results achieved.

2   Importance of Assuring Quality in Upstream Processes

The cost required to correct software problems increases exponentially the further downstream the problems are discovered. Solving problems downstream requires redoing development. Extra processes are generated, and the proper number of processes can no longer be performed for the original development work. The result is a drop in the quality of the work, which in turn leads to a drop in the quality of the completed product.

When given a short development schedule, ultra-large-scale systems (such as the one referred to in this report) don't enable development work to be redone, so assuring quality in the upstream processes is the first step to successful system development.

3   Conventional Quality Evaluation Method and Its Problems

3.1   Conventional Quality Evaluation Method

In the conventional quality evaluation method, the blueprints created by the design work are reviewed during the upstream processes, and design errors are removed to increase quality. Quality evaluations are then performed based on the review records, to determine whether the quality has reached a level permitting the product to proceed to the next process. NTT Comware integrates all its accumulated expertise into these procedures to standardize the development process. Figure 1 summarizes the flow of the conventional quality assurance procedure.

The blueprint is created by carrying out the design work in line with the information input into the process (such as the design guidelines and required specifications).

1.   The created blueprint is reviewed, and review records are created (listing reviewer and date/time of review, along with information such as comments and error causes).

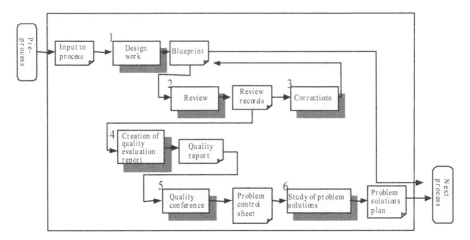

Fig. 1 Overall flow of conventional quality assurance work for upstream processes

2. The blueprint is corrected according to the review records. If needed, another review is carried out.
3. When all the reviews have been completed, the designers evaluate the quality based on the review records, and compile the results into a quality report. The evaluation must include the review time concentration (time spent on review per 100 pages) and error concentration (number of errors discovered per 100 pages). The rest of the evaluation is a free-form expression of the designers' opinion of the quality.
4. A quality conference is arranged by the quality control department. At this conference, the designers report on the status of the quality to the quality control staff, using the quality report. The quality control staff question and critique the reported information, and ask about items not reported. Any remaining problems uncovered by these questions are listed in the problem management sheet, and the quality control staff make the final determination of whether to proceed to the next process.
5. Methods of solving the problems are studied, and a solutions plan is created.

3.2   Problems with the Conventional Quality Evaluation Method

The conventional evaluation method has two problems. Each is discussed below.

3.2.1 Possibility of Overlooking Points Needing Evaluation

The conventional method only has two mandatory evaluation points: the review time concentration and the error concentration. These points don't enable a sufficient quality evaluation. Since no other standard evaluation points are specified, points may be left out of the report if its creator doesn't consider them or feels they might reflect badly on his work.

While the report is critiqued by its examiners and other participants in the evaluation process, these critiques are also not based on predetermined criteria. As a result, the points in the evaluation aren't comprehensive, and problems can be overlooked and sent on to downstream processes.

3.2.2 Lack of Objectivity (Bias of Report's Creator)

Since the creator of the evaluation report is the development group leader for the process under evaluation, there is psychological pressure to avoid making evaluations that might reflect poorly on himself. And even if the group leader conscientiously tries to make an unbiased evaluation, the evaluation can become skewed by the self-interest of other parties. The conventional evaluation method is therefore biased by the report's creator. It lacks objectivity and can often fail to properly evaluate quality.

4   Improvements Enabled by Our Quality Evaluation Methods

4.1   More Comprehensive Quality Evaluation Points

4.1.1 Comprehensive I-P-O Evaluation Method

Ideally, the information input into the design process is accurate, and any problems will be eliminated when the reviews of the design that was created using this information have been completed. Therefore, when all the reviews have been completed, the quality is assured. However, in actual practice, reviews aren't always complete. Information input into the design process may contain pre-existing problems carried over from upstream processes, reviewers lack sufficient competency, and there may be time constraints. To solve these problems, quality evaluations need to be redone, and the remaining problems discovered. The points that need to be included in these quality evaluations are discussed below.

Evaluations of overall process quality need to include evaluations of the accuracy of the input (I), process (P) and output (O). I includes the information contained in the documents needed to start the process, such as the required specifications or design policies. P includes the design work (the work of executing the process), the reviews, and the management work needed to proceed with the process. O is the product manufactured as the result of the process.

The importance of these points is discussed in [1] listed in the reference. We further broke down this framework of input, process and output, to re-examine the points that need to be covered by evaluations. We listed these points in our 'analysis/evaluation sheet,' summarized in Table 1 below. Our evaluations were carried out by filling out each item in this sheet.

Table 1. Analysis/Evaluation Sheet (Overview)

		Check point	Evaluation point
Input accuracy		Accuracy of design policies	Whether written in design policy, description
		Accuracy of objectives	Whether written in implementation objectives (achievement level), description
		System completeness	List of experienced workers, IT engineers (worker skill, checker skill)
			List of whether lists of information to share exist
			Descriptions of revision management procedures, spreadsheet, system, staff
		Finality of specifications	Whether list of requirements exists
			Descriptions of work processing volume and performance objectives
		Accuracy of design criteria	Whether design criteria exist, descriptions
Process accuracy	Design process accuracy	Method of carrying out design policies	How to familiarize members with design policies
		Method of carrying out objectives	Special implementation procedures
		System effectiveness	Items for study, study conference, participation in reviews
			Method of sharing information
		Method of finalizing specifications	Method of checking that specifications have been finalized
			Method of determining which specifications to implement
			Ways to prevent user misunderstandings
		Interface design accuracy	Method of discovering processing conditions
			Method of carrying out walk-throughs for major routes (comparisons, conferences)
		Database design accuracy	Method of extracting data items (procedures, systems, checking, standardization, non-standardization, data item definitions)
		Screen/spreadsheet design accuracy	Method of assuring consistency (special ways of assuring operation ease)
			Method of studying movement from screen to screen
	Review process accuracy	Review accuracy	Conference review performed after self-review (creating quality that can withstand review)
			Participation of needed reviewers
			Preliminary distribution/clarification of objectives /use of check lists/preliminary measures for review planning
			Method of assimilating points brought up in previous review
			Method of organizing points brought up in reviews
			Reviews focusing on degradation
			Method of evaluating performance (Model used? Basic numerical values?)
		Accuracy of error solutions	Completion check method (procedure, system, staff)
		Accuracy of error discovery/results analysis	Errors, causes, severity analysis
			Method of recognizing unrecoverable errors
			Method of recognizing error convergence
	Management accuracy	Completeness of assimilation of changes (in specifications/design)	Revision spreadsheet (staff approval, effect study/solutions/checking, method of tracking revision history)
		Problem/task management accuracy	Method of management from generation of problem/task to completion of solution
		Progress management accuracy	Method of progress of staff and team (Standard used?)☐
			Has the plan been completely assimilated in the last phase of the process?
			Has a catch-up diagram been proposed after analyzing the causes of lags in progress?
Output accuracy		Accuracy of descriptions in documentation	Whether design documentation exists
			Documentation descriptions
			Method of assuring description level accuracy (comparison to similar existing systems or previous descriptions, evaluation of description concentration)
			Major items covered by conventional evaluation method

Major items covered by conventional evaluation method

4.1.2   Evaluation of Effectiveness of Comprehensive I-P-O Evaluation Method

We surveyed the conventional evaluation reports used for the development of other systems to determine how many more evaluation points our comprehensive I-P-O evaluation method uses. We found that the number of evaluation items had increased by a factor of between 5 and 9 (increase in number of items = items in comprehensive I-P-O evaluation/items in conventional evaluation).

The use of a comprehensive evaluation with a predetermined set of evaluation points ensures that points that may be overlooked with the conventional method are evaluated, reducing the number of problems that can be missed.

4.2   Improvement in Quality Evaluation Objectivity

4.2.1 Objective (Multilateral) Evaluation Method

Objective evaluations require a third party other than the designer of the process under evaluation, but thought is required to make an appropriate selection. Since third parties not involved in the development of the system would require a considerable amount of time to understand the quality conditions, they were deemed unsuitable for reasons of efficiency and effectiveness. We therefore decided to use an evaluator involved in the development, but realized that using a single individual would skew the evaluation. We ultimately decided that the best option was to use multiple evaluators who were not entirely unrelated to the project, and whose involvement in it differed.

To evaluate the accuracy of the process input and output, we used pre-process workers involved in creating the information input to the process (B), along with workers on the next process who would receive the information output by the process (C). To evaluate the process itself, we used the process workers (D), since the designer of the process being evaluated would find it difficult to be unbiased.

Since subsystems are interrelated, the quality of the subsystem under evaluation can affect other related subsystems. In other words, related subsystems are continually affected by the quality of the subsystem under evaluation. We therefore deemed it necessary to add developers of other subsystems (E) as evaluators involved in other aspects of development. The flow of the evaluation is described below (see Figure 2).

Procedures through Quality Conference

1.   Using the analysis/evaluation sheet, the designer of the process under evaluation (A) gives a quality evaluation, and submits it to the quality control staff (F).
2.   When it has received analysis/evaluation sheet (a), the quality control staff (F) requests evaluations from the multilateral evaluators ((B) to (E)), using analysis/evaluation sheets (b) to (e). These evaluators note whether each item on their sheet is in agreement with the corresponding item on analysis/evaluation sheet (a). If an item is different, they confer in detail on the difference.

3. Before the quality conference is held, the quality control staff (F) lists each of the disputed evaluation items in analysis/evaluation sheets (a) through (e) on the multilateral evaluation differences sheet (f).

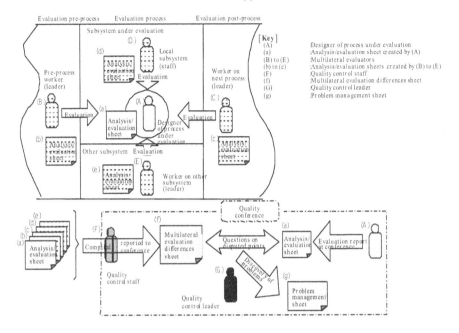

Fig. 1. Multilateral Evaluation Method

Steps Taken during Quality Conference

4. Based on the evaluation/analysis sheet (a) created by the designer of the process under evaluation (A), a quality evaluation report is created that covers each quality evaluation point. (This step is performed before the multilateral evaluation differences sheet (f) has been distributed.)

5. Questions on the evaluation of each point are answered to clarify the opinion of the designer of the process under evaluation (A) about the quality.

6. The multilateral evaluation differences sheet (f) is distributed to the conference members. Questions on points that differ from the opinion of the designer of the process under evaluation (A) (disputed points) are answered again to check that no quality problems exist.

7. In the steps above, opinions of poor quality are emphasized, to enable discovery of problems that can be added to the problem management sheet (g).

Step Taken after Quality Conference

8. Solutions to problems are studied, and a plan for solutions is created. The plan's implementation is followed up in the next process.

The points to note in Steps (1) to (8) are described below.

i.   In Step (6), the multilateral evaluators are not asked to give evaluations directly. Instead, they give a preliminary evaluation during the discussion in Step (2), to list the disputed points that will be brought to the conference. This method is used to avoid the psychological resistance that would occur at the conference if they were asked to voice different opinions to the designer of the process under evaluation (A).

ii. The discussion of Step (2) is held after checking the evaluation of the designer of the process under evaluation (A) (who carries out Step (1)), and determining the points to focus on. This procedure enables the discussion to focus on the important points, making it easy to clarify the disputed points.

iii. In Step (6), the disputed points are outlined on the multilateral evaluation differences sheet (f). The disputed points that were noted in Step (2) are given anonymously to enable the multilateral evaluators to give unbiased evaluations freely.

4.2.2 Evaluation of Effectiveness of Multilateral Evaluation Method

The true quality of a process becomes clear in the post-process. To evaluate the effectiveness of the multilateral evaluation method, we checked the next process (the internal design process) to determine the accuracy of the method's result for the external design process (see Figure A-1 in Appendix).

We examined the accuracy of the evaluations given by the designer of the process under evaluation (A) in comparison to those given by the multilateral evaluators (B) to (E). We found that for subsystems in which the evaluations were highly disputed (high rate of disputed points), the evaluations given by the multilateral evaluators (B) to (E) were more correct than those of the designer of the process under evaluation (A).

However, for subsystems with a low rate of disputed points, the multilateral evaluators had a slightly lower hit (accuracy) rate than the designer of the process under evaluation (A). We will continue to study this point in future.

4.3 Process Improvements
and Effects Created by Our Quality Evaluation Methods

As previously described, we used a set of comprehensive I-P-O evaluation items to conduct a multilateral objective evaluation of the finished process. Our evaluation methods were used to discover and clarify problems, and to enable solutions. They enabled problems to be discovered and corrected earlier. Table 2 gives an overview of the use of our evaluation methods for the external design process, and the solutions implemented in the internal design process.

The use of our evaluation methods significantly improved the development process. When applied to the example subsystems above, the methods were able to effectively clarify disputed points. The number of bugs they discovered was equal to 12% of the total number of bugs discovered in the internal design process and later processes. We were able to eliminate these errors in the internal design process. If the conventional evaluation method had been used, these 12% of the errors would have been passed along to downstream processes, increasing the cost of correction, interrupting the smooth flow of the development process, and ultimately endangering the project's success.

Table 2. Use of our quality evaluation methods to discover/solve problems

Evaluation item		Evaluations (multilateral evaluations) of ED process					Overall evaluation	Problem, solution
Category	Item	ED process designer	User	ID process designer	Staff of local subsystem	Staff of other subsystems		
Design input accuracy	Clarification of scope of functions, meeting user expectations	OK	NG Disputed	OK	NG Disputed	OK	Fail	Detailed specifications adjustments hadn't been discussed with user. □The specifications adjustment toward a created to date were ⊞reorganized, to clarify the undecided items. Items were ⊞formulated, planned and followed upon.
Accuracy of design's achievement level	Implementation of specifications in blueprint	OK	OK	NG Disputed	OK	OK	Fail	Didn't understand terminal operation. Description in documentation was vague. □Reviewed format of diagrams showing movement from ⊞screen to screen, removed vague descriptions.
	Management and assimilation of revisions in specifications/ design	OK	OK	NG Disputed	OK	OK	Fail	Many aspects of ED process design hadn't been implemented □Items that weren't implemented were discovered and plans ⊞for their assimilation were created.
	Designs (functions, interface, performance)	OK	OK	NG Disputed	OK	OK	Fail	Contradictions between TB1 elements existed due to vagueness of interrelationship. □Chart showing interrelationships of TB1 elements was ⊞improved. Interactions between terminal and host were unclear. □New dialog process diagram was defined, added.
	ED* review method	OK	NG Disputed	OK	OK	OK	Fail	User couldn't understand whether ED blueprint correctly reflected required specifications. □Matrix was created to link user requirements to the ⊞positions at which those requirements were implemented ⊞in the design, a service asked to give review again.
	Assimilation of schedule, coordination, transfer of responsibilities to ID** staff	NG	OK	OK	NG	OK	Fail	Some points hadn't been explained to ID process designer. □ED process designer repeated explanation of missing ⊞points, participated in ID review, provided follow-up
Design output accuracy	Descriptions in documentation	OK	OK	NG Disputed	OK	OK	Fail	Documentation was vlacking, couldn't read screen operations. □New dialog process diagram was defined, added.

*External design **Internal design

In this report, we focused on the upstream process of external design. But, our evaluation methods are available for the cases such as the information output by the process are received between the groups. For typical example in Japan, the group of the programming process are different from one of the testing process.

5   Tasks for the Future

As previously described, we succeeded in assuring the quality of upstream processes by using two new quality evaluation methods, one based on a comprehensive approach, the other on an objective approach. These methods helped us develop an ultra-large-scale system, and achieve cutover on schedule. The tasks remaining for future study are described below.

1. Earlier evaluation

Our quality evaluation methods evaluated quality and discovered problems after completion of the process. Solutions to problems were implemented in the next process. If problems can be discovered and solved earlier, the cost required for corrections can be further decreased. To this end, items related to input accuracy could be evaluated before the start of the process, and items related to process accuracy could be evaluated during the process.

2. Improving the hit rate

While our quality evaluation methods improved the hit rate, further improvement will require a study of the following points:

i. An even more comprehensive set of evaluation points needs to be created. Bugs created in upstream processes and discovered in downstream processes could be analyzed to discover points that hadn't been considered or thought necessary.

ii. We observed that in processes with few disputed points, our multilateral evaluation method didn't improve the hit rate, but actually decreased it. We would therefore like to gather more data on the use of the multilateral evaluation method, to clarify the conditions under which its use is effective.

References

1. Tom Glib, Dorothy Graham, "Software Inspection", Addison-Wesley, 1993
2. Mamoru Wakaki, "Daihyo Kigyo ni Okeru Software Test Case no Sekkei to Hyoka no Jissai: Hinshitsu no Tsukurikomi to Hyoka no Jissai" ('The Design and Evaluation of Software Test Cases at Representative Corporations: Quality Creation and Evaluation'); material from a seminar given by J-Techno Incorporated, 2001
3. Sumitaka Horiuchi, Yaku ni Tatsu Design Review ('Useful Design Reviews'), JUSE Press, 1992
4. Minoru Itakura, Super SE, JUSE Press, 1993

Appendix

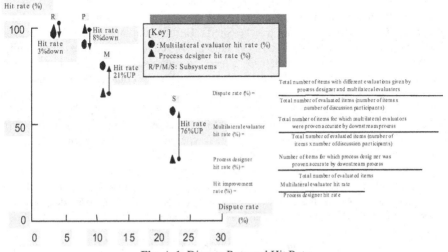

Fig. A-1. Dispute Rate and Hit Rate

Classifying COTS Products

Letizia Jaccheri and Marco Torchiano

Department of Computer and Information Science, Norwegian
University of Science and Technology, Trondheim Norway
{letizia,marco}@idi.ntnu.no

Abstract. Classes of COTS products can be derived by classification attributes, which define a Cartesian space. Examples of such attributes are the architectural level, the kind of the COTS product (is it a standard, or a service, or an executable component?), and the software life cycle phase in which the product is used (is it a development tool or an executable component?). COTS products belonging to the same class can be evaluated and compared by means of evaluation attributes, such as price or type of license. This work has been conceived mainly for learning purposes. Building a classification schema and filling it with products is a way for COTS product familiarization. In addition, the process of defining classes and filling them with COTS poses new research questions, like "why is this class empty?", or "which are the relationships between these two classes?". The result of classification and evaluation process cannot have general validity if it not customized for special organization goals. These customization issues are outside the scope of this work.

1 Introduction

The requirements for being on the market today can be summarized by three keywords: faster, better and cheaper. A key factor in this strive for faster-better-cheaper is the use of innovative software technologies and the related implementations, i.e. software products available on the market, often dubbed with the buzz-word COTS (Commercial-Off-The-Shelf). Before adopting a COTS product, an organization must learn about it, and evaluate it, particularly with reference to similar products. One way to facilitate the COTS learning process is that of classifying COTS into classes of similar items and to make comparisons in the context of each class.

The classification process gives a set of principles and themes, which may result in research issues for the field [3]. Our classification of COTS is intended to partition items into sets whose elements are comparable. Classes cannot be defined one time forever, but they are organization and goal specific. Classes can be defined by intuition, like the class of all DBMS, the class of all web browsers, etc..

Several works deal with classification of commercial products; either proposing taxonomies of application domain [3] or defining a set of attributes, which define a Cartesian space used to characterize COTS products [2][5]. Other works deal with the problem of evaluating and selecting COTS products using a set of attributes [1][4][6][7].

The idea underlying our work is that attributes can be divided into classification and evaluations ones. Some attributes are clearly classification ones. An example is

J. Kontio and R. Conradi (Eds.): ECSQ 2002, LNCS 2349, pp. 246–255, 2002.

the phase in which the CsOTS is used, which can be either during development or as a component of the final system. Other attributes are evaluation ones. Price is the typical attribute one wants to use to make comparisons about different COTS. On the other hand one could be interested in studying the category of COTS, within a given price class, thus making the price attribute a classification one.

This work has been conceived in the context of a fifth year course in software technology, which was run for first time at the Norwegian University of Science and Technology during the Autumn 2001. The goal of the course is to make the students reflect over how to learn, evaluate, and start to use software technology. Central in the course is a COTS classification and evaluation process. The process consists of several activities; the most important being Classification Attributes definition, COTS Classification, Evaluation Attributes definition, COTS Evaluation.

Apparently, a possible outcome of this work is a software technology database which records information about COTS and their relationships and which can be used during technology selection and evaluation. However, this is not the goal of our work. We are in fact skeptical about the general validity of such a database as technology changes too fast and the information contained in the database would be doomed to become soon obsolete. Moreover, to keep the database up to date requires a huge effort, which is not affordable for most organizations whose mission is different from that of developing and maintaining such kind of information (see for instance *www.ovum.com* as an example of organization, which has the main mission of providing and updating such information).

The process of investigating COTS product features in order to classify them is a useful activity. On one end it forces the classifier to look at products from an unusual point of view, which can uncover otherwise unnoticed features; on the other end it stimulate reflection on the results of the classification process, resulting in interesting research questions, like "why is this class empty?" or "which are the relationships between these two classes?".

This paper is mainly about the classification attributes definition phase. For more information about the whole process or the single phases, refer to [8]. The rest of the paper is organized as follows: section 2 elaborates the concept of classification attributes and proposes a set of three classification attributes. Section 3 reports about the process of assigning COTS items, to the classes and to evaluate such items. Section 4 analyze the relationships with related works. Section 5 is a preliminary evaluation of our work which has been performed in the context of a University undergraduate course. Conclusions are given in section 6.

2   Finding Classes

The first step in our proposal is the definition of the criteria for classifying COTS products. The approach we adopt is to define attributes that define a Cartesian space.

2.1   Classification Attributes

We identified three attributes that are useful in order to classify products: architectural level, artifact kind, and life-cycle phase. These attributes can be associated with orthogonal axes: architectural level, product kind, life-cycle phase. Thus a given COTS product can be characterized by means of three coordinates in the resulting Cartesian space.

These three attributes have to be regarded as three possible classification attributes and not as "the" classification attributes. Other interesting attributes, which can supplement or even substitute these three or can be found. For instance, the domain for which the COTS component is conceived, or its functionality, etc..

2.1.1   Architectural Level

Architectural issues concern both the top-level architectural pattern (or style) chosen for the system and the role the item plays in the architecture. Examples of top-level architectural patterns are: centralized, client-server, 2-tier, 3-tier, peer-to-peer, pipe and filter, and blackboard.

The possible values of the architectural level attribute consist of a pair composed of:
- an architectural pattern,
- a role defined in that pattern.

E.g. with the architectural pattern 3-tier, each COTS can play the role of either the client, server, or data.
- Examples of COTS for which the attribute architectural level assumes the value client are Html language, and the WEB browser Opera.
- Examples of COTS for which this attribute assumes the value server are: java servlet and Oracle application server.
- Examples of COTS having architectural level "data" are MySQL and Oracle DBMS.

2.1.2   Product Kind

COTS components deal with different kind of artifacts, not only with the software properly said. We say that the attribute "kind" of a COTS component can assume one of the following values:
- *executable* statements either in source or binary form, e.g. Java Compiler "javac" and Macromedia flash.
- *standard* publicly available and approved, e.g. the HTML specification.
- *service* provided by other through some network, for instance web-based development services (such as project hosting, version control, bug and issue tracking, project management, backups and archives, and communication and collaboration resources), e.g. SourceForge.net.

2.1.3   Life-Cycle Phase

Another distinction can be found when looking at when, during the life cycle of a system, a given COTS product is used. Each COTS product can be used during:
- *development* of the system, for instance Macromedia Flash,
- *execution* as a part of the running system, e.g. Opera and MySQL.

Table 1. Classification dimensions.

Attribute	Possible values		
Architectural Level	c (*client*)	s (*server*)	d (*data*)
Artifact Kind	e (*executable*)	st (*standard*)	sv (*service*)
Life-cycle Phase	d (*development*)	e (*execution*)	

2.2   Generating Classes

After deciding a set of attributes and their possible values, classes can be derived. This process leads to a number of classes (N_c), which can be calculated starting from the number of possible values along the three axes:

$$N_c = V_a \cdot V_k \cdot V_p . \qquad (1)$$

If we consider three attributes described above:

V_a : number of architectural combinations is equal to 3   (client, server, data);

V_k : number of possible kinds is equal to 3 (executable, standard, service);

V_p : number of phases is equal to 2 (development, execution).

Thus the number of possible classes $N_c = 18$. There can be items for which it is not possible to assign a given value to an attribute. In this case we can say that its value is not applicable. This would lead to a greater number of classes.

3   Classification and Evaluation

3.1   Classification

Once the classes have been defined, COTS products can be assigned to classes. To do that, for each COTS product, values must be assigned to the classification attributes.

It happens that it is not possible to assign a single value to an attribute. Consider for example the XML standard. XML can be used in every layer of the 3-tier architecture. Possible uses of XML include:

- data storage format or query language (XQuery) in the data layer
- distributed object communication format (SOAP) in the server layer
- presentation (XHTML) in the client layer

XML is not a COTS, but the SOAP standard (which is based on XML) is a classifiable COTS. Another possible solution, when an item leads to ambiguity, is to try splitting it into smaller items and classify them. E.g. for Java Run Time Environment (JRE), the question architecture level may lead to the answers "client" and "server". If we split the JRE up into components the client compiler is at client level and the beans component is at server level. Adopting this approach, the list of COTS to be evaluated may grow as new items obtained by splitting existing items are added.

For some COTS items, it is not possible to assign a unique value to a given classification attribute. For example a CASE development tool can be used to develop models at client, server, and data level. In this case we say that the attribute cannot be specified. When considering also the non-specified value, a greater number of classes arise. For simplicity reasons we choose not to generate a-priori classes for al combinations of attribute values that include the not-specified values, but we rather delay the creation of these classes when items belonging to them are found.

3.2   Evaluation

3.2.1   Attributes Definition

In addition to the classification above, each COTS product can be characterized by evaluation attributes. By help of these attributes and their values it will be possible to compare items belonging to the same class. While several of these attributes are common across the classes, some attributes are specific of a single class. Examples of common attributes are: price, market share, license type, compatibility issues, etc. Examples of attributes for DBMS are transaction speed, scalability issue, etc..

For each attribute, we must define its measurement scale, which can be: nominal, ordinal, ratio, and absolute. Examples of evaluation attributes, which can be applied to several classes, are presented in the following Table 2.

Table 2. Evaluation attributes.

Attribute	Scale
Acquisition cost	Ratio
Ownership cost	Ratio
Market size	Ratio
Market share	Ratio
License type	Nominal

The cost of a software product can be split into two parts: the cost of acquisition of the product or of its license and the cost derived from its support, maintenance, and setup.

The diffusion of a COTS product can be defined in terms of market size and market share. The market size is an absolute number representing the number of people that use items similar for the given one. For instance the market size for Internet Explorer (IE) is the number of user web browsers. Market share is the fraction of the market that uses the specific product. For instance the market share for Internet explorer is the number of user of Internet Explorer itself.

Another interesting attribute for evaluating a software product is the type of license under which it is sold, e.g. single user, open source, or GNU.

3.2.2   Assigning Values to Evaluation Attributes

The assignment of values to an attribute must respect the scale for that attribute. The operations on attributes must also respect scale constraints, e.g., while is it possible to assert that an item is better than another one with respect to its price, we will not able to assert any ordering based on the maturity attribute unless we change its scale.

4   Related Works

Glass et al. [3] survey taxonomies of application domains. They emphasize the confusion between problem-oriented criteria and solution-oriented ones. This distinction is somehow related to the distinction we propose between classification and evaluation attributes. Classification can be seen as a problem oriented operation, while evaluation deals with solution related issues.

Carney and Long [2] propose the classification of COTS products using a bi-dimensional cartesian space. In addition they reports some examples that populate this space. The dimensions they define are origin and modifiability. The origin dimension addresses the way the product is produced; ranging from products developed on purpose to commercial components with a large number of customers. The modification dimension describes to which extent the product either can or must be modified by the system developer that uses the component.

Morisio and Torchiano [5] propose a classification framework for COTS products. The purpose of their framework is twofold: first it is a tool to precisely define what is the meaning of COTS product, second it represents a way of specifying which sub-classes of products are addressed by a given work. The aim of their work is mainly classification. It is similar to the approach presented in this paper.

Boloix et al. [1] propose a framework for evaluating technology; it is based on metrics that address three perspectives (or dimensions): the project, the system and the environment. Each dimension encompasses three factors. In order to keep the process simple, only three ratings are used: basic, intermediate, and advanced.

One of the first approaches proposed for COTS selection is Off-The-Shelf Option (OTSO) [4]. Starting from a set of requirements specifying the system component, using the analytic hierarchy process approach, a decision taxonomy and a set of measures is defined to select the most suitable COTS component in a given requirements context.

The IusWare methodology [6] is based on the multi-criteria decision aid approach and consists of two main phases: design of an evaluation model and application of the model. The design phases can be broken into: identification of relevant actor, identification of evaluation type, definition of a hierarchy of attributes, definition of the measures, choice of an aggregation technique.

A recent approach based on metrics for COTS selection is COTS Acquisition Process (CAP) [7]. This process is made up of three parts: Initialization, Execution and Reuse. The first part deals with the acquisition process planning and its cost estimation. Second part provides guidance for performing the COTS assessment and taking the make-or-buy decision. The third part is responsible for storing all the information gathered for reuse in future COTS acquisition processes.

Provided suitable measurement and comparison criteria are defined, the evaluation attributes can be used for COTS selection purposes. In this phase one of the above methodologies can be adopted.

5   Experience

The initial assessment of our framework has been performed in a fifth year course in the field of Software Technology at Norwegian University of Science and Technology. In this section we concentrate about the use of our classification proposal in this course. Students were ask to perform two individual assignments, each lasting three weeks:

1. Assignment 1: students are asked to propose a list of COTS components; classify them according to the classes generated by the three attributes in section 2.1; propose a list of at least six evaluation attributes. Students can choose COTS components freely. As a starting point, a list of web sites was provided in [8].
2. Assignment 2: starting from a list of 18 evaluation students are asked to assign values to these attributes to four COTS components (assigned to each student by the teacher). The 18 evaluation attributes are designed by the teacher and other researchers.

At the end of the course there was a workshop during which students worked together with 12 panelists from research centers and universities, 10 being local and two being foreigners.

There were 34 students that participated to the project. Each of them proposed a variable number of products, ranging from a minimum of 4 to a maximum of 36. A total of 162 different products were suggested.

Table 3 shows the main results of the classification process. The classes that got the most numbers of items were: server-side languages (s, st, e) (23 items), client development tools (c, e, d) (19 items), client execution engines (c, e, e) (19 items), client-side languages (c, st, e) (14 items), server-side engines (s, e, e) (9 items), DBMS (d, e, e) (10 items).

Several items could not be fully classified. In particular 57 items get not applicable on the architectural level attribute, 3 get not applicable on the artifact kind attribute, and 6 items get not applicable on the life-cycle phase attribute.

Fig. 1 shows the frequency of occurrence of the 18 classes during the classification of the COTS products. The 6 classes collected 90% of items while the remaining 10% was scattered across other 7 classes, which accounted each for a percentage of items ranging from 1% to 3%. Finally 5 classes remained empty, they are (s, sv, e); (s, sv, d); (c, sv, d); (d, e, d); (d, sv, d).

Focusing the attention on the empty classes, we can observe that four of them have the "sv" value for the artifact kind dimension. This may imply that there are few service products available on the marketplace, and thus there is a lack of products in a certain area of software technology, this is a suggestion for new commercial opportunities.

The discussions at the workshop confirmed our hypothesis that the process we followed is useful for COTS product familiarization and that this process may be extended by COTS product evaluation by prototyping. The panelists agreed about the fact that an evaluation database should be considered as a learning medium rather than a final contribution.

The main drawback that was highlighted during the workshop about our classification framework was the lack of concern about the domain. In a real world instantiation of the framework the application domain should be taken into account. In a cross-domain context it could appear directly as a dimension; in a more simple case it could appear indirectly by introducing a dimension that deals with the functionalities of the COTS products.

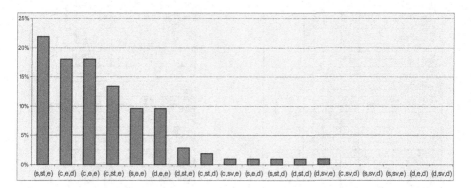

Fig. 1. Distribution of items

6   Conclusions

We have proposed a framework for COTS classification, which is based on a set of attributes. This paper proposes three attributes: kind, architectural, level, and phase. These three attributes must be regarded as an example of possible classification and not as the attributes for classification.

Classification attributes are different from evaluation attributes. Evaluation and comparison of COTS products can be performed on a homogeneous set of products, i.e. those that classification process put into the same class.

COTS classification is useful for several purposes. First, our classification attributes lead to classes, some of which denote well known classes of elements, like for example the class of all browser, while some other are empty classes. Empty classes lead to the research question "Why is this class empty?" A class may be empty because existing COTS have been forgotten or because there do not exist COTS with those characteristics on the market. If such COTS do not exist, an obvious reason may be that that class does not make sense. A more interesting reason may be that COTS like that have not been yet developed, and this may open for new research. One can for example ask: "Is the class of tools for development of server level standard not interesting?"

Other research questions may be generated by looking at the existing or not existing relationships between classes of COTS. Like, "are there any relationships between the COTS for client standard development and the COTS for server standard development?".

Table 3: Items and their classification.

COTS Product	Classification archi	kind	phase	Class Name	Size
CORBA	s	st	e		
Perl	s	st	e		
Java Language	s	st	e		
SMIL	s	st	e		
MS ASP	s	st	e		
Java Servlet	s	st	e		
Java Beans	s	st	e		
Java RMI	s	st	e		
Java Server Pages	s	st	e		
MS DCOM	s	st	e		
CGI	s	st	e		
CORBA IIOP spec.	s	st	e		
Java EJB	s	st	e		
SOAP	s	st	e		
Ada Language	s	st	e		
Java Connector	s	st	e		
Java Message Queue	s	st	e		
Java NDI	s	st	e		
Java SSE	s	st	e		
PHP	s	st	e		
RPC	s	st	e		
SSH	s	st	e		
XQL	s	st	e		23
Java IDL	s	st	d	(s, st, d)	1
Orion Application Server	s	e	e		
Oracle Application Server	s	e	e		
Sybase Adaptive Server	s	e	e		
IBM HTTP Server	s	e	e		
MacroMedia ColdFusion Srv.	s	e	e		
Apache HTTP server	s	e	e		
Jigsaw	s	e	e		
MS Biztalk server 2000	s	e	e		
MS Exchange 2000	s	e	e		
ORBacus	s	e	e		9
IBM Websphere	s	e	d	(s, e, d)	1
Jasmine asp	d	sv	e	(d, sv, e)	1
Java JDBC	d	st	e		
SQL 91	d	st	E		
MS ODBC	d	st	e	(d, st, e)	3
Clustra C++ API	d	st	d	(d, st, d)	1
IBM DB2	d	e	e		
Oracle DBMS	d	e	e		
Sybase DBMS	d	e	e		
MS SQL Server	d	e	e		
MS Access	d	e	e		
Borland Interbase DBMS	d	e	e		
Clustra DBMS	d	e	e		
MS project central db	d	e	e		
MySQL	d	e	e		
Sybase industry Warehouse	d	e	e		10
Yospace	c	sv	e	(c, sv, e)	1
HTML	c	st	e		
XHTML	c	st	e		
Java Applet	c	st	e		
Dynamic HTML	c	st	e		
WML	c	st	e		
CSS	c	st	e		
Java ME MIDP	c	st	e		
MS Pocket PC Jscript	c	st	e		
Java Phone	c	st	e		
JavaScript	c	st	e		
MacroMedia ColdFusion ML	c	st	e		
MathML	c	st	e		
WebTV	c	st	e		
XSLT	c	st	e		14
Java 3d	c	st	d		
MS Pocket PC PoketC	c	st	d	(c, st, d)	2
Winamp	c	e	e		
Opera	c	e	e		
MS Internet Explorer	c	e	e		
Lynx	c	e	e		
Fetch!	c	e	e		
MacroMedia Shockwave	c	e	e		
Neoplanet	c	e	e		
Java ME runtime	c	e	e		
Java Plugin	c	e	e		
Netscape Communicator	c	e	e		
MS Pocket PC IE	c	e	e		
Palm Reader	c	e	e		
Acobat Reader	c	e	e		
Java ME preverifier	c	e	e		
MS Media Player	c	e	e		
MS Pocket PC Media Player	c	e	e		
Open SSH	c	e	e		
Palm Multimail	c	e	e		
Shoutcast	c	e	e		19

COTS Product	archi	kind	phase	Name	Size
Paint Shop Pro 7.0	c	e	d		
MacroMedia Flash	c	e	d		
Amaya	c	e	d		
Macromedia Dreamweaver	c	e	d		
Macromedia Fireworks	c	e	d		
WAP Emperor	c	e	d		
WAP Pro	c	e	d		
Java ME compiler	c	e	d		
SmartPhone Emulator	c	e	d		
Macromedia homesite	c	e	d		
Java ME wl. Emulator	c	e	d		
MS emb. VC++ Emulator	c	e	d		
Code Warrior for Palm	c	e	d		
IBM perfect photo	c	e	d		
Java ME wl. Compiler	c	e	d		
MS Frontpage	c	e	d		
Netscape Composer	c	e	d		
Oracle think9i	c	e	d		
Palm Mobile iNet kit	c	e	d		19
AltaVista	-	sv	e	-,sv,e	1
Mobile Access	-	st	e		
C++	-	st	e		
Java Speech	-	st	e		
MS ActiveX	-	st	e		
XML DTD	-	st	e		5
UML	-	st	d		
Rational RUP	-	st	d		
XMI	-	st	d		3
XML	-	st	-		1
MS Excel	-	e	e		
MS Office	-	e	e		
MS Word	-	e	e		
MS Office XP	-	e	e		
MS Outlook	-	e	e		
Age of Empire	-	e	e		
Java HotSpot Runtime	-	e	e		
Java VM	-	e	e		
MasterBooter	-	e	e		
MS Powerpoint	-	e	e		
MS RegClean	-	e	e		
Oracle 8i	-	e	e		12
Rational Rose	-	e	d		
Argo UML	-	e	d		
MS Visual C++	-	e	d		
Java SDK	-	e	d		
Together Control Center	-	e	d		
Java Compiler	-	e	d		
Java ME SDK	-	e	d		
MS Visual Studio	-	e	d		
MS Visual Studio .NET	-	e	d		
MS emb. VC++ Compiler	-	e	d		
MS emb. VC++ Editor	-	e	d		
Rational Purify +	-	e	d		
Text Pad	-	e	d		
GNU Emacs	-	e	d		
IBM VisualAge	-	e	d		
Java Forte	-	e	d		
Java IDE	-	e	d		
Jbuilder	-	e	d		
Jedit	-	e	d		
MacroMedia ColdFusion Studio	-	e	d		
MS emb. Remote Spy++	-	e	d		
MS emb. VC++ RegEdit	-	e	d		
MS Sourcesafe	-	e	d		
MS Visio	-	e	d		
MS Visual FoxPro	-	e	d		
PowerBuilder	-	e	d		
Rational Apex	-	e	d		
Rational family	-	e	d		
Rational Requisite Pro	-	e	d		29
MS Windows	-	e	-		
IBM OS/2	-	e	-		
MS Windows XP	-	e	-	-,e,-	3
MS .NET	-	-	-		
Palm	-	-	-		
Oracle	-	-	-	-,-,-	3

Another interesting consequence of our work is to assess its validity for learning purposes both in academia and in industry. We believe that one gets a deep knowledge of COTS components by taking them in use. Another interesting question is "which is the relationship between a classification work like the one we propose and a learning program based on active use of COTS components for, for example, prototype development?".

Finally, to our knowledge, there is no work in the literature that either proposes the distinction of classification and evaluation attributes or emphasizes the benefits of classification for learning new technologies.

Further steps will be. First, for each of the available class, study the evaluation data and try to make comparisons, if possible, among the items of each class. This may lead to further evaluation steps to improve the quality of our evaluation data. Second, change the classification attributes, like making domain as a classification attributes. This will lead to different classes. For the new classes, comparisons among items in single classes will be made. Finally, we have to add several COTS components to our pool of components and eventually remove some items, or even classes of items if we discover that they cannot be regarded as COTS components.

References

1. Boloix, G., Robillard, P.N.: A software system evaluation framework. IEEE Computer, 28(10): 17–26, December 1995.
2. Carney, D., Long, F.: What Do You Mean by COTS? Finally a Useful Answer. IEEE Software, 17(2): 83-86, March/April 2000.
3. Glass, R., Vessey, I.: Contemporary Application Domain Taxonomies. IEEE Software, 12(4): 63–76 July 1995.
4. Kontio, J.: A Case Study in Applying a Systematic Method for COTS Selection. Proc. of IEEE-ACM 18th Int. Conf. on Software Engineering (ICSE), pp 201-209, Berlin, Germany, March 25-29, 1996.
5. Morisio, M., Torchiano, M.: Definition and Classification of COTS: a proposal. Proc. of International Conference on COTS Based Software Systems (ICCBBS), pp 165-175, Orlando (FL), February 4-6, 2002.
6. Morisio, M., Tsoukiàs, A.: IusWare: A methodology for the evaluation and selection of software products. IEE Proceedings Software Engineering, 144(3):162-174, June 1997.
7. Ochs, M.A.; Pfahl, D.; Chrobok-Diening, G.; Nothhelfer-Kolb, B.: A Method for Efficient Measurement-based COTS Assessment ad Selection – Method Description and Evaluation Results. Proc. IEEE 7th International Software Metrics Symposium, pp 285-296, London, England, 4-6 April 2001.
8. SIF80AT - A course in new software technologies, home page at http://www.idi.ntnu.no/emner/sif80at/

Understanding Software Component Markets: The Value Creation Perspective

Nina Helander[1], Pauliina Ulkuniemi[2], and Veikko Seppänen[3]

[1] Ph.D. Student, Project Researcher, University of Oulu, Finland
Nina.Helander@koti.tpo.fi
[2] Ph.D. Student, Assistant in Marketing, University of Oulu, Finland
Pauliina.Ulkuniemi@oulu.fi
[3] D.Tech, D.Econ, Professor, University of Oulu, Finland
Veikko.Seppanen@oulu.fi

Abstract. The purpose of this study is to analyse and create understanding of the emerging software component markets. The phenomenon is studied through the theoretical perspective of value creation in business relationships. Furthermore, the theoretical perspective is mirrored on empirical data that we have gathered during the last two years. In the end of the paper the possible development directions for software component markets are presented and the factors enabling this development discussed.

1 Introduction

Although the idea of large-scale reuse of standard software components was introduced as early as in the late sixties, rather little has happened during the past thirty years when it comes to systematic reuse of *commercial off-the-shelf (COTS) software components*. Intra-organisational software reuse has emerged during the nineties, but software component business in terms of recognisable markets including sellers, buyers and possible intermediaries, is still at its early stage of development. Apparent reasons behind the slow development are, for example, difficulties in defining the future-to-be roles of actors in the markets and problems in developing and managing interactions between software component sellers and buyers, in practice. Moreover, it is not obvious what kind of value is created in the interaction between component sellers, buyers and possible intermediaries.

Many software component acquisition projects have faced difficult contract negotiations between the interacting parties, and have been involved in problematic co-operation schemes after the purchase of software components. Parties have often had more or less differing views on, for example, pricing, liability, quality and future development needs related issues.

In other words, there seem to be quite many interaction problems to be solved in the road towards effectively functioning software component markets. We expect that some of the problems could possibly be overcome, if the value created by and for the interacting parties in business relationship was better understood and managed. The objective of the study described in this paper is therefore to develop a preliminary

J. Kontio and R. Conradi (Eds.): ECSQ 2002, LNCS 2349, pp. 256–266, 2002.

understanding of value creation in the context of the emerging software component markets, through theories on business relationships and value creation that have been addressed in industrial marketing and purchasing research.

This theoretical discussion is applied to the specific industry context of software components, which is studied based on empirical data that we have gathered during the last two years from companies operating in the software industry and in other industries where software is being used. The empirical material includes both secondary data gathered through Internet and primary data acquired in several interviews among professionals that represent potential software component sellers, buyers and intermediaries (see Table 1). The data gathering was done in a semi-structured way, so that only some basic themes for the interviews were prepared in advance. Most of the interview data was tape recorded and all the data was transcripted. This empirical material was then analysed by following the qualitative analysis method, including comparison of between the material gathered from suppliers and buyers. This provided a more thorough understanding of the research phenomenon.

Table 1. Illustration of the Empirical Material

	Component Buyer	Component Seller	Industry Professionals
Telecommunications industry	1 company, 20 interviews	2 companies, 3 interviews	7 interviews
Automation industry	9 companies 15 interviews	7 companies 7 interviews	3 interviews

2   The Software Component Business

In the field of software engineering, one of the most recent issues has been increasing interest in software components and on component-based software engineering [11]. A software component can be defined as a piece of reusable and independent computer program that is accessible through specified interfaces [e.g. 16]. Due to their reusable and independent nature, software components are expected to make software development more effective by offering not only cost and time savings, but also quality improvements.

It is also important to acknowledge that many software products can be seen as "large" components and platforms on which different applications are being built. The best-known examples of the latter include not only Windows and other operating systems, but also databases, communication protocols and user interface software packages. In this research we do not refer only to COTS software components, but also to MOTS (modified-off-the-shelf) components.

By COTS we mean standardised software components, without any or little modifications done for the customer, whereas MOTS components are modified for the customer either by the supplier or as in a co-operation (cf. the phrase Original Software Component Manufacturing, OCM) with the customer. In both cases, the business idea is to sell an explicit piece of software to several customers, not as an independent stand-alone application, but as a building block for such applications. However, customer-specific modifications of MOTS components may result in additional, even very large development costs to the seller or purchaser, compared to standard software pieces that can be sold at such a low cost that the supplier can gain considerable economies of scale and the buyer benefit from the price, availability, standardisation and quality.

Even though the possible benefits of commercial software components are many, also several problems in the use of such components have been raised [19]. In practice, component-based software engineering (CBSE) has presented significant risks related to, for example, the software development process, the nature of COTS software components, component technologies and vendor support [10]. It has been cited in many sources that the software component markets are far from being mature, e.g. the lack of industry standards and management guidelines characterise the markets [19]. Software component markets seem to be at a stage in which most market actors are facing problems related to the interactions in which they wish to engage with the other actors. To understand these difficulties, we will first discuss some basic aspects of inter-organisational business relationships.

3   Business Relationships as a Setting for Value Creation

Business relationships have been one of the major themes during the last few decades in the industrial marketing and purchasing research (see e.g. [8]; [1]; [5]; [3]). In relationship marketing the central focus is to understand the role of business relationships [6] whereas the more traditional approach to marketing has been more or less focused on seeing the role of marketing only as a series of decisions related to the marketing mix of product, price, place or promotion [9]. Moreover, emphasis on relationship marketing in the industrial purchasing research has caused a shift from analysing organisational buying behaviour, buying situations etc. into developing supplier relationships, supplier networks and other forms of co-operative structures between firms.

Webster [18] has presented a classic model of the relationship continuum, illustrating different kinds of interactions in which organisations may be involved. Accordingly, not all business relationships are close and long-term oriented, but instead, relationships vary between a continuum from pure market transactions at the one end, to fully integrated hierarchical firms at the other end. In the middle of this kind of a continuum there are the so called partner relationships, characterised by close co-operation, but in terms of two separate actors. We are going to concentrate on transactional relationships and partnerships, leaving out of the scope the other extreme of the relationship continuum, e.g. vertical integration, acquisitions and mergers.

Möller [12] has studied both transactional relationships and partner relationships. He uses the term *relational exchange* to refer to partner relationships that are characterised by different kinds of economic, social, legal, technical, informal and procedural bonds. Discrete transactions, on the other hand, are described as predominately governed by market forces [12]. In these so-called *transactional relationships* buyers and sellers are seen as interacting only with rather selfish consideration, aiming at merely finalising the single transaction at hand. Future co-operation is not actively considered in the transaction, and the seller is usually valued according to its current products and prices.

Several other researchers have ended up with a similar kind of conclusion regarding the differences between transactional and partner relationships in their research on business relationships (e.g. [13]; [4]; [7]). According to these studies, partner relationships require *open information sharing* based on both person-to-person and electronic communication. The relationship involves a high level of *trust* and *commitment* over time, *joint conflict resolution* and the *sharing of risks and rewards*. Such collaboration affords many of the benefits of vertical integration without the attendant loss of strategic flexibility. In contrast, transactional buyer-supplier relationships are characterised by *sourcing from multiple suppliers*, the use of *competitive bidding*, fully developed bidding specifications, and *short-term contracts* to achieve *low purchase prices*. This distinction between strategies of interacting with market participants helps us to understand the situation in the software component markets.

Evidently, the parties may also have differing views on the kind of relationship they would want to engage themselves with the other party. In the industrial marketing and purchasing research, the portfolio view has been used to illustrate both the buyer's purchasing strategy and the seller's marketing strategies, as well as the combination that different strategies make from the relationship point of view.

Campbell [2] has presented a classification of buyer-seller relationships illustrating the interplay between buyers strategies and the sellers strategies. According to this classification, both marketers and purchasers have three alternative strategies to use in relation to the counterpart and thus the business relationship can be understood through the interplay between these strategies. The competitive strategy refers to a company's aim to engage in more transactional relationship, whereas the co-operative strategy can be described as a more partner-type relationship. The command strategy illustrates a situation where the other party has dominance over the other, for some reason, and aims to use this one-sided dependence. Furthermore, different kinds of interdependencies result from these strategies, and some of the interplay situations are even evaluated as "Mismatch". Figure 1 (in Appendix 1) illustrates these kinds of interdependencies.

Campbell's classical illustration provides us with the basic understanding of the alternative buyer-seller relationship interfaces from the strategy point of view. Reflecting upon the software component markets, Campbell's model allows us to make one conceptualisation of the basic problem facing the buying and selling organisations. One could easily assume that the ultimate aim of CBSE, from the viewpoint of both parties, could be positioned to the upper-left corner, where the competitive strategy is adopted by both parties in the relationship.

The seller aims at selling standard pieces of software to several customers at as high price as possible. Also, the customer's ambition would be to buy components from a marketplace where all the suppliers would sell their components and where all the product and price information would be available for the customers to make comparisons between suppliers. However, based on our preliminary empirical findings, the situation is not this at the moment. Clearly, the suppliers are not willing to adopt "too" co-operative mode, e.g. they may modify components only if the customer is willing to pay for the development of the whole component. They even aim at having the right to sell the developed modifications further to any other customers.

This could probably be described as the command strategy. On the other hand, the problems faced by component buyers would suggest a more co-operative purchasing strategy, because customer-specific modifications and the future development of the component and the seller company become often critical. To conclude, ideally the situation in the software component business would be the independent perfect market type, but in practice sellers are adopting a more co-operative strategy during contract negotiations and more command type strategy after the purchase.

Buyer's, on the other hand, are hoping to use a command type strategy as they, for example, want to choose a supplier over which they would have some power, but in practice they may be forced to try to use a co-operative relationship strategy to have even something to say to the future development of the component, and to ensure "correct" future evolution of the component on which they own offering is based.

To provide some suggestions on how to deal with these kinds of difficulties in relation to the parties' purchasing and marketing strategies, we will now take a look at one of the key driving forces behind business transactions, value creation. We suggest that by understanding the way value is created in business relationships, one can more thoroughly foresee and avoid difficulties in the emerging software component markets.

4 Value Creation in Business Relationships

"To create value" can be seen as the very basic aim of any business operation or transaction. In order to understand the kind of value that can be created in business relationships and to whom value is created, we need to first define the term *value*.

Many differing as well as overlapping definitions has been presented in the literature, but according to a rather general view the concept of value can be regarded as the *trade-off between benefits and sacrifices*. Some define value in business markets purely in monetary terms, whereas other use a broader value definition, which also includes non-monetary revenues, such as developed competence, market position, and social rewards [17]. In this paper, we emphasise the broader definition of value: value is something that includes the monetary benefits, but also much more.

The meaning of *value creation* can be looked from a function-oriented point of view, as Walter et al. [17] suggest. They have discovered seven different value creation functions. The *volume function* contributes to the success of the supplier by securing the necessary "break-even" volume and thus, allows the company to operate on a profit-making basis. A positive cash flow to the supplier is provided through the *profit function* of a customer relationship. Obtaining stability and control in sales terms within a dynamic marketplace is represented by the *safeguard function*.

Through the *innovation function* technological know-how and creative ideas are obtained from the customers. Gaining access to new markets (i.e., new customers) is represented by the *market function*. The *scout function* of a customer relationship captures the possibility to gain critical information through customers. The *access function* allows access to third parties and makes those actors reachable, open, and understandable.

However, often the definition of value creation is based on a process view, instead of separate functions: every company has its own value creation process, through which it creates value in various business operations. The ultimate purpose of the company's value creation process is to achieve its goals and mission. Looked from the buyer's point of view, this implies that the buyer always measures value in relation to its own goals. Therefore, the seller aiming at building a good and long-lasting relationship with the buyer, i.e. with the customer, has to have a thorough understanding of the buyer's mission, goals, vision and strategy [14], [15].

5   Value Creation in Software Component Business

One basic question in the emerging software component business is to analyse the kind of value that software components bring for both the potential buyers, sellers and any possible intermediaries. According to many industry sources and our empirical data, even the monetary benefits are not always very clear and easy to measure.

According to our empirical research material, companies operating in the software component markets mentioned the pricing issues, component acquisition and lifetime cost analysis as the biggest problems hindering the effective use and selling of components. Non-monetary value benefits, such as market position, learning and reference value are even harder to measure by the actors in the component markets. We argue that for both component sellers and buyers it is equally important to understand also the non-monetary value benefits than the directly monetary ones, and any possible intermediaries must in most often base their offering on nothing but this kind of value. For example, it may be a typical situation that the buyer is requiring lots of resource demanding and costly services, such as component evaluations, modifications and guarantees.

In such a case, the seller may feel that due to small purchase volumes of that particular buyer, the relationship is not worth the additional effort measured in strictly monetary terms. However, this kind of a conflict could be solved by analysing also the other kinds of benefits that the particular relationship can create for the seller than just the monetary ones. As earlier discussed, besides of the profit function, the relationship can create also volume, safeguard, innovation, market, scout and access benefits. The relationship with the buyer may create innovation value for the seller through, for example learning from the customer's requirements and modification needs or through after-sales co-operation that is needed due to the long guarantee times. Additionally, the particular relationship can provide reference value for the seller in regard to, for example other customers and through offering an access to new customers. A third party, a kind of relationship broker, may be needed to make these benefits explicit and to help the parties to associate their value creation processes together. For example, reference value may be gained by using the same marketing communications organisation.

In addition to analysing both the monetary and non-monetary value benefits, it is also important to understand the create value both from the software component buyer's and seller's perspective. When both relationship parties recognise each other's value creation logic, the possible "mismatches" in the relationship might be easier to overcome. Based on our empirical findings, it is not, for example, unusual that software component sellers try to understand only the software component *acquiring process* of the buyer, although the buyer itself is more concerned with the component's actual *reuse process*. This is to say that sellers are investing in providing certain kinds of trial licences, and component functionality documentation related to the acquisition process, whereas the actual value for the customer related to the purchased component is in fact created as the component is put into use as a part of the final product's system engineering process.

Additionally, there are also other important value creating processes from the buyer's perspective, such as the *identification process* of the actual component need, in which the key features for the component are defined. Also, the *maintenance process*, which includes e.g. guarantees and upgrading entails a significant value creation for the customer. These customer's processes, however, aren't usually well understood by the seller – because it provides only partial solutions, the components, and may not be familiar with the customer's entire product architecture. Of course, the situation is similar also vice versa; usually the buyers are requiring too much from the sellers, although they aren't offering enough value for the seller as a customer. For example, for buyers that have become familiar with software development subcontractors, it may be difficult to realise that the profit margin of a COTS software seller can be three to four times bigger compared to a software subcontractor.

However, according to our empirical material, these kinds of relationship and value creation questions are always related to the specific characteristics of the software components in case. From the buyer's point of view the three most important questions are 1) how *critical* the component is for the overall functionality, 2) is there a need for *modifications,* and 3) how closely *related* that specific component is *to the core competence* of the buyer. These three questions usually define how important such other component related questions are IPRs, documentation, testing, quality and maintenance services are. Furthermore, the three questions determine also much of the requirements set for sellers, i.e. software component suppliers, and the heaviness of the software component acquiring process, including evaluation of the potential suppliers. For example, if the component is not that critical for the buyer, the evaluation of the potential seller may be light, and it is possible that the component is bought from a company that sells the same component to competitors, too.

From the seller's point of view, based on our empirical findings, the most important component related value question is the *generality* of the component. The more general the component is, the wider markets there are. Additionally, the seller usually owns the IPRs of components that do not need any modifications, and the need for giving the source code to the buyer is not evident. However, the problem is if it is possible to produce and sell 100% general components – all software products are used by some specific organisations and person, unique compared to any other actors. These actors usually benefit from the recognition of their particular characteristics.

There are also other important questions besides of the generality of the component, from the seller's point of view. For example, the question of the purchase volume of the buyer is relevant for the seller, when trying to define how valuable that specific customer in fact is. Referring to the two kinds of positions in the relationship continuum, we summarise the aspects of relationships and components related to differences in value creation in Table 2 (in Appendix 1).

6 Conclusions

This study has tried to shed some preliminary light to understanding the emerging software component markets. We have taken the perspective of analysing the markets through the existing buyer-seller interfaces and relationships on the basis of our empirical material. Through analysing the markets from relationship perspective, we aimed at illustrating that some of the difficulties faced by the companies in the component markets may be understood through analysing the relationship interfaces between the market participants.

More specifically, through using the marketing and purchasing strategy interface analysis, we illustrated how the component sellers and buyers relate to each other at the moment. Furthermore, through the value creation analysis we could analyse some of the apparent software component market problems. The interplay between the purchasing and marketing strategies could be harmonised through analysing value creation in business relationship. If both sellers and buyers of software components would understand the way value is created to the other party, better functioning business relationships could be developed, as the mutuality and compatible strategies could enable the parties to develop joint value creation.

This would allow companies operating in the emerging software component markets to develop their market offerings and market behaviour so that the existing problems in the emerging markets could be diminished. In all, the question of *information exchange* seems to play the critical role in the software component markets and buyer-seller relationships. This is due to the special nature of components; the heavy requirements on documentation, testing, quality etc.

Although one important goal of utilising commercial software components has been seen as improved quality, we argue that at this moment there are still several pitfalls in achieving these kinds of quality improvements. Based on our empirical findings, quality problems in commercial software components are usually caused by insufficient information exchange between the seller and the buyer: the seller doesn't give enough information of what he is selling and on the other hand the buyer does not define well enough what he wants to buy and thus what he thinks he is buying. As several researchers (see e.g. [1], [3], [6]) have pointed out that important aspect of product quality is the customer's expectations and how those expectations are filled, it would be necessary to improve the information exchange between the two parties of the relationships. This kind of improved information exchange would also be needed in order to solve those quality problems that are related to demanding integration work and different kinds of environments, in which the component should function.

On the basis of our preliminary analysis, we propose that the efficient information exchange in regard to value creation would enable a better functioning component markets to develop. Naturally, despite our attempt to define the analysed software component as unambiguously as possible, a vast amount of different kinds of software products are included into the definition. Our point is that as there exist many different kinds of software components in the markets, and more or less close and co-operative relationships are needed in the component markets between the buyers and sellers. The perfect market kind of situation described in the marketing and purchasing strategy interface model is very unlikely to come true in the software component markets, due to the complex nature of the trade object, software.

However, we do not see that component markets are only to be characterised by extremely close and co-operative relationships, in which companies are determined to stay for a long time. According to our view, the development of the component markets would more likely be characterised as markets in which companies develop means of effective information sharing within the whole markets as well as within a specific business relationship. Through this, the managerial implication would be better defined purchasing and marketing strategy interfaces, open value creation and a more simple and lighter acquisition processes.

References

1. Anderson, J.C. and Narus, J.A. (1999). Business Market Management. Understanding, Creating, and Delivering Value. Prentice Hall, Upper Saddle River, New Jersey.
2. Campbell, N.C.G. (1997) An Interaction Approach to Organizational Buying Behavior. In: Ford, D. ed. Understanding Business Markets. The Dryden Press, London.
3. Christopher, M.; Payne, A. and D. Ballantyne (1991). Relationship Marketing. Bringing quality, customer service and marketing together. Butterworth-Heinemann Ltd. Oxford.
4. Ellram, L.M. (1990). The Supplier Selection Decision in Strategic Partnerships. Journal of Purchasing and Materials Management, Vol. 26, No. 3, pp. 8-14.
5. Ford, D. eds. (1997). Understanding Business Markets. Second edition. The Dryden Press. London.
6. Grönroos, C. (1994). From marketing mix to relationship marketing: Towards a paradigm shift in marketing. Management Decision, Vol. 32, Iss. 2; pg. 4, 18 pgs.
7. Heide, J. and John, G. (1990). Alliances in Industrial Purchasing: The Determinants of Joint Action in Buyer-Supplier Relationships. Journal of Marketing Research, 27, No. 1 pp. 24-36.
8. Håkansson, H. and Snehota, I. (1995). Developing relationships in business networks. Routledge, London.
9. Kotler, P. (1997) Marketing Management. Analysis, Planning, Implementation, and control.Rentice Hall, Upper Sadle River, New Jersey.
10. Kotonoya, G. and Awais, R. (2001). A Strategy for Managing Risk in Component-based Software Development. Proceedings of the 27th Euromicro Conference, pp.12-21.
11. Morisio, M.; Seaman, C.B.; Parra, A.T.; Basili,V.R.; Kraft, S.E. and Condon, S.E. (2000). Investigating and Improving a COTS- Based Software Development Process. ICSE 2000 Limerick Ireland. AMC.

12. Möller, K. (1994). Interorganizational Marketing Exchange: Metatheoretical Analysis of Current Research Approaches. In: G. Laurent, G.L. Lilien and B.Pras eds. Research Traditions in Marketing. Kluwer, Boston.
13. Spekman, R. (1988). Strategic Supplier Selection: Understanding Long-term Buyer Relationships. Business Horizons, 31, No. 4 pp. 75-81.
14. Storbacka, K.; Blomqvist, R.; Dahl, J. and Haeger, T. (1999). Asiakkuuden arvon lähteillä. CRM Finland Oy. WSOY – Kirjapainoyksikkö, Juva. (in Finnish)
15. Storbacka, K.; Sivula, P. and Kaario, K. (1999). Create Value with Strategic Accounts. Kauppakaari Oyj, Helsinki.
16. Szyperski, C. (1997). Component Software. Beyond Object-Oriented Programming. New York: Addison Wesley Longman Ltd. 411 p.
17. Walter, A.; Ritter, T. and Gemünden, H.G. (2001). Value Creation in Buyer-Seller Relationships. Industrial Marketing Management, Vol. 30, Issue 4, May 2001. pp. 365-377.
18. Webster, Jr. and Frederick, E. (1992). The changing role of marketing in the corporation. Journal of Marketing. Oct92, Vol. 56, Issue 4.
19. Xia, C.; Lyu, M.R.; Wong, K-F and Roy K. (2000). Component-Based Software Engineering: Technologies, Development Frameworks, and Quality Assurance Schemes. Proceedings of the Seventh Asia-Pasific Software Engineering Conference, APSEC 2000., pp.372-379.

Appendix 1

		Marketing strategies		
		Competitive	Cooperative	Command
Purchasing strategies	Competitive	Independent Perfect Market	Mismatch	Independent Seller's Market
	Cooperative	Mismatch	Interdependent Domesticated Market	Dependent Captive Market
	Command	Independent Buyer's Market	Dependent Subcontract Market	Mismatch

Figure 1. Campbell's classification of buyer-seller relationships (Campbell in Ford eds. 1997)

Table 2. Comparison of partner and transactional relationships from the viewpoint of value creation.

Value creation	Partner relationship	Transactional relationship
Nature of Relationship		
Information Exchange	More open sharing of information, e.g. future product development plans	Standard and narrow information exchange
Legal Bonds	"Handshake" agreements preferred, IPRs shared or buyer owned	Standard legal agreements, mostly license based trade, seller owned IPRs
Operational Linkages	Operational linkages exist a lot, e.g. in terms of shared product development	Indirect operational linkages, mainly concentrated on selling and purchasing activities
Closeness	Close cooperation, including shared risks and mutual adjustments	Arm's length relationship, lack of direct contacts, utilization of an intermediary
Nature of Component		
Generality	Mostly application domain specific components	Mostly general components
Adaptability	MOTS, modifying and tailoring done in cooperation	COTS, standardized components, narrow possibilities to have tailoring
Importance	Usually quite critical for the buyer, e.g. important piece of the final product	Not so critical and important parts, at least not closely related to the buyer's core competence area

Collaboration between a COTS Integrator and Vendors

Tuija Helokunnas[1] and Marko Nyby[2]

[1] Nokia, P.O.Box 301, FIN-00045 Nokia Group, Finland
`Tuija.Helokunnas@nokia.com`
[2] Tampere University of Technology, P.O.Box 541, 33101 Tampere, Finland
`Marko.Nyby@tut.fi`

Abstract. This paper describes the acquisition and management of the Commercial Off The Shelf (COTS) and Open Source software components. The paper focuses on approaches to organize the relationship between a large global company and small software vendors on telecommunications area. The large company integrates both in-house and externally developed components into products and deliveries the products to end customers. Long-lasting and deep partnership relation between the component integrator and vendor is needed to reduce the efforts and time spent on the commercial negotiations. The paper is based on information gathered during last ten months. In addition to literature study, several detailed interviews have been held among people working for the component integrator.

1 Introduction

This paper describes approaches to acquire and manage external software components such as the Commercial Off The Shelf (COTS) software and Open Source software components. Software component as a concept has attracted software development organizations during past thirty years. Principles of the component based software development have been considered to provide the software developing organizations with means to manage complexity of the software systems, e.g. [1]. In addition to develop components in-house many organizations have recently studied and deployed the acquisition and delivery of externally developed components, i.e., components developed outside the product development organization.

All companies lack competent human resources. It is practically not possible to develop all the needed software from scratch. Companies need to acquire external components for reducing time-to-market, i.e. to speed up product development. Attempts to utilize external software components include the use of very small pieces of code such as a sorting algorithm implementation as well as the integration of large subsystems like embedded database management system and distribution management system. However, widely accepted approaches to the acquisition and delivery of software components do not exist yet.

The term component has many definitions, which are quite inconstant and context-dependent. Szyperski [2] defined software component as follows: "The component is

J. Kontio and R. Conradi (Eds.): ECSQ 2002, LNCS 2349, pp. 267–273, 2002.

a unit of composition with contractually specified interfaces and explicit context dependencies only. Context dependencies are specified by stating the required interfaces and the acceptable execution platform(s)." He went on to state that a component can be deployed independently in binary form and is subject to composition by third parties. This definition means that the component is a black-box concept, which interacts with its environment.

According to Dion Hinchcliffe and Michael J. Gaffney cited by P. Valenca [3] this view of components is incomplete, so they complemented it with nine other points. These twelve items constitute what they believed are the "unequivocal requirements a software entity must meet in order to claim to be a 'true' component". They emphasized that component interface shall be clearly defined and a component shall contain interoperability capabilities, e.g., a component must use and expose services through standardized middleware services.

A component-based software system consists of components. The structure of the component system is defined in the software architecture of the system. The term software architecture does not have widely accepted definition, e.g., CMU/SEI [4]. One of the most comprehensive definitions was given by Meyers & Oberndorf [5]: "Architecture is a representation of a system or a subsystem characterized by functionality, components, connectivity of components and mapping of functionality onto components". There is no universal rule about the feasible size of a component of a large system. However, the size of a component is a very important issue when the work effort required for the acquisition, integration and maintenance of an external component is compared to in-house component development and maintenance work. For example, Szyperski [2] felt that too small components with a variety to choose from, e.g. hundreds of different implementations of stacks and queues, are not likely to increase software development productivity.

This paper uses the term external component as an umbrella concept that covers the terms free software, public domain, shareware, Open Source Software (OSS), COTS, Original Component Software Manufacturing (OCM) and Modified Off-The-Shelf (MOTS). This umbrella concept was introduced mainly to cover COTS and Open Source components that are the most widely recognized external component types in large product development organizations. Meyers & Oberndorf [5] defined the COTS product as a product that is sold, leased or licensed to the general public in multiple, identical copies. It is offered by a vendor, which supports and evolves it and tries to profit from it. The COTS product is being used without internal modification from the customer. The definition of MOTS software is based on [6]: MOTS software is similar to COTS software; however, the MOTS software is tailored to buyer-specific requirements by the component vendor. If the buyer modifies the COTS components the vendor is an Original software Component Manufacturer (OCM).

This paper focuses on the external component acquisition and delivery between a large global company and small software vendors on telecommunications area. The large company integrates self-made and external components into products and deliveries the products to end customers. The small companies deliver software components to several integrators. The paper is based on information gathered during last ten months. Information gathering has included literature study, study of information available on the Internet and discussions with component business professionals in Finland. In addition, several detailed interviews were held among people working on component integrator's side. 22 people with technical, commercial and legal interest were interviewed. The interviews were conducted by having a rough questionnaire based discussion with each of the interviewees. A typical interview took one to two hours. The arguments presented in this paper are derived from the conclusions of the interviews and authors' understanding of the subject.

2   Roles in Collaboration

This paper's view to collaboration follows Harju's [7] definition: Collaboration is working together to achieve a shared goal. According to Marmolin et al. [8] collaboration can be viewed as a social process, which is controlled by social conventions. Collaboration consists of information sharing, knowledge integration, communication and co-working. This paper focuses on the collaboration between a large component integrator and small software vendors. Defined, deployed and well managed collaboration process between the integrator and vendors is vitally important to meet all the integrator's customer requirements.

During recent years the component integrators' relationships with the component vendors have varied from body shopping and software project subcontracting to buying of widely used software products such as SQL-database management systems. A deep partnership relation has often been the goal of an integrator when it has developed its relationship with an excellent software project subcontractor. On the other hand, there are cases where an integrator's relationship with a vendor is very weak such as the use of a piece of free software downloaded from the Internet. The variety of the relationships has made the efforts to manage the relationships quite a demanding task.

Body shopping and software project subcontracting typically have longer history in an integrator's organization than the use of OSS or COTS components. This paper follows Merriam-Webster's [9] definition of subcontracting: an individual or business firm contracting to perform part or all of another's contract. Instructions and guidelines for the management of software project subcontracting have been defined [10]. So, it is especially the management of the relationships with OSS and COTS sources where the integrators need to focus on.

An integrator whose aim is to produce reliable products has to very carefully evaluate the risks of using unknown source of software. Therefore, an integrator typically needs a reliable vendor to work together with. The tasks of the preferred vendor, i.e., a partner include providing the integrator with external components that originally were free software, public domain software, shareware, OSS or COTS. Particularly with OSS originated software the partner delivers the modified OSS components back to the OSS community too.

One of the main drawbacks of the use of external components, especially COTS components, has been identified to be the very long-lasting commercial negotiations between the integrator and the vendors. 8 out of 22 interviewed people mentioned this drawback. Negotiations have lasted even longer than one year. While the negotiations are going on the technical requirements often change and when the commercial and legal negotiations are finished the component to be bought is already outdated. Therefore, long-lasting and deep partnership relation between the component integrator and few preferred COTS vendors are needed to speed up the negotiations. In addition, partnership relation is required for developing technically feasible COTS components.

The acquisition and delivery activities of the software components have been compared to the more traditional acquisition of hardware components. However, there are only few standardized software component interfaces. Even if there is an interface specification or the integrator writes a specification to be able to order a component, the specification is often inaccurate and time-demanding to test. This makes the buying and selling of software components more demanding than the buying of hardware components.

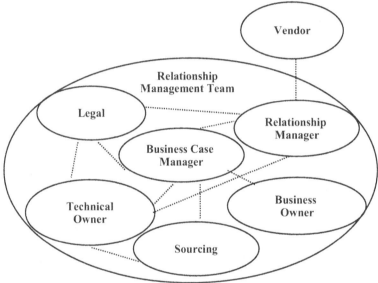

Fig. 1. Relationship management team

There are many software technology areas such as memory-resident database management systems where there are only a few or even none software components available. An integrator may start horizontal component markets by ordering components as a subcontracted development work and allowing the developer to sell the components to other companies too. However, a vendor organization moving to software product business faces many challenges.

When the subcontracting of software development become popular a new job role was created in the integrators' organisations. This new role was a vendor manager whose task is to take care of the relationship between the two companies. This type of a job role is very essential with component acquisition too. However, instead of resource management that is one of the main tasks of the vendor manager, the component acquisition requires that information sharing and co-working are emphasized. Especially, the more deep the relationship becomes the more confidential information sharing is required. A new job role - relationship manager - is needed to enable efficient information sharing.

In addition to relationship management the external component acquisition requires technical, business, legal and sourcing competence. An integrator representative interviewed during this study proposed a relationship management team to be organized for all the significant software component acquisition efforts (Figure 1). None of the interviewees resisted the establishment of these teams. The team is launched during the definition phase of the product to be developed and the team finishes its work when the acquired external component is acceptance tested. However, the relationship manager continues to work during the product maintenance phase too.

The leader of the relationship management team is the business case manager. He is responsible for the component acquisition activities in general. He provides the team with business competence and he is able to understand the technical and legal requirements of the external component and its vendor. He receives instructions from the business manager. The business manager has business responsibility of the product where the external components will be integrated. The business manager, i.e., selects pricing models and defines cost limits for the negotiations. The technical owner is responsible for the technical requirements and technical contents of the agreements between the integrator and the vendor. The sourcing people are the main negotiators. They manage all the existing agreements with software vendors. The legal people provide legal advice and assess agreement drafts.

The primary activities of the relationship management team include the business, technical and legal evaluations of external components. The evaluations shall be carried in parallel to reduce the total duration of the evaluations. Before the evaluations shall be performed the business owner has to define and prioritize the evaluation criteria. The evaluation criteria, i.e., external component attributes to be studied include both technical and business aspects such as maturity of the vendor, price of the component, applied pricing model, partnership agreement conditions, maintenance of the component and the required integration work with the component. In addition, criteria are needed for the financial comparison of the use of external components versus the development of in-house components.

3 Aspects of the External Component Management

The acquisition and management of the external components differs from the development and management of in-house developed components in many ways. When a company starts to use external components, the nature of the company changes from a producer to a consumer organization [5]. Approaches are needed for making decisions about external component upgrade and replacement. In addition, the funding profile during the life-cycle of an external component, the security issues and software quality issues have to be considered [11]. The changing of the technical, business and legal people's mindset from production-oriented to consumer-oriented is a challenging task. Many technical people feel that software developed in-house is always better, because they can keep the control and customize it whenever needed.

Experience of the transition shows that the initiative to use external components should become from senior management and the message to search for external component alternatives should be communicated to all the technical, business and legal people. The technical middle management and software developers have the best knowledge of their area particular technical problems, so they should be able to affect the make/buy decisions according to agreed and accessible criteria.

Changing from a producer to a consumer of external components in an open system environment means adapting to the marketplace: you cannot control the implementation or specification of a component any more, so you need to concentrate on visible interfaces. These interfaces have to be standard, because standard-conforming implementations provide some assurance of the product behavior [5]. On the positive side, you get a freedom of choice between multiple products in a competitive marketplace, if you use standards, which are commonly accepted [5].

The technical middle management generally cannot control the frequency or the content of new software releases [11]. Failing to upgrade to the latest version can result in loss of vendor support for previous versions that are installed and in use and the inability to buy new copies or more licenses for additional copies of previous versions [11]. A live example of this is Microsoft today: the company offers support only to latest two Windows and Office versions [12]. Therefore, the management of the external components have to be considered already when the first implementations of the components are integrated into the final product. A typical problem is that the integration of the second implementation of a component requires the same work effort as the integration of the first implementation did.

4 Summary

Software component development as well as collaboration approaches between component integrator and vendors should be further developed so that they support the acquisition and management of external components. When a company starts to use external components, the nature of the company changes from a producer to a consumer organization. This means that the mindset of the technical, business and legal people has to be changed. The changing of the mindset is a challenging task. People typically resist change. The utilization of external components brings up a plethora of new concepts; thus a great deal of change management is needed.

The relationship between the component integrator and vendor has to become a collaborative one to minimize work effort and time spent on the technical, legal and business negotiations. The lack of standardized software component interfaces makes the need for a working relationship even more obvious. A new job role called a relationship manager was created in the integrator's organisation to take care of the relationship between the two companies. The aim of the implementation of the new job role was to tackle difficulties, which often arise with this new way of software development.

Acknowledgement

This paper was funded by Nokia, Tekes and VTT Electronics.

References

1. Helokunnas, T. Component Architecture Based Planning System. Proc. of GIS/LIS'98. Forth Worth, Texas, USA, 1998.
2. Szyperski, C. Component Software: Beyond Object-Oriented Programming. ACM Press & Addison-Wesley, 1997.
3. Valenca, P. Developing with plugins and components, 2000. http://wwwinfo.cern.ch/pdp/as/papers/plugins/components.html, 2001-09-21.
4. CMU/SEI. How do you define software architecture? http://www.sei.cmu.edu/ architecture/definitions.html, 2001-11-06.
5. Meyers, B.C., Oberndorf, P. Managing Software Acquisition. Open Systems and COTS Products. SEI Series in Software Engineering, Addison-Wesley, 2001.
6. IEEE STD 1062-1993. IEEE Recommended Practice for Software Acquisition, 1993.
7. Harju, R. Groupware Support for Collaboration in Distributed Software Projects. Master's Thesis. The University of Jyväskylä, 2000.
8. Marmolin, H., Sundblad, Y. and Pehrson, B. An Analysis of Design and Collaboration in a Distributed Environment, Proc. of the Second European Conference on Computer-Supported Cooperative Work, ECSCW 91, Netherlands, 1991.
9. Merriam-Webster Dictionary http://www.m-w.com/cgi-bin/dictionary, 2001-10-02.
10. CMU/SEI. Capability Maturity Models. http://www.sei.cmu.edu/cmm/cmms/cmms.html, 2002-02-12.
11. Clapp, J. A., Taub, A. E. A Management Guide to Software Maintenance in COTS-Based Systems.http://www.mitre.org/resources/centers/sepo/sustainment/ manage_guide_cots_base.html, 2001-10-30.
12. Berger, M. Office 97 Users Lose Free Support. http://www.pcworld.com/news/ article/0,aid,51565,00.asp, 2001-11-12.

Creation of a Guideline for Tailoring Development Processes Using Project Metrics Data

Kazutoshi Shimanaka, Masato Matsumoto, Junji Koga, and Hiroyuki Domae

SE Department, System Integration Headquarters, NTT Comware Corporation
1-6 Nakase Mihama-ku Chiba-shi, Chiba 261-0023 Japan
{shimanaka.kazutoshi,m.matsumot,koga.junji,doumae.hiroyuki}
@nttcom.co.jp

Abstract. A project management process for an organization is usually defined to be adapted to a wide range of projects in order to minimize costs and risks. Consequently, the project management process is usually customized to suit each particular project in its planning stage. This customization work is relatively easy for a proficient and experienced project manager, but it is very difficult for an inexperienced manager. To assist these inexperienced managers, we have created a guideline for customizing the project management process using project metrics data. This paper introduces the guideline in part, and presents the review process as an example of method of how to create a tailoring guideline.

1 Introduction

At the beginning of a development project, a manager faces the task deciding which type of project management process to apply to the development. Especially for a manager who will develop a new system and has no experience of a similar project, this decision will not be easy. A management guideline for the project management process will be greatly helpful to such a manager. However, in most cases management guidelines are designed to cover all projects of an organization and are not customized to each project. Therefore, the guidelines are often too heavy for smaller projects. This is one reason managers tend to dislike management guidelines.

We have tried to create a standard that allows even inexperienced managers to tailor project management processes to their particular project needs. The standard is designed not to apply imposing impractical ideals onto projects but to consider projects in practical situation.

We focused on the fact that, as shown Figure 1, project metrics data is the result of activities in a series of processes and reflects the status of the project management process. By inventing a process assessment method in which the project metrics data is assessed and the project management process efficiently grasped, we have tried to create a practical guideline for tailoring the project management process.

J. Kontio and R. Conradi (Eds.): ECSQ 2002, LNCS 2349, pp. 274–287, 2002.

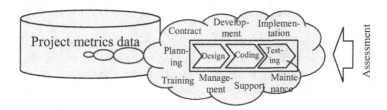

Fig. 1. Project Metrics Data and the Evaluation of the Project Management Process

2   Process Assessment Using Project Metrics Data

2.1   Project Metrics Data

NTT Comware Corporation has a standard under which all projects are developed and a system of managing projects using project metrics data. Figure 2 shows the basic concept of the project management system employed by NTT Comware.

As shown Figure 2, the project metrics data is input with help of a project management support tool and is utilized in managing the project. The project metrics data is also kept in a database after the project is complete so it can be used as a management model for future projects and as a basis for estimating their cost. The database contains the development plan, a review of the output and milestones of the project, test results and records, a project completion report, and field quality data.

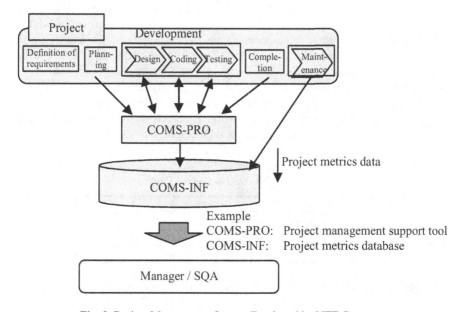

Fig. 2. Project Management System Employed by NTT Comware

2.2 Goal of Process Assessment

Process assessments are usually carried out by a specialized assessor who interviews key people in the project or in the managing organization. Therefore, the larger the organization, the more management resources are required for process assessments.

In contrast, a self-assessment method for assessing project metrics data does not affect the progress of the project, so assessment is easier to implement. Systematizing the assessment procedures makes automated assessment and immediate feedback of results possible. However, the output from this type of self-assessment tends to be superficial compared to the interviewing method. Inevitably, we narrowed the goals of the assessments to the following three:

- To reflect the entire organization
- To stimulate continuous management commitment
- To utilize assessment results as a valuable source of information when planning process improvements

3 Process Assessment Method

3.1 Evaluation Model and Levels

We have designed our self-assessment method based on the SPA (ISO/IEC15504). However, it was difficult to apply the SPA's five capability levels to assessment using a process metrics database. Therefore, we modified the SPA's five levels to three as shown in Table 1 for our evaluation. We used SLCP-JCF98 as the process model for assessment. SLCP-JCF98 is a common frame that was created by modifying the working items defined in the Software Life Cycle Process (ISO/IEC12207), which became an international standard in 1995, to suit Japanese software industry. A common frame defines system development work groups and is used as a common ruler for transactions between two entities. It also clearly defines such aspects as the scope and content of system development work. The items that were added to suit the Japanese software industry include 1: Increased scope (to include planning and system audit processes), 2: Task names, and 3: Additional working items.

Table 1. Process Assessment Levels

Level	Meaning
Defined	How was the process defined?
Performed	Was the defined process implemented?
Managed	Was the implemented process audited/managed?

We evaluated the process by comparing our in-house working standards and project metrics data definitions to tasks defined by SLCP-JCF98. We applied the following rules for mapping the project metrics data to the levels shown in Table 1.

- To compare activities defined by SLCP-JCF98 and activities defined by our in-house working standard to assign "Defined" levels.

- To separate management tasks from other tasks and assign a "Managed" level to management tasks and a "Performed" level to other tasks. (This is in recognition of the fact that some tasks in the activities defined by SLCP-JCF98 have the meaning of managing other tasks)

Tables 2 and 3 show the mapping of level assignment.

Table 2. Mapping SLCP-JCF98 to the "Defined" Level

Number		SLCP-JCF98		In-house standard	
ISO [1]	JCF [1]	Task	Output	Working standard name	Output
5.2.4.5	1.2.4.5	Draft a Project	Project Management Plan	Project Management	Project Plan

Table 3. Mapping SLCP-JCF98 to the "Performed" and "Managed" Levels

Number		SLCP-JCF98		In-house standard	Performed		Managed	
ISO [1]	JCF [1]	Task	Output	Output	Table	Data item	Table	Data item
5.3.5.3	1.4.6.3	Design uppermost level of DB	DB Type Design	DB Design	Process Records	Number of records pages	-	-
5.3.5.7	1.4.6.7	Joint review of SW method design	Design evaluation report	Design review	-	-	Error analysis	Error phenomena

3.2 Evaluation Criterion

1. Evaluation Criterion for the "Defined" Level
   The question of whether or not output has been defined is converted to the question of whether or not there is activity. The evaluation criterion is yes or no; "0" or "1".
2. Evaluation Criterion for the "Performed" and "Managed" Levels
   The project metrics database is searched for the data items in the table to check whether or not effective data exists. After the search, the data is evaluated from the percentage (hereinafter called the project management process implementation rate) obtained by dividing the number of projects for which effective data is registered by total number of projects for the organization.

3.3 Image of Survey Results

The analysis results are summarized in the Project Management Maturity Analysis Chart (hereinafter called the PMMAC) shown in Figure 3 so that the project management status can be effectively grasped. The PMMAC is a chart with three layers in which the implementation status is evaluated for each SLCP-JCF98 activity. Each layer indicates the different levels shown in Table 1: "Defined", "Performed" and "Managed", arranged from inside to outside. The core pie chart corresponds to the sections of the outer layers. Each section of the pie chart indicates a different process defined in SLCP-JCF98. The numbers in the layers correspond to the item numbers of

---

[1] ISO is used here to indicate ISO/IEC12207 and JCF to indicate SLCP-JCF98.

SLCP-JCF98 activities. Each cell of the layers indicates the level for each activity by a different color, as shown in Table 4. However, because this paper will be printed in black and white, the higher implementation rate is indicated by a lighter shade. The PMMAC is evaluated by activity, and each activity is made up of different tasks. Therefore, we specified a representative task for each activity. The evaluation result for the task shown in3.2 (2) was applied to the evaluation result of the activity.

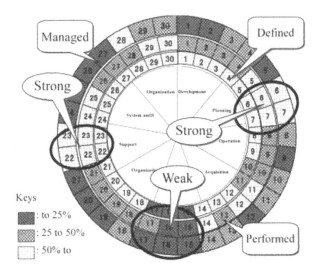

Fig. 3. Image of PMMAC

Table 4. Keys for PMMAC (Colors and Levels)

Color	Level	Remarks
Red	0 ~ Achievement ~ 25%	Low implementation rate
Yellow	25% ~ Achievement ~ 50%	Insufficient implementation
Green	50% ~ Achievement	High implementation rate

4   Example of Survey Results

4.1 Result of Analysis with PMMAC

Figures 4 and 5[2] show the PMMAC's created from the results of surveys actually conducted for NTT Comware's Organization A, in telecommunications, and Organization B, in business. The survey covers about 1600 projects over the past 5 years and the organization ratio is roughly half and half. The main life cycle of SLCP-JCF98 was used for indication. An empty cell indicates that there was no table entry in

---

[2] Missing numbers in the PMMAC indicate that no output was entered for the activity defined in SLCP-JCF98.

the project metrics database. In other words, the empty cells indicate that organizational data management is not performed. However, empty cells are not necessarily bad, because they could occur due to strategic management. The PMMAC reflects the management system of the organization and thus will be used when developing the future management system.

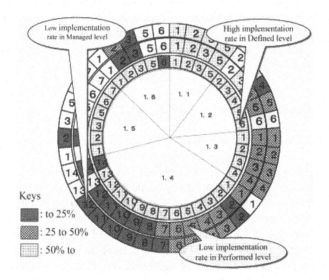

Fig.4. PMMAC for Organization A

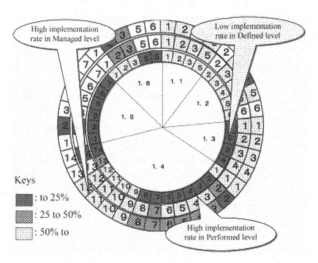

Fig. 5. PMMAC for Organization B

Both organizations A and B have higher implementation rate in the processes of 1.1[3] Acquisition and 1.2 Supply, which indicates that these processes are thoroughly implemented throughout the entire company. For the processes of 1.5 Maintenance and 1.6 Operation, processes are defined, but there are many empty cells in Performed and Managed levels. This indicates that the company does not seem to grasp the status of the processes very well.

Organization A has a low implementation rate in the Performed and Managed levels, but it has an excellent level of process definition. In the process 1.4 Development, it seems that a higher implementation rate achieved for the upper processes but a lower rate for lower processes. Organization B is superior to Organization A in the implementation rate in the Performed and Managed levels. However, the organization seems to be not good at defining tasks. For the 1.4 Development process, it seems that lower processes are superior to higher processes in implementation rate.

4.2   Consideration of Results of Analysis with PMMAC

From the company point of view, the good results for the 1.1 Acquisition process is a reflection of the company's high dependence on outsourcing.

From the perspective of each organization, Organization A has a higher outsourcing rate than other organizations in the company. The organization seems to make more effort on the upper processes and is demonstrating that they are analysis/design-oriented. In contrast, Organization B emphasizes the lower processes. This comes from their policy of maintaining quality of software by conducting tests. Actually, they have special test environment equipped with actual equipment. The PMMAC for Organization B has many lightly shaded cells. This indicates that process activities are well rooted in the organization. In contrast, Organization A has many heavily shaded cells; indicating that the activities are not well rooted. It can be said that Organization B has a higher maturity in process capability than Organization A. Organization A puts emphasis on making close definition on development processes while it has low maturity; indicating a top-down approach. Organization B lays emphasis on allowing autonomy for each project rather than making definitions for the entire organization; indicating a bottom-up approach.

For an organization with ambiguous process definitions, defining processes clearly is an obvious suggestion for improvement. However, analysis of the PMMAC's shows that the organization with a bottom-up approach has a higher implementation rate and the organization with top-down has lower implementation rate. Another in-house survey also reported that the top-down organization tends to have more problems with their projects. The PMMAC analysis shows us that rooting process activities to organizations is more important than making a half-baked effort to defining processes. This finding, very interestingly, supports the fact that CMM addresses systematic standardization for its level 3 KPA.

---

[3] The numbers are the item numbers of the processes defined in SLCP-JCF98 and are the same as the numbers shown in the pie chart within the PMMAC

As shown above, PMMAC clearly shows the status of the project management process of an organization. Our self-assessment method is sufficiently effective in terms of the goals we set for it.

5 Constructing a Strategic Project Management Process

5.1 Ideal Project Management Process

We succeeded in creating a method for showing the status of project management in an organization. On the other hand, this showed us that the entire company had stagnated with a poor implementation rate of the project management process. Before conducting the survey, we expected that Organization B, which has produced many exemplary projects, would have implemented the project management process very well, as modeled by CMM and SPA. The model for the organization was affirmed in terms of comparison with Organization A. However, Organization B's implementation rate for the project management process is not high in terms of absolute value. It does not seem to be appropriate to measure an organization's process capability maturity level by applying ideal models. However, this conclusion contradicts the fact that Organization B has fewer problems with their projects, which indicates high maturity. Therefore, we made this hypothesis to explain the phenomenon: projects do not always follow the prepared standard, and an organization creates project management processes as they are necessary; resulting in a low implementation rate of the project management process. The following points will support this hypothesis.

- The results of analysis using the PMMAC show that process activities are basically rooted.
- Because output definitions and process descriptions are ambiguous, process defintion can be efficiently implemented as circumstances demand.

By further analyzing the details of the project management process in Organization B, we aimed to verify our above hypothesis and to make a tailoring guideline for the construction of a strategic project management process. Constructing a strategic project management process does not imply pointless 100% compliance with a fixed standard, but rather the creation of an appropriate project management process which does not bring chaos to the project nor result in poor quality or delayed delivery. Incidentally, our activities are restricted to within our company. In terms of activities involving the entire company, such as the processes 2. Support Life Cycle and 3. Organizational Life Cycle defined by the SLCP, there is no difference between organizations. Therefore, from here, we will continue the discussion by limiting the range of processes to the 1.4 Development process, for which survey data may vary among organizations. We also assume that all projects surveyed have been completed and we exclude failed projects. We analyze the project management process for only successfully completed projects.

5.2 Analysis of Project Management Process

As defined in the previous chapter, we will analyze the 1.4 Development process activities defined by SLCP-JCF98. Table 5 shows the activities of the 1.4 Development process and the item numbers for them.

We analyzed the characteristics of the project management process by the following procedures.

- Grouping projects in layers using project metrics data indicating project properties (hereinafter called project property values), in layers.
- Using the method described in Chapter 3 to summarize the process data of the grouped projects.
- Showing the summarization results in a lines graph which has a horizontal axis for the activities shown in Table 5 and a vertical axis for the implementation rate defined in Chapter 3.2 (2).

Table 5. 1.4 Development Process Activities Defined by SLCP-JCF98

JCF	ISO[3]	Activity name	JCF	ISO	Activity name	JCF	ISO	Activity name
1.4.2	5.3.2	System requirement analysis	1.4.6	5.3.5	Software type design	1.4.10	5.3.9	Software conformance check
1.4.3	5.3.3	System type design	1.4.7	5.3.6	Software details design	1.4.11	5.3.10	System integration
1.4.4	—	Work details design	1.4.8	5.3.7	Software code creation and test	1.4.12	5.3.11	System Conformance check test
1.4.5	5.3.4	Software requirement analysis	1.4.9	5.3.8	Software integration			

We decided the number of groups to be created first, and then determined a criterion to minimize the difference in the number of projects between groups. For project property values, we decided on appropriate person-months, project duration and development scale, which are basic project metrics that are easy to grasp from the project metrics database. However, due to limitations of space, we mention about only the development scale as project

For the same reason, we mention hereunder about only the "Managed" level to analyze the correlation between project property values and the project management process. In the meantime, feature of each of the "Performed" and "Managed" can be considered almost to be similar, and therefore we think that the analysis results can represent the whole analysis result.

5.3 Feature of Project Management Process

Figure 6 is a graph of projects of Organization B, in which project management processes (Managed) are grouped in terms of the scale of development. An examination of the correlation between development scale and the project management process reveals the following:

- On the whole, projects of smaller development scale tended to have simplified project management processes.
- The larger the development scale is, the more the lines graph levels, which indicates more emphasis on the upper processes.
- Projects of smaller development scale tended to have simplified project management processes for the production process.

5.4   Consideration of the Results of Grasping the Project Management Process

It is said that the larger the project scale is, the more risk there is that the project will fail. As clearly shown in Figures 6, when each project property value related to project scale increases, the implementation rate of the project management process increases accordingly. In our opinion, this comes from the increased implementation rate of the project management process against the risk of failure of the project, as shown in Figure 7. We think the risk for a project equals the implementation rate of the project management process. The projects we analyzed, including those for which the project management process was simplified by omitting some activities, were all successful projects, as described in Chapter 5.1. It seems that projects for which the project management process was simplified by omitting some activities had management processes established appropriate to their risk. From the graph, it is evident that the implementation rate of the project management process for large-scale projects is high. This is reasonable as a basis for the high process capability maturity. The hypothesis we set forth above is well explained. We think it is possible to create a project management process appropriate to the level of project risk.

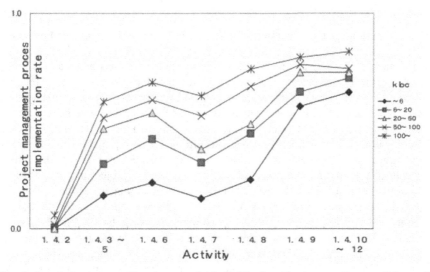

Fig. 6. Correlation between Development Scale and Project Management Process (Managed)

Organizations with low process capability maturity commonly produce many failed projects. The type of process capability maturity model represented by CMM states that the maturity level increases with increased coverage of activities that comprise the project management process. However, the result of our analysis demonstrated that it is possible to reduce activities that comprise the project management process without producing failures. Therefore, depending on the characteristics of a project of the organization, the criteria for judging process capability maturity can vary. From the point of view of company cost reduction, it can be said that a pointlessly detailed

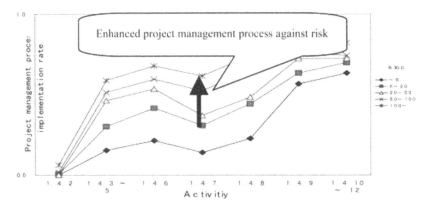

Fig.7. Development Scale and Project Risk

management process that will require more person-months is not always necessary, depending on project characteristics.

5.5   Application for Construction of a Strategic Project Management Process

Development projects cannot avoid risks. In order to beat the risk and lead the project to success, the enhancement of the project management process is definitely key. However, if project risks are overestimated and an excessive project management process is introduced, this will result in increase of unnecessary overhead costs and naturally will not satisfy the customer. It is necessary to tailor a standard process to create a project management process according to the project risk. From the consideration in the previous section, the implementation rate of the project management process is interconnected with the size of the project property value. In other words, project risk can be estimated from the project property value.

In order to grasp the project risk and create a process appropriate to the risk, we aimed to set an allowable risk value to which the process can be simplified, as shown in Figure 8. It is necessary to show that there is a difference in the implementation rate of the project management process below the allowable risk value. We will prove the existence of such a difference in implementation rate for the grouped processes, using the statistical evaluation method, and calculate the allowable risk value.

We propose the following procedure for tailoring project management process when planning a project.

<Setting an allowable risk value>

- To edit the assessment results according to the procedure outlined in items 1 through 3 in Section 5.2.

- From the edited assessment results, to consider process in the layered group that has the highest average of process implementation rates as the process for comparison.

- To make a null hypothesis that "there is no difference in average of process implementation rate among different groups." in order to examine the difference between the process for comparison and other processes.

- To consider the group with the highest average of process implementation rate in which the null hypothesis is dismissed as the allowable risk value.

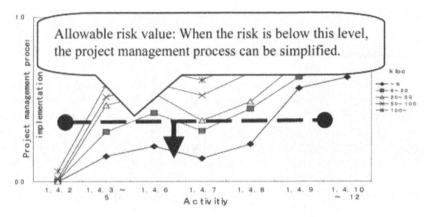

Fig.8. Project Risk and Allowable Risk Value

<Tailoring Work>

- To estimate the property values (development scale) for the project.

- To consider the implementation rates (= base data of Fig.9) of the project management process as the project risk, and determine the risk value for the data range corresponding to the estimated project property value.

- To adjust the allowable risk value depending on the project properties (skill, experience of members, application of new technology and etc.)

- To compare the risk value with the allowable risk value of the project.

- After comparing them, to pick up activities with risk values in excess of the allowable risk value as the project management process.

- It is recommended that activities with risk values that do not exceed the allowable risk value should not be included in the project management process.

6   Conclusion

6.1   Efficient Self-assessment Method Using Project Metrics Data

We have created a unique self-assessment method using project metrics data and have proved its effectiveness. Our assessment method is not perfect but it is satisfactory considering its cost performance. We think our activity can be applied to other organizations in which working standard and project metrics data is prepared. We have proposed an efficient self-assessment method in the procedures described in this paper.

The self-assessment method does not deal with the data content of project metrics data but deals with whether or not the data exists. Because of this, low accuracy data that could not be used before and even missing data can be utilized as information. Data is fully utilized.

6.2   Utilization of Self-assessment Results

Through the self-assessment method, we have proved that it is possible to create a project management process appropriate to project risk. Based on this consideration, we have explained that the criterion for the process capability maturity level is not always a matter of coverage of activities comprising the project management process; rather, it can vary depending on project properties. From the point of view of cost reduction to the company, the assessment model should not be blindly believed, nor is a pointlessly detailed management process that results in increased person-months necessary. With this proposal, we hope that our self-assessment method will pave the way for more efficient and strategic improvement proposals.

6.3   Guideline for Tailoring the Project Management Process Using Project Risk

We have created a guideline for tailoring the project management process using project risk to help project managers to plan their projects. This result is not one that can be applied to all other organizations. However, it can be a realistic tailoring guideline in the organization surveyed. The analysis method can be applied to any organization. We have proposed a method of creating a tailoring guideline for a strategic project management process.

References

1. Mark C. Paulk, Charles V. Weber, Suzanne M. Garcia, Mary Beth Chrissis, Marilyn W. Bush: "Key Practices of the Capability Maturity Model, Version 1.1", Software Engineering Institute, CMU/SEI-93-TR-25
2. SLCP-JCF98 committee edition: Common frame 98 - SLCP-JCF98 -(1998 edition) common frame for software system development and transaction / International standard compliance Trade and industry document research office, 28th Oct. 1998
3. Capers Jones: Assessment and Control of Software Risks, Kyouichi shimazaki, Hisashi Tomino supervised trans., Kyoritsu Shuppan, 25th Aug. 1995
4. Robert B. Grady: Successful Software Process Improvement / Spiral model for obtaining core competence, Tsuneo Koyama, Shu Tomino supervised trans., Kyoritsu Shuppan, 25th Nov. 1998

5. Shimanaka Kazutoshi, Koga Junji: The utilization case of the project metrics data towards the improvement of the process capability maturity level., Software symposium 2001 Collection, Software Engineers Association
6. ISO/IEC TR 15504(TR): 1998 Software Process Assessment.
7. ISO/IEC 12207 Software Life Cycle Process - 1995

Comparison of CMM Level 2
and eXtreme Programming

Jerzy R. Nawrocki[1], Bartosz Walter[1], and Adam Wojciechowski[1]

[1] Poznan University of Technology, ul .Piotrowo 3A, 60-965 Poznan, Poland
{Jerzy.Nawrocki,Adam.Wojciechowski}@put.poznan.pl,
Bartosz.Walter@cs.put.poznan.pl

Abstract. Lightweight software development methodologies promise an easy way to deliver products of high quality without excessive cost. On the contrary, classical heavyweight processes are well-defined and proven, but require a lot of effort. Two approaches: eXtreme Programming (XP) and CMM Level 2 have been used in joined industry-academic software projects run at the Poznan University of Technology. Running concurrently those two software approaches allowed us to compare them on the basis of experimental data. After the projects were completed, major risk factors connected with both approaches have been collected and some improvements have been proposed.

1 Introduction

In 1960's big software producers, such as IBM, encountered serious problems concerning software development. Since then a lot of ideas, methods and tools have been proposed to make software development easier, more predictable, and more effective in the sense of customer satisfaction. Structured programming [7], modularity [17, 26], structured analysis [5], object-oriented programming [23], object-oriented analysis [3], CASE tools and many others have been proposed to produce software of better quality.

In this quest for quality, many software developers and researchers advocated to look to other, more mature, areas of engineering to bring from there some useful ideas and adapt them to the context of software development. One of such proposals was the ISO 9000 suite developed around 1987 with classical consumer goods in mind [24] and then used also for software development. Unfortunately, ISO 9000 in many cases proved to be too restrictive, resulting in too much paper work, and too 'heavy' [21].

Capability Maturity Model (CMM for short) developed a few years later at the Software Engineering Institute (Pittsburgh, USA), much better suited the needs of software developers [18]. It was supported with two other products of SEI: Personal Software Process [10] (PSP) and Team Software Process (TSP) [11]. CMM was developed in a few versions oriented toward different aspects of software development: Systems Engineering, Software Engineering, Integrated Product and Process Development, People CMM, and so on. In 2000 first three CMM models have been combined into so called CMM Integration (CMMI for short) [4].

J. Kontio and R. Conradi (Eds.): ECSQ 2002, LNCS 2349, pp. 288–297, 2002.
© Springer-Verlag Berlin Heidelberg 2002

Unfortunately, CMM models and PSP are also perceived by many people as too heavy and too bureaucratic. So, no wonder that in late 1990's so called 'lightweight' software development methodologies appeared. Perhaps the most popular one is Extreme Programming (XP for short) proposed by Kent Beck [1]. In XP artifacts are reduced to code and test cases. There are no inspection meetings. Planning horizon is very short, so advanced planning tools (such as Function Point Analysis) are getting useless. Many people admire XP. Among them is Tom de Marco, who expressed his great support for XP during his keynote speech at the joint IEEE Metrics and ESCOM 2001 conference (see also [6]).

The problem is that we know very little about lightweight methodologies. There are books presenting the idea and practices [1, 2, 12] but we lack experimental data that would clearly assess when one approach is better than another. Many years ago Tom De Marco said: 'You can't control what you can't measure'. Unfortunately, we still lack measures concerning XP. The only data that have been published so far concern pair programming [16, 25, 14] but those experiments are very limited.

The aim of the paper is to compare some aspects of exemplary XP and CMM Level 2 implementations (Level 2 of CMM is, like XP, project-oriented, while higher levels of CMM are oriented toward the whole organization) and to describe important risk factors related to both methodologies. Recent publication by Paulk [19] gave some light into the subject, though it was focused rather on mapping between XP and CMM practices. In this papers experimental data that has been collected during laboratory-like experiments and some came from student projects developed as part of the Software Development Studio [13] is presented. Next section describes the Software Development Studio and the student projects. The student projects have been split into two groups: SDS-CMM and SDS-XP. Section 3 describes practices adopted by the CMM group, while Section 4 concerns the XP group. Then, in subsequent sections we discuss main risk factors that can serve as comparison criteria. In Section 5 software maintenance issues are analyzed. In Section 6 both approaches are compared from the point of view of customer involvement. Section 7 deals with pair programming and presents results of laboratory-like experiments that aimed at comparison of pair programming with individual programming. The last section contains conclusions and directions of further research.

2   Software Development Studio

Software Development Studio is a 2 years (4 semesters) long academic module run at the Poznan University of Technology. It is intended to teach students the software development in projects   for external customers (either industry companies or different units of the university). Every project involves eight students: four from 3rd year, two from 4th and two from 5th year of study. Students play different roles in two different, one-year long projects in subsequent years, gaining experience in programming, software project management and quality assurance. The educational outcome of the project is bachelor thesis written by 3rd year students.

The projects are proposed and defined by prospective customers. Project subjects vary very much, from scientific ones (e.g. *Assembling DNA sequences, Managing users in meta-computing environment*) to commercial ones (like *Defect tracking system, Multi-project management at a software company*).

In year 2000 all eleven projects were divided into two Project Areas: SDS-XP and SDS-CMM, devoted respectively to eXtreme Programming and CMM Level 2. Since some of the projects were run concurrently according to both processes (by different project teams), we could observe the impact of methodology on the process quality.

XP defines a very different set of roles and responsibilities than the classical methodologies. Therefore, team structure and roles were different in both Project Areas. Moreover, the processes had to be suited for academic environment, what resulted in some modifications of the original approaches.

3 Implementation of CMM Level 2

Software Engineering Institute's (SEI's) Capability Maturity Model[SM] (CMM) is a framework representing improvement paths for software organizations. It is a domain-independent hierarchical structure built on five levels; except level 1 (Initial), each maturity level is decomposed into a number of Key Process Areas (KPA). Each KPA indicates a cluster of activities that performed collectively, help to achieve a set of goals important for organization's software process.

Among the five levels, the Level 2 (*Repeatable*) is directly project-oriented, whereas the others focus on the whole organization. It is important that the first step towards process maturity concentrates on individual projects and team internal communication, leaving more general issues for higher levels. CMM puts stress on initial identification of the crucial for the process and product quality practices. This allows to concentrate on the most important success factors.

The Level 2 comprises 6 Key Process Areas: *Requirements Management, Project Planning, Project Tracking and Oversight, Subcontract Management, Quality Assurance* and *Configuration Management*[18].

At university it is difficult to be fully compliant with all the areas defined at the Level 2. Some deviations are inevitable. For example one of the areas – *Subcontract Management* - has been entirely omitted, since the SDS project teams must develop the software by themselves. Therefore the process defined for SDS-CMM does not meet all the CMM requirements, but it is close to them.

The team is organized hierarchically: 4 students from 3rd year of study are *Programmers and Designers* (PDs), 4th year students act as *Project Managers* (PMs), whereas the oldest and most experienced ones (5th year of study) play roles of *Quality Assurers* (QAs). Moreover, a senior management layer is established for every Project Area (Project Area Managers are university teachers). Detailed responsibilities assigned to roles are presented at Table 1.

In order to support SDS-CMM Project Area projects, two university modules were introduced: Requirements Engineering and Quality Assurance. Besides, every project team is assigned a dedicated university supervisor to support the project and assess the educational outcome. This Project Area follows a modified CMM-based process presented at Table 2.

Table 1. SDS – CMM project team - roles and responsibilities

Role	Responsibilities
Customer	Requirements Management, Acceptance tests
Quality Assurers (5th year)	Inspections, QA, Configuration Management (*Software Cnfiguration Control Board*, SCCB)
Project Managers (4th year)	Planning, Progress tracking, Configuration Management (*Software Configuration Management Board*, SCMB)
Programmers & Designers (3rd year)	Design, Coding, Unit testing

Table 2. Most important activities in SDS – CMM process implementation

Level 2 Key Proces Area	Most important activities implemented
Requirements Management	• requirements are documented, reviewed and managed; • IEEE/ANSI Std 830-1993 is used;
Project Planning	• plan is documented and managed; • size and effort are estimated; • risk factors are identified, monitored and mitigated;
Project Tracking and Oversight	• the plan is a basis for progress tracking; • effort, schedule and progress are tracked; • formal reviews are perfomed twice a semester;
Quality Assurance	• the SQA group reviews documents and activities; • Fagan-like inspections are used;
Configuration Management	• a repository of software baselines exists; • CVS is used;
Subcontract Management	not implemented

4   Extreme Programming Process for SDS

Extreme Programming is relatively new (about five years old) lightweight methodology of software development. It was proposed in response to problems concerning rapidly changing (dynamic) requirements and new technologies. In opposition to CMM, XP offers a light approach, going on the edge of chaos. It is suited for small software teams (up to 10 people).

The general assumption in XP is that the customer, not the documentation is the heart of project. It means that customer is a privileged team member, and he is able to make all business decisions, which drive the project development process. This leads to instant orientation towards customer's goal: whenever the project objectives change, the focus of the project is changed as well.

Table 3. SDS – XP project team - roles and responsibilities

Role	Responsibilities
Customer	User stories, Business decisions, Acceptance tests
Testers (5th year)	Implementing and running acceptance tests
Coach (4th year)	Managing the team
Tracker (4th year)	Risk management, Progress tracking
Programmers (3rd year)	Development, Coding, Unit testing

XP also prefers informal, oral communication within the team in place of written documentation. This allows both for avoiding documentation maintenance and speeds up the process.

Here the most distinctive features of XP are listed:

- The software development is split into a number of small increments (each one about 2-3 weeks long), giving the developers fast feedback from the customer; planning is performed just-in-time, only for the forthcoming increment.
- The customer role is crucial; he provides the programmers with user stories (informal, customer-written description of the functionality) and he is capable of changing them at any time. They also specifies the aceptance tests.
- Quality assurance is test–centered: writing every piece of code should be preceded by preparation of a set of test cases for the implemented function. If a defect is detected, the programmer writes new test cases that detect the defect if it reappears.
- Programming is done in pairs. This is a technique thought as substitution for reviews and inspections – a pair of programmers work on a single piece of code, so they can review it continuously.
- The code is co-owned by all team members, so that everyone can change anything. It requires a defined coding standard;

For the purpose of SDS we implemented a modified version of the XP approach. The roles and responsibilities for the SDS-XP Project Area are listed in Table 3.

The project time span was divided into 2 releases, each consisting of 2 iterations, each iteration took approx. 4 weeks.

In year 2000 SDS-XP Project Area consisted of 5 projects.

5   Software Maintenance Issues

Software maintenance is a real test for the organization's software process: it shows whether the knowledge about projects is kept and can be recalled at further stages at low cost. In real environment the maintainability (and its cost) is a very important factor for the software process assessment.

Although SDS projects last one year only, it is long enough to experience problems with maintainability. In both project areas several artifacts were produced, and keeping them up-to-date was one of key success factors.

In case of SDS-XP Project Area, the reduction of documentation to code and test cases makes the software maintenance particularly difficult. The process for that project area assumed only two written artifacts: user stories (it was our deviation from XP – we asked our students to keep user stories documented) and the code with accompanying test cases. Since no other documents existed, it was hard for teams to keep the track between changing user stories, the code implementing them and the associated test cases. Changes in source code, which might trigger redefinition of test cases, were difficult to follow and track. Since we did not have a board for user stories, the person designated to maintain the artifacts, became a key team member.

The other drawback was lack of an intermediate layer similar to the architectural design in our CMM implementation process. The system metaphor (informal system description understood by all team members including the customer), despite its simplicity and customer-readability, is not well suited for maintenance.

One of symptoms of problems in project maintenance in XP were the difficulties the 3rd year students had in writing their bachelor thesis at the end of the project. Thesis describes the process and system developed during the project. Several students could hardly recall details of the work after just three months. Unfortunately, refactoring was not a common practice in SDS-XP projects, and this could be the reason for the maintenance problems we encountered.

In order to improve the process, we suggested several changes into our XP implementation, which were implemented next year. First, for each user story a business rationale should exist. This gives a chance to keep all user stories tied to the customer goal. Secondly, some kind of architectural model appears inevitable. We suggest to use UML as a unified and commonly used by software engineers language, though it may not be readable for the customer. On the other hand, it improves the communication within the team if programmers are not used to do it orally.

In XP changes drive the process. Beck claims that *"maintenance is really the normal state of an XP project"*[1]. Unfortunately, infrequent refactoring and lack of written artifacts make inexperienced programmers to forget the specifics of user requirements and to miss the goal. We found it difficult to implement XP in newly formed teams, which was the case.

In the SDS-CMM Project Area the maintenance was based on the documentation. The students in this project area had significantly less problems with writing their bachelor theses. Moreover, one of the SDS-CMM projects was continued by a new team and the new team did not report important problems.

This shows that the risk connected with maintenance in XP is much higher than for the CMM-based approach. Code and test cases seem to be insufficient.

6 Customer Involvement

In XP, customer is the central person of a team. His presence *in the team* (not *beside the team*) is a prerequisite for customizing the project to the needs immediately after the needs arise. The customer should make or approve every decision concerning the project scope and schedule. Therefore, the insufficient customer involvement seems to be an important risk factor. Lack of the legitimated decision maker in the team leads to decision guessing. Then the pass of acceptance tests is in danger.

XP assumes on-site customer. Unfortunately, in our experiment there was no single project where customer would be available all the time. Also in other XP experiments [8, 20, 22] customer was not continuously present. To manage this, our project teams organized on-line chat sessions with customers, which provided a partial solution for customer absence. Many teams had to go to the customer's premises to get necessary knowledge, which was not so effective.

In most SDS-XP projects the close contact with customer resulted in a higher customer satisfaction, while in one case lack of decision-maker hold the project for a few weeks. Therefore we conclude that a close, personal contact with customer and their instant presence is a must for XP-like processes.

For SDS-CMM Project Area it was not assumed that customer will be available all the time. Customers were supposed to meet the team quite frequently at the initial stages (before coding) – at least once a week, and once a fortnight during the implementation phase. For that projects we observed noticeably lower actual customer involvement: sometimes they did not have time for reading documents, which led to costly refactoring at further stages. On the other hand, most of customers attended at least the inspection meetings, making important remarks. In the SDS-CMM Project Area none of the customers changed their requirements once they had been defined.

It appears again that the assumptions made in XP process, concerning the customer involvement, are much stronger and needs appropriate risk management. Although all projects in SDS-XP Project Area succeeded in general (products were delivered with only minor delays), it appears that fast decision making and almost immediate feedback from the customer is crucial for lightweight methodologies.

7 Pair Programming

Pair programming is one of the most important and characteristic features of XP. It means that all the production code is programmed in pairs. While one programmer is in control of keyboard and enters the code, the other looks at screen and checks if the code is correct. After some time they switch the roles. Next day they change their partners.

Kent Beck claims that pair programming removes the need for inspection meetings because there is continuous inspection – all the time there is someone checking quality of the produced code [1]. However, there are some problems concerning pair programming:

Not everybody likes working in pairs. In a software company that decided to join our experiment to provide large-scale empirical data one of very clever programmers did not want to program in pairs at all. He could not stand someone watching him working.

Even if people are ready to program in pairs, it does not mean that everybody will be able to work with anybody. It is common observation that with some people we have very good contact and communication is very effective, while with other people it is very hard to communicate. In case of programming it is even more difficult. It can happen that two people have very good social contacts, but while they start to work together one of them is much faster than the other, and after some time they cannot work together because they work at very different speed.

Thus, we cannot assume that *all* the production code is pair programmed (in experiment described by Schuh [22] pair programming took 30% of developer time). Consequently, one cannot remove inspections. It is important to realize that inspection meetings serve two purposes:

- It is well known that through inspections one can assure quality.
- Moreover, inspection meetings make all the parties present at the meeting responsible for prospective defects. That is of great importance from psychological point of view. When a defect appears, it is easier to focus attention on what to do and prevent people from blaming anybody else.

If there is a person in a project team that hates pair programming, inspection meetings can be the only solution. Obviously, they should be well organized and not too long (Fagan advocated inspection meetings lasting not longer that 1.5 hour [8]). It means that frequent inspections are better than rare. If inspection meetings are organized frequently, the size of artifacts subject to inspection is relatively small. Then inspection meeting can be short and more effective. While observing student projects we have found that inspection meetings should be once a week (students working on SDS projects are expected to spend about 15 hours per week on a project). In industry setting inspection meetings should be probably even more frequent (at least twice a week).

Even if programmers are ready to program in pairs, it does not mean that they will be allowed to. Our students reported that in one company senior management was very enthusiastic about XP but very skeptical about pair programming (similar observations were reported in [9]). From management point of view pair programming was waste of time and money. Why to assign two people to a task that one person can do? It is an important question concerning pair programming: what is overhead connected with pair programming? Is pair programming effective from economical point of view? That question seems to be still open. Very few experiments concerning pair programming have been performed till now. According to an experiment described by John Nosek [16] pairs consumed 43% total effort more than individuals. Unfortunately, that experiment concerned only one very short programming assignment (the allotted time was 45 minutes). The second experiment has been conducted at the University of Utah [25]. The results were more optimistic. The authors report that '*the pairs completed their assignments 40% to 50% faster*'. That means that total effort in case of pairs was not greater than in case of individual programmers. On the other hand, from our experiments follows that pairs need at least 50% more effort than in case of individual programming (see [14] for more details). So, it is not obvious if pair programming really pays-off and further research is necessary.

8 Conclusions

After completion of all projects in both Project Areas (SDS-XP and SDS-CMM), several conclusions can be deduced. First of all, XP has some critical risk factors, which can lead to project failure. The factors we described appeared to be important in SDS projects, that do not claim to be real industry ones, although in many aspects (like full-time students involvement, progress tracking) they were very similar. Therefore, special care should be paid when introducing XP into organization's practice. We suggested several improvements that allowed the teams to finalize the projects successfully (i.e. with delivering both the product and master thesis without excessive delay). Anyway, it proved to be non-trivial for newly-formed teams, which members are inexperienced and do not know one another very well.

On the other hand, the SDS-CMM process implementation seems more stable and less failure-prone, but also the work is more tedious (e.g. keeping the numerous documents consistent). In the SDS-CMM Project Area, the customer involvement, appropriate CASE tools and strict process definition seem to be the most important success factors.

The comparison of the processes shows that SDS-CMM process is less failure-prone, since it puts stress to the process organization, whereas XP process stresses personal team members involvement and experience. Still, the impact of risk factors we encountered may be dependent on the team itself. Anyway, XP appears to be an interesting alternative for teams with some experience in working together, members of which can communicate easily.

References

1. K. Beck, Extreme Programming Explained: Embrace Change, Addison-Wesley, Boston, 2000.
2. K. Beck, M. Fowler, Planning Extreme Programming, Addison-Wesley, Boston, 2001.
3. G. Booch, Object-Oriented Analysis and Design with Applications, Redwood City, Addison-Wesley, 1991.
4. CMMI Models, http://www.sei.cmu.edu/cmmi/products/models.html (February 2002)
5. T. DeMarco, Structured Analysis and System Specification, Englewood Cliffs, Prentice-Hall, 1978.
6. T. DeMarco, The Agile Organization, http://www.escom.co.uk/conference2001/papers/keynote-tom-demarco.pdf (February 2002)
7. C. Elgot, Structured programming with and without GO TO statements, IEEE Trans. Soft. Eng., No 1, 1976, 41-53.
8. M. Fagan, Design and code inspections to reduce errors in program development, IBM Systems Journal, vol. 15 (1976), No. 3.
9. J. Grenning, Launching Extreme Programming at a Process–Intensive Company, IEEE Software, vol. 18, No. 6, 27-33.
10. W. Humphrey, A Discipline for Software Engineering, Addison-Wesley, Reading MA, 1995.

11. W. Humphrey, Introduction to the Team Software Process, Addison-Wesley, Reading MA, 2000.
12. R. Jeffries, A. Anderson, C. Hendrickson, Extreme Programming Installed, Addison-Wesley, 2001.
13. J. Nawrocki, Towards educating leaders of software teams, in: P. Klint, J. Nawrocki (eds), Proceedings of Software Engineering Education Symposium SEES'98, Scientific Publishers OWN, Poznan, 1998, 149-157.
14. J. Nawrocki, A. Wojciechowski, Experimental evaluation of pair programming, in: K. Maxwell, S. Oligny, R. Kusters, E. van Veenendaal (eds), Project Control: Satisfying the Customer (Proceedings of ESCOM 2001, 2-4 April 2001, London, UK), Shaker Publishing,   2001,   269-276, http://www.escom.co.uk/conference2001/papers/nawrocki.pdf (February 2002)
15. J. Nawrocki, B. Walter, A. Wojciechowski, Toward maturity model for eXtreme Programming, Proceedings of the 27th EUROMICRO Conference, Los Alamitos, IEEE Computer Society, 233-239.
16. J. T. Nosek, The case for collaborative programming, Communications of the ACM, vol. 41 (1998), No. 3, 105-108.
17. D. L. Parnas, On the criteria to be used in decomposing systems into modules, Communications of the ACM, vol. 15, No. 12 (1972), 1053-58.
18. M. C. Paulk et al., The Capability Maturity Model: Guidelines for Inproving the Software Process, Addison-Wesley, Reading MA, 1995.
19. M. C. Paulk, Extreme Programming from a CMM Perspective, IEEE Software, vol. 18, No. 6, 19-26.
20. Ch. Poole, J. W. Huisman, Using Extreme Programming in a Maintenance Environment, IEEE Software, vol. 18, No. 6, 42-50.
21. J. Seddon, The Case Against ISO 9000, Oak Tree Press, Dublin, 2000.
22. P. Schuh, Recovery, Redemption, and Extreme Programming, IEEE Software, vol. 18, No. 6, 34-41.
23. B. Stroustrup, The C++ Programming Language, Addison-Wesley, Reading MA, 1985.
24. R. Tricker, B. Sherring-Lucas, ISO 9001:2000 in Brief, Butterworth-Heinemann, Oxford, 2001.
25. L. Williams et al., Strengthening the case for pair programming, IEEE Software, vol. 17 (2000), No. 4, 19-25.
26. N. Wirth, Programming in Modula-2, Springer-Verlag, Heidelberg, 1982.

An Empirical Study
with Metrics for Object-Relational Databases

Coral Calero[1], Houari Sahraoui[2], and Mario Piattini[1]

[1] Departamento de Informática University of Castilla-La Mancha
Paseo de la Universidad, 4
13071, Ciudad Real (Spain)
{Coral.Calero,Mario.Piattin}@uclm.es
[2] DIRO, Université de Montréal, CP 6128 succ Centre-Ville,
Montréal QC H3C 3J7, Canada
sahraouh@iro.umontreal.ca

Abstract. Object-relational databases are supposed to be the substitutes of relational ones because they are a good mixture between the relational model and object-oriented principles. In this paper we present the empirical work we have developed with four metrics for object-relational databases (Percentage of Complex Columns (PCC), Number of Shared Classes (NSC), Number of Involved Classes (NIC) and Table Size (TS)) defined at different granularity levels (attribute, class, table and schema). The empirical work presented is the validation made with the aim of proving the usefulness of the four metrics in estimating the complexity of an object-relational schema . This study can be considered to be a replica of another one we made with the same purpose but with two main differences: the dependent variable and the way we analyze the results. The results obtained from the empirical work seem to prove the usefulness of the TS metric in estimating the complexity of an object-relational schema however, conclusions about the other metrics are difficult to extract.

1 Introduction

Relational databases are the most important ones in the database world. This success can be explained because they are not too difficult to understand and also because there is a standard (SQL) for them. However, relational databases are not capable of working with the new kind of data (as complex data, image, sound, GIS, CAD) modern applications require.

In response to these new necessities, object oriented databases were created as the successors of the relational ones, but they have not been successful. Perhaps because, unlike the relational model, OO databases have not had a widely accepted standard until the appearance of the ODMG, but also because it is very difficult to convince 85% of the market of this revolutionary change: another technology, another way of thinking for their workers, another kind of data types, etc.

In order to allow the possibility of working with new data and applications without a revolutionary change in the market, the relational industry has reacted and has created object-relational databases that can be considered to be an evolutionary

J. Kontio and R. Conradi (Eds.): ECSQ 2002, LNCS 2349, pp. 298–309, 2002.

solution. The idea is to allow the adaptation of the relational market by supporting some object orientation capabilities. So, these databases have all the elements of the relational model (relations connected by referential integrity relationships) but with the particularity that the columns of a relation can be defined over a class. In fact, some studies predict that object-relational databases will substitute the relational ones by the year 2003 ([4]). Perhaps the data is not so accurate, but the change seems to be possible.

Taking into account the brilliant future predicted for the object-relational databases in the database market and to ensure that it becomes a reality, it is essential to have quality designs. One widely accepted mechanism for assuring the quality of a software product in general and of object-relational database designs in particular, is the use of metrics specifically designed for this kind of databases.

Metrics must be defined for capturing a specific attribute of a product (in our case object-relational databases). We think one of the most important internal factors to be captured is complexity. If we have a set of metrics for capturing complexity, we are also capturing understandability ([5]) and hence maintainability, one important dimension in software product quality ([3]).

In this paper we present the empirical work we have developed in order to know if the metrics defined for object-relational databases are good mechanisms for measuring their complexity and, hence, for assuring the quality of the schema design of this kind of databases. The controlled experiment presented is a replica of a previous one. However, there are two main differences between the study presented here and the previous one: the dependent variable and the way we analyze the results. We decided to change these two factors to see if the results obtained on the first study were independent of these factors and hence could be generalized.

A deeper explanation about object-relational databases and the metrics we have designed for them will be presented in the next section. Section Three will present the problem statement and the experiment planning will appear in Section Four. Analysis and interpretation will be discussed in Section Five and conclusions and future work will appear on the last section.

2   Metrics for Object-Relational Databases

As we have said in the previous section, object-relational databases can be considered a mixture of relational databases with object oriented characteristics.

So, an object-relational database schema is composed by a number of tables related by referential integrity, which have columns that can be defined over simple or complex (user-defined) data types. Simple data types may be one of the classic data types as integer, number or character (correspond to the relational columns). A complex or user-defined data type (also called classes), can be related with other data types by generalization associations.

In Table 1 we present an example of an object-relational database schema whose definition is in SQL:1999. The example defines two tables (agency and houses). Table agency has 2 simple columns (idAgency and name) and 1 complex column (situation) and table houses has 7 simple columns (idHouse, idAgency, price, rooms, size, description and photo) and 1 complex column (situation). We can also see that in table houses we have two columns defined as LOB type, this data type is used to store multimedia data (even GB).

Table 1. Example of an object-relational schema

create **type** address as(
    street varchar(15),
    city varchar(10),
    county varchar(10),
    zip varchar(8));
	create table **agency**(
	    idAgency integer,
	    name varchar(10),
	    situation address
	        primary key (idAgency));

	create table **houses**(
	    idHouse integer,
	    idAgency integer,
	    price double,
	    rooms integer,
	    size float(4),
	    situation address,
	    description clob(100K),
	    photo blob(100K)
	        primary key idHouse;
	        foreign key (idAgency)
	        references agency);

Considering all the characteristics explained, we present the next metrics (the detailed explanation of these metrics can be found in [1]:

- **TS** (Table Size). This metric is calculated by adding the size of the simple columns (in our case we consider that a simple column has a size equal to one) of the table (TSSC) plus the size of the complex columns of the table (TSCC). The size of a complex column is defined as the size of the class hierarchy above which the column is defined divided by the number of complex columns that are defined over this hierarchy (SHC/NHC). The size of the hierarchy is defined as the sum of the classes of the generalization hierarchy. The size of a class is calculated as the sum of its attributes plus the size of its methods. It is necessary to take into account that a class can also have simple attributes (with a size equal to one) and complex attributes (attributes related to other classes by an aggregation relationship and its size are calculated as the size of a class). It will also be necessary to divide the size of a class by the number of classes which are related to the class with an aggregation relationship.
- **NIC** (Number of Involved Classes). Number of classes needed for defining all the columns of a table.
- **NSC** (Number of Shared Classes). Number of classes that are used by more than one table.
- **PCC** (Percentage of Complex Columns). Number of the columns of a table that are complex related with the total number of columns of the table.

Table 2. Relationships among the characteristics of the object-relational database levels and the metrics

	TABLE	CLASS	SCHEMA	ATTRIBUTE
PCC	X			
NIC	X	X		
NSC	X	X	X	
TS	X	X	X	X

Table 3. Relationship between our metrics and coupling and size

	SIZE	COUPLING
TS	X	x
NIC	X	x
NSC		x
PCC	X	

Table 4. Metrics values for the example presented in Table 1

	TS	NIC	NSC	PCC
Agency	4	1	1	1
Houses	9	1	1	1

We have selected these metrics because they cover all the possible levels of an object-relational database (attribute, class, table and schema). In Table 2, we reflect the different levels involved on the definition of each of the metrics. For calculating the PCC metric, it is necessary to look at the information of the table. For the NIC metric, it is necessary to look at the information of a table and the classes used by this table. For the NSC metric, we work at a table level. We also need to consider all the classes involved in the definition of this table and the rest of the schema tables that also use these classes. Finally, the calculation of the TS metric requires the consideration of a table: its simple attributes, the classes the table uses for the definition of its complex columns and whether or not these classes are used by other tables

We can also relate the metrics with two important factors related to complexity, size and coupling (see Table 3).

Applying these metrics to the example presented in Table 1, we obtain the values shown in Table 4.

The next step is to try to prove if our metrics can be considered complexity metrics.

3 Problem Statement

As we indicated previously, the main goal of this paper is to prove that the presented metrics can be used as complexity metrics.

The experimentation presented in this paper can be considered a replica of another controlled experiment carried out with the same objective. However, with the aim of being able to generalize the results, some changes were included in this second controlled experiment with respect to the first one:

- the dependent variable is now measured as the time needed by the subjects to answer a set of questions about the object-relational schemas, unlike the dependent variable in the previous study that was measured as the number of correct answers obtained in a fixed time.
- the way we analyze the results. In this study we use traditional statistics and in the previous one we used advanced techniques (RoC and C4.5).

In the next section, we will briefly present the results obtained from the original experiment. At the end of this paper we will discuss the conclusions we can draw from the experimentation process as a whole.

3.1 Previous Work

In [2] the previous experimental work made with these and other metrics is presented. In that case we also sought to prove the utility of our metrics as complexity indicators. Our hypothesis was that *complexity is itself impacted by the size and the coupling between the elements of an object-relational database schema (tables and classes)*. We worked with six object-relational schemas and the dependent variable was measured as the time needed by the subjects to make some operations with the schemas. To analyze the usefulness of the metrics, we used two machine learning (ML) techniques: C4.5 ([6]), a Top Down Induction of Decision Trees algorithm, and RoC ([7]), a robust Bayesian classifier. As for subjects, we worked with people from both Canada and Spain. As a conclusion, both techniques indicated that the table size metric (TS) is a good indicator for the complexity of a table. The rest of the metrics do not seem to have a real impact on the complexity of a table.

3.2 Current Work

As previously indicated, the main goal of this paper is to explain the empirical work we developed in order to know if the results obtained with the previous study about our metrics were repeated and, hence, could be generalized. The hypothesis did not vary in the replication of the experiment. However, we did change the way in which the dependent variable was measured (we wanted to capture complexity in another way in order to confirm if the previous results were independent of the way it was captured) and the way we analyzed the results (to know if the results are independent of the technique used). By carrying out this kind of replication in which the same hypothesis is studied but some details of the experiment are changed, our aim is to make the results of the experiment more reliable.

The goal definition of our experiment can be summarized as:
- *To analyze* the metrics for object-relational databases
- *for the purpose* of evaluating if they can be used as a useful mechanism

- *with respect to* the object-relational databases complexity
- from the designer *point of view*
- *in the context of* students of a database course with knowledge of object-relational databases, relational databases and object-oriented programming.

4 Experiment Planning

Nine students from the University of Montreal (Canada) and six students from the University of Castilla-La Mancha (Spain) participated in the experiment. All of them were finishing a course on advanced databases and knew all the concepts related with object-relational databases. They were also familiar with relational databases and object-oriented programming.

We tried to define the tests involved in the experiment in such a way that they would be representative of real cases. The use of a simple experiment allows other experimenters to replicate it because the number of examples is not too large. All the experimental materials (laboratory package) of this experiment can be found in http://alarcos.inf-cr.uclm.es.

4.1 Hypotheses Formulation

Our hypothesis is that complexity is itself impacted by the size and the coupling between the elements of an object-relational database schema (tables and classes).

4.2 Variables in the Study

Independent variables. In our experiment these variables correspond with the metrics under study: TS, NIC, NSC and PCC. Each of these metrics (factors) can take different values (levels) .

Table 5. Descriptive statistics of each metric

	Minimum	Maximum	Average	Stan.Dev.
NIC	,00	7,00	2,6410	1,9532
NSC	,00	5,00	1,0513	1,1459
PCC	,00	,66	,2982	,1736
TS	2,00	25,00	9,9474	6,4840

Dependent variables. As we have previously stated, the complexity of the tests was measured as the time each subject used to perform all the tasks of each one of the 21 object-relational database schemas. Taking into account the experience of the subjects in relational and object-relational database design and object-oriented programming, and the fact that the tasks were not too difficult, we thought that all of them would give the right answers. We were proved right as all the subjects (except one whose results were discarded) answered the tests correctly. Therefore, we were able to work with the results of fourteen subjects.

Regarding the time, it is necessary to point out that it included the time to analyze the schema and the time to answer the questions about it.

4.3 Analysis

Taking the hypotheses into account, the experiments must consider the relationship between the metrics and the time. So, we decided to made a correlation among these factors. For the correlation test we used two different correlation tests: the Pearson correlation, and the Spearman´s non-parametric correlation to identify potential relationships between the time needed by the subjects and the metrics defined.

4.4 Data Used in the Study

Twenty-one object-relational database schemas were used for performing the experiment. The documentation was approximately twenty-four pages long and included, in addition to the database schemas, a general description of the metrics and a requirements document.

For each design, four operations were performed. The subjects had to calculate the values of four structural metrics for each table of each one of the 21 schemas. With the results they had to complete a questionnaire. Part of this questionnaire is shown in Figure 1. In this questionnaire, the result of each metric in each table of each schema had to be recorded along with the time needed to calculate these values.

Table Name	Schema Name	Begin (Hour :Minute)	O1	O2	O3	O4	End (Hour :Minute)
Laboratories	Laboratory_Reports						
Books	Library						
Activities	Sport_2						
Houses	Housing						
Categories	Directory						
Cities	Regions						

Figure 1. Question/Answer Paper

Before the subjects took the test, the experiment was conducted with a small group of people in order to improve it, if necessary and ensure that both the experiment and the documentation were well designed. No changes were necessary.

Tests were given to the subjects and they had a week to answer and return the results. Before giving them the material, the complete experiment was explained to the subjects, what kind of exercises they had to do, the material they would be given, what kind of answers they had to provide and how they had to record the time spent solving the problem. The metrics with an example was also explained.

Before starting each test, the subjects had to record the start time, and when they had completed the test, they had to record the end time. As the annotation of the time was the responsibility of the subjects and in order to avoid fatigue effects in the subjects (because the experiment had a lot of schemas) we decided to give the subjects one week to carry out the experiment.

In order to avoid learning effects we required subjects to calculate the metrics of the tables in a determined order, in this way they never worked with two tables of the same schema consecutively. As all the metrics were correctly answered, to obtain the results of the experiment we used the number of minutes needed by each subject. We may indicate here that one test were discarded because we detected very strange results on the time annotated by a subject and he told us that he had not respected the order given in the question/answer paper.

4.5 Validity of the Results

We are aware that different threats to the validity of the results of an experiment exist. In this section we are going to discuss threats to internal and external validity and to construct.

Construct Validity

Construct validity is concerned with the relationship between theory and observation ([8]). We propose, as a reasonable measure of complexity, the time for calculating the values of the metrics taking into account that this time comprises not only the time needed to calculate the metrics but also the time needed by the subject to analyze and to understand the object-relational database schema.

To assure construct validity it would be necessary to perform more experiments, varying the operations to be developed.

Internal Validity

Internal validity is related to the assurance that the relationship observed between the treatment and the outcome is a causal relationship, and that it is not a result of a factor over which we have no control or which we have not measured ([8]). Regarding internal validity the following issues must be considered:

- Differences among subjects. Although we worked with subjects of different countries, we think there were no significant differences among them because they had approximately the same experience on relational and object-relational databases and on object-oriented programming. In fact all of them (except for one) calculated the metrics correctly.
- Differences among schemas. We tried to define the tests involved in the experiment in such a way that they were representative of real cases. However, the domain of the schemas was different and this could influence the results obtained in some way.
- Precision in the time values. The subjects were responsible for recording the start and finish times of each test. We think this method is more effective than having

a supervisor who records the time of each subject. However, we are aware that the subject could introduce some imprecision.

- Learning effects. We required subjects to calculate the metrics of the tables in a determined order, in this way they never worked with two tables of the same schema consecutively. In this way, we think we prevent learning effects.
- Fatigue effects. In order to avoid fatigue effects in the subjects (because the experiment had a lot of schemas) we decided to give the subjects one week to carry out the experiment. We think this could be dangerous (from the plagiarism perspective, for example) if the subjects were be forced to made the experiment but, as we used volunteers, we think this is not a problem.
- Persistence effects. Not present because the subjects had never performed a similar experiment.
- Subject motivation. The experiment was made by volunteers so we think they were sufficiently motivated.
- Other factors. Subjects were informed they should not share answers with other subjects. Nevertheless, the subjects were not watched or controlled during the experiment so we cannot assure that the mentioned effects do not appear, although we think it is improbable.

External Validity

External validity is concerned with generalization of the results ([8]). Regarding external validity the following issues must be considered:

- Materials and tasks used. We tried to use schemas and operations representative of real cases in the experiments although more experiments with larger and more complex schemas are necessary.
- Subjects. In general, more experiments with a larger number of subjects, students and professionals, and with different kinds of operations are necessary to obtain more conclusive results about the metrics.
- We tried to increase external validity by performing the replica with some changes (in the dependent variable and in the technique used to analyze the results), so the results can be more general.

5 Analysis and Interpretation

As we have explained previously, we had fourteen data sets for each table of each schema, one of which corresponded to the answer of each subject of the experiment. For applying the tests of correlation we decided to work, for each table, with the time average for calculating each metric.

First we had to check the normality of the data obtained after the calculation of the average. If the data were normal, the best option in our case was to use parametric tests because they are more efficient than non-parametric tests and because they require fewer data points (this point is very important in our case because we only have eleven data points), and therefore smaller experiments than do non-parametric tests.

Among the tests we can apply to ascertain if a distribution is normal, we have the Shapiro-Wilk test and the Kolmogorov-Smirnov test. Both tests were applied to our data and we found that they were normal. In Figure 2 the normality test graph is shown. As we can see, the points are near the line, so the data can be considered normal and the parametric tests can be applied.

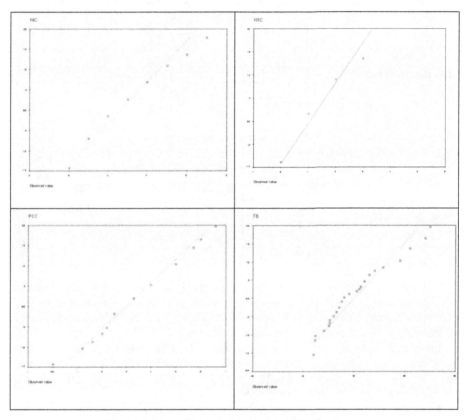

Figure 2. Normality tests for the data of the four cases

To proceed to the analysis, we first have to preset a level of significance. Several factors have to be considered when setting α because we can commit a Type I error (probability of incorrectly rejecting the null hypothesis). We decided to select α=0.05 which means a 95% level of confidence.

Although we knew our data were normal and the parametric tests could be applied, we decided to apply both, parametric and non-parametric tests in order to check if we would obtain the same results. So, we applied both Pearson and Spearman correlation tests to our data. We present the results obtained from the Pearson (Table 6) and Spearman (Table 7) correlations below.

From the Pearson correlation we can conclude that the number of involved classes, the percentage of complex columns and the table size seem to be significant metrics as complexity indicators. The number of shared classes does not seem to be significant. This can be explained because the NSC is easily calculable (it is only the number of classes that are shared by more than one table) and does not add complexity to the schema.

Table 6. Pearson correlation results

		NIC	NSC	PCC	TS	TIME AVG
Pearson Correlation	**NIC**	1,000	,267	,826	,829	,607
	NSC	,267	1,000	,130	-,172	,164
	PCC	,826	,130	1,000	,694	,575
	TS	,829	-,172	,694	1,000	,513
	TIME AVG	,607	,164	,575	,513	1,000

Table 7. Spearman correlation results

		NIC	NSC	PCC	TS	TIME AVG
Rho de Spearman	**NIC**	1,000	,299	,805	,807	,733
	NSC	,299	1,000	,188	-,082	,331
	PCC	,805	,188	1,000	,605	,650
	TS	,807	-,082	,605	1,000	,648
	TIME AVG	,733	,331	,650	,648	1,000

From the Spearman correlation we can conclude the same as from the Pearson's one, the number of involved classes, the percentage of complex columns and the table size seem to be significant metrics as complexity indicators, unlike the number of shared classes which does not seem to be significant.

From both tests we can conclude that the NIC, PCC and TS seem to be good indicators of the complexity of an object-relational database schema. Also, we can see that there is a correlation among TS and the rest of the metrics (except NSC), so perhaps it would be enough to use the TS metric.

From the experiments as a whole, the previous one and the one presented in this paper, we can conclude that TS seems to be a good indicator of the object-relational databases complexity and it is not possible to obtain a conclusive result for the other metrics.

It would be necessary to carry out more experiments with the set of metrics to determine if the PCC, the NIC and the NSC metrics are useful complexity mechanisms of the object-relational database schemas or not. The new experiments can also help us to know if the statistic technique applied also has impact on the results obtained.

It would be also interesting to carry out new experiments with the participation of professionals instead of students, and make not only controlled experiments but also case studies with real data. In this way, the experimental work would be complete and the results would be more conclusive.

6 Conclusions and Future Work

Object-relational database are considered to be the substitutes of the relational ones in the database market. For assuring that the designs obtained have quality, it is fundamental to have metrics for the designs of these databases. However, it is more important to be sure that the metrics proposed are useful for the aim they seek to achieve. Performing empirical validation with the metrics is fundamental in order to demonstrate their practical utility. In this paper we have presented part of the empirical work we are developing with a set of metrics for object-relational database schema designs (TS, NIC, NSC and PCC).

The controlled experiment presented here can be considered as the replica of a previous one. The objective of this empirical validation is to know if the metrics can be considered indicators of the complexity of the database design.

As a result of the experiment we have concluded that the TS, NIC and PCC metrics seem to be good complexity indicators. Also, we have indicated that there is a correlation among TS and the rest of the metrics (except NSC), so perhaps, it would be enough to use the TS metric.

As a result from the whole empirical work, we can only obtain conclusive results for the TS metric.

Looking at these results it is necessary to follow up to learn more about the metrics. Perhaps, the experimental process would be improved by changing the subjects (working with practitioners), and developing real cases (working with real data). However, we think this study was necessary in order to have preliminary results about the metrics.

References

1. Calero, C., Piattini, M., Ruiz, F. and Polo, M. Validation of metrics for Object-Relational Databases, *International Workshop on Quantitative Approaches in Object-Oriented Software Engineering (ECOOP99)*, (Lisbon ,Portugal. June 1999), 14-18
2. Calero. C., Sahraoui, H, Piattini, M., Lounis, H. Estimating Object-Relational Database Understandability Using Structural Metrics, *12th International Conference and Workshop on Database and Expert Systems Applications, (DEXA 2001)*, (Munich, Germany, 3-7 September 2001).
3. ISO (1999). ISO 9126. Software Product Evaluation-Quality Characteristics and Guidelines for their Use. *ISO/IEC Standard 9126*. Geneva.
4. Leavitt, N. (2000). Whatever happened to Object-Oriented Databases?. Industry Trends, *IEEE Computer Society*. pp. 16-19. August
5. Li, H.F. and Cheng, W.K. An empirical study of software metrics. *IEEE Trans. on Software Engineering*, (1987), 13 (6): 679-708.
6. Quinlan, J.R., *C4.5: Programs for Machine Learning, (1993)*, Morgan Kaufmann Publishers.
7. Ramoni, M. and Sebastiani, P. Bayesian methods for intelligent data analysis. In M. Berthold and D.J. Hand, editors, *An Introduction to Intelligent Data Analysis*, (New York, 1999). Springer.
8. Wohlin, C., Runeson, P., Höst, M., Ohlsson, M.C., Regnell, B. and Wesslén, A. *(2000). Experimentation in Software Engineering. An Introduction.* Ed. Kluwer Academic Publishers

Extended Model-Based Testing
toward High Code Coverage Rate

Juichi Takahashi[1] and Yoshiaki Kakuda[2]

[1] SAP Labs, 2-43, Aomi, Koto-ku, Tokyo 135-0064, Japan,
`juichi.takahashi@SAP.com`
[2] Hiroshima City University, Faculty of Information Sciences, 3-4-1,
Ohzuka-higashi, Asaminami-word, Hiroshima 731-3194, Japan,
`kakuda@ce.hiroshima-cu.ac.jp`

Abstract. Recently, it has become popular to use applications on window operating systems, such as Microsoft Windows and GNOME, and for this we attempt to use the GUI specific testing approach. Legacy type of approaches, such as control flow path and data flow path testing, are not always effective testing methods for GUI application. Thus, model-based testing was newly established and often used in GUI application testing. But the model-based testing method is not yet mature and has not been researched enough. Our developed model-based testing focuses not only on application behavior but also on data and external factors. In addition, we realized that model-based testing lacks the ability to find some types of defect. In this paper, we will clarify which factors are lacking and offer solutions with case studies.

1 Introduction

Many researchers have investigated code-based and white box testing. However, the software is complicated and lines of code are much bigger than a decade ago. For commercial software, we often rely more on black-box testing than white-box testing since it is not feasible for all testers to understand developed code. Using development code to test requires too much time and expense. Only risk control software, such as rail and flight control systems may be suitable for white box testing. For instance, in SAP Co., most testing is executed using the black box testing method without the testers knowing developed code. On the other hand, a formal specification can generate certain models [1]. However, whereas people recognize the importance of specification, in business software, we often start development before finishing the design specification because marketing pressure obliges software developers and designers to start writing code as soon as they can. In addition, a lot of application has designed by using GUI, and model based-testing is perfectly adapted for GUI specific testing. Due to the above factors, we naturally use the black box and the model-based testing approach. Yet, the problem is that little is known about black box and model based testing in the theoretical testing research area. First, in this research, we analyze our developed extended model-based testing and check whether it can find all types

J. Kontio and R. Conradi (Eds.): ECSQ 2002, LNCS 2349, pp. 310–320, 2002.

of bugs, besides more finding code defect than using existing model-based testing. Also, by using code coverage rate, we will demonstrate that the extended model-based testing can increase software quality. Second, there is the problem that existing model-based testing uses only the black box testing method. Thus, we are aware only of experimental achievements obtained by this method. We analyze our extended model-based testing using both black box and white box testing and then we demonstrate how efficient extended model based testing.

1.1 Model-Based Testing

In most model-based testing [2][3]and automatic test case generation [4] [5] the modeling generates a set of data and operations, as well as executing test cases by the black box testing method. Before turning to extended model-based testing, it would be useful to examine existing model-based testing using Microsoft(R) Notepad(R), which is commonly used by many people. A simple scenario is that users open a file using Microsoft Notepad. During the opening of a file, users may have 4 states and 7 transitions (Fig. 1, 2). Using those transitions and states, we can, for instance, generate series of transitions, such as:

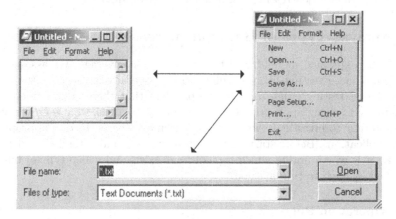

Fig. 1. Notepad Application

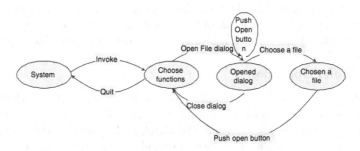

Fig. 2. Transition diagram

"Invoke -> open file dialog -> choose a file -> push open button -> open file dialog -> close dialog -> quit". In another case: "Invoke -> quit". Testers can make thousands of paths to cover every possible users' behavior. The model-based testing is seen to be of value in simulating users' behavior and to execute some combined operations. But just simulating user behavior is not sufficient to prove if the model-based testing can contribute to raise software quality and find bugs.

1.2   Code Coverage

Since testing research started, coverage analysis has been used [6][7]. It is known that more code coverage means higher quality. We recommended 100% code coverage before releasing software [8]. Thus, in this paper, we use the code coverage rate to assess software quality and the extent to which extended model-based testing contributes to increase software quality. There are several coverage methods, namely: decision coverage, condition coverage, C/D(condition/decision) coverage, and so on [6]. Because C/D coverage is more accurate than other methods, we use this to assess the application quality. The current problem is that model-based testing does not provide theoretical evidence for increased software quality. Thus, at present, we use the code coverage rate to provide evidence of whether extended model-based testing can increase software quality.

2   Analyse Types of Bug and Increase Coverage Rate

We briefly explained model-based testing and code coverage. We assume existing model-based testing likely simulates users' operations. Besides, the current model-based testing issue, there is the problem that there is no evidence that model-based testing appropriately tests application. Thus, we use C/D coverage data in order to investigate whether existing model-based testing appropriately tests applications. Before starting to analyze existing and extended model-based testing, it is worth noting which type of bugs exist, and which type of bugs can be found by each testing method.

2.1   Operation Bugs

Existing model-based testing tries to find bugs when users use various operation. Yet, the existing model-based testing does not distinguish between operation and data inputting. In extended model-based testing, we handle the operation and the data input separately. We will begin by considering operational bugs.

2.1.1   Mono Operation

When developing test cases, testers try to keep them simple so they be easily maintained. For instance, Yamasura[9] suggests developing test cases can be classified into three groups: normal, abnormal, and boundary test cases, as minimum testable units. Using Yamaura's method, we can expose most of the mono operational defects and any testing method can find these types of bugs.

2.1.2   Multiple Operation

Beizer [10] describes this as "The testing you do when you put yourself in the software user's place to verify that it behaves the way it's supposed to, no matter how it may be build." Testers design a number of test cases from users' behavior, and then they separate them into each unit test component. This is not a true use case as when users use real software. They usually use software to achieve a goal. Until reaching the goal users keep using software and use various functions sequentially. But the exiting model-based testing method tends to execute paths which are as short as possible (using the shortest path and Markov model [11]) and avoids testing the same operation because it is verbose. We should also add that the existing model-based testing method does not anticipate the user performing the same function multiple times. However, users may initiate the same function multiple times, and then the operation may find more bugs than mono operation. Also these multiple operations sometimes extend code coverage rate. Thus, we insist that this multiple operation should be added to extended-model based testing. The following are a couple of examples of multiple operation bugs:

Memory Leak: When an application uses static memory to store data, memory leak does not occur. Yet, in commercial products, an application may be required small amount of memory while running. Consequently, developers often use dynamic memory instead of static memory. When employing dynamic memory usage, developers explicitly free the memory after use, for example by using *free*, *delete* functions in C language. Usually leaking memory is not harmful if it occurs only once. However, if it occurs multiple times it may cause critical bugs. In order to reveal this type of bug, testers are required to operate the same function multiple times.

Running Out of Memory: When users operate a function multiple times, the application often uses much more memory than for a single operation. Therefore, the application is supposed to check if the memory runs out. Yet, sometimes developers do not implement the memory checking code, and the application may stop. In this case, using existing model-based testing, we rarely find these types of bug because the existing model-based testing tend to cover operation paths as short as possible. On the other hand, using extended model based testing, testers are recommended to operate the same function multiple times and find these 'running out of memory bugs'. An example of a combined and multiple operations' bug is: when using PowerPoint and creating more than 8000 slides, PowerPoint becomes erratic because of memory shortage. As shown on Fig.3, after making over 8000 sheets, even if the letters "aaaa" are typed, they do not appear on screen. We assume that PowerPoint does not check if memory is available in the operating system.

Expanding Used Code: When users perform multiple operations, the application may run on another part of code which does not run in mono operation.

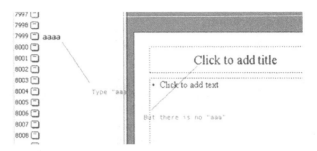

Fig. 3. An example of shortage memory

An example will be shown in a later chapter (3.2). As we showed above, we often see multiple operation bugs when we input data multiple times. Normally, a model based testing diagram (Fig. 2) is modeled on the same rule for all functions. However, we suggest using a guideline when testers model the application. It is applicable that inputting functions will be executed as many as possible. For example, in Markov modeling[11], the testers can assume that users employ the inputting function much more than other functions. Another recommended guideline for applying extended-model based testing, is that when an application use a lot of memory, extended model-based testing allows it to be tested with limited memory condition.

2.2   Data Inputting Bugs

Using existing model-based testing, testers may not find bugs that are related to data because the testing method often ignores data. We assume the data are used for calculation and control application, and analyze both in this section.

Data Calculation: Computers originally calculate data and show the result to users, such as spreadsheet. You may often see calculation errors in real life computing. In data calculation, we cannot offer any solution for finding bugs and increasing coverage using our extended nor existing model based testing.

Data Which Control Application Behavior: Data is not only used for calculation, but also for control of applications. Existing model-based testing only considers pre and post conditions. If only if the data change state, the existing model-based testing requires input data. To put it another way, when the data inputting does not effect a change of state, the existing model-based testing does not consider data at all. If testers know the data will impact application control, they expect to input those data in extended model-based testing. However, there is no doubt it is difficult testing with such an incredible number of combinations [6]. For example, an application with two edit boxes and an input parameter might accept integers in the range of 0, 255. Combination pattern are 255 x 255. Even we use automated testing, inputting those combinations is extremely difficult. In such cases, we may use boundary analysis and AETG[12]. AETG

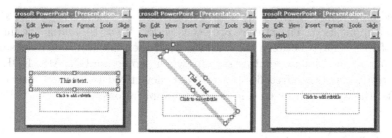

Fig. 4. PowerPoint bug

Fig. 5. xclock application

could be the best solution when testers use extended model-based testing since it can dramatically reduce the number of combination test cases. There is an interesting bug, which is caused by unique data inputting. In fig. 4, when rotating a string to 180 degrees, there are no problems. However, when rotating the screen 45 degrees twice, the screened text disappears. This example shows not to reveal this bug without inputting various data. Existing model-based testing cannot find this type of bugs since they do not distinguish between inputting 45 and 90 degrees. Both degree input values can be regarded as the same states in existing model-based testing.

External Invoking: One problem is that current model-based testing does not consider external invoking factors such as timers, network communications, and so on. For example, when we develop the clock application (Fig. 5) the application is invoked by the user, and after a certain time passes, the software is invoked by a system call which tells that a certain time has passed. Whittaker mentions [13] that software is operated by users and invisible users. When modeling extended model-based testing, we have to consider 'invisible users' such as clock invoking and network communication. A case study using a clock application is taken up in a later section.

3   A Case Study: Analysis for x11 Project

We demonstrated our idea on how to increase the code coverage rate to ensure software quality. This case study attempted to provide evidence that our extended model-based testing can increase the code coverage rate by using xfree86 project application. The xfree86 project is widely used [14] and is the underlying software that is between the hardware and the graphical user interface. For example, in the Linux operating system, when people use GNOME, KDE, they are already using the xfree86 software. We believe if we use the software and get results, the result can be used in other real applications.

3.1   Xclock Application

In order to demonstrate our case study, we chose a xfree application called the xlcock. Xclock is a simple application which tells the current time either digitally or by analog means. The code includes 9282 lines. We demonstrated the percentage of external invoking during 1 min. of running. What was demonstrated was that the clock program may have at least 6 % of timer related code, and the code can be covered by our extended-model based testing. This result suggests the existing model-based testing may lose this timer related code coverage.

3.2   Xclipboard Application

Another sample is the Xclipboard application that is included with the Xfree86 project. The Xclipboard program(see Fig. 6) is used to collect and display text selections that are sent to the clipboard by other clients. It is typically used to save clipboard selections for later use. Modeling by existing model based testing is shown in Fig. 7. We show a simple example that expands the code coverage rate by multiple operations. The first operation is:

    Invoke -> Type "a" character -> Push the New button
Coverage rate is 12%. The second operation is:

    Invoke -> Type "a" character -> Push the New button
    -> Push the New button again
Coverage rate is 13%. In this example, the second operation can increase coverage rate by 1%. The reason for the increase in coverage is that the first operation gets a memory area for a new operation, and the second operation checks if there is already memory storing input data. Therefore, there are different code

Fig. 6. Xclipboard application

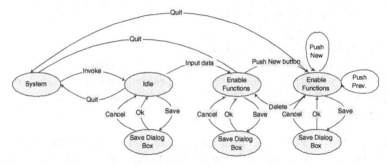

Fig. 7. Transition diagram for Xclipboard

executions between the first and second operations. This example clearly shows that multiple operations can increase coverage rate.

4   Analysis Using White Box Testing

We demonstrated how to increase the code coverage rate in model-based testing from the black-box point of view. The question we have to ask here is whether our extended model-based testing can cover the whole developed code and can find more bugs than existing model-based testing. We already know it is extremely difficult to obtain 100% coverage rate by black box testing. In this section, we approach testing from the white box testing point of view and show how our extended model based testing could be affected and limited. We now consider which factors decide whether branch code exists or not, since the coverage is decided by branch coding. Interestingly, checking both the xclock and the xclipboard applications, we can categorized the branches into following four parts:

- **Branches Decided by Condition**
  ```
  if (currentClip -> prev)
    newCurrent = currentClip -> prev;
  ```
  The above code check if there is previous clipboard data. If such is the case, we can cover those branches by existing model based testing. In fact, existing model-based testing focuses only on these types of branches.
- **Branches Decided by Data Inputting**
  The below code is a part of the xclipboard application. The branch decision is made as a result of the width of the screen. The data(the width of screen) decide the branch. We hardly know or cover this type of branch by the black box testing. We may cover some cases by AETG in extended model-based testing.
  ```
  x = x - (int) width / 2;
  if (x < 0) x = 0;
  ```
- **Branches Caused by Error Handling**
  Users somehow mistakenly input the wrong data. The application is, of course, supposed to check user inputting data or tell users' errors. In that case, the application requires branch code.

```
if(w -> clock.update <= 0)
   w -> clock.update = 0;
```

– **Branches Decided by Configuration**
   The code below checks if there is enough free memory in the operating
   system. If no extra memory exists, the program returns from sub-routine.

```
newClip = (ClipPtr) malloc (sizeof (ClipRec));
   if (!newClip) return newClip;
```

We hardly discussed the operating system and configuration related topics
because black box testing rarely executes this type of branch. A large number
of applications use the operating system and depend on operating system ability. For example, we usually encounter difficulties when checking those memory
functions by black box testing. Unfortunately, dynamic memory allocation is a
critical part of code since failing memory allocation easily causes application
crash in the operating system. Also, a large number of bugs are not found by
their testers but by users. In PCs, there are millions of configurations throughout
the world, including factors such as different memory size, CPU speed, hard drive
speed, etc. Naturally not all bugs occurring on the user side can be reproduced
[15]. Thus, chasing covering/testing the code, which may cause the various types
of operating system bugs, is difficult and time consuming. Table 1 shows the percentage for each type of branch in the xclipboard application. Through the table, we can see the rate of percentage in each branch type. Configuration-related
branches do not occupy a small area. It is difficult to cover those configuration-
related branches even using extended-model based testing. On the other hand,
we testers can achieve 82%(condition:49%+data inputting:33%) code coverage
rate by extended model based testing for the clipboard application. The 82%
figure represents quite a high code coverage rate by using black box testing.
Though it is debatable wether any application has the same rate of branch, we
now show the basic result of coverage rate of extended-model based testing.

Table 1. xclock application

Function Name	No. of C/D *	Data inputting	Condition	Config.
DeleteClip	6		6	
NextCurrentClip	2		2	
PrevCurrentClip	2		2	
InsertClipboard	2	2		
WMProtocols	20		20	
NewCurrentClip..	10	2		8
SaveClip	8	8		
AcceptSaveFile	6	6		
main	6			6
DeleteCurrentClip	4		4	
CenterWidgetAt..	8	8		
NewClip	4		4	
SaveToFile	2		2	
Total	80	26	40	14
%	100%	33%	49%	18%

* C/D Condition/Decision

5   Conclusion

In this research, we have achieved the goal of developing the concept of extended model-based testing. First, we offered a new approach for increasing code coverage rate. Increasing code coverage rate is difficult without knowing the source code structure. When designing and executing model-based testing, testers sometimes do not reach certain code coverage rate planed (the project and test plan often define code coverage rate to ship a product). If the planned code coverage rate is not reached, our only option was to use the white box testing approach which is an extremely time and cost consuming method. Now we can offer a method for increasing code coverage rate by black box and extended-model based testing. Second, a foreseeable extension of this research would be to conduct expanded model-based testing which is more efficient at finding bugs, such as memory related bugs, than the existing model-based testing method.

6   Future Work

The idea of this project is to increase code coverage rate and to find more bugs than the existing mode-based testing method does. Thus, our novel extended model based testing requires a more complicated model than existing model-based testing. Though we have offered some guideline and concepts for extended model based testing in this paper, we will be required to precisely model applications using this research idea and develop automated testing for our next research, which may be on a subject such as how many times a repeated operation can be applied. The capacity of the automated testing tool is now very much improved and the tool handles many graphical objects [16]. This new automated testing technology may be appropriate for handling this type of complicated model-based testing. In addition, though we have analyzed only two applications at this time, we will research more of various types, such as applying real complex business applications.

References

1. Apfelbaum, L. "Spec-based tests make sure telecom software works" *IEEE Spectrum*, Nov. 1997, Vol. 34, Issue 11, pp. 77–83
2. Robinson, H. "Intelligent Test Automation ", *Testing and Quality Eng.*, Sep. 2000
3. Dalas, S. R., Jain, A., Karunanithi N., Leaton, J. M., Lott, C. M., and Patton, G.C., "Model-Based Testing in Practice" ICSE 99, 1999
4. Memon, A. M., Pollack, M. E., "Hierarchical GUI Test Case Generation Using Automated Planning" *IEEE Tran. on Soft. Eng.*, Vol. 27, No. 2, Feb. 2001
5. Esmelioglu, S. and Apfelbaum L. "AUTOMATED TEST GENERATION, EXECUTION, AND REPORTING" *Pacific N. W. Software Quality Conf.*, 1997
6. Myers, G. J., *The Art of Software Testing*, New York: John Wiley & Sons, 1979
7. Hetzel, B., *The Complete Guide to Software Testing*, John Wiley & Sons, Inc., 1976
8. Beizer, B., *Software Testing Techniques*, Van Nostrand Reinhold Inc., NY, 1983

9. Yamaura, T., "How To Design Practical Test Cases" *IEEE Soft.*, Nov. 1998, pp. 30–36
10. Beizer, B., *Black-Box Testing*, John Wiley & Sons, Inc., 1995
11. Whittaker, J. A. and Thomason, M., "Markov Chain Model for Statistical Software Testing" *IEEE Trans. on Soft. Eng.*, Vol. 20, No. 10, pp. 812–824, Oct. 1994,
12. Cohen, D. M. and Dalal, S. R., "The AETG System: An Approach to Testing Based on Combinational Design" *IEEE Trans. Soft. Eng.*, Vol. 23, No. 7, July 1997
13. Whittaker, J. A., "Software's Invisible Users" *IEEE Soft.*, Vol. 8, No. 8, 2001
14. X86Free project Inc., http://www.xfree86.org/
15. Takahashi, J., "Is Special Software Testing Necessary Before Releasing Products to an International Market?" *Quality Week 2000*
16. Takahashi, J., "An Automated Testing Oracle for Verifying GUI Objects" *ACM Software. Eng. Note.*, July 2000, pp. 83–88

Restricted Random Testing

Kwok Ping Chan[1,*], Tsong Yueh Chen[2], and Dave Towey[1]

[1] Department of Computer Science and Information Systems,
University of Hong Kong, Hong Kong
`{kpchan,dptowey}@csis.hku.hk`
[2] School of Information Technology,
Swinburne University of Technology, Hawthorn 3122, Australia
`tychen@it.swin.edu.au`

Abstract. This paper presents a novel adaptation of traditional random testing, called Restricted Random Testing (RRT). RRT offers a significant improvement over random testing, as measured by the F-measure. This paper describes the ideology behind RRT and explains its algorithm. RRT's performance is examined using several experiments, the results of which are presented and discussed.

1 Introduction

Software testing is an important aspect of software development, and to ensure high quality software is being developed, thorough testing is a must. Exhaustive testing (checking of all possible inputs) however is not usually feasible, and so effective testing strategies are therefore needed to maximise the probability of uncovering any errors in the software.

Random Testing (hereafter referred to as *RT*) is the simplest strategy of testing software. In addition to alleviating the overheads associated with the design of test cases, efficient algorithms exist to generate random test cases, and reliability estimates and statistical analyses are also readily calculable [7].

In its most basic form, Random Testing consists of no more than repeatedly drawing test cases randomly from a specified input range. It has been found however, that by requiring the testing candidates to be more evenly distributed, and far separated from each other, the program failure can be more efficiently identified for some types of defects. This forms the basis of a testing methodology proposed by Chen et al., namely, Adaptive Random Testing (hereafter referred to as *ART*) [5]. In tests, *ART* has been shown to outperform Random Testing by as much as 50%.

Motivated by the same goals underlying *ART* of ensuring a good distribution spread of test cases while maintaining low overheads, we have investigated an alternative testing methodology based on restricting the regions of the input space from which random test cases may be generated. This Restricted Random Testing method (hereafter referred to as *RRT*) compares favourably to *ART*, and has, in experiments, been found to outperform ordinary Random Testing by as much as 55%.

---

* All correspondence should be addressed to: K. P. Chan, Department of Computer Science and Information Systems, University of Hong Kong, Hong Kong. Email: kpchan@csis.hku.hk

J. Kontio and R. Conradi (Eds.): ECSQ 2002, LNCS 2349, pp. 321–330, 2002.
© Springer-Verlag Berlin Heidelberg 2002

In the next section we introduce the notation used in this paper, and describe some of the background and preliminaries of the study. We then outline the **RRT** method and explain its philosophy and algorithm (section 3). In section 4, we detail a simulation and some experiments carried out using **RRT** and describe their results. Finally, these results are discussed in section 5, where we also offer some conclusions and suggestions for when to apply the **RRT** method.

2   Preliminaries

When conducting testing using a random selection strategy, apart from avoiding repetition of test cases (elements of the input domain for testing the software for errors), no use is made of the information related to previous, non failure-causing test cases. Random test cases are repeatedly generated until a failure-causing input is selected. Failure-causing inputs are elements of the input domain which cause a failure [6].

Following the notation of Chen and Yu [6], for an input domain D, d, m and n denote the domain size, number of failure-causing inputs and number of test cases, respectively. The failure rate, θ, is defined as m/d.

As explained by Chen et al. [5], the effectiveness of testing techniques have traditionally been measured according to their ability to detect at least one failure (the *P-measure*), or the total number of failures successfully detected (the *E-measure*). Because these measures are less than ideal however, Chen et al. propose instead to use the total number of test cases required to find the first failure (the *F-measure*) as a gauge of how effective the testing method is. In support of this they point out that, in practice, testing usually stops when a failure is found. Therefore, the *F-measure* is not only intuitively more appealing than either the *E-* or *P- measures*, but also is more realistic and informative from a practical viewpoint. In keeping with their methodology, we also adopt the *F-measure* to evaluate the testing strategies presented in this paper.

For Random Testing with replacement of test cases, the expected value for F is equal to $1/\theta$, or equivalently, d/m. In this paper, as with the study of Chen et al. [5], we assume that the random selection of test cases is based on a uniform distribution without replacement. (For a fuller discussion of test case selection with and without replacement, see Leung et al. [8]).

In their study, Chan et al. [3] report on how the performance of some partition testing strategies vary with the failure patterns (the patterns of the failure-causing inputs). They classify these patterns into three categories: *point*: stand alone points or small groups of contiguous, failure-causing input patterns; *strip*, characterised by a narrow strip of failure-causing inputs; and *block*, characterised by the failure-causing inputs being concentrated in either one or a few regions. Figs. 1a-1c give examples of each of the three categories of pattern (the outer boundaries represent the borders of the input domain, and the shaded areas represent the failure-causing inputs' region).

In the Adaptive Random Testing (*ART*) method [5], to achieve a good distribution spread of test cases, a set of test case candidates selected randomly from the input

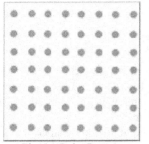  

| Fig. 1a. Point Pattern | Fig. 1b. Strip Pattern | Fig. 1c. Block Pattern |

Fig. 1. Types of Failure Patterns

domain is maintained. Each time a test case is required, the element from this set which is farthest away from all previously executed test cases is selected.

3   Our Methodology

The *RRT* method is motivated by Chen et al.'s suggestion [5] that, for non-point failure patterns, the failure detection capability can be significantly improved by slightly modifying the ordinary Random Testing technique. Specifically, by requiring the testing candidates to be more evenly distributed, and far separated from each other, it should be possible to lower the *F-measure* for *RT*.

While the *ART* method makes use of a candidate set of test cases, and selects that element of the candidate set which lies furthest away from all previously executed (but non failure-causing) test cases, *RRT* uses exclusion zones around each previously executed test case, and generates a new random test case from outside of these zones. *RRT* thus ensures a minimum distance between all executed test cases.

As we continue generating test cases and testing for failures, we continue to assign exclusion zones around each non failure-causing input. Additionally, although the exclusion zone around each test case is the same size for all test cases, the area of each zone decreases with successive cases. The purpose of decreasing the area for each new test is twofold: Firstly, to attempt to maintain a constant amount of excluded area; and secondly, to enable points increasingly close to previously tested points to also be tested.

For convenience, we correlate the size of the exclusion zones with the size of the entire input domain. By attempting to maintain this area, it is possible in advance to calculate the radii for all potential points' exclusion zones (e.g., for an input domain with 2 dimensions, if there are n points around which we wish to generate exclusion zones, and the target exclusion area is A, then each exclusion zone radius will be $\sqrt{A/(2n\pi)}$).

Because of the effects of overlapping zones and of portions of the zones lying outside the input domain, the actual coverage within the input domain may be significantly less than the target coverage. Since the actual coverage depends on the magnitude of the target coverage, we refer to the target coverages when discussing our methods and results.

4   Analysis of RRT

4.1   Simulation

According to Chen et al., for non-point type failure patterns, it should be possible to improve upon the failure detection capability of ordinary Random Testing by ensuring a more even spread of the test cases over the input domain [5]. To test this, we conducted a simple simulation within a square input domain.

Firstly, we specified a certain percentage of the entire input area to be an error zone (a region from which an input drawn would cause the tested program to fail). The method of assigning this zone was to pick a point randomly in the input domain (*error_center*), and then, according to the desired percentage of the input domain to be failure-causing (θ), the radius of the circle whose area corresponds to this is calculated (*error_radius*). When testing a given point to check whether it is failure-causing or not, its distance from the *error_center* is compared to the *error_radius*: if the distance is less, then the point is said to be failure-causing.

For the simulation, we defined the size of the error zone to be 0.001 of the entire input domain area (i.e., $\theta = 0.1\%$), and then varied the target exclusion zone (R) between 10% and 150%. (From experiments it was found that, within a square input domain, even with target coverage of 150%, the actual coverage was still less than 100%.) The results are summarized in Fig. 2.

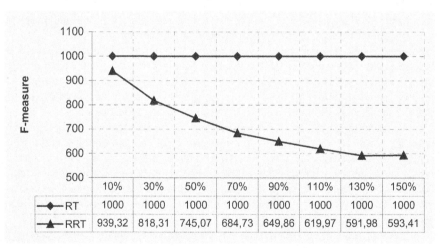

Fig. 2. Expected F-measures for Random Testing (*RT*) compared with the calculated F-measure, averaged over 10,000 trials, for Restricted Random Testing (*RRT*). The *error_zone* (θ) is 0.1% of the entire input domain. The target coverage (R) varies from 10% to 150%

As can be seen from the figure, the calculated *F-measure* for *RRT* lies below the expected values for Random Testing, and the efficiency appears to improve as the target coverage increases. These results give strong support to our hypothesis that the *F-measure* of ordinary random testing can be improved by ensuring a more even spread of the test cases over the input space.

4.2   Adaptive Random Testing

In the Adaptive Random Testing (*ART*) method [5], two sets of test cases are maintained: the candidate set, a set of test cases selected randomly from the input domain; and the executed set, a set of those test cases which have been executed but without causing failure. Each time a test case is required, the element in the candidate set which is farthest away from all elements of the executed set is selected.

Two variations of *ART* are: the Fixed Size Candidate Set (*FSCS*) version, where each time a test case is used, the entire candidate set (of fixed size) is regenerated; and the Growing Candidate Set (*GCS*) version, where a fixed additional number of elements are added to the candidate set each time a test case is used [5].

4.3   Error-Seeded Programs

Seven of the twelve programs studied by Chan et al. [4] and Chen et al. [5] were written in C. We converted these programs to C++, and tested them using the *RRT* method. They are published programs [1, 9], all involving numerical calculations, and varying from 30 to 200 statements in length.

Mutation Analysis [2] was used to insert errors, in the form of simple mutants, into the different programs. Four types of mutant operators were used to create the faulty programs: arithmetic operator replacement (*AOR*); relational operator replacement (*ROR*); scalar variable replacement (*SVR*) and constant replacement (*CR*). These mutant operators were chosen since they generate the most commonly occurring errors in numerical programs [4]. Fig. 3 summarizes the seeded error details.

Program Name	D	Error Type				Total Errors
		AOR	ROR	SVR	CR	
bessj	2	2	1		1	4
bessj0	1	2	1	1	1	5
cel	4	1	1		1	3
erfcc	1	1	1	1	1	4
gammq	2		3		1	4
plgndr	3	1	2		2	5
sncndn	2			4	1	5

Fig. 3. Dimension (D), seeded error types, and total number of errors for each of the error-seeded programs. The error types are: arithmetic operator replacement (*AOR*); relational operator replacement (*ROR*); scalar variable replacement (*SVR*) and constant replacement (*CR*)

4.4   ART Applied to Error-Seeded Programs

The results of Chen et al.'s experiments [5] using the *ART* method on the error-seeded programs are given below. In the experiments, the Fixed Size Candidate Set (*FSCS*) version maintained the candidate set size at 10, and the Growing Candidate

Set (*GCS*) version added 4 new elements to the set each time a test case was used. Included in the results are the calculated values for Random Testing without replacement, also taken from Chen et al.

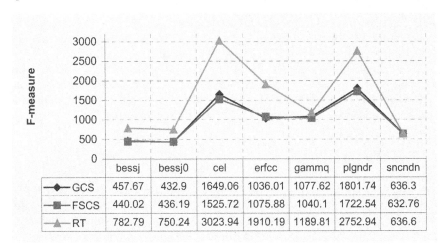

Fig. 4. F-Measures for Adaptive Random Testing (*ART*) and ordinary Random Testing (without replacement) when applied to the seeded programs. *GCS* is the Growing Candidate Set version of *ART*, *FSCS* is the Fixed Size Candidate Set version, and *RT* refers to Random Testing (Taken from Chen et al. [5])

As the figure shows, both forms of the Adaptive Random Testing method (*GCS* and *FSCS*) give comparable results, and, for most programs, appear to improve upon the *RT* results. The results, expressed in terms of their improvement over the *RT* F-measure are shown in Fig. 5.

From the figure it is clear that, for most of the programs, both styles of *ART* (*GCS* and *FSCS*) offer significant improvement over the calculated F-measure for *RT*.

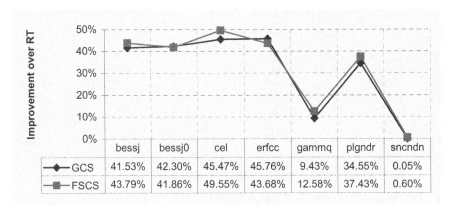

Fig. 5. Improvement in F-Measures for Adaptive Random Testing (ART) compared to Random Testing (RT), when applied to the seeded programs. GCS is the Growing Candidate Set version of ART and FSCS is the Fixed Size Candidate Set version (Taken from Chen et al. [5])

4.5   RRT Applied to Error-Seeded Programs

We applied the **RRT** method to the seven error-seeded programs described above (section 3.3). As with the simulation (section 4.1), we varied the target coverage ratio (R), and obtained an **F-measure** for each ratio by repeating the experiments 5,000 times and calculating the mean value. Because the input domains and sizes of failure-causing areas varied, the maximum target coverage (R) also varied for each program. A summary of these results is given in Table 1. In the table, an asterix (*) indicates a situation where failure could not be detected and hence no F-measure could be calculated. This is anticipated to occur when the actual coverage is close to 100%, as then the failure patterns may always be excluded.

Table 1. F-Measures for Restricted Random Testing (**RRT**) when applied to the seeded programs. The target coverage (R) varies from 10% to up to 220%. The results are averaged over 5,000 iterations

(R)	bessj	bessj0	cel	erfcc	gammq	plgndr	sncndn
10%	726.499	669.909	2986.49	1633.79	1146.06	2052.46	628.04
20%	685.495	614.452	2978.01	1483.03	1131.42	2002.62	637.037
30%	638.442	601.361	2951.72	1380.09	1127.58	2011.12	626.444
40%	622.008	554.405	2879.36	1273.74	1101.57	1944.8	624.504
50%	594.845	520.449	2915.15	1225.47	1104.24	1892.76	625.81
60%	575.952	497.884	2928.33	1130.43	1095.78	1900	620.653
70%	541.766	465.448	3002.39	1088.33	1103.72	1852.8	634.568
80%	517.18	455.298	2916.04	1041.04	1100.76	1816.75	625.678
90%	499.486	441.125	2973.55	993.801	1105.38	1812.66	629.552
100%	483.987	418.172	2939.72	969.588	1090.52	1827.56	633.571
110%	480.981	*	2942.58	*	1098.36	1794.81	633.432
120%	459.256	*	2909.57	*	1071.91	1789.94	617.071
130%	446.62	*	2940.67	*	1069.87	1774.85	626.33
140%	427.076	*	2866.28	*	1073.27	1795.86	631.072
150%	428.592	*	2912.58	*	1071.27	1819.14	629.522
160%	406.732	*	2874.89	*	1068.89	1782.55	*
170%	402.207	*	2922.1	*	1050.22	1778.71	*
180%	400.82	*	2860.06	*	1083.94	1800	*
190%	384.102	*	2940.76	*	1067.97	1802.7	*
200%	366.541	*	2921.31	*	1061.2	1820.51	*
210%	369.295	*	2924.71	*	*	1832.16	*
220%	351.083	*	2886.23	*	*	1836.81	*

The results of the comparison between **RRT** and Random Testing are summarized in Fig. 6, where the values shown are the percentage improvement of **RRT** over **RT**.

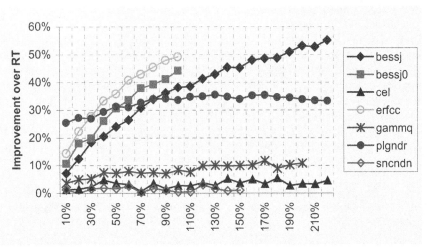

Fig. 6. Comparison of the F-Measures for Restricted Random Testing (***RRT***) when applied to the seeded programs. The target coverage (R) varies from 10% to up to 220%. The figures show the improvement of ***RRT*** over RT

As with the simulation, for most of the programs there appears to be an increase in the improvement over ***RT*** corresponding to the increase in target coverage area (***R***), particularly for the bessj, bessj0, and erfcc programs, but also for gammq. The cel program shows some small overall improvement, but does not seem to vary with ***R***. The plgndr program, while showing an average improvement of about 35%, does not monotonically improve as ***R*** increases. The sncndn program, as with the ***ART*** methods, shows no real improvement, nor does it appear to vary with ***R***.

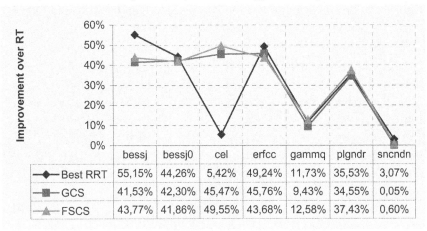

	bessj	bessj0	cel	erfcc	gammq	plgndr	sncndn
Best RRT	55,15%	44,26%	5,42%	49,24%	11,73%	35,53%	3,07%
GCS	41,53%	42,30%	45,47%	45,76%	9,43%	34,55%	0,05%
FSCS	43,77%	41,86%	49,55%	43,68%	12,58%	37,43%	0,60%

Fig. 7. Comparison of best improvement of F-Measures for Restricted Random Testing (***RRT***), and Adaptive Random Testing (***GCS*** and ***FSCS***), when applied to the seeded programs. The figures show the improvement over ***RT***

A comparison between *ART* and the best *RRT* results is given above in Fig. 7. As the figure clearly shows, *RRT* outperforms the calculated F-measure for Random Testing (*RT*). The improvement, however, is not uniform, and varies from as low as 3.07% (sncndn) to a maximum of 55.15% (bessj). In addition, except for the cel program, the results for the *RRT* method compare favourably with those of the *ART* methods.

5   Discussion and Conclusions

In this paper, a novel method for improving upon Random Testing (*RT*) techniques has been presented. This method, called Restricted Random Testing (*RRT*), has been shown to consistently outperform *RT*, when evaluated using the F-measure. In addition, when applied to seven error-seed programs, *RRT* compared favourably with another methodology, Adaptive Random Testing (*ART*). Four of the error-seeded programs (bessj, bessj0, erfcc and gammq) showed an increase in the improvement over *RT* as the target coverage increased for the *RRT* method.

That the sncndn program did not respond favourably to either the *RRT* or the *ART* techniques is explained by examining the failure patterns. From experiments, it is revealed that the error patterns for sncndn are similar to the point patterns discussed in section 2, and therefore, the failure detection efficiency for sncndn was not expected to improve according to our hypothesis.

For the cel program, the rather disappointing results for *RRT* were not reflected in those for *ART*. A closer inspection revealed that the problem was connected with the shape of the input domain for this program. The cel program requires input from a 4 dimensional space whose dimensional magnitudes are 0.99, 299.99, 9999.99 and 999.99. Because *RRT* imposes a regularly shaped exclusion zone on the input domain regardless of the relative sizes of the dimensions, for those programs of which the sizes of the various dimensions of the input domain do vary significantly, the goal of achieving a good spread of test cases is harder to achieve.

Although the plgndr program shows significant improvement with *RRT* over both *RT*, this improvement does not continue as the target coverage increases. Preliminary investigations suggest that this phenomenon is related to the program's input requirements: the program takes three inputs, the first two of which are integers in the ranges [10, 499] and [0, 10], respectively. Because this represents a relatively small, finite domain, it is probable that the optimum spread of test cases is achieved comparatively quickly using *RRT*, even with a lower target coverage. Attempts to improve upon this already optimum spread by increasing the target coverage are unsuccessful. This is currently being investigated further.

It appears that the shape and nature of the input domain have a strong influence on the *RRT* method, not just for the extreme case of cel, but for all the programs. This relationship, and ways of adapting *RRT* to better suit different input spaces, is currently the focus of more investigation.

Although the *RRT* method is computationally relatively inexpensive, there is some overhead with the random number generation. To generate valid test candidates for the *RRT* method, it is necessary to first generate a random point, and then check if this point lies within any exclusion zone (by comparing its distance to each other point with the exclusion zone radius). If it does, we discard the point, and make a second attempt to generate a valid test candidate. This process of generating and discarding random points continues until a point lying outside of the exclusion zones is produced. As the target coverage increases, so too do the required number of generations and discarded random points. Therefore, for those systems where random point generation is expensive, it may be more advisable to use lower target coverages. In spite of these overheads associated with the *RRT* technique, compared with *RT*, when the execution overheads of a test case far exceed the generation of a random test case, then the *RRT* method offers a clear advantage.

Acknowledgement

This research was supported by a grant from the Hong Kong Research Grant Council (HKU 7007/99E).

References

1   Association for Computer Machinery, 'Collected Algorithms from ACM, Vol. I, II, III', *Association for Computer Machinery*, 1980

2   T. A. Budd, 'Mutation Analysis: Ideas, Examples, Problems and Prospects', Computer Program Testing, B. Chandrasekaran and S. Radicci (eds.), North-Holland, Amsterdam, pp. 129-148, 1981.

3   F. T. Chan, T. Y. Chen, I. K. Mak and Y. T. Yu, 'Proportional Sampling Strategy: Guidelines for Software Testing Practitioners', *Information and Software Technology,* Vol. 28, No. 12, pp. 775-782, December 1996.

4   F. T. Chan, I. K. Mak, T. Y. Chen and S. M. Shen, 'On the Effectiveness of the Optimally Refined Proportional Sampling Testing Strategy', *Proceedings of the 9th International Workshop on Software Technology and Engineering Practice (STEP '99)*, S. Tilley and J. Verner (eds.), IEEE Computer Society, Los Alamitos, California, pp. 95-104, 1999.

5   T. Y. Chen, H. Leung and I. K. Mak, 'Adaptive Random Testing', *submitted for publication.*

6   T. Y. Chen and Y. T. Yu, 'On the Relationship Between Partition and Random Testing', *IEEE Transactions on Software Engineering,* Vol. 20, No. 12, pp. 977-980, December 1994.

7   R. Hamlet, 'Random Testing', *Encyclopedia of Software Engineering*, edited by J. Marciniak, Wiley, pp. 970-978, 1984.

8   H. Leung, T. H. Tse, F. T. Chan and T. Y. Chen, 'Test Case Selection with and without Replacement', *Information Sciences*, 129 (1-4), pp. 81-103, 2000.

9   W. H. Press, B. P. Flannery, S. A. Teulolsky and W. T. Vetterling, *Numerical Recipes*, Cambridge Universoty Press, 1986.

Quality-Adaptive Testing:
A Strategy for Testing with Focusing
on Where Bugs Have Been Detected

Yasuharu Nishi

SQC Inc., Pastoral Shin-Yuri II 2F, 1-7-14 Kami-Asao, Asao-ku,
Kawasaki-shi, Kanagawa-ken, Japan
nsh@mtd.biglobe.ne.jp

Abstract. It is important in developments of software systems with quick
delivery and high quality how developments are conducted adaptively. This
paper presents an add-on process for developments of software systems, namely
Adaptive Development Framework. ADF consists of Quality-adaptive testing,
ATLM/prototyping and Predictive Trial and Error. ADF can improve
traditional development cycles by spinning a cycle more rapidly, condensing a
cycle to turn it more and adding small cycles to compare what they are with
what they should be. ADF will lead development processes to deal swiftly and
flexibly with changes of conditions. Next we propose a test strategy to detect
many fatal failures by fewer test cases, namely Quality-adaptive testing.
Quality-adaptive testing is a test strategy focusing on where bugs have been
detected and test where many bugs will lurk based on knowledge of production
patterns and bug patterns. We also detail a Quality-adaptive testing tactic and
the procedure, namely Quality-adaptive Resource Path Testing.

1 Introduction

Creatures are adaptive. They survive severe nature by dealing swiftly and flexibly
with changes in conditions. They adapt the behavior to their health and situations.

Developments of software systems should be adaptive like creatures, for the spread
of networks and the Internet have changed circumstances of developments. The
increase in speed of business decision-makings makes delivery dates sooner and
sooner. The diversification of values among customers makes system requirements
variable and variable. The wide circulation of information about system failures,
especially about security holes, makes quality consciousness strong and strong.

This paper presents an add-on process for adaptive development of software
systems, called the Adaptive Testing Framework (ADF). Section 2 describes the
concept and overview of the ADF. Section 3 presents the Quality-adaptive Testing
(QAT), a major element of the ADF. QAT is a adaptive strategy for testing with
focusing on where bugs have been detected. Section 4 details a procedure of QAT by
application of the Resource Path Testing, a test method focusing on architecture of the
system under testing.

J. Kontio and R. Conradi (Eds.): ECSQ 2002, LNCS 2349, pp. 331–339, 2002.

2   Adaptive Development Framework

2.1   A Concept of Adaptive Development Framework

To be adaptive, that is, to deal swiftly and flexibly with changes of conditions you should keep on improving your development process by comparison of what they are with what they should be. The software engineering has improved development process paradigms from waterfall to spiral development, and besides, to agile development like eXtreme Programming, briefly speaking, into being more adaptive.

Development processes generally consist of a production phase (specification, design and implement) and a testing phase (unit testing, integration testing, function testing and system testing). They are also a cycle as shown in the left part of Figure 1.

In order to improve development processes into being more adaptive, you should spin a development cycle more and more to an appropriate direction as follows:

     1. Spin a cycle more rapidly.
     2. Condense a cycle to turn it more.
     3. Add small cycles to compare the real with an ideal and improve.

The Adaptive Development Framework (ADF) is a software development process paradigm based on these concepts as shown in the right part of Figure 1. First, the ADF spins development cycles by testing with focusing on where bugs have been detected, called the Quality-adaptive testing. Second, the ADF condense a cycle by early automation of testing. Third, the ADF add small cycles by estimating total development effort in consideration of test effort and testability in design phase.

The ADF, however, do not define a whole development process. The ADF is an add-on and optional process, because various development organizations use various development processes, methodologies, or paradigms. It is better that organizations should not modify their familiar processes radically.

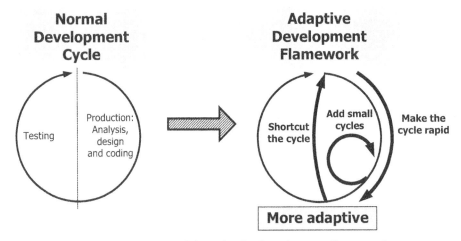

Fig. 1. A concept of the Adaptive Development Framework

2.2 Elements of Adaptive Development Framework

The ADF has three elements as shown in Table 1. Table 1 also shows contrast with traditional development

To spin a development cycle more rapidly, it is important to reduce what is not directly led to deliverables. We do not discuss a way to improve production phase because a lot of ways have always proposed as what was called development methodologies and any of them will have been adopted. In testing phase, you should not design and execute test cases that cannot detect failures, namely test cases that cannot directly contribute quality of the system under testing (SUT).

We propose a test strategy to design earlier test cases that can detect failures, called *the Quality-adaptive testing* (QAT). With QAT you can design test cases with focusing on where bugs have been detected and test where many bugs will lurk. It costs less effort than traditional test strategy that you should cover functions or paths of the SUT. We detail QAT in Section 3 and 4.

To condense a development cycle to turn it more, it is down-to-earth to shortcut a cycle by automation of production and/or testing, especially of test execution which needs no wisdom. It is late, however, that test automation begins from testing phase because changes of test cases are difficult to adapt to changes of specifications.

Dustin et al.[1] presented the Automated Testing Lifecycle Model (ATLM), a method for test automation from production phase to adapt to changes of specifications. We advanced the ATLM to begin test automation from prototyping phase as *ATLM/prototyping*[2]. We call these concepts *Early Automated Testing.* They can save test effort that occupies most of development effort.

To add small cycles to compare what development cycles are with what they should be and to improve them, you should validate design in production phase. In design phase, though you have already validate your design by small cycles as trial and error, they are not necessarily appropriate validations. They consider effort and complexity of only design and/or implement, not of testing. As a consequence, development projects fail to deliver software systems in time.

We propose a concept for more appropriate validation in design phase, called *the Predictive Trial and Error* (PTE). With the PTE you should design test cases in production phase and consider effort and complexity not only of design and/or implement, but of testing to reduce total development effort and complexity. This concept is advanced "Test First" concept in eXtreme Programming. As space is limited, we do not detail the PTE in this paper.

Table 1. The Elements of the Adaptive Development Framework

	Traditional development	Adaptive Development Framework
Test strategy	Covering functions or paths	Quality-adaptive Testing (focusing on where bugs have been detected)
Test automation	Only in testing	ATLM/prototyping (before testing)
Design validation	Only of design and/or implement	Predictive Trial and Error (also of testing)

3 Quality-Adaptive Testing

3.1 A Concept of Quality Adaptive Testing

Testing is practically conducted in a seat-of-the-pants style. The principle is a rule of thumb, "Bugs are maldistributed"[3]. In other word, you should test where many bugs will lurk. Kaner et al. also says that you should understand the condition how bugs are detected and do test cases that are likely to detect bugs[4]. You can aim at weak points of the SUT by recognizing patterns of bugs.

The concept of QAT is you can do testing efficiently by flexibly re-design test cases with information where bugs will be maldistributed, suppose bugs are maldistributed. In QAT, you can more detect more fatal failures earlier by fewer test cases.

3.2 Guessing Where Bugs Will Be Maldistributed

Many books and papers about programming and project management also introduce software have weak points that is causes of bugs[5]. Major examples of the bug-prone production conditions to embed bugs is as follows:

- Specification changes and/or design changes.
- Difficult and/or complex design.
- Production by poor engineers.
- Confusion of project management.

In QAT, test cases are re-designed by guessing where a lot of bugs will similarly lurk from information of parts where many bugs have already detected. The parts guessed in QAT have bug-prone production conditions similar to the parts where many bugs have already detected. You design test cases based on information of the bug-prone production conditions.

To guessing weak points, you have to understand similarities of bug-prone production conditions by abstracting production conditions as *production patterns*. Design patterns[6] are typical of production patterns.

In this paper we call where you recognize a production pattern, *a resource*. Resources are functions, method, modules such as DLL, structure, architecture and so on. Resource is an abstract notion indicating an instance that has a pattern.

3.3 Bug Patterns

In QAT, you have to consider production patterns and bug patterns together. First, you extract production patterns of bug-prone resources. Second, you search for resources of similar pattern. Third, you draw the particular bug patterns of the resources found out. Finally, you do testing aiming at the resources and the bug patterns.

For example, buffer is a primitive design pattern (i.e. also a production pattern) such as array, queue and stack. Buffer has a popular bug pattern, "buffer overflow", that so long data are overflowed from a fixed-length buffer into memory allocated for other programs. If test designers using QAT know where buffers are in an SUT and target the buffers, they can detect buffer overflows more frequently than if they don't know where and do area bombing. They can design test cases to bring about buffer overflow with long and long test data into the target buffers. If they don't use QAT and put very long data into every input field, they shall exhaust their test effort or test schedule. Because they design using QAT, they can efficiently detect the bug.

When we tested an old version of Netscape Navigator and Internet Explorer[7], bugs lurked in buffers for a part of HTML tags[1]. Targeting the buffers, our team succeeded in detection of buffer overflow bugs including a serious failure such as General Protection Failure (i.e. system crash). The other test team missed most of the bugs in spite of executing test cases about four times as many as ours due to unconsciousness of the buffers. We detected the bugs effectively and efficiently.

Several researches have been conducted on bug patterns such as Anti-patterns[2] [8]. Traditional bug taxonomies[4][9] are bug patterns. Test patterns[10][11] are also researched independently of bug patterns.

It is important in QAT to accumulate knowledge of links between production patterns and bug patterns. In order to design and implement test cases rapidly, it is better to prepare test skeleton of links between production patterns and bug patterns.

3.4   A Strategy of Quality-Adaptive Testing

By the notions mentioned above, we can present a strategy of QAT, which consists of two strategy called *Backtracking* and *Analogical Backtracking*.

Backtracking Strategy

1. To test and increase test cases of resources where many bugs are detected.
2. To test and decrease test cases of resources where few bugs are detected.

Analogical Backtracking Strategy

3-1. To test and extract production patterns of resources where many bugs are detected.
3-2. To search for resources that have similar production patterns.
3-3. To enumerate particular bug patterns of the resources found out.
3-4. To design test cases aiming at the resources found out and the bug patterns enumerated.
4-1. To test and extract production patterns of resources where few bugs are detected.
4-2. To search for resources that have similar production patterns.
4-3. To decrease test cases of the resources found out.

---

[1] A part of Font Style, Headings, Phrase and Table tags needs buffers so that web browsers can store information of levels or order of nested tags.
[2] Anti-patterns can be recognized as production patterns.

4   Quality-Adaptive Resource Path Testing

4.1   Resource Path Testing as a Test Tactic

In QAT, a tactic is necessary to design test cases tracing from bug patterns to failures affected by the bug patterns if the resource considered has the bug patterns. We select a tactic for QAT, Resource Path Testing (RPT)[12], as *Quality-adaptive Resource Path Testing*.

RPT is a method for test design. First, you aim at an important resource. Second, you search for resources that affect the resource aimed at. Third, you search for resources that are affected by the resource aimed at. Fourth, you tie the chain of these resources, called *resource path*. Finally, you design test cases considering resource paths.

In order to tie resource paths, it is necessary to identify dependency among these three resources:

- Target Resource (TR)   : a resource that has bug patterns.
- Activation Resource (AR)   : a resource where functions are executed.
- Observation Resource (OR)   : a resource where failures are detected.

Test cases are on AR-TR-OR paths, namely resource paths, which imply functions of the SUT. To design test cases appropriately, you should understand dependency of resources on a graph, called *Resource Dependency Graph* (RDG), as shown in Figure 2.

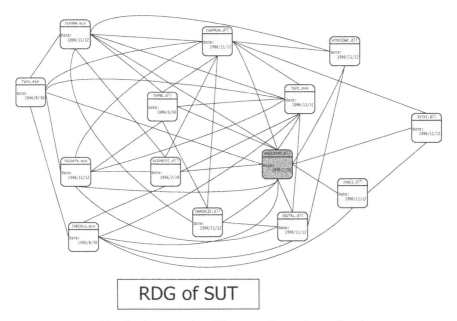

Fig. 2. An example of Resource Dependency Graph

4.2 Common Resources

If two or more resources have the same patterns, which test cases should be executed previously? Resources that customers will use more frequently should be tested previously, because the less frequently customers will use buggy resources, the less frequently bugs will be exposed as failures.

Resources that will be frequently used satisfy either or both two conditions as follows:
-    To be included in resource paths (i.e. functions) that customer will frequently use.
-    To be included in more than one resource path.

A resource that satisfies the latter condition is called *common resource*.

We, therefore, can define a metric that consists of these two conditions, and we can decide which resource should be tested previously. The metric, called *Resource Frequency of Use* (RFU), is the sum of frequency of use of each resource path that includes the common resource.

In practice when you have to decide an order of test cases, you, however, should consider not only RFU but importance of function from the viewpoint of a marketing division.

4.3 The Procedure for Quality-Adaptive Resource Path Testing

Quality-adaptive resource path testing is managed using the procedure shown in this section, which consists of the five phases.

I. Primary Testing Phase
  1. Draw an RDG of the SUT.
  2. Test the SUT using traditional test strategy and method.

II. Analyzing Phase
  3. Analyze the failures detected in 2., and enumerate resources in descending order of number of bugs considering RFUs.
  4. Extract production patterns of the resources enumerated in 3.
  5. Identify bug patterns that can be caused by the production patterns
  6. Arrange the resources enumerated in 3. in ascending order of number of bugs.

III. Backtracking Phase
  7. Pick out resource paths including the resources enumerated in 3.
  8. Design test cases aiming at the ARs of the resource paths so as to cause the bug patterns identified in 5.
  9. Derive expected results of the test cases and the ORs of the resource paths.
  10.Pick out resource paths including the bug-less resources arranged in 6.
  11.Choose test cases aiming at the resource paths picked out in 10.

IV. Analogical Backtracking Phase

    12.Search for resources with the same production patterns as the bug-ful resources enumerated in 3. considering RFUs.

    13.Pick out resource paths including the resources found out in 3.

    14.Design test cases aiming at the ARs of the resource paths picked out in 13. so as to cause the bug patterns identified in 5.

    15.Derive expected results of the test cases designed in 14. and the ORs of the resource paths picked out in 13.

    16.Search for resources with the same production patterns as the bug-less resources arranged in 6. considering RFUs.

    17.Pick out resource paths including the resources found out in 16.

    18.Choose test cases aiming at the resource paths picked out in 17.

V. Adaptive Test Design Phase

    19.Increase the test cases designed in 8. and decrease the test cases chosen in 11. considering remainder of test effort.

    20.Increase the test cases designed in 14. and decrease the test cases chosen in 18. considering remainder of test effort.

5 Discussion

5.1 Testing That Should Not Conduct in Quality-Adaptive Way

The purpose of QAT is to detect many fatal failures by fewer test cases. But the purpose of acceptance testing or regression testing is not only to detect failures. Acceptance testing may be conducted to get assurance or guarantee of proper operation, and regression testing may be conducted to verify that bugs embedded in debugging are "NOT" exposed.

These concepts are low-level of testing mentioned by Myers[13] and Beizer[9]. They assert that testing falls through if testing cannot detect bugs from the viewpoint that testing improves quality with detecting and modifying failures. This concept of quality is, however, a narrow definition.

When the concept of quality is widen from how failures are few to how customers feel reliable, testing that cannot detect failures does not fall through. Testing succeed , though it cannot detect failures, because test results provide customers with peace of mind. We think this peace of mind very important now that "good enough quality" software have overwhelmed our market.

Therefore, testing for assurance of proper operation such as acceptance testing and regression testing should not be Quality adaptive testing but cover requirements of customers in order of their importance.

6   Conclusion

We have presented an add-on process for developments of software systems, namely Adaptive Development Framework.   ADF consists of Quality-adaptive testing, ATLM/prototyping and Predictive Trial and Error.   ADF can improve traditional development cycles by spinning a cycle more rapidly, condensing a cycle to turn it more and adding small cycles to compare what they are with what they should be. ADF will lead development processes to deal swiftly and flexibly with changes of conditions.

We have proposed a test strategy to detect many fatal failures by fewer test cases, namely Quality-adaptive testing.   Quality-adaptive testing is a test strategy focusing on where bugs have been detected and test where many bugs will lurk based on knowledge of production patterns and bug patterns.   We have also detailed a Quality-adaptive testing tactic and the procedure, namely Quality-adaptive Resource Path Testing.

For effective test design, it is important to accumulate many and proper production patterns and bug patterns.   Accumulating properly them beyond companies and organizations awaits further researches.

References

1. Dustin, E. et al.: Automated Software Testing: Introduction, Management, and Performance. Addison-Wesley (1999)
2. Nishi, Y. et al.: Prototyping with automated test execution tools (in Japanese). Proc. 31th conf. of JSQC (2001)
3. Davis, A: 201 Principles of Software Development. McGraw-Hill (1996)
4. Kaner, C. et al.: Testing Computer Software 2nd Edition. John Wiley & Sons (1995)
5. McConnel, S.: Code Complete. Microsoft Press (1995)
6. Gamma, E. et al.: Design Patterns. Addison-Wesley(1995)
7. Nishi, Y et al.: Design of Stress Testing focused on Resource (in Japanese). IEICE Transactions on Information and Systems(D-I), Vol.J83-D-I, No.10(2000) 1070-1086
8. Brown, W. et al.: AntiPatterns: Refactoring Software, Architectures, and Projects in Crisis. John Wiley & Sons (1998)
9. Beizer, B.: Software Testing Techniques 2nd Edition. Van Nostrand Reinhold (1995)
10. Rising, L. et al.: System Test Pattern Language. http://www.agcs.com/supportv2 /techpapers/patterns/papers/systestp.htm (2000)
11. Marick, B.: Software Testing Patterns. http://www.testing.com/test-patterns/ (2001)
12. Nishi, Y. et al.: Resource Path Testing :A Framework for Design of System Testing. Software Quality Professional, Vol.3, Issue 3 (2001) 34-39
13. Myers, G.: The Art of Software Testing. John Wiley & Sons (1979)

Peer Reviews as a Quality Management Technique in Open-Source Software Development Projects

Jacqueline Stark

School of Computing and Information Technology
Griffith University, Q 4111, Australia
J.Stark@cit.gu.edu.au

Abstract. This paper focuses on peer review as a quality management technique used in open-source software (OSS) development and the similarities and differences with those of traditional development. The organizational commitment of OSS developers to quality is also explored. A comprehensive web-based questionnaire was completed by OSS and traditional developers. It was found that peer review is generally considered very useful for detecting both defects and flaws in code, as well as being important in contributing to the quality of the software. It is suggested that OSS developers commit to quality through internalization – adopting the ideas as their own, as the majority of the developers indicated that they would perform peer reviews without management direction. Encouragement to perform peer reviews and an organizational culture of peer review make it more likely for the developers to perform peer review under their own initiative, but neither are essential.

1 Introduction

Feller and Fitzgerald [1] state that "the software crisis… clearly illustrates that traditional modes of development do not work very well, specifically in the areas of speed, quality, and cost of development". Mockus et al [2] state that open-source software (OSS) is "often claimed to be equivalent, or even superior to software developed more traditionally"; there is evidence that OSS development is able to produce high quality software of excellent functionality. OSS development is rapid, and the software evolves quickly by its "frequent, incremental release, and by interaction in 'Internet time'" [1].

Yet, OSS development, which is asserted to be able to produce high quality software, does not seem to apply the same quality management techniques as those in traditional software development. Mockus et al [2] note that OSS development does not seem to use any of the "traditional mechanisms to coordinate software development" that are considered even more important in distributed environments. Open-source software development "openly challenge[s] much of the conventional wisdom surrounding software development methodologies, life-cycle models, and project management" [3]. Yet the processes in developing OSS are not yet fully understood [2] and thus require research. There has been little research into OSS development as yet, and no studies have been reported in the literature regarding

J. Kontio and R. Conradi (Eds.): ECSQ 2002, LNCS 2349, pp. 340–350, 2002.
© Springer-Verlag Berlin Heidelberg 2002

quality management techniques and the organizational commitment of open-source software projects to quality.

This paper focuses on peer review as a quality management technique employed by open-source software development projects. Open-source software is software that is freely available and modifiable, and includes the source code. It must be distributed under a license whose terms comply with the criteria given by the Open Source Initiative [4]. Peer reviews are an informal style of review, where a person or group of persons other than the author read through the artifact with the purpose of detecting defects and flaws, and to make suggestions and comments. This paper also considers the organizational commitment in open source development to quality management.

The next section gives an overview of the literature on open-source software development and its characteristics. In Section 3, peer review and organizational commitment to quality is discussed. Section 4 provides the research design used for this paper, and finally Section 5 discusses the results from the research.

2 Open-Source Software Development

Open-source software development is highly iterative; the core methodology is of "massive and parallel development and debugging" [1] – many different developers undertake the development in parallel [5]. Open-source software development is asynchronous and distributed; the developers are located in various countries and do not necessarily work at the same time and rarely, if ever, meet face to face [1, 2, 5].

Open-source software projects typically do not have a set plan [2]. Rather, the project is continually improved when the developers choose to undertake the work. The projects usually have a central person or body who selects the modifications contributed by developers to be incorporated into the official version [2] and who provides direction and leadership for the project [1, 2]. Co-developers have full access to all code, and submit their changes to the control person or group [1].

The contributors to OSS development are not assigned work; rather they choose to undertake any tasks that they perform [2]. Some projects have TODO lists – lists of tasks to be done, and the developers select those tasks that they wish to undertake [6]. In a case study conducted by Yamauchi et al [6], they state that the programmers made all implementation choices – the task lists state the task, not how it should be performed. When making modifications to the source code, the programmer first downloads the current source code from the Concurrent Versions System (CVS) [2, 6]. The developer then makes and tests changes on their local copy of the system, and then submits the new code for review. Open-source software developers typically do not perform rigorous system testing – users perform most of the system testing [2].

There is agreement in the literature that the open-source software community is based on a meritocracy. "OSS community norms ensure a strict meritocracy where quality speaks for itself. Contributors cannot confer expert status on themselves; rather, it arises through peer recognition" [1]. Yamauchi et al [6] state that "technologically superior options are always chosen in decision-making". Raymond [7], a noted open-source developer states that there is "a very strict meritocracy... quality should (indeed must) be left to speak for itself". The leader of an OSS project generally has little formal authority, as the developers working on the project are volunteers and cannot be forced to undertake certain tasks. However, the leader is usually respected and their recommendations followed [8]. The "owners of the project make the binding decisions" [7]. For this to work well, the leader's goals must be compatible with the goals of the developers; the leaders must be flexible and accept that the project is not completely under their control [8].

Project processes and decisions are usually made transparent to the public [9]. For example, anyone on the Apache (an open source web server) mailing list may vote on decisions, "expressing their opinion on what the group should do" [9].

Open source developers communicate via email, bulletin boards, mailing lists and distribution lists [2, 6]. A number of difficulties and limitations arise from the sole use of electronic forms in communicating between software developers. Such limitations include lack of spontaneous conversation, little real-time knowledge of other developers, difficulty in conveying complex messages and complications in achieving agreement between members [6]. There are however potential benefits of using electronic media for communication; it may "favour the rational decision-making." and "computer-mediated communication is inherently impersonal and prompts task-oriented and focused exchanges" [6]. The extensive use of electronic media in communicating between OSS developers may have an effect upon all development activities, including the management of quality.

It is suggested that OSS developers are highly motivated and usually work as professionals in traditional software development environments [1]. Lerner and Tirole [8] note several different motivations for OSS developers, such as "career concern incentive" which include "future job offers", and the "ego gratification incentive [stemming] from a desire for peer recognition". Feller and Fitzgerald [8] support the argument that open source developers work on projects to increase their own learning and skill advancement. Open source development is usually performed on a voluntary basis, which differs markedly from "traditional" development.

3 Software Quality Management

Quality assurance is the "planned and systematic actions necessary to provide adequate confidence that a product or service will satisfy given requirements for quality" [10]. Quality management is the "management function that determines and implements the quality policy" [10]. A quality system is the "organizational structure, responsibilities, procedures, processes and resources for implementing quality management" [10]. The construction of the software quality management system "involves the identification and formalization of all business processes that can affect delivered quality" [10].

Verification and validation (V&V) techniques are part of quality management. There are various V&V techniques, such as peer reviews, formal inspections, walkthroughs and testing. The use of peer reviews is the focus of quality management in this paper. The definition of peer review that is used in this paper is an activity where someone (or a group of people) other than the author of the artifact reads through the artifact with the purpose of finding errors, omissions or flaws and making suggestions and recommendations to the author. This definition of a peer review is regarded as informal [13], as there is not a structured process, resulting documentation is not required, and data is not collected to improve the process. Peer review in open source includes peer review conducted before its public release or when it is available to the public. No distinction has been made regarding the timing.

There has been little mention of peer reviews in traditional forms of organization in the literature. Most of the review literature has focused upon the use of inspections, or discusses possible alternatives to the inspection. Research has been conducted regarding distributed, asynchronous review, which is suggested by the author to share many similarities with the peer review conducted in OSS development. Distributed, asynchronous inspection "allows participants to conduct meetings independently of time and space, making inspections more convenient" [12].

Perpich et al [13] conclude, based on empirical data, that "meetingless inspections are no less effective than inspections with meetings" and that "asynchronous code inspections are more cost effective and at least as quality effective as synchronous inspections". Stein et al [12] also conclude that distributed asynchronous inspections are just as effective in terms of defects found as synchronous inspections.

It has been noted that more software development is being carried out in geographically distributed locations [14]. Caivano et al [15] recognize that the traditional inspection process is inappropriate for distributed development of "temporary groups of developers collaborating on projects over the Internet" and state that there is much that can be learnt from open source development for inspections. It has also been suggested that if members are working in different locations, then "the formal code inspection process needs to be redefined to suit the new criteria" [14].

From the research into the suitability of, and possible alternatives to formal review techniques, there seems to be agreement that these alternatives are at least as effective as formal techniques and are worthy of further research.

Commitment is necessary to successfully implement quality management in organizations [16] and the. There are three types of response to quality management commitment [16]:

1. *Compliance:* the member complies because they feel they are forced to: if there are rules and a member in authority constantly enforces them.
2. *Identification:* the member commits as they are "influenced by another person to such an extent that they adopt the views of that person"
3. *Internalization:* the member "accept[s] the ideas as their own, together with the associated change in behaviour and work practices".

Internalization is the strongest type of response, and requires little maintenance once it has been established. Compliance and identification are transient; if the authority or influential person leaves, the commitment will disappear [16].

4 Research Method

The data used in this paper has been revisited from that of a larger research project, of which an extensive literature review has been completed [17]. Twenty-three open source and nine traditional developers participated in the web-based survey that was created. Messages were posted to newsgroups and websites to gain participation from open source developers, and traditional developers were sought through the author's contacts in industry.

The survey consisted of several types of questions. There were semantic differential scale questions, such as "How important do you think peer reviews are in contributing to the quality of the software in your organization?" with a five point scale rated from "essential" to "little or no use". Five point scale questions asking for agreement or disagreement were also asked, such as "I would ask others to peer review my code without management direction", with the options of strongly agree, agree, neural, disagree and strongly disagree. Comments regarding certain questions were also asked. These were mainly asking "why" the developer chose the answer in the previous question. Yes and no question were also asked.

5 Discussion

5.1 Quality Management Techniques in OSS and Traditional Development

Ljungberg [18] states that quality assurance is central to open-source software development, with "testers, debuggers, and programmers [contributing] to the development". Feller and Fitzgerald [1] state that the quality aspect of the software crisis is "addressed by the OSS approach" in that the developers are "reckoned to be the most-talented and motivated 5% of software developers". Additionally, they state that the peer review process is completely independent, as the reviewers have "no vested interested, consciously or unconsciously, in turning a blind eye to deficiencies in the product" [1].

The research conducted for the larger project [17] focused quite specifically upon peer reviews and did not address other quality management techniques such as testing. A comment made by an OSS developer was that he feels more comfortable releasing open-source software with less testing than he would proprietary or commercial code, as he knows that the "open source code will receive extensive real-world testing on far more machines and under more circumstances than I or my project team could possibly have access to internally".

There seems to be a consensus in the literature that peer review is a widely used, and often the most employed, quality assurance technique in OSS development. McConnell [19] states that "open source's best-known element is its extensive peer review". Bollinger and Beckman [20] state that the "only traditional software practice that open-source software developers do follow is peer review, and they do that with a vengeance". Yamauchi et al [6] noted that "all the work required 'peer-review'" in the two OSS projects they observed, and Mockus et al [2] also state that any changes to the Apache project are usually reviewed before being committed.

From the survey, only 9% of OSS developers indicated that all of their code was reviewed, compared to 40% of traditional developers. However, 40% of OSS developers responded that most of their code was reviewed. Taken together, almost 50% of OSS developers have most or all of their code reviewed, compared to 40% of traditional developers. Thirteen percent of OSS and 20% of traditional developers indicated that none of their code was reviewed at all.

Table 1. Perceptions of peer reviews by OSS and traditional developers.

	OSS	Trad		OSS	Trad
Usefulness of peer reviews to find "flaws"					
Disagree	0%	0%	Agree	40%	50%
Strongly Disagree	0%	0%	Strongly Agree	56%	50%
Usefulness of peer reviews to find defects					
Little use	4%	0%	Useful	35%	30%
No use at all	0%	0%	Very useful	52%	60%
Contribution peer reviews make to quality					
Not much use	13%	11%	Important	44%	33%
Little or no use	0%	0%	Essential	30%	44%

The research conducted somewhat supports the statements in the literature that peer reviews seem to be the most prevalent quality management technique in open-source software development.

The survey results suggest that most OSS and traditional developers consider peer reviews useful for detecting both defects and flaws, and important in contributing to quality (Table 1). About 90% of both OSS and traditional developers rated peer reviews as useful or very useful in detecting defects, and none indicated that they were of no use at all. Additionally, 96% of OSS developers and all traditional developers either agreed or strongly agreed that peer reviews are useful for finding flaws. Three-quarters of OSS developers rated peer reviews as essential or important in contributing to quality in their organization, as did 78% of traditional developers.

Fifty-seven percent of OSS developers agreed or strongly agreed that peer reviews are part of their organizational culture, as compared to about 45% of traditional developers. No OSS developer strongly disagreed, but a third of traditional developers did. However, 22% of OSS developers did disagree.

It seems as if peer reviews are more widely accepted, and more part of the organizational culture in OSS development than in traditional development. While the actual OSS development team may not perform many of the quality management techniques, this may be because they are confident that these techniques will be applied by the users of the software.

5.2 Organizational Commitment to Quality

Using electronic forms of communication reduces the social context of the communication, equalizing the participants. Accordingly, the traditional authority held by a person decreases in meaning [6]. Yamauchi et al [6] further state that "no authoritative leaders monitor the development" of open-source software. Therefore, it may be suggested that wielding traditional authority would be insufficient to ensure that the open-source software developers were using quality management techniques.

The research into OSS seems to suggest that the only appropriate, and indeed, the only available, option for organizational commitment to quality management in open-source software development is internalization.

Since users are free to use and modify the code as they wish, according to the Open Source Definition, there is no real formal authority present within open-source software development. Furthermore, the medium of communication usually precludes the use of formal authority unless the figure is particularly well known [6]. However, the developers do tend to respect the decisions of the leader [8]. Nevertheless, the leader of the developer cannot force the other developers to do anything that is inconsistent with their own goals, as it is their own time and resources that the developers volunteer – they can simply decide to stop contributing. The leader cannot afford to attempt to control others or stifle contradictory opinions lest they lose their volunteer base.

Formal authority is necessary for compliance; "compliance will occur if there are definite rules in place which must be followed, and someone with suitable authority constantly checks to ensure that the rules are being obeyed" [16]. As open-source software development generally precludes the use of formal authority, the author suggests that compliance is not a valid alternative for organizational commitment to quality in OSS development.

There is no evidence in the literature that identification does or does not play an important part the volunteers' commitment to quality. While the leader of the particular OSS project's decisions are usually respected, no particular research has been found to evaluate the leader's influence over the other developers. The research carried out by the author does not address this factor, either. However, some research has been conducted that may reflect the level of internalization of the OSS developers towards quality, where the developers take the quality ideas as their own.

Since peer review was regarded by the majority of the survey respondents as a very useful technique and an important contributor to the quality of the software (as discussed in the previous section), it is suggested that the degree to which peer review is used as a quality management technique in OSS development may be an indicator of the individual's commitment to quality. Furthermore, there is a consensus in the literature that peer review is a widely used, and often the most employed quality assurance technique in OSS development.

Table 2 shows the level of encouragement developers received from their organization to perform peer reviews. Table 3 shows the agreement or disagreement of the developers that they would ask others to peer review their code without management direction. This particular question is important for judging internalization of quality. Table 4 shows the percentage of OSS developers with the particular trait who indicated that they strongly agree or agree that they would ask others to peer review their work without management direction. Ninety-five percent

Table 2. Level of encouragement received by OSS and traditional developers.

Encouragement	OSS	Traditional
Very encouraged/mandatory	9%	44%
Encouraged	39%	11%
Neutral	48%	22%
Discouraged	4%	22%
Very discouraged/forbidden	0%	0%

Table 3. Developers who would ask others to peer review their code.

I would ask others to peer review my code without management direction	OSS	Traditional
Strongly disagree	0%	0%
Disagree	9%	0%
Undecided	9%	22%
Agree	44%	67%
Strongly agree	39%	11%

Table 4 Percentage of OSS developers who agree or strongly agree that they would perform peer review without management direction.

OSS Developers who:	Agree/strongly agree
Regard peer reviews are useful for finding defects.	95%
Encouraged or very encouraged by their organization.	82%
Regard peer reviews as important/essential to contributing to quality.	88%
Believe that peer reviews are part of their organizational culture.	77%

of developers who indicated that peer reviews are useful for finding defects would perform peer reviews without management direction.

Of those developers who indicated that they would perform peer reviews without management direction, 11% of those were very encouraged by their organization, 37% were somewhat encouraged and 53% received neither encouragement nor discouragement. Most developers (83%) who were encouraged or very encouraged would perform peer reviews without management direction. However, for those developers who did not receive encouragement or discouragement (neutral), 91% indicated that they would perform peer reviews without management direction.

The majority of those who thought that peer reviews were essential or important in contributing to quality indicated that they would perform peer reviews on their own initiative. Of the OSS developers who would perform peer reviews without management direction, 53% agreed or strongly agreed that peer reviews was part of their organizational culture. A fifth indicated that peer reviews were not particularly part of their culture, and 26% indicated that they disagreed that peer reviews are part of the organizational culture. Of OSS developers, 77% who believe that peer reviews are part of their organizational culture (strongly agreed or agreed) would perform peer reviews without management direction.

These findings suggest that encouragement to perform peer reviews from within the project group would make the developers more likely to perform peer reviews without management direction. However, encouragement from the project is not essential; as shown by the 91% of OSS developers who were not encouraged or discouraged, who would still perform peer reviews. This is similar to the peer reviews in the organizational culture. Most of the OSS developers who believe peer review is part of their culture would perform peer review on their own initiative.

However, about half of those who would perform peer reviews on their own initiative indicated that peer reviews are not particularly part of their organizational culture. OSS developers have an interest in making their software high quality, but do not have anyone forcing them to undertake any particular technique. They seem to be generally committed to quality – as a respondent stated, "Peer reviews are usually done because you want to help someone out by checking their code".

6 Conclusion

This paper has discussed the use of peer review as a quality management technique in open-source software development, and compared these with those in traditional development organizations. The key findings from this study are:
1. Although the literature states that reviews are widely carried out in open-source software development, this is not entirely supported by the research findings, with approximately half of the OSS developers stating that they have most or all of their code reviewed.
2. Peer reviews seem to be more widely accepted and more part of the organizational culture in OSS development than in traditional development.
3. Peer reviews are generally considered to be useful for detecting defects, flaws and in contributing to the quality of the software in OSS projects.
4. It is suggested the only appropriate option for organizational commitment in OSS projects is internalization.
5. The developer's attitude to peer reviews may be an indication of the organizational commitment to quality within OSS development.
6. Encouragement to perform peer reviews seems to make the developers more likely to perform peer reviews without management direction.
7. However, this encouragement does not seem essential, as over half of the developers who would perform peer review on their own initiative were not actively encouraged.
8. An organizational culture of peer review seems to make it somewhat more likely that the developers would peer review without direction, but it again does not seem essential.
9. OSS developers seem to be generally committed to quality in their projects.

The following suggestions that follow from the findings may be useful for practitioners:
1. Organizations should encourage their developers to perform informal peer reviews as much as possible.
2. Organizations should foster a culture of peer review.

6.1 Limitations of the Study and Future Research Directions

The research for this paper is somewhat restricted in that it focused quite narrowly upon peer reviews in open-source software development. Additionally, the survey was quite small, with only thirty-two respondents, which makes generalizations more difficult and any conclusions drawn tentative. It is recommended that further research be conducted into the other quality management techniques into open-source software development to see how these compare with the techniques in traditional development. This will assist in achieving a greater understanding of the overall quality management of open source development. It is also recommended that a more detailed study be made of the organizational commitment that open-source software developers have towards quality in their projects.

References

1. Feller, J. and Fitzgerald, B.: A Framework Analysis of the Open Source Software Development Paradigm. In: 21st International Conference on Information Systems Brisbane, Australia (2000) 58-69
2. Mockus, A., Fielding, R. T. and Herbsleb, J.: A Case Study of Open Source Software Development: The Apache Server. In: 22nd International Conference on Software Engineering (2000) 263-272
3. Feller, J.: Thoughts on Studying Open Source Software Communities. In: N. L. Russo, B. Fitzgerald, and J. I. DeGross, eds. Realigning Research and Practice in Information Systems Development: The Social and Organizational Perspective. Kluwer Academic Publishers Idaho (2001)
4. Open Source Initiative: Open Source Definition. Accessed on 1 March 2001, (2001) www.opensource.org/osd.html
5. Bollinger, T., Nelson, R., Self, K. M. and Turnbull, S. J.: Open-Source Methods: Peering Through the Clutter. In: IEEE Software, July/August 1999 (1999) 8-11
6. Yamauchi, Y., Yokozawa, M., Shinohara, T. and Ishida, T.: Collaboration with Lean Media: How Open-Source Software Succeeds. In: ACM 2000 Conference on Computer Supported Cooperative Work (2000) 329-338
7. Raymond, E. S.: Homesteading the Noosphere. Accessed on 23 January 2001, (2000) http://tuxedo.org/~esr/writings/homesteading/homesteading/homesteading.ps
8. Lerner, J. and Tirole, J.: The Simple Economics of Open Source. Accessed on 23 January 2001, (2000) http://www.people.hbs.edu/jlerner/simple.pdf
9. Fielding, R. T.: Shared Leadership in the Apache Project. In: Communications of the ACM, April 1999/Vol 42 No 4. (1999) 42-43
10. von Hellens, L. A.: Quality Management Systems in Australian Software Houses: Some Problems of Sustaining Creativity in the software Process. In: Australian Journal of Information Systems, Vol 3 No 1. (1995) 14-24
11. Johnson, P. M.: Reengineering Inspection: The Future of Formal Technical Review. ics-tr-95-24 University of Hawaii Honolulu (1995)
12. Stein, M., Riedl, J., Harner, S. J. and Mashayekhi, V.: A Case Study of Distributed, Asynchronous Software Inspection. In: International Conference on Software Engineering Boston, USA (1997) 107-117.
13. Perpich, J. M., Perry, D. E., Porter, A. A., Votta, L. G. and Wade, M. W.: Anywhere, Anytime Code Inspections: Using the Web to Remove Inspection Bottlenecks in Large-Scale Software Development. In: International Conference on Software Engineering, Boston, USA (1997) 14-21.
14. Doherty, B. S. and Sahibuddin, S.: Software quality through distributed code inspection. In: Software Quality Engineering, C. Tasso, R. A. Adey, and M. Pighin, eds., Computational Mechanics Publications, Southampton, UK, (1997) 159-168.
15. Caivano, D., Lanubile, F. and Visaggio, G.: Scaling up Distributed Software Inspections. In: Proceedings of the 4th ICSE Workshop on Software Engineering over the Internet, Toronto, Canada (2001).
16. Nielsen, S. and Timmins, R.: Organisational Commitment and Software Quality Management: A Framework for Analysis. In: Proceedings of the 4th International Conference on Achieving Quality in Software Venice, Italy (1998) 235-242
17. Stark, J.: Peer Reviews in Open-Source Software Development. Honours Dissertation Griffith University Brisbane (2001)

18. Ljungberg, J.: Open Source Movements as a Model for Organizing. In: Proceedings of the European Conference on Information Systems Vienna, Austria (2000)
19. McConnell, S.: Open-Source Methodology: Ready for Prime Time? In: IEEE Software, July/August (1999) 8-11
20. Bollinger, T. and Beckman, P.: Linux on the Move. In: IEEE Software, January/February (1999) 30-35

An Evaluation of Inspection Automation Tools

Vesa Tenhunen and Jorma Sajaniemi

University of Joensuu, Department of Computer Science,
P.O. Box 111, FIN-80101 Joensuu, Finland

Abstract. A key element in manufacturing quality software is the early detection of defects which can be fostered by inspection techniques. Inspections may be boosted by automated tools that help in various tasks during the whole inspection process. We present a framework for inspection automation tool evaluation and use it to evaluate four tools. The framework divides tool requirements in two dimensions: phase and viewpoint. The former deals with the successive phases of the process, and the latter considers various issues that must be dealt with during the process.

1 Introduction

A key element in manufacturing quality software is the early detection of defects throughout the whole software production life cycle. If defects are not removed as soon as possible they give rise to other defects which may be hard to trace and are expensive to remove. Early defect detection can be fostered by inspection techniques [3,4] yielding an effective way to quality [1,11]. It is, however, sometimes hard to motivate people to spend enough time doing inspections. Especially, when customers are needed for inspections, e.g., in inspecting a Requirements Document, proper participation is often found to be a problem. Any mechanism that helps to show that inspections are an important premise for project success is therefore helpful for achieving good quality products.

Software process improvement (SPI) is only possible if the state of a process can be measured and articulated in a rigorous way so that the effect of improvement acts can be evaluated [5]. Measurements should be automated as far as possible to get objective data and to relieve developers from extra work [7]. A good solution is to integrate measurement collection into the tools that are used for software production.

Inspection automation tools may provide a solution for both of the above problems: they can give the customer – and other inspectors as well – an increased feeling of the importance of inspections, and help SPI in providing metrics of the inspected product and the inspection process itself.

Existing inspection automation tools [6,12,13,10] vary in their scope for inspection process phases and tasks, and support for various document formats and computer platforms. Therefore, a framework for tool evaluation is needed. The framework should take into account the whole inspection process and provide a possibility to make judgments based on individual needs and emphasis.

J. Kontio and R. Conradi (Eds.): ECSQ 2002, LNCS 2349, pp. 351–361, 2002.

In this paper, we will present such a framework (Chap. 3) and use it to evaluate major inspection automation tools (Chap. 4). To get a basis for the framework we will start with an overview of the inspection process (Chap. 2).

2   Inspection Process

Inspection as a method for finding defects within software engineering process was first described by Fagan [3] in the early 1970's. Since then, inspections have become quite popular and they are used during the entire life cycle. Inspections have been tested empirically and they have been found to be an effective way to ensure quality [1,11].

Despite some variations, most inspection processes still follow closely Fagan's original proposal. Fagan divides the process into five separate stages: (1) Overview, (2) preparation, (3) Inspection, (4) rework, and (5) follow-up.

The people involved are cast into well-defined and distinct roles: moderator, producer (or author), inspectors, reader, and recorder.

Usually the process goes as follows: In the overview, the moderator selects the inspection team members and assigns them their roles. The producer then introduces the product (code, document etc.) that is to be inspected.

During the preparation stage, the inspectors familiarise themselves with the material. In Fagan's original description, the inspectors are supposed to gain an understanding of the work – defect detection is only a by-product. In a variation suggested by Gilb and Graham [4], the inspectors should explicitly focus on finding defects.

In the inspection the moderator oversees the event; the reader (or the producer) paraphrases the document in full. The inspectors can stop the reader at any time and tell their comments which they have found in advance or at the meeting. All comments are written down by the recorder. No attempt to fix the defects is made – the inspection must focus solely on finding defects. The end product of this stage is a document containing all the found defects and problems.

It is also possible to have an inspection as distributed (non-local). The participants "meet" electronically using a suitable conferencing software to send their comments to each other. Another possibility is to replace the meeting by an asynchronous inspection, where the moderator oversees that the inspectors complete their tasks before the inspection moves forward [9].

The next stage is rework, where the producer reviews all defects. In the final stage, the follow-up, the moderator ensures that all comments are addressed and then decides whether there is a need for a full or partial re-inspection.

In the following, we will use a slight variation of these inspection stages. We rename overview as planning, for even in Fagan's proposal, there are more activities in this stage than just overseeing the start of the process. Preparation of materials, assignment of tasks to roles and assignment of roles to participants cannot be done without proper planning.

Phase	Moderator	Producer	Inspector	Reader	Recorder
Planning	Start process	Provide materials			
Preparation			Search for defects		
Familiarisation		Check findings			
Inspection	Oversee meeting	Clarify findings	Search for defects	Go through the materials	Record findings; write a summary
Rework		Remove defects			
Follow–up	Check rework				

Fig. 1. Roles and tasks in inspection process

The preparation is the same as above, but we add a new phase between that and the inspection: familiarisation, where the producer steps through the inspectors' remarks and makes her own comments about them. The rest of the inspection process follows as stated previously. Figure 1 lists the phases and participants' major tasks in them.

In practice, companies often have their own inspection process, where some phases may be joined and some tasks done in a different phase. This has no effect on the evaluation framework, as we have used the phases as an analysis tool rather than a fixed process description.

3   Framework for Tool Evaluation

There are several goals in automating the inspection process. Among the most important ones are increasing rigour, effectivity, and efficiency [8,9].

MacDonald et al. [8] have presented requirements for inspection support tools. They look for each phase in the inspection process and point out the elements that could or should be automated. We use a similar approach, but create a more detailed view of the process. We examine each phase from four viewpoints:

- Material Handling (all document-related issues such as file format, versions, navigation etc.)
- Comment Handling (all comment-related functions, such as adding, viewing, reviewing, reporting, summarising etc.)
- Support for Process (features that automate or otherwise benefit the inspection process)
- Interfaces (use of external software or other tools)

In each case, we determined whether there's a possibility for automation and if so, what kind of support the tool should provide. With this division, it was possible to get a more detailed view of tool requirements. We included previously reported requirements [9,2], but the viewpoints suggested some new requirements, too. We have left out voting support suggested by MacDonald et al. [9], as we feel that support for voting is not a necessity in a process where defects are supposed to be found but not resolved.

Phase	Material Handling	Comment Handling	Support for Process	Interfaces
Planning	Distribute materials		Defining tasks for roles; casting persons for roles	Different document types; paper documents
Preparation	Navigation; automatic defect detection; support for comprehension	Recording; summary reporting	Monitoring time usage, completeness of review, and completeness of checklist usage	Checklists
Familiarisation	Navigation	Walkthrough; reviewing comments		
Inspection	Navigation	Selecting and modifying final comments; summary reports	Time tracking; summaries for time usage etc.	Checklists
Rework		Listing unfinished comments; bundling corrections		Change control system
Follow–up		Checking for rework		

Fig. 2. Requirements for inspection automation tools

The resulting evaluation framework is presented in Figure 2 and described in more detail below.

Planning. A tool can support material handling by automating the distribution of materials. It can help in support for process, when the moderator defines tasks for roles and casts persons to those roles. The tool may automate interfaces by supporting various kinds of documents, like different file formats (including paper documents).

Preparation. The tool should provide support in every category for this phase. In material handling, it should help navigation, i.e. moving around and searching in the document, even though this may contradict the previous requirement of supporting different document formats. It should also find (at least some) defects automatically and support inspectors' needs to gain understanding of the material.

In comment handling, the tool should enable the recording of comments with information about the comment's location, classification, explanation and references. Another requirement is the ability to create summary reports as needed.

For process support, the tool should monitor inspector's use of time and check that the inspector has completely gone through material and checklists.

The tool should support interfaces by facilitating the use of checklists.

Familiarisation. In this phase, the tool should provide support for the producer: walkthrough and review of comments, and navigation within the material as the producer evaluates the comments.

Inspection. The tool should help comment handling by supporting selection and modification of final comments, and also creation of summary reports (even covering several inspection meetings). It should also support the moderator's tasks in inspection meeting by keeping track of time, so that if too much time is consumed in secondary issues, the moderator can urge to move on. It should also make summaries of time usage. As for interfaces, the tool should support the use of checklists in this phase, too.

Rework. In rework, automation is most useful in comment handling. The tool can help by listing unfinished comments and by enabling the producer to bundle corrections together. For interfaces, the tool can work in cooperation with a change control system.

Follow-Up. The tool should support comment handling by automating the moderator's overview of finished rework.

4 Tool Evaluation

We will now apply the evaluation framework to four inspection automation tools: CSRS, ReviewPro, sfia and Microsoft Word. This selection of tools is based on our search for currently supported inspection automation tools. Selected tools are particularly designed for inspection automation except Microsoft Word, which is included as an example of word processors that are sometimes used for inspection purposes. A summary of the analysis is presented in Figure 3.

4.1 CSRS

CSRS, Collaborative Software Review System [6], is a tool for Formal Technical Asynchronous review method (FTArm), which is a modification of Fagan's inspection. In FTArm, nearly all parts of the inspection process are managed asynchronously: all participants have certain tasks, and when they are completed, the inspection can continue to the next stage. CSRS works on Unix operating system.

Material Handling. CSRS manages material using a database where documents are stored as nodes which are linked together. A node can be a whole file or a portion of it (e.g. a function within code). Different file formats are not supported. Only plain text files can be used, because CSRS is built on XEmacs editor.

The pages of a document can be easily navigated, and standard XEmacs search functions are available. There is no automatic fault detection, neither there is any special support for comprehension. Automatic fault detection can be added by using CSRS's process modelling language.

Comment Handling. There can be three different types of comments, or annotations, as they are called in CSRS: a *comment* is a public note available to all inspectors and it is used for making questions and answering them in a general level. An *issue* is a private inspector's note which is used to address a defect. An *action* is also a private note and used to suggest an action to correct a defect.

All comments are stored as nodes and they are linked to the relevant parts of the document, so that they can be viewed concurrently with the content which they refer to.

Comments can be categorised with pre-made classifications of the types of the defect and its severity. When inspectors have finished their preparation tasks, comments can be reviewed in a public review which corresponds to an inspection meeting. CSRS ensures that all comments are visited.

	CSRS	ReviewPro	sfia	MS Word
Material Handling				
distribution	−	++	−	+
navigation	++	−	+	+++
automatic defect detection	−	−	−	−
comprehension support	−	−	−	−
Comment Handling				
comment attributes	+++	+++	+++	−
walkthrough	++	+	+++	+
summary reports	++	++	++	−
reviewing & modifying	++	++	++	++
listing unfinished	+	+	++	−
Process				
tasks & roles	−	+	−	−
monitoring time usage	+	+[1]	−	−
summaries of time usage	+	+[1]	−	−
monitoring completeness	+	+	−	−
monitoring checklists	+	+	−	−
Interfaces				
different document types	−	++	++	+
checklists	+	+	−	−
change control system	−	−	−	−

− = not supported, + = supported, ++ = good support, +++ = extensive support
[1] partially manual

Fig. 3. Summary of the inspection tool analysis

Support for Process. CSRS keeps logs of each inspector's usage of time. It also sees that every node is reviewed and that checklists are completely gone through. CSRS doesn't support role casting and task assignments unless they are added using the system's programming language.

CSRS is not meant to provide support for inspection meetings. It only helps the moderator to summarise decisions and to produce a report of results.

Interfaces. CSRS does not support different file formats or paper versions. It does support checklists which are included in the node database.

Summary. CSRS is aimed to support FTArm, a method that differs from traditional Fagan inspection. Yet the program is quite versatile because of its built-in process modelling language, so it can be tailored to support many variations of inspection processes. However, it works only with text files.

4.2   ReviewPro

ReviewPro[1] 3.0 [12] is a web-based groupware application that supports both synchronous and asynchronous inspections. All inspection data is kept in a server database and the reviewers need only web browsers. ReviewPro is available for Windows and Unix.

Material Handling. Material can be of any type as ReviewPro is not used to handle it. ReviewPro can store copies of documents in different file formats. These documents are downloadable from the server and other programs are used to manage them.

Navigation or searching of the documents cannot be done with ReviewPro. It is meant to be used simultaneously with a word processor that shows the document, or with paper versions. ReviewPro is used to record inspectors' comments.

Comment Handling. Comments are linked to documents manually by a separate log page describing their place within the document (page, paragraph etc.). Attributes of a comment include type, severity, status, and description. All comments are saved into the database.

ReviewPro can create several types of reports from comment information. Comments can be reviewed and modified both in synchronous and asynchronous inspections.

Support for Process. ReviewPro includes some support for defining roles and tasks. The moderator can create task lists for every participant.

The use of checklists and the control of their usage is automated. Tracking and summarisation of time usage requires that inspectors enter the data manually.

Interfaces. ReviewPro requires that the inspected material is available to inspectors in some form. There are no restrictions to document types or their file formats.

As many as six checklists can be created to be used in preparation and inspection. ReviewPro checks that inspectors have completely gone through them before the inspection moves to the next phase. There is no support for a control change system.

Summary. ReviewPro serves as a versatile note pad that inspectors can use to save and review their comments. It leaves the handling of inspected materials to other tools. As a web-based application, ReviewPro provides support for distributed, asynchronous and traditional inspection processes.

---

[1] This evaluation is based on the demo version of ReviewPro. Consequently, some functionality could not be assessed.

4.3   sfia

sfia 1.0 (software for inspection automation) [13] is a tool for inspection of code and documents in every stage of software development. It uses pictures to represent documents and XML-type plain text files for inspection data. By utilising GIF files as document pages and Tcl/Tk as the implementation language, sfia can be used with basically any document type and in various operating systems (including Unix, Linux, Windows and Macintosh).

Material Handling. sfia does not use the material per se; instead it manages images of the material, a graphic representation in GIF format of each page of the original document. Thus it gets around the problem of different file formats and works also with scanned paper documents.

sfia does not convert files to pictures, but there's an abundance of tools which can be used to do that. The producer can create the pictures and then write a definition file, which tells sfia what files comprise the document and what classifications of comments are used.

There is no automatic fault detection nor support for document comprehension. The pages of the document can be easily navigated, but there's no search function for document content.

Comment Handling. The main feature of sfia is its ability to handle comments. Inspectors can add comments and at the same time attribute classification, severity and other criteria to them. These classifications are freely definable by the moderator (or company). Comments are shown as semitransparent marks in the insertion point and they can be viewed simultaneously with their content texts. Inspectors can also view at any time detailed or summary reports of the comments.

For inspection meeting, all comments made by several inspectors can be combined into a single file. Comments can be deleted as necessary and also marked according to their status: finished, unfinished and notified.

Using summary reports, the producer can view unfinished comments, make modifications to original material and edit comments and change their status.

Support for Process. sfia does not support definition of roles or tasks. It does not record logs of time usage and neither does it track completeness of preparation or inspection.

Interfaces. Based on the use of standard graphics format it is possible to use sfia with any kind of file formats, including paper. However, sfia does not support any third party software like change control systems. Also, there is no support for checklists: they can be used only separately and manually.

Summary. sfia works in virtually all systems and it provides all necessary support for comment handling. However, it leaves process support and content-related issues like search and comprehension to be managed with other content-aware tools.

4.4   Microsoft Word

Microsoft Word 97 [10] is a word processor, but it is widely used in many organisations also for document handling. The program has some characteristics that can be used to automate inspections, so it is appropriate to review it. Word can be used on Windows and Macintosh.

Material Handling. Word can keep track of different versions of documents. The producer can prepare the material using Word's protection functions: the inspectors can be granted rights to add only comments, add comments and modify the text, or add comments and tracked changes. Documents can be distributed directly from Word via e-mail.

Navigation through document is supported as well as search of content, but there is no fault detection or comprehension support.

Comment Handling. Inspectors can add comments to documents. Comments can be either text or recorded sound files. Depending on the granted rights, inspectors may also modify documents.

By using track changes feature, Word keeps track of any modifications inspectors make and it is later possible to merge all copies into a single document with all the comments and modifications.

The comments can not be classified automatically: the inspectors must add manually the appropriate class, severity and other information into each comment's text. Word also lacks all summarising or reporting features; it can only show a listing of comments made by every inspector or by one selected inspector.

In rework, the producer can step through the comments, make necessary modifications and edit comments to show that they are dealt with. If there are any tracked changes, the producer can accept or discard them.

Support for Process. Word does not offer any support for the inspection process. There is no functionality regarding roles and tasks; it does not keep track of time usage (although it records the time when a modification is made); and there is no way to create reports about comments, although it is possible to print a list of comments and modifications.

Interfaces. Word provides some support for different file formats, but added comments can only be saved in Word's own format. This can cause a variety of problems, if the members of the inspection team have different versions of the program.

By using Word's macro language, Word can be made to support the use of checklists (which must be also in Word document format). There is also a possibility to ease distribution of the material by using e-mail directly from Word. The e-mail connection provides also some sort of support for asynchronous meetings, even though the program has no direct facilities for them.

Summary. Word is a familiar tool for many users. It does have some functionality usable in an inspection process, but it does not recognise any special features of inspection, so it requires disciplined working from users. It can be utilised with Word documents only.

5   Conclusions

Inspection automation tools motivate inspectors, especially customers, to do their best by providing an increased feeling of the importance of inspections. Furthermore, tools can automate metrics collection and help in SPI.

We have presented a framework for inspection automation tool evaluation. The framework divides tool requirements in two dimensions: phase of the inspection process and viewpoint of the contemplation. Our viewpoints are: material handling, comment handling, support for process, and interfaces. Using this framework we evaluated four tools: CSRS, ReviewPro, sfia and Microsoft Word.

CSRS is based on a special inspection method and it supports plain ASCII files only. ReviewPro serves as a versatile note pad with a manual connection to the inspected material. sfia supports any document type and gives good support for comment handling but has no process support. Finally, Microsoft Word is a word processor that provides no special support for inspections, and can be used with caution when Word documents are inspected by disciplined users.

The number of inspection automation tools is quite limited and a need for new tools applicable in different environments is apparent. Our evaluation framework can be used in tool design, too. It lists the major tasks that inspection participants encounter and thus poses requirements for future inspection automation tools.

References

1. Doolan, E. P.: Experience with Fagan's inspection method. Software – Practice and Experience, Vol 22, No. 2 (1990) 173–182
2. Dunsmore, A. P.: Comprehension and visualisation of object-oriented code for inspections. Technical Report, EFoCS-33-98, Computer Science Department, University of Strathclyde (1998)
3. Fagan, M. E.: Design and code inspections to reduce errors in program development. IBM System Journal, Vol. 15, No. 3 (1976) 182–211
4. Gilb, T., Graham, D.: Software inspection. Addison-Wesley (1993)
5. Humphrey, W. S.: Managing the software process. Addison-Wesley (1989)
6. Johnson, P. M., Tjahjono, D.: Improving software quality through computer supported collaborative review. Proceedings of the Third European Conference on Computer Supported Cooperative Work (1993)
7. Kitchenham, B.: Measuring software development. In Software Reliability Handbook, Ed. by P. Rook, Elsevier Applied Science (1990) 303–331
8. MacDonald, F., Miller, J., Brooks, A., Roper, M., Wood, M.: A review of tool support for software inspection. Proceedings of the Seventh International Workshop on Computer Aided Software Engineering (1995) 340–349
9. MacDonald, F., Miller, J., Brooks, A., Roper, M., Wood, M.: Automating the software inspection process. Automated Software Engineering Vol. 3, No. 3–4 (1996) 193–218
10. Microsoft Corporation. http://www.microsoft.com/office/word/
11. Russell, G. W.: Experience with inspections in ultralarge-scale developments. IEEE Software, Vol. 8, No. 1 (1991) 25–31

12. SoftWare Development Technologies (SDT). http://www.sdtcorp.com
13. Tenhunen, V.: sfia – software for inspection automation. http://www.cs.joensuu.fi/
    pages/saja/se/sfia

Author Index

Aaltio, Tapani 73
Abrahamsson, Pekka 175
Anttila, Juhani 25
Arami, Mikako 124

Calero, Coral 298
Chan, Kwok Ping 321
Chang, Wen-Kui 42, 63
Chen, Tsong Yueh 321
Chuang, Min-Hsiang 42

Dehli, Einar 17
Domae, Hiroyuki 274

Ferber, Stefan 165
Fuji, Hitoshi 135
Fukui, Shinji 217

Gantner, Thomas 186
Goldin, Leah 226
Gotou, Isao 135
Grütter, Georg 165

Häberlein, Tobias 186
Hashino, Nobuyuki 236
Helander, Nina 256
Helokunnas, Tuija 267
Hon, Shing-Kai 63

Jaccheri, Letizia 246
Johansen, Jørn 207

Kakuda, Yoshiaki 310
Kanayama, Toyohiro 53
Kauppinen, Marjo 73
Kautz, Karlheinz 175
Kimijima, Hiroshi 53
Kitajima, Yoshihiro 135
Koga, Junji 274
Kujala, Sari 73
Kurokawa, Satoshi 236
Kusanagi, Takumi 124

Larvet, Philippe 156

Matsumoto, Masato 274

Nakasone, Junji 236

Nakata, Masahiro 82
Nawrocki, Jerzy R. 288
Nishi, Yasuharu 331
Nyby, Marko 267

Ogasawara, Hideto 53, 124
Ohsugi, Hitoshi 135
Okazaki, Yasuko 197
Olesen, Robert 207
Oono, Hitoshi 135

Pfleeger, Shari Lawrence 7
Piattini, Mario 298

Raghavan, Gopalakrishna 90
Richardson, Ita 100
Rifkin, Stan 13
Rochell, Lilach 226
Rombach, H. Dieter 1
Rosendahl, Esa 146

Sahraoui, Houari 298
Sajaniemi, Jorma 351
Satou, Seiichiro 135
Schneider, Kurt 114
Seppänen, Veikko 256
Shimanaka, Kazutoshi 274
Stark, Jacqueline 340

Takahashi, Juichi 310
Tenhunen, Vesa 351
Terho, Mikko 2
Torchiano, Marco 246
Towey, Dave 321

Ulkuniemi, Pauliina 256

Vallée, Frédérique 156
Vullinghs, Ton 146

Wakaki, Mamoru 236
Walter, Bartosz 288
Watson, Gregory H. 36
Wojciechowski, Adam 288

Yamada, Atsushi 124
Yang, Chao-Tung 42
Yasuda, Katsuyuki 82

Lecture Notes in Computer Science

For information about Vols. 1–2269
please contact your bookseller or Springer-Verlag

Vol. 2270: M. Pflanz, On-line Error Detection and Fast Recover Techniques for Dependable Embedded Processors. XII, 126 pages. 2002.

Vol. 2271: B. Preneel (Ed.), Topics in Cryptology – CT-RSA 2002. Proceedings, 2002. X, 311 pages. 2002.

Vol. 2272: D. Bert, J.P. Bowen, M.C. Henson, K. Robinson (Eds.), ZB 2002: Formal Specification and Development in Z and B. Proceedings, 2002. XII, 535 pages. 2002.

Vol. 2273: A.R. Coden, E.W. Brown, S. Srinivasan (Eds.), Information Retrieval Techniques for Speech Applications. XI, 109 pages. 2002.

Vol. 2274: D. Naccache, P. Paillier (Eds.), Public Key Cryptography. Proceedings, 2002. XI, 385 pages. 2002.

Vol. 2275: N.R. Pal, M. Sugeno (Eds.), Advances in Soft Computing – AFSS 2002. Proceedings, 2002. XVI, 536 pages. 2002. (Subseries LNAI).

Vol. 2276: A. Gelbukh (Ed.), Computational Linguistics and Intelligent Text Processing. Proceedings, 2002. XIII, 444 pages. 2002.

Vol. 2277: P. Callaghan, Z. Luo, J. McKinna, R. Pollack (Eds.), Types for Proofs and Programs. Proceedings, 2000. VIII, 243 pages. 2002.

Vol. 2278: J.A. Foster, E. Lutton, J. Miller, C. Ryan, A.G.B. Tettamanzi (Eds.), Genetic Programming. Proceedings, 2002. XI, 337 pages. 2002.

Vol. 2279: S. Cagnoni, J. Gottlieb, E. Hart, M. Middendorf, G.R. Raidl (Eds.), Applications of Evolutionary Computing. Proceedings, 2002. XIII, 344 pages. 2002.

Vol. 2280: J.P. Katoen, P. Stevens (Eds.), Tools and Algorithms for the Construction and Analysis of Systems. Proceedings, 2002. XIII, 482 pages. 2002.

Vol. 2281: S. Arikawa, A. Shinohara (Eds.), Progress in Discovery Science. XIV, 684 pages. 2002. (Subseries LNAI).

Vol. 2282: D. Ursino, Extraction and Exploitation of Intensional Knowledge from Heterogeneous Information Sources. XXVI, 289 pages. 2002.

Vol. 2283: T. Nipkow, L.C. Paulson, M. Wenzel, Isabelle/HOL. XIII, 218 pages. 2002.

Vol. 2284: T. Eiter, K.-D. Schewe (Eds.), Foundations of Information and Knowledge Systems. Proceedings, 2002. X, 289 pages. 2002.

Vol. 2285: H. Alt, A. Ferreira (Eds.), STACS 2002. Proceedings, 2002. XIV, 660 pages. 2002.

Vol. 2286: S. Rajsbaum (Ed.), LATIN 2002: Theoretical Informatics. Proceedings, 2002. XIII, 630 pages. 2002.

Vol. 2287: C.S. Jensen, K.G. Jeffery, J. Pokorny, Saltenis, E. Bertino, K. Böhm, M. Jarke (Eds.), Advances in Database Technology – EDBT 2002. Proceedings, 2002. XVI, 776 pages. 2002.

Vol. 2288: K. Kim (Ed.), Information Security and Cryptology – ICISC 2001. Proceedings, 2001. XIII, 457 pages. 2002.

Vol. 2289: C.J. Tomlin, M.R. Greenstreet (Eds.), Hybrid Systems: Computation and Control. Proceedings, 2002. XIII, 480 pages. 2002.

Vol. 2290: F. van der Linden (Ed.), Software Product-Family Engineering. Proceedings, 2001. X, 417 pages. 2002.

Vol. 2291: F. Crestani, M. Girolami, C.J. van Rijsbergen (Eds.), Advances in Information Retrieval. Proceedings, 2002. XIII, 363 pages. 2002.

Vol. 2292: G.B. Khosrovshahi, A. Shokoufandeh, A. Shokrollahi (Eds.), Theoretical Aspects of Computer Science. IX, 221 pages. 2002.

Vol. 2293: J. Renz, Qualitative Spatial Reasoning with Topological Information. XVI, 207 pages. 2002. (Subseries LNAI).

Vol. 2294: A. Cortesi (Ed.), Verification, Model Checking, and Abstract Interpretation. Proceedings, 2002. VIII, 331 pages. 2002.

Vol. 2295: W. Kuich, G. Rozenberg, A. Salomaa (Eds.), Developments in Language Theory. Proceedings, 2001. IX, 389 pages. 2002.

Vol. 2296: B. Dunin-Kęplicz, E. Nawarecki (Eds.), From Theory to Practice in Multi-Agent Systems. Proceedings, 2001. IX, 341 pages. 2002. (Subseries LNAI).

Vol. 2297: R. Backhouse, R. Crole, J. Gibbons (Eds.), Algebraic and Coalgebraic Methods in the Mathematics of Program Construction. Proceedings, 2000. XIV, 387 pages. 2002.

Vol. 2298: I. Wachsmuth, T. Sowa (Eds.), Gesture and Language in Human-Computer Interaction. Proceedings, 2001. XI, 323 pages. 2002. (Subseries LNAI).

Vol. 2299: H. Schmeck, T. Ungerer, L. Wolf (Eds.), Trends in Network and Pervasive Computing – ARCS 2002. Proceedings, 2002. XIV, 287 pages. 2002.

Vol. 2300: W. Brauer, H. Ehrig, J. Karhumäki, A. Salomaa (Eds.), Formal and Natural Computing. XXXVI, 431 pages. 2002.

Vol. 2301: A. Braquelaire, J.-O. Lachaud, A. Vialard (Eds.), Discrete Geometry for Computer Imagery. Proceedings, 2002. XI, 439 pages. 2002.

Vol. 2302: C. Schulte, Programming Constraint Services. XII, 176 pages. 2002. (Subseries LNAI).

Vol. 2303: M. Nielsen, U. Engberg (Eds.), Foundations of Software Science and Computation Structures. Proceedings, 2002. XIII, 435 pages. 2002.

Vol. 2304: R.N. Horspool (Ed.), Compiler Construction. Proceedings, 2002. XI, 343 pages. 2002.

Vol. 2305: D. Le Métayer (Ed.), Programming Languages and Systems. Proceedings, 2002. XII, 331 pages. 2002.

Vol. 2306: R.-D. Kutsche, H. Weber (Eds.), Fundamental Approaches to Software Engineering. Proceedings, 2002. XIII, 341 pages. 2002.

Vol. 2307: C. Zhang, S. Zhang, Association Rule Mining. XII, 238 pages. 2002. (Subseries LNAI).

Vol. 2308: I.P. Vlahavas, C.D. Spyropoulos (Eds.), Methods and Applications of Artificial Intelligence. Proceedings, 2002. XIV, 514 pages. 2002. (Subseries LNAI).

Vol. 2309: A. Armando (Ed.), Frontiers of Combining Systems. Proceedings, 2002. VIII, 255 pages. 2002. (Subseries LNAI).

Vol. 2310: P. Collet, C. Fonlupt, J.-K. Hao, E. Lutton, M. Schoenauer (Eds.), Artificial Evolution. Proceedings, 2001. XI, 375 pages. 2002.

Vol. 2311: D. Bustard, W. Liu, R. Sterritt (Eds.), Soft-Ware 2002: Computing in an Imperfect World. Proceedings, 2002. XI, 359 pages. 2002.

Vol. 2312: T. Arts, M. Mohnen (Eds.), Implementation of Functional Languages. Proceedings, 2001. VII, 187 pages. 2002.

Vol. 2313: C.A. Coello Coello, A. de Albornoz, L.E. Sucar, O.Cairó Battistutti (Eds.), MICAI 2002: Advances in Artificial Intelligence. Proceedings, 2002. XIII, 548 pages. 2002. (Subseries LNAI).

Vol. 2314: S.-K. Chang, Z. Chen, S.-Y. Lee (Eds.), Recent Advances in Visual Information Systems. Proceedings, 2002. XI, 323 pages. 2002.

Vol. 2315: F. Arhab, C. Talcott (Eds.), Coordination Models and Languages. Proceedings, 2002. XI, 406 pages. 2002.

Vol. 2316: J. Domingo-Ferrer (Ed.), Inference Control in Statistical Databases. VIII, 231 pages. 2002.

Vol. 2317: M. Hegarty, B. Meyer, N. Hari Narayanan (Eds.), Diagrammatic Representation and Inference. Proceedings, 2002. XIV, 362 pages. 2002. (Subseries LNAI).

Vol. 2318: D. Bošnački, S. Leue (Eds.), Model Checking Software. Proceedings, 2002. X, 259 pages. 2002.

Vol. 2319: C. Gacek (Ed.), Software Reuse: Methods, Techniques, and Tools. Proceedings, 2002. XI, 353 pages. 2002.

Vol.2320: T. Sander (Ed.), Security and Privacy in Digital Rights Management. Proceedings, 2001. X, 245 pages. 2002.

Vol. 2322: V. Mařík, O. Stěpánková, H. Krautwurmová, M. Luck (Eds.), Multi-Agent Systems and Applications II. Proceedings, 2001. XII, 377 pages. 2002. (Subseries LNAI).

Vol. 2323: À. Frohner (Ed.), Object-Oriented Technology. Proceedings, 2001. IX, 225 pages. 2002.

Vol. 2324: T. Field, P.G. Harrison, J. Bradley, U. Harder (Eds.), Computer Performance Evaluation. Proceedings, 2002. XI, 349 pages. 2002.

Vol 2326: D. Grigoras, A. Nicolau, B. Toursel, B. Folliot (Eds.), Advanced Environments, Tools, and Applications for Cluster Computing. Proceedings, 2001. XIII, 321 pages. 2002.

Vol. 2327: H.P. Zima, K. Joe, M. Sato, Y. Seo, M. Shimasaki (Eds.), High Performance Computing. Proceedings, 2002. XV, 564 pages. 2002.

Vol. 2329: P.M.A. Sloot, C.J.K. Tan, J.J. Dongarra, A.G. Hoekstra (Eds.), Computational Science – ICCS 2002. Proceedings, Part I. XLI, 1095 pages. 2002.

Vol. 2330: P.M.A. Sloot, C.J.K. Tan, J.J. Dongarra, A.G. Hoekstra (Eds.), Computational Science – ICCS 2002. Proceedings, Part II. XLI, 1115 pages. 2002.

Vol. 2331: P.M.A. Sloot, C.J.K. Tan, J.J. Dongarra, A.G. Hoekstra (Eds.), Computational Science – ICCS 2002. Proceedings, Part III. XLI, 1227 pages. 2002.

Vol. 2332: L. Knudsen (Ed.), Advances in Cryptology – EUROCRYPT 2002. Proceedings, 2002. XII, 547 pages. 2002.

Vol. 2334: G. Carle, M. Zitterbart (Eds.), Protocols for High Speed Networks. Proceedings, 2002. X, 267 pages. 2002.

Vol. 2335: M. Butler, L. Petre, K. Sere (Eds.), Integrated Formal Methods. Proceedings, 2002. X, 401 pages. 2002.

Vol. 2336: M.-S. Chen, P.S. Yu, B. Liu (Eds.), Advances in Knowledge Discovery and Data Mining. Proceedings, 2002. XIII, 568 pages. 2002. (Subseries LNAI).

Vol. 2337: W.J. Cook, A.S. Schulz (Eds.), Integer Programming and Combinatorial Optimization. Proceedings, 2002. XI, 487 pages. 2002.

Vol. 2338: R. Cohen, B. Spencer (Eds.), Advances in Artificial Intelligence. Proceedings, 2002. X, 197 pages. 2002. (Subseries LNAI).

Vol. 2342: I. Horrocks, J. Hendler (Eds.), The Semantic Web – ISCW 2002. Proceedings, 2002. XVI, 476 pages. 2002.

Vol. 2345: E. Gregori, M. Conti, A.T. Campbell, G. Omidyar, M. Zukerman (Eds.), NETWORKING 2002. Proceedings, 2002. XXVI, 1256 pages. 2002.

Vol. 2347: P. De Bra, P. Brusilovsky, R. Conejo (Eds.), Adaptive Hypermedia and Adaptive Web-Based Systems. Proceedings, 2002. XV, 615 pages. 2002.

Vol. 2348: A. Banks Pidduck, J. Mylopoulos, C.C. Woo, M. Tamer Ozsu (Eds.), Advanced Information Systems Engineering. Proceedings, 2002. XIV, 799 pages. 2002.

Vol. 2349: J. Kontio, R. Conradi (Eds.), Software Quality – ECSQ 2002. Proceedings, 2002. XIV, 363 pages. 2002.

Vol. 2350: A. Heyden, G. Sparr, M. Nielsen, P. Johansen (Eds.), Computer Vision – ECCV 2002. Proceedings, Part I. XXVIII, 817 pages. 2002.

Vol. 2351: A. Heyden, G. Sparr, M. Nielsen, P. Johansen (Eds.), Computer Vision – ECCV 2002. Proceedings, Part II. XXVIII, 903 pages. 2002.

Vol. 2352: A. Heyden, G. Sparr, M. Nielsen, P. Johansen (Eds.), Computer Vision – ECCV 2002. Proceedings, Part III. XXVIII, 919 pages. 2002.

Vol. 2353: A. Heyden, G. Sparr, M. Nielsen, P. Johansen (Eds.), Computer Vision – ECCV 2002. Proceedings, Part IV. XXVIII, 841 pages. 2002.

Vol. 2359: M. Tistarelli, J. Bigun, A.K. Jain (Eds.), Biometric Authentication. Proceedings, 2002. XII, 373 pages. 2002.